THE CREATION OF DEATH AND LIFE

THE CREATION OF DEATH AND LIFE

by

RACHEL H. KING

Philosophical Library
New York

MANUFACTURED IN THE UNITED STATES OF AMERICA

Dedicated to the memory of
Dr. Eleanor Benjamin Gutman,
in whom I first saw the coexistence
of the Biblical and the Scientific
ad majorem Dei gloriam

Contents

PREFACE

In controversy it is often good strategy to look carefully at facts which the other side acknowledges to be true, but would be glad to sweep under the rug. When trying, therefore, to set the general scientific view within the over-all Christian belief, I have emphasized as my starting-point science's basic—but unadvertised—*second law of thermodynamics,* which is the belief that the over-all tendency of matter is toward increasing randomness, with the implication that the universe is progressing to a "heat-death," a time when the whole show will be over because matter will have achieved maximum randomness, and action will cease because all energy will have passed from the available to the nonavailable state.

In other words, it has been said that death is as much a taboo subject in the twentieth century as sex was in the Victorian era. I therefore chose the death of the universe as the starting-point for my thought. When I did this I discovered to my surprise that what had seemed the insoluble problem of evil fell normally into place in the total robust Christian picture of the carrying out of God's plan, and that the question of man's freedom in relation to God's omnipotence became less perplexing.

The book attempts to relate the over-all scientific view to the over-all biblical view of God and the world and men. No apology is being made for the restrained anthropomorphism which characterizes the book: it characterizes the Bible also. For if the Lord's Prayer is valid the Ultimate Power is also a Conscious Intelligence with whom men can have an I-Thou relationship. This means that the restrained anthropomorphism of the Bible is a more accurate picture of the Ultimate Power than is the picture which emerges from the philosophically conditioned abstractions of high theology, although these, too, have their usefulness to Christian thought. But a man's relation to abstractions is an I-it relationship, and if abstract expressions are considered more valid than the so-called naive biblical language, the whole Christian perspective can be subtly falsified. I have contented myself with trying to stay true to the basic trend of biblical thought, and to stay in line with the teaching of the Apostles', Nicene, and Chalcedon Creeds, and with the full Trinitarianism of the Athanasian Creed. Beyond this I have made use eclectically of theological and philosophical insights.

One curious fact has emerged in trying to think and write under these freedoms and limitations. I have found it easier to relate the biblical God to science than to relate the God of theology to science. The reason is that both the biblical God and the creation as described by science are characterized by tremendous, specifically active power. By contrast, the Greek thought which the early centuries wedded to Christianity, is static. One finds it difficult to make an intellectual or emotional linkage between a philosophically somewhat static Divine, and the powerfully active universe which science portrays.

The reader is begged not to prejudge the book, which, although couched in everyday language, nevertheless presents a comprehensive and carefully interrelated theological position.

My gratitude is due to Dr. Marianne Beran, (now Mrs. William J. Lipton) who, when we were both teaching at Northfield, once mentioned to me in conversation that Nature is characterized by basic patterns which repeat themselves with variations. Now, twenty-five years later, her casual remark has borne fruit. I also wish to thank Dr. Margaret Dann and Mrs. Jean P. Hatheway for reading and commenting upon portions of the manuscript.

Rachel H. King

New York City
February 1970

CHAPTER 1

The Point of Departure

In the last chapter of my book, *The Omission of the Holy Spirit from Reinhold Niebuhr's Theology*,[1] I have called for an all-out attempt, on the part of theologians, to rework the doctrinal framework of our religion to include harmoniously both the biblical view of God and man and the scientific picture of the universe. The present work is my own contribution to this most important twentieth century theological problem.

If Christianity is to assume that the findings of science have any validity, then any reworking of Christian doctrine must take into consideration both the theory of evolution and the equally important theory of entropy, which is called *the second law of thermodynamics*. Popular thought is highly conscious of evolution and the over-all impression that it gives of the world's built-in escalation from small beginnings to bigger and better eventualities. For a hundred years the concept of evolution has seemed to popular thought to give scientific corroboration to the socially optimistic confidence in progress. But equally important for a philosophy of life is *the second law of thermodynamics* which presents a contrary and pessimistic picture of the universe's over-all existence. Yet I find that a large proportion even of educated people are not aware of this "law," and those who do recognize it when it is mentioned give little evidence of its having an integral place in their philosophy of life. For that reason entropy's implications need to be clearly stated as a point of departure for our thinking:

Although it is true that the amount of matter in the universe is perpetually changing, the change appears to be all in one direction — toward dissolution. All the phenomena of nature, visible and invisible, within the atom and in outer space, indicate that the substance and energy of the universe are inexorably diffusing like vapor through the insatiable void. The sun is slowly but surely burning out, the stars are dying embers, and everywhere

---

[1] Published by Philosophical Library, New York, 1964.

1

in the cosmos heat is turning to cold, matter is dissolving into radiation, and energy is being dissipated into empty space.

The universe is thus progressing toward an ultimate "heat-death," or as it is technically defined, a condition of "maximum entropy." When the universe reaches this state some billions of years from now all the processes of nature will cease. All space will be at the same temperature. No energy can be used because all of it will be uniformly distributed through the cosmos. There will be no light, no life, no warmth — nothing but perpetual and irrevocable stagnation. Time itself will come to an end. For entropy points the direction of time. Entropy is the measure of randomness. When all system and order in the universe have vanished, when randomness is at its maximum, and entropy cannot be increased, when there no longer is any sequence of cause and effect, in short when the universe has run down, there will be no direction to time — there will be no time. And there is no way of avoiding this destiny. For the fateful principle known as the Second Law of Thermodynamics, which stands today as virtually the only pillar of classical physics left intact by the march of science, proclaims that the fundamental processes of nature are irreversible. Nature moves just one way.[2]

No structural innovations should ever be made in Christian theological theory except with extreme caution and the understanding that they should undergo a sufficient probationary period in which the new ideas can be tested by learned Christian thinkers to see whether the new theory is compatible with the biblical revelation. For this reason, as well as because of the present fluid state of astronomical and other scientific theory, I have labeled the present book "an hypothesis", because *the cornerstone of its reworking of the theological edifice is the denial of the standard doctrine that God sustains the universe.* The book takes as its point of departure the picture of cosmic creation *ex nihilo* (II Maccabees 7:28; Hebrews 11:3; Romans 4:17 and see Psalm 33:9 and Job 26:7) and the dissolution quoted in the first chapter of Hebrews from Psalm 102:

Thou, Lord, didst found the earth in the beginning,
and the heavens are the work of thy hands;

---

[2] Lincoln Barnett, *The Universe and Dr. Einstein;* New York: Mentor Books, 1957, pp. 110, 111.

2

they will perish, but thou remainest;
they will all grow old like a garment,
like a mantle thou wilt roll them up,
and they will be changed.
But thou art the same,
and thy years will never end.

What God upholds does not perish.

As the years have passed it has increasingly come to seem to me that one of the great difficulties in making a working relationship between Christian and scientific thought has been that our religion has been hampered in this regard by its large admixture of Greek philosophy. For most educated Christians the highly active, highly specific, and highly discriminating God of the Bible has seemed primitively anthropomorphic and less intellectually respectable than a more generalized, pervasive, and static picture of God who upholds nature in its standard activities. However, this more sophisticated picture of God, which is of Greek rather than Hebrew extraction, has become pale and ineffectual in most people's minds when contrasted with the picture science has given us of a cosmos of breathtaking immensity, intricate specific detail, and dynamic power. So God seems to have been taken away, and modern man knows not where he has been laid. But what has really been lost is this Hellenized picture of God. I personally find it easier to picture science as related to the active anthropomorphic God of the Old Testament than to the Hellenized God of Western theology.

In the present essay I shall attempt to describe a relationship between the scientific picture and the Christian God depicted as the Creator in the Old Testament and the Father in heaven in the New. Philosophical insights I shall make use of only eclectically, as they contribute positively to this overall picture. I insist on the intellectual right to make this tentative approach to the science-religion problem, because the basic authoritative book of Christianity, the Bible, is non-philosophic. As the biblical description of God is non-philosophic but is expressed in personal terms, this approach is necessary to create a picture harmoniously linking the anthropomorphic God of the Bible with science.

By using a picture of a personal anthropomorphic God to link to science, the weak point in scientific theory as a complete description of reality is made good use of in the interests of Christian

3

apologetics. For science is the magnificent investigation of the objectively measurable universe, and so the question of God and his relation to the cosmos is beyond the range of its investigation. But science assumes the relation to the universe of the anthropomorphic scientist for whom it has no place within its scientific theory. Since this is so, science can also assume the relation to the universe of an anthropomorphic God. (Of course the picture of God which this book will outline is not *crudely* anthropomorphic.)

Life presents us with two types of reality, the knower and the known. Each human knower knows himself directly, and understands about others by analogy with himself. But although each human individual knows himself directly by being himself, he cannot have scientific, i.e., objective, knowledge of even himself as a knower, for as soon as he tries to focus his attention upon himself he finds that he, as the experiencing but non-objectifiable knower, is only looking objectively at his historical past of the previous split second. Subjective reality, whether divine or human, would therefore be permanently out-of-bounds for science's objective investigation.

All attempts to construct a unified theology in accordance with biblical teaching have been selective of corroborating Scripture passages. The present work is no exception. But the choice has not been purely arbitrary. There is a general trend in biblical thought with which theology can align itself. While the writers of the New Testament could not have believed the specific arguments here presented, because they did not know science, I am confident that they *could have* fitted this argument to their Christian beliefs had they had the modern scientific picture with which to work. Furthermore, while the Bible does not precisely *foretell* the modern scientific view, certain passages in it, like the Psalms-Hebrews extract quoted above, fit the present situation more exactly than the writers of Scripture realized. It is typical of human creativity in general to feel pulled in the creative act to just-beyond the mind's intellectual knowledge, so that the created work when completed can serve in turn as an objective source to help educate the rational intellect of its creator. Therefore it does not take a very robust faith to believe that the writers of Scripture, writing under the guidance of the supernatural God, could sometimes write more adequately than they themselves fully understood, even though in

4

guiding them God made use of, and did not do violence to, their humanly acquired knowledge and their humanly intellectual thinking.

One of the great problems involved in writing this book is that of science's incomplete knowledge within its own realm, so that there is no assured scientific picture of the cosmos with which to relate Christian belief. For example, in harmonizing the biblical account of creation with astronomy's "big bang" theory, it makes considerable difference for religious interpretation whether what exploded in all directions at the beginning of our universe was pristine or "reconditioned" neutrons. That is, was the "big bang" at the beginning of our universe a unique happening, starting the universe expanding endlessly into infinite space, or is space a closed system, pulsating regularly with a "big bang" every multibillion year period?

Either alternative will fit our basic Psalms-Hebrews quotation. But as a Christian I would intellectually and emotionally much prefer the alternative to be true which considers the "big bang" a unique event, and this book is written oriented to that alternative.

The reason the single cosmic explosion theory is more easily absorbed by Christian thought is that Christianity denies the everlastingness of matter and claims that God created the universe ex nihilo. If the matter or "stuff" of the universe is thought of as everlasting and God is thought of as Spirit, one has the insoluble problem of how two things *completely unrelated* could interact. What seems the easy way out of this dilemma is to see God's relation to the universe as analogous to our own relation to our bodies: as we are mind-matter organisms so God is thought of as a Spirit-matter totality. This solution does not escape the pantheistic taint. What most people do not see clearly is that pantheism undercuts Christianity by denying the basic biblical claim that God is actively righteous. (In Judaism and Christianity God's love is never a mere togetherness divorced from his righteousness.) For if God is described as having an all inclusive togetherness with the world, then God includes the evil of the world and so it is not forever at variance with it.

It is a curious thing that the modern pulsating universe theory characterized by successive "big bangs" is not new in human thought, but resembles with superficial differences the basic cosmological picture of two great pantheisms, Stoicism and Hinduism. According to Stoicism, after a time-age the world will be destroyed by fire. Then a new cycle of development begins and earth will repeat its history down to the last detail. Again Cicero will deliver his orations against Cataline and again Caesar will land in Britain. This will be repeated, without ultimate purpose, forever. In Hinduism, the three stresses within the Power of Brahman go out of equilibrium and multiplicity occurs, and a universe, referred to as the Day of Brahma, takes place. After millions of years the three stresses within the Power of Brahman go back to equilibrium, and a state of no-universe, referred to as the Night of Brahma, takes place. This is repeated, without purpose, forever. Neither Hinduism nor Stoicism believes in the righteous God.

The pulsating universe theory, if it were proved to be correct, would not necessarily entail pantheism. But an endlessly pulsating universe is cyclical, rather than indicating the straight line of history progressing from the past to the future, which is the Hebrew conception. Also a pulsating universe theory, if established, might lead to a theory of scientific naturalism instead of pantheism. People might argue that it is just as easy to assume the original factor in existence to be endlessly enduring matter as it is to assume that it is a God who is a personal (i.e., a consciously purposive) spirit.

However, the scientific picture is not complete unless it accounts for biological evolution and human social evolution. Biological evolution fits more easily into the Hebrew theory of history moving in a straight line from the past to the future to accomplish something of value than it does with the cyclical theory of existence with its associated idea of ultimate purposelessness. And human evolution, when man reaches the intelligent reflective state, involves something more than the increasing complexity of matter with increasing reactiveness. For complexity and reactiveness are objective and measurable and within the scope of science. But reflective intelligence is subjective, and the thinker cannot study himself objectively as thinking, he can only study objectively the product of his thought. The realm of value, both ethical and aesthetic, is also beyond the domain of a materialistically explained universe. Aesthetic and ethical values and reflective intelligence presuppose the existence of a mind of a very high sort, and cannot

6

be accounted for by matter, although they appear on this earth when matter becomes highly complicated and highly reactive.

One cannot get around the problem by saying that a mental aspect was associated with matter from the beginning, if by mental aspect one only means an aspect of matter. For the "mental aspect" of the original atoms, or even of the comparatively highly developed amoeba is *not* the same as self-conscious, reflective, value-understanding mind.

Furthermore, since the "big bang" that marked the beginning of our universe erased all traces of what went before it, the claim that there *was* a preceding universe is speculation and not a scientifically verifiable statement. Even if there seemed to be sufficient evidence that there is now deceleration in the rate of expansion of the present universe, and the theory seemed justifiable that space is closed and finite, with the resulting probability that after our universe reaches its maximum expansion it will contract and eventuate in another explosion and another universe, there is no guarantee that this will happen, and still less a guarantee that our present universe is not the first in the series. The great field of science, in which it won recognition as an authority for men's understanding of existence, was that of the repeatable, and thus verifiable, experiment. One can attempt to deduce history and to prophesy the future on lines of direction seen in the present. But neither are subject to validation by means of the repetition of the experiment.

This is being said as an explanation for this present book's building its argument around the "single big bang" theory. One of the problems that besets religion in trying to make a picture of existence that will include both biblical religion and modern science is that science keeps changing its picture that it asks us to accept as authoritative for the human life-view. There have been various cosmologies current in science even in my lifetime. This present book does not claim to be more than an hypothesis. What I very much hope it will succeed in doing is to convince people that there is a closer tie-up possible than has hitherto been made between the scientific picture and biblical religion, and that the book will encourage further and more adequate attempts to relate the two fields, and that it will contain seminal insights that will prove permanently valid.

It is my personal belief that the validation of the truth of Chris-

7

tianity does not depend upon the adjustment that can be made between it and scientific theory. It is within the realm of human history, of which the Bible records the key segment for the interpretation of the whole, and in the realm of values, especially ethical and aesthetic, and especially in the area of the constant recognition of the subject-object relationship as being a mystery impenetrable to our intellectual understanding, that material for Christian apologetics is found.

However, Christianity cannot permanently hold men's confidence without taking the scientific picture into account. For biblical religion is not world-denying as Hinduism and Buddhism are. Christianity claims that this is God's world, that he made it, loves it, and acts purposively with regard to it. Thus, while Christianity can never get its religion from science, it nevertheless thinks that the world and cosmos that science investigates are the stage-setting in which God acts to carry out his purpose relative to men. Christianity must therefore be able to show that the stage-setting, which is also investigated by science, is adequate as a stage-setting for the Christian religion. Love is active, and, if God loves the world and acts in it, it must be the same world and universe the physical aspects of which science investigates. If this working harmony does not seem attainable, then, since it is axiomatic of all thought that truth is interrelated and self-consistent, whether or not men have made much progress toward discovering it, the unavoidable implication is that either Christianity or science is not true, or else that the thinking associated with one or the other or both is mistaken at some points,or inadequately advanced to the point at which a working harmony of the two disciplines could be seen.

Although, in reworking the theoretical relationship of Christianity to secular scientific belief, it is necessary at times to lift the biblical teaching from its context in the ancient cosmological and secular world-view and reset it with some minor modifications in the modern secular scientific world-view, three things should be noted. One is that Christian teaching in its biblical form, that is, shorn of the philosophical accretions it acquired when it became acclimated to Greco-Roman civilization, is easier to correlate with modern scientific thought than is usually believed. The second is, that there is as vast an accumulation of evidence for basic Christian belief as

8

there is for any of the theories of modern scientific belief. The Christian evidence is admittedly not as neat and tidy as that offered by science, and it is evidence of a different sort, involving the mystery of the subjective-objective, the recognition of the authoritative status of aesthetic and especially of ethical values, and the present experience and the recorded history of men's experience, especially that recorded in the biblical revelation. Over the centuries quite as many intelligent men have tested the truth of the Jewish-Christian faith by personal relationship to God in lives devoted to his service, as there are men who have had more than superficial direct knowledge of science. The Western world's knowledge of science, even the educated Western world's knowledge, has been largely hearsay evidence accepted on the authority of the research knowledge of comparatively few investigators. The number of men who have any genuine *evidence* that the universe is expanding or that our sun is dying is an infinitesimal fraction of all the college graduates in the world. All the other college graduates and all the high school graduates who accept these beliefs do so simply on the authority of the SCIENTIST, whose pronouncements are now taken as truth as unquestioningly as the pronouncements of the CHURCH were accepted as true in the Middle Ages, because of men's confidence in the Church's authority.

The third important point is that, in recasting the Christian account of the world milieu to coordinate it with the modern scientific picture, care must be taken that a theoretical world-universe view that undercuts basic Christian belief is not attached to Christianity. It has been carelessness at this point that has played havoc with Liberal Christianity. On the other hand both the birth-right-heritage-conservatives and the neo-conservatives have tried to avoid this disaster by taking their stand on the biblical revelation without coming to grips with the problem of its relation to modern secular scientific knowledge. William Temple tried to write an apology for basic Christianity without ignoring the actual world about us that is known to secular thought. I agree heartily with Temple's insistence that the full basic claim of Christianity has to be united with a theology that *is* a Christian theology. He says:

I am very sure that the conception of the Divine Personality is only tenable if it is taken in bitter earnest. . . . If the belief in divine transcendence be abolished, religion is in a parlous state, for a mechanically constant order (which is all that is then left, however much it be called divine immanence) is no object of worship or fount of love. . . . We are left with this result: a purely transcendent God, who intervenes often to give special direction to the course of events, is incompatible with a scientific apprehension of the world; while a purely transcendent God who never intervenes at all, or has done so only once or twice in recorded history, is incompatible with vital religion. . . . The governing principle of reality is a living and righteous God. . . . The hope of immortality is strictly dependent on and subordinate to faith in God. If God is righteous—still more if God is Love—immortality follows as a consequence.[3]

The merely immanent picture of God that was theologically fashionable in the 1920s was ruthlessly shattered by the philosophy of Sartre, to whose consistent atheism the gloom engendered by the great depression and World War II lent immediate popularity. For science does not really give us an optimistic picture of a scientifically discernible unconscious Cause moving through all things ever onward and upward, and coming to fruition in man's struggle to attain ever higher values, so that man is in a sense God-in-the-making. On the contrary, science knows nothing of causes either great or small. It can only record observable sequences. Therefore all we can say scientifically is that, at a particular point in the increasing complexity of biological sequences, men, in Sartre's phrase, "turn up". Sartre drew the ruthless conclusion: There are therefore no values outside of men for men to find or attain, for all values are men's creation and depend on men for their existence and continuation. There is therefore no moral imperative to which men can cling to give a sense of guidance and direction to their actions. All men's attempts to create values are an attempt to build a bridge over nothingness. As Sartre says, "Man is forlorn." Scientific naturalism cannot create a picture of God, and Sartre has done Christianity the service of eliminating it as a possible philosophical basis for theology.

---

[3] William Temple, *Nature, Man and God;* 1934, 1951, pp. 269, 287, 293, 452, 457.

CHAPTER 2
Inadequacies in Teilhard de Chardin's Great Attempt

In the problem of the relation of science and theology Christianity owes a great debt to Pierre Teilhard de Chardin for throwing the weight of his expert knowledge of biology and paleontology behind the construction of a theory that combines that scientific knowledge with a Christ-centered interpretation of man's nature and destiny. The resultant picture of man and his future is as optimistic as Sartre's is depressed. However, as far as my own thinking is concerned, I can only say that the theory of this present book was formulated, and three quarters of the book was written before I read any of de Chardin's writings; so as far as I know my own thinking has not been influenced by him. He was obviously a great and good Christian and his works are a joy to read, and in all probability future theologians will make use of his writings in the coming intellectual reformulation of the faith.

But I doubt whether his belief can be made the basic scheme for the reformulation of theology in relation to science. One reason is that the deep springs of his theoretical insight lie within the predominantly mystical bent of his personal piety. And structurally mysticism, when it builds exclusively on its own insights, tends to be dangerously monistic. De Chardin was a Roman Catholic mystic, and the non-mystical elements in Roman Catholicism can steady the mystical strain, where it appears, into an uneasy correlation with more orthodox belief. Whether an adequate structure for Christian faith can be grounded in mystical insight is, however, an open question. Because of the mystical strain, there is lacking in de Chardin's work that tang of the specific that characterizes the Hebrew Scriptures, which are the normative documents of our Faith. Mysticism tends toward a monistic philosophy in which salvation is seen in man's loss of personal identity by reabsorption in the Ground of Being. Since Catholicism has other strands in it besides the mystical—the Scriptural, the charitable, the organizational, the legal, and the intellectual—and since Catholicism keeps

11

its mystics within the total discipline of the Church, the mystical tendency is minimized there, and its danger is not as great as it is in Hinduism where it is the controlling factor. De Chardin strongly insists that he is against the idea of monistic reabsorption, and that the final denouement of the human enterprise as he sees it is an organic unity of the entire human race at the intense intellectual-spiritual level, where the physical body is no longer needed, but the whole human race, and under it the whole creation, will be united as the body of Christ. In this state the individual personal experience will be heightened and intensified instead of cancelled out. This convergence of humanity at the Omega point is, in Tennyson's words, the "one far-off divine event to which the whole creation moves." This is de Chardin's belief. But it can be questioned whether his thought provides the intellectual safeguards that are necessary to save it from misunderstanding when interpreted by those less steeped than he is in traditional Christianity.

As a biologist and paleontologist his main thinking is along evolutionary lines. Critics say that there is no sufficient place for evil in his system. I would agree, and I would also add that there is no sufficient emphasis on either creation or the cosmos. The two subjects are of course linked. It is instructive that the final uniting of men in the great spiritual organism "in Christ" as the goal of evolution, is regularly referred to by de Chardin as "the Omega point." The expression is obviously taken from the last chapter of the Book of Revelation: "I am the Alpha and the Omega, the first and the last, the beginning and the end." It seems to me that "the Alpha" is insufficiently dealt with. Specifically, I would say that, in dealing with the relation of science and Christian doctrine, the second law of thermodynamics, or entropy at the cosmic level, must be firmly dealt with.

My own book, I believe, provides for this lack that I find in his thought; for I work through the doctrine of creation in relation to entropy and then throughout the book rework the doctrine of evil in relation to entropy with I think new and fruitful results.

The other areas in which I feel there is a lack in his thought have to do with the modus operandi *of evolution in relation to God.* He claims that he avoids the monistic trap and instead thinks of God as a personal Spirit and so not part of nature but everywhere present in or with nature. According to his teaching this God

12

created the universe—there is no detailed discussion of how—and the nature he created was a nature that could evolve by the process of evolution. Granted. Then comes the main emphasis in his thought, the discussion of how evolution, by evolving into increasing complication, brings forth first life, then consciousness, then reflection-and-spirit. But he does not explain how this is done, and he gives one the general impression that "The earth produces of itself, first the blade, then the ear, then the full grain in the ear. But when the grain is ripe, at once he puts in the sickle, because the harvest is come." (Mark 4:28, 29.) *One only gets a clear impression of God interacting with his creation after evolution has reached the reflective or human stage.*[1]

In-as-much as de Chardin does not believe that the soul is a special endowment inserted into the evolutionary process to make a creature into man, but instead believes that the line is unbroken —from the scientific point of view—from inanimate matter to man, there ought to be some explanation in his theory of how pre-human evolution could take place. It is my impression that the transition from the barely alive to the fully alive, and from the fully alive to reflective consciousness, is accomplished in his thought by a confusion of terms, in which he uses anthropomorphic words in de-

---

[1] "It may be said that for a long time, under pressure of external forces engaged in concentrating it, the Human developed in a fashion that was mainly automatic—spurred on principally, in Bergson's expression, by a *vis a tergo,* a 'push from behind.' But when intelligence, which originally, as has been well said, was simply a means of survival, became gradually elevated to the function and dignity of a 'reason for living,' it was inevitable that, with the accentuation of the forces of free will, a profound modification should become discernible in the working of anthropogenesis, and one of which we are only now beginning to experience the full effects. . . . Which is to say that, given a sufficient degree of hominisation, the 'planetary sequence' generating the Human can only continue to operate in an atmosphere of *consent*—meaning, finally, under the impulsion of some desire. . . . The 'pull' after the 'push,' as the English would say. . . . Indeed . . . it seems essential that there should be a field of attraction at once powerful and irreversible, and such as cannot emanate collectively from a simple nebula of reflecting atoms, but which requires as its source a self-subsisting, strongly personalized star." Pierre Teilhard de Chardin, *The Future of Man;* New York: Harper & Row, 1964, pp. 276, 277, 279.

This change from the "push" to the "pull" seems to me unwarranted, if the "push from behind" means nature causing evolution to take place. For we know that nature's "push from behind" is entropy which is the opposite of evolution. My theory sees evolution as God's "pull" from the beginning at work against the natural force of entropy.

scribing the aliveness of the earliest stages of evolution, and a vocabulary drawn from the inorganic sciences in describing man.[2]

---

[2] I have italicized the key words in the following. The following are examples of de Chardin's application of anthropomorphic words to matter early in the evolutionary sequence:

"The essential originality of the cell seems to have been the *discovery* of a new *method*. . . ." (p. 86, line 22, 23). [Life at the beginning of the evolutionary process] "must . . . have *enjoyed* an exceptional *aptitude* to branch out. . . ." (p. 93, line 25.)

"Matter seems dead. But could not the next pulsation be slowly *preparing* around us?" (p. 99, line 23.)

"At first sight reproduction appears as a simple process *thought up by nature* to *ensure* the permanence of the unstable in the case of these vast molecular edifices." (p. 104, lines 17-19).

"Once more, this time on the plane of animate particles, we find the fundamental *techniques* of *groping*, the specific and invincible *weapon* of all expanding multitudes. . . . Groping is *directed chance*. It means pervading everything so as *to try* everything. . . . ["Directed chance" and the first "groping" are italicized by the author.] To accumulate characters in stable and coherent aggregates, life has to be very clever indeed. Not only has it to *invent* the machine but, like an engineer, so *design* it that it occupies the minimum space and is simple and resilient." (p. 110, lines 5-7, 10-12, 18-21.)

The following quotations are examples of words normally used to describe matter in an unconscious state, as used by de Chardin to describe the human self-conscious state. The italics are mine:

". . . *constituents* of consciousness. . . ." (p. 59, line 22.)

"But in one well-marked region at the heart of the mammals, where the most powerful brains ever made by nature are to be found, *they became red hot*. And right at the *heart of that glow burns a point of incandescence*. . . . *Thought is born*." (p. 160, lines, 4-8, 12.)

"When the anthropoid, so to speak, had been brought 'mentally' to *boiling point* some further *calories* were added. Or, when the anthropoid had almost reached the *summit of the cone*, a final effort took place along the *axis*. No more was needed for the whole inner *equilibrium* to be upset. What was previously only a *centred surface* became a *centre*. By a tiny 'tangential' *increase*, the 'radial' was turned back on itself and so to speak took an infinite leap forward. Outwardly, almost nothing in the organs had changed. But in *depth*, a great revolution had taken place: consciousness was now leaping and *boiling* in a *space* of super-sensory relationships and representations; and simultaneously consciousness was capable of perceiving itself in the concentrated simplicity of its faculties.. And all this happened for the first time." (p. 168, line 28 to p. 169, line 5.)

"After the grain of matter, the *grain* of life; and now at last we see constituted the *grain of thought*." (p. 173, lines 18-20. *Grain of thought* italicized by the author.)

"From now onwards it was not merely *animated grains* which the *pressure* of evolution *pumped* up the living stem, but *grains of thought*." (p. 174, lines 21-23.) (All of the above quotations are from Teilhard de Chardin, *The Phenomenon of Man;* New York: Harper & Row, Harper Torchbook edition, 1961.)

14

Creative hypotheses are constructed like the good detective story. The brilliant denouement occurs to the author and he marshals the incidents leading up to it, testing each as he goes to see that the account "holds water" and could have occurred. The brilliant denouement in de Chardin's theory, described in the imagery of the Omega point, and the cone imagery in his evolutionary hypothesis by which he describes evolution as leading to this point, can I think be traced in their pictorial origins in the medieval view of existence as pictured in the *Divine Comedy*.

In Dante's great work it will be remembered that the descent into hell is the descent into the interior of a cone. When the apex of the cone is passed in the center of the earth the next stage of the journey is that of climbing the mountain (another cone) of Purgatory. When in turn the apex of that cone is reached Vergil may no longer guide the poet, but instead the heavenly Beatrice guides Dante ever upward to the empyrean, and he sees at last the ineffable Beatific Vision, where, at the center of all existence he sees God, its flaming Source, surrounded, like the petals of a great rose, by the concentric circles of the saints who are incandescent as they burn in reflection of the burning Love at the heart of all existence, the Love that, as an unmoved Mover, moves evenly the sun and the other stars.

In *The Phenomenon of Man* de Chardin often resorts to the "cone" imagery as we have seen in his description of the anthropoid animal becoming man (*ante*, footnote 2). The "cone" imagery becomes even more marked in his theory of the prolongation of evolution past the biological stage, by means of the social and cultural history of man. He makes the important point that with the full "hominization" of man the line of evolution takes a distinct turn. In the beginning of life, after the stage of the one-celled organisms had been reached, the course of evolution branched out into several great stems, which in turn branched into innumerable species and sub-species, until we have the multitude of present-day living forms. But we find a centripetal movement beginning with the social evolution of the species man. Man has spread over the earth and as population increases individuals are forced into closer proximity to one another. We have voluntarily highly increased this proximity by the rapid modern methods of travel and communication. There is increasing not only a cross-fertilization of

15

races but also of cultures. We are becoming socially "one world."

Thus according to de Chardin, we are becoming united in our progress. It is again the cone imagery rather than the prolongation of parallel lines. The full drawing together of the human race at the Omega point is end as *finis* of the evolutionary progression—although not end as *finis* for the individual human beings involved in the evolutionary progression—and it is end as *telos* for men and through them for the whole evolutionary development.

What, according to de Chardin, brings about the evolutionary development? As we have seen, at the beginning it was the "push from behind" of matter acting upon matter, forcing it into one combination after another until those that facilitated the course of evolution were hit upon. After the human stage is reached the pull of the desired goal is exerted upon man's choices without destroying his freedom. (See *ante,* footnote 1.) Suggestions of the picture of God as the unmoved Mover, to the lure of whose intellect and love the order of the universe is due, and who influences men by their desire to conform freely to his perfection, are found in Roman Catholic thought, which is heavily influenced by Greek philosophy. Dante is of course in the Roman Catholic theological tradition.

I myself am neither Roman Catholic nor mystical, and I find such a picture of God too static to be congenial to my religious insight which is formed on the Bible and therefore thinks of God in Hebraic terms as intimately, constantly, but sporadically at work upon the created nature in which he is at all times and all places intimately interested (Luke 12:6), but to which he always remains supernatural. *This is why my account of evolution in this present book differs in an important way from that of de Chardin, although like him I see evolution as an unbroken line of development from inanimate matter to modern civilized man, and like him I see freely obedient union with God through Christ forever as the great goal.* But if one is combining the Old Testament picture of God with science's picture of the evolutionary process, then a *modus operandi* must be sketched by which the supernatural God can act *upon* nature throughout the entire evolutionary process in the interests of his overall plan.

This I have tried to do. I say intentionally that God's action is *upon* nature rather than *through* or *within* nature. *Through* and *within* are words that blur the biblical picture of God's supernatural status. *In the Old Testament God's relation to the world at both the human and the subhuman level is always seen as intercourse, never as immanence. This biblical description of the relation of God to the universe I have tried to adjust to the general outlines of its entire cosmological and evolutionary (biological) history.*

Of course in insisting that God is not *within* the universe I am not describing God as localized "up there" and as the absentee landlord of his creation. I subscribe wholeheartedly to the doctrine that God is not localized anywhere in the creation or in the creation as a whole, but that nevertheless God is totally available at all times at each and every point in the cosmos simultaneously. The reason that statements about God working *within or through* nature need to be avoided in the twentieth century is that they blur the distinction between the Creator and the creation in order to seem to by-pass what has appeared the intolerable difficulty of finding some way of reconciling the Christian picture of God with the picture science has offered us of the universe's activity. If, when Christians talk about God working *within* and *through* nature they mean God related to nature according to Old Testament insights, then they have thrown no light on the problem at all but have simply appeared to extricate themselves from the difficulty of relating science and Christianity by using words that blur the point at issue. For if no further explanation is given of *how* God works *within* and *through* nature, *within* and *through* can only ease the problem intellectually by surreptitiously accepting the pantheistic position that makes the universe an aspect of God, and so, by not positing anything outside the universe whose relation to the universe needs to be accounted for, comes to harmonious terms with science by denying the Hebrew-Christian faith.

Modern science could be adjusted easily to Hinduism's formula: *Brahman is the Ground of Being; Brahman is Atman; Atman is the Ground of Being in its multiform differentiation as ourselves and the universe about us.* Individuals in their personal lives have linked the Christian God with pantheistic theology only by the saving inconsistencies of their thinking. But even with the non-intellectual layman, the bedrock of intellectual presuppositions eventually has an effect upon the "practical" religious outlook and life. Liberalism has been playing with the edges of pantheism too long and too dangerously.

There is one type of statement that recurs so often in de Chardin's writings that I think it must have been important to him, and I find it distressing. More than any other type of thing that he says it makes me think that his theory is lacking, as others have claimed, in the area of insight into the problem of sin. The problem lies in de Chardin's central use of the word "reflection" with emphasis on both its *thought* and *reflex* implications. He thinks that the species became fully human when there occurred an "in-folding of a psychic core upon itself."[3] He believes "that this separate Human element cannot achieve its final equilibrium except by coiling and concentrating, through both compulsion and attraction, on a planetary scale upon itself. . . ."[4] These quotations are by no means isolated ones. The following quotations are all taken from *The Phenomenon of Man*:

> And we are happy to admit that the birth of intelligence corresponds to a turning in upon itself, not only of the nervous system, but of the whole being. (pp. 170, 171)
>
> Man discovers that *he is nothing else than evolution become conscious of itself,* . . . On this summit and on this summit alone are repose and illumination waiting for us. (p. 220)
>
> From our experimental point of view, reflection is, as the word indicates, the power acquired by a consciousness to turn in upon itself, to take possession of itself *as of an object* endowed with its own particular consistence and value. . . . (p. 165)
>
> The ego only persists by becoming ever more itself, in the measure in which it makes everything else itself. (p. 172)
>
> . . . . it is mankind that seeks itself and grows. (p. 177)
>
> In short, the further the living being emerges from the anonymous masses by the radiation of his own consciousness, the greater becomes the part of his activity which can be stored up and transmitted by means of education and imitation. (p. 224)[5]

One cannot help feeling that at this point his theory is spiritually questionable, and that he is lauding as the key to social evolution

---

[3] de Chardin, *The Future of Man*. New York: Harper & Row, 1964, p. 271.

[4] *Ibid.*, p. 280. And note the mechanistic vocabulary that gives the illusion of bridging the gap between the subhuman and the human.

[5] Pierre Teilhard de Chardin, *The Phenomenon of Man*. New York: Harper & Row, Harper Torchbook, 1961, pp. 170-171, 220, 165, 172, 177, 224.

the self-centeredness in which Christianity has identified basic sin. Of course the third chapter of Genesis sees the tie-up between the possession of reflective intelligence and the sin of self-centeredness, but according to the Bible self-centeredness is perversion of the reflective intelligence, and not its essential nature. It is very much to be questioned whether mind *increases* by concentrating upon itself, although with the gropings of the increasing mind goes an increased awareness of the self. I would agree in general with the opposite insight of Martin Buber, who was a Jew and who saw mind functioning by the "I-it" and still more by the "I-thou" relationship.

It is the insight of Buber's that I have made basic to my own attempt to relate over-all biblical teaching to the basic scientific outlook. De Chardin's belief about the intelligence growing by turning in upon itself shows that he had not watched closely enough what his own vigorous and creative mind had done. As at once a scientist and a Roman Catholic religious, he centered his attention upon God and upon the world as the world appeared as itself, and this was a means of clarifying his vision of the world in relation to God. And both these turnings of the attention to God and to the world were forms of mental extroversion, the turning of the attention to the other-than-the-self. This is true even when he found God within himself, unless he actually falls into the mystical trap of identifying God with himself.

The words that you speak and the sight of your face are for me originally my sensations that give the illusion of being exterior to myself, and are practically assumed by me to give genuine evidence of something other than myself, although as states of consciousness they occur as part of my consciousness. As these sensations pass over into my perception I am much more aware of the total situation as involving myself-as-interacting with the outside world. But even the memory of the perception would involve fading traces of the sensation. Thus, although all that I know of you occurs within me, I am not tempted to fall into the subjective trap of thinking that my consciousness of you is your existence and that when I remember you I am turning my mind inward upon itself. The difference between this type of experience and man's awareness of God is that when the supernatural God makes his presence known to a human soul he by-passes sensation, and the human experience begins with perception which may or may not borrow from the memories of past ordinary sensational experience to supply the perception with as much of the audio-visual accompaniment of normal social intercourse as the individual finds necessary to his thinking, or that God finds desirable in making the situation useful to the individual.

Even in ordinary human experience not all perception is initiated by immediately preceding sensation. I can perceive a characteristic of you for the first time when the perception depends upon memories accompanied by almost no audio-visual imagery. The memories of two of your well known characteristics may suddenly intersect in my mind, and the spontaneous relating of these two characteristics may make me suddenly perceive a third characteristic of your nature that I had never before identified, but once identified, the memory's correlating it with my knowledge of your past behavior corroborates immediately the accuracy of this new perception. This is perception not initiated by immediate audio-visual experience.

But even in this type of perception, the mind of the thinker is turned outward to the other and is not bent back upon itself. For the thinker is aware—if he is really thinking of the other person's characteristic and not all bound up with interest in what practical advantage or disadvantage the other person's characteristic is going to be to himself—that his mind in thinking is relating itself to *the other*, and is not bent back upon itself.

When a man is in relation to God as the Other, he is related to a God outside of himself although his point of knowing is within his own spirit, as is all of his knowing. It is within our spirits that we know that it is raining. But we assume that the rain is taking place outside of us. God's otherness and relation to the individual is nontheless real because God is able to by-pass sensation entirely and begin the human awareness of himself as a perception that usually involves no audio-visual accompaniments. It is the fact that the Divine-human relationship is usually unaccompanied by any impression of sensation that leads men into the mystical trap of identifying the Divine as the ground of existence within the human. Christian mysticism tries to avoid this trap by identifying God as Love and its Source. This is less dangerous than the Hindu way of identifying God simply as the Absolute, the All, or

20

the Ground of Existence. But although Christian love is active, it is easy for a Christian, if he does not also stress righteousness as a governing characteristic of God, to allow his idea of love to be predominantly a somewhat static state of radiant contemplative togetherness. From this point it is much easier to slip into the pantheistic error and describe man as part of God. On the other hand, since righteousness in any sense that means anything to us involves specific discriminating choices which involve specific activity in time, if a firm emphasis is kept on God's righteousness, he has to be thought of in the sufficiently anthropomorphic terms of an actively discriminating personal spirit and this militates against the pantheistic trap. Furthermore, if the emphasis on God's discriminating righteousness is never lost, the individual will sometimes discover the God whom he met in his consciousness to be actively *discriminating against* some of the man's own actions and desires, and thus the pantheistic trap of identifying man with God is easily avoided.

No, it must be affirmed that, on any Christian understanding of life, when a man's reflective ability is heightened by an "I-it" relationship with the physical world, or by an "I-thou" relationship with another human being or with God, the intellectual life of the man is heightened by turning outside itself, not by turning in upon itself.

The same extroversion can exist in those states in which the man shuts out sense impressions temporarily and concentrates upon ideas in his own mind. All readers who like myself are slow, independent thinkers, remember the strain of the intellectual house-divided of the college and graduate-study years, when the technicalities of the academic regime forced the mind to absorb knowledge faster than it could be critically assimilated. The novice thinker, weighted down with the large accumulation of learning that the mind has forced the brain to "tape-record", suffers from chronic intellectual and spiritual indigestion, since what he has learned is as yet largely extraneous to the genuine experience and working knowledge of his independent thinking, and is simply stored, as a camel stores water and nourishment, preparatory to a long journey. Under these circumstances, when, in later years, a person with such an experience, in forging ahead where the trails run out and stop, turns his mind inward to feed upon his stored

21

knowledge, he is quite conscious of the spiritually extrovert character of this mental activity.

When we work with knowledge that has very recently come to us through sensation, as for example when we see and hear that a dish is boiling over and immediately turn down the gas on the stove, we think of ourselves as dealing with the outside world. *And when the mind deals with knowledge that it has gathered months and years previously, it is still in a sense dealing with the exterior world at one or two removes. The mind is not reflexively turned in upon itself as de Chardin believes.*

The subtlety of the distinction between the thinking mind itself and some of the ideas it has available to it by means of memory is implied in Jesus' famous dictum that "there is nothing outside a man which by going into him can defile him; but the things which come out of a man are what defile him." (Mark 7:15) The Church has rightly extended "outside" to include information which is acquired by the mind from without, (Matthew 4:1-11, James 1:14, 15) before that information gets to be "within" the person by being taken up by his will.

Reflective thought, in the sense of being able to hold ideas in the memory, and then at a later time take two ideas from the memory, put them together and draw a conclusion from them, does not seem to be the exclusive ability of the human race. The rudiments of the ability seem to occur in the higher animals. On one occasion my sister saw her saddle-horse walk over to the locked gate and with his nose move back the wooden bar that pinned the gate to the gate-post as he had seen her do it with her hand, and push open the gate and walk out.

Reflection in the sense of the mind making itself the object of its concern seems to me to be an ability of which slight traces can also sometimes be found in the higher animals. These traces can I think be identified in some instances of worry, which is a state in which the mind does turn inward on itself. Worry does not normally occur in a strong primary emotion. For example, if a fierce dog suddenly comes into the immediate vicinity of a cat, the cat will be afraid and climb a tree. The cat's fear is healthily extrovert. It fears the dog. The cat's fear is not unhealthily introverted to worry about states of its own consciousness.

Worry, which we usually think of as a distinctly human experience, is a complex emotional state involving fear. But worry might be called distress at a fear foreseen in tranquility. Here the mind is conscious in advance of the unpleasant state it may in the future experience, and a state of worry is a state in which the consciousness is to some extent turned inward unhealthily upon itself, the "reflex" meaning of "reflection" which de Chardin praises as the greatness of man, and which Jesus thought in the case of worry could indicate an unhealthy state of the human spirit. He said, "Do not be anxious." (Matthew 6:25) But I have seen an intelligent small dog exhibit all the signs of worry and dread as he saw his master preparing to give him his accustomed bath. So there would not seem to be the absolute line of demarcation that de Chardin thinks there is between the ordinary consciousness of the higher animals and the "reflective" consciousness of man.

In what sense is de Chardin right, then, in making man's distinctiveness his ability to look consciously within himself, to be aware that there is another kind of "space" than the physical space his body occupies, and that this different space really exists, so that by becoming man, man in truth enters a new space? It is my belief that the truth of this situation can be expressed more subtly than de Chardin expresses it. In his children's story, *The Magician's Nephew*, C. S. Lewis describes a "wood between the worlds" which is the intersection point of many universes. The two children, with the aid of magic rings, journey by way of this wood to a different universe. When, again via this wood, they return to England, they find that the time taken by the adventure has not elapsed upon earth, because the strange other universe had not been physically far away. It had been in a different space-time altogether.

Now it seems to me that when man discovers his inner life, what he is discovering is that new sorts of spaces are suddenly and mysteriously available to him by means of his mind which is the wood between the worlds. He cannot look directly *at* the space of our physical world, but can only identify it by the objects in it. Neither can he look directly at the strange newly discovered "spaces" in his mind any more than he as thinker can look directly at himself-thinking. (The acting subject cannot make himself-acting the object of his thought. His nearest approach is making his immediate past the object.) Man identifies the inner space of

23

his mind as he does physical space, by means of that which fills it, which, in the case of the inner space, is thoughts. In this newly discovered space man finds that he can bring together and relate in new ways things originally far separated in space and time, so that by means of the inner space he can combine things heretofore not combinable, and then impress the influence of the combination upon the exterior world to which he has full access by evolutionary involvement. But in all this man is making "the other," not himself, the object of his thought. For the external world is only known to us at two removes, by sensation as catalogued for our minds by perception and combined with memory. To deal with much of the world at once one has to deal with it in connection with that which is stored in the memory, but such dealing is still the turning of the mind outward, to the not-self. That this is so is seen from the fact that the great regimes of meditative mysticism regularly prescribe the emptying of the mind of the clutter of specific thoughts, impressions, and memories of the world as an advanced step toward the simplification of life, after the simpler step of the renunciation of worldly possessions has been taken.

This long discussion has been inserted because I believe that the secret of evolution lies in the "I-it" and "I-thou" relationships, in the story of how God has loved the world and related himself to it from the beginning. *Man, as fulfillment of evolution, is not created mind turning inward upon itself, but is the creation as successfully brought by God to the point at which it is possible for it to cooperate voluntarily in a fully I-thou relationship with its Creator.*

One other point needs to be mentioned. As this present book takes the scientific picture of man's existence as over against the Christian biblical picture, and then tries to make a working relationship between the two pictures, it may look at times as if I thought that modern scientific thinkers have been working against Christianity. I realize that many scientists are deeply religious people and that there are also a wide variety of opinions held by scientists themselves on the subject of the relation of science and religion and of the interpretation and implication of scientific knowledge itself. So the expressions that I constantly use "science holds that . . ." or "scientists believe that . . ." are glittering generalizations and therefore not altogether accurate. But I plead that

I must over-simplify in order to make headway in correlating a wide range of material, and that in the use of these expressions— the easiest ones available—I am not casting reflections on any one scientist. What is really referred to by those expressions is the total impact that the rise of modern science has had in the last hundred years on the mind of the Western man-on-the-street, the scientific layman whether he be philosopehr, novelist, Doctor of Divinity, sociologist, or the rank and file of Americans whose thinking is molded by these specialists and by the accounts of science that appear in popular journals. This pervasive outlook on life as largely colored by the findings of science might be called "scientism" or "the science image". But by whatever name it is called its impact upon the thought of this century has been heavy, and has made it increasingly difficult to convince earnest and thoughtful younger people of the truth of Christianity. I do not think that the difficulty is entirely that of the layman's interpretation of science. As de Chardin said, "For most modern biologists ... there is no sharp line to be drawn between instinct and thought, neither being very much more than a sort of luminous halo enveloping the play—the only essential thing—of the determinisms of matter."[6]

This description of the role of consciousness was the frank basis of the Behavioristic psychology that I was taught in my undergraduate days in the 1920s. It is now fashionable to say that science is less dogmatic and no longer claims that the universe is a neat mechanism, but instead admits that nature's regularities are only statistical, and looks upon Behaviorism as an outmoded fashion in psychology. It is true that the Behavioristic position blatantly advocated is now seen by science to be an embarrassment, and the claims of the physiological determinism of human conduct are not blatantly publicized. But the change would seem to be more a cautious approach to the subject rather than a hearty advocacy on the part of science of an alternate hypothesis which scientists see as adjustable to Christianity's claim that God is the righteous Father in heaven who actively cares for human beings, that human beings can respond to God and as a result of this response initiate action in the world that otherwise would not have been initiated, and that by the power of this God through Christ it will be possible for the individual consciousness of these persons to continue

---

[6] *Ibid.*, p. 166.

after death without their present physical bodies, so that after death they can know and serve God in vigorous active conscious fellowship with him. This Christian claim has to be made by Christianity, not as a mythological statement, but as true, or the religion advocated under the Christian name would really be another religion masquerading as Christianity.

* * * * * *

One omission requires an explanation. A writer can scarcely try to harmonize science and theology without indicating briefly why he is making no structural use of the process philosophy of Alfred North Whitehead. In the present instance there are two reasons. The first is that Whitehead's God is so completely entwined with the process that he cannot be described as the active, discriminating, supernatural, personal God required by the Bible's insistence on the unswerving, powerful, acting-righteousness of the Divine character. The second is that his system does not really face the implications of *the second law of thermodynamics*.[7] The very occasional passing references that he may make to the disintegration of the universe are not built into the structure of his thought.[8]

In this regard the relation of Whitehead the man to the structure of his thought should be noted. Alfred North Whitehead was born in 1861. He taught mathematics and theoretical physics at Cambridge 1911-14, and at the University College, London, 1914-24.

---

[7] This is true at least of the only works of Whitehead's that I have read, namely: *Science and the Modern World, Religion in the Making, Adventures of Ideas, Process and Reality,* and his lecture on "Immortality." However my conclusion as to my second reason is corroborated by the complete lack of mention of entropy both in *Whitehead's Philosophy of Physics* by Laurence Bright, O. P. (New York: Sheed and Ward, 1960) and in the extended references to Whitehead's philosophy in *Issues in Science and Religion* by the physicist Ian G. Barbour, (Englewood Cliffs, N. J.: Prentice-Hall, Inc., 1966).

[8] Alfred North Whitehead, *Religion in the Making,* (New York: Meridian Books, 1960) pp. 93, 153-154; *Process and Reality,* (New York: Harper & Row, Torchbooks TB 1033, 1960) pp. 122 lines 1-3; 142 lines 5-21; *Adventures of Ideas,* (New York: The Macmillan Company, FP93517, 1967) p. 46 lines 8-11. Whitehead declares that "What is inexorable in God, is valuation as an aim towards 'order'; and 'order' means 'society' permissive of actualities with patterned intensity of feeling arising from adjusted contrasts. In this sense God is the principle of concretion." *Process and Reality* pp. 373, 374. And he explicitly claims that "The immanence of God gives reason for the belief that pure chaos is intrinsically impossible. At the other end of the scale, the immensity of the world negatives the belief that any state of order can be so established that beyond it there can be no progress." *Ibid.* p. 169.

When past sixty years of age he became professor of philosophy at Harvard, 1924-38, and it was during this American period that his famous books of philosophy were published. He died in 1947. Thus the early formative period of his life was spent in an intellectual climate in which a dominant problem concerned the absorption of the doctrine of evolution into the intellectual scheme of things. The idea of evolution's biological *crescendo* and the unrelated awareness of the British Empire's political *crescendo* were part of the early environment of a young man of such outstanding personal vigor that he was able to begin his new career as a philosopher at an age when most men are thinking of laying down the burdens of professional life. His great philosophical works were written before the gloom of World War II.

Although Whitehead was aware that evil and degeneration can occur on earth, the overall assumption of his philosophy is that "The universe is . . . a creative advance into novelty,"[9] and in general is productive of an ever more desirable and spiritually enhanced situation.

> The 'consequent nature' of God is the physical prehension by God of the actualities of the evolving universe.[10]
> This final phase of passage in God's nature is ever enlarging itself.[11]
> In the philosophy of organism this ultimate is termed 'creativity'.[12]

His choice of words is at least weighted towards optimism.

But according to the picture presented by *the second law of thermodynamics*, biological evolution is only a small-scale phenomenon in a universe that in its overall aspects is "dying". When the universe as a whole arrives at its final state of disintegration at a low temperature all biological life will have become extinct. Since in Whitehead's thought God is never dissociated from the processes of the universe,[13] it should follow that, although the unconscious

---

[9] *Process and Reality;* New York: Harper & Row TB 1033, 1960, pp. 339, 340.
[10] *Ibid.* p. 134.
[11] *Ibid.* p. 530.
[12] *Ibid.* p. 11.
[13] *Religion in the Making;* New York: Meridian Books, LA28, 1960, p. 104, lines 18-26.

primordial nature of God would remain unchanged,[14] the content of the consequent nature of God would perish when "maximum entropy" was reached and all the energy of the universe had gone into the non-available state. For according to Whitehead all God's consciousness and realized values are serially attained by and enjoyed in the process of the universe.[15] But when the universe has disintegrated the show will be over and that will be that.

The idea that the content of the consequent nature of Whitehead's God is ultimately dying would not be contradicted even by the more recent theory of the "expanding universe" and the theory that matter, after its farthest expansion, will again coalesce and another cosmic explosion initiate a new universe. For such a God, as to his attainments and consciousness, would completely perish with the end of the present universe, and his consequent nature would only reattain actualized values and consciousness when and if a new process of organic evolution took place.[16] The consequent nature of God in this new universe would not in any way be enriched by memory of our universe and its attainments, all traces of which would be completely wiped out by the cosmic explosion that would initiate the new universe. For on Whitehead's theory God, having attained consciousness and realized values in and by the earthly process, would not then hold the consciousness and actualized values in himself as supernatural to and dissociated from the process,[17] in the interim between the two instances of biological evolution. For Whitehead's God is always fully enmeshed in the process of the universe.

Because of entropy it is difficult to see how Whitehead's robust philosophy can have a structural—as distinct from a temperamental —optimism.

For the fateful principle known as the Second Law of Thermodynamics, which stands today as virtually the only pillar of classical physics left intact by the march of science, proclaims that the fundamental processes of nature are irreversible. Nature

---

[14] "This side of his nature is free, complete, primordial, eternal, actually deficient, and unconscious." (*Process and Reality;* New York: Harper & Row, TB1033, 1960, p. 524.)

[15] *Ibid.* pp. 134 lines 33-35; p. 340 line 1; p. 362 lines 7-9; pp. 521 line 29 to p. 522 line 3.

[16] *Ibid.* p. 531, lines 18-24, 30-36; and p. 531, lines 1-6.

[17] *Ibid.* pp. 528, 529.

moves just one way. . . . Time itself will come to an end. For entropy points the direction of time. Entropy is the measure of randomness.[18]

In view of the fact that, as against the static philosophy of the ancients, time has an important place in process philosophy, I do not see how Whitehead's theory can adequately take the outlines of the scientific view of the universe into account, as it attempts to do, because it does not have in it a place for entropy.

Since the sum total of all processes that go on in the universe entails an increase in entropy, and since such processes go only one way in time, it may be expected that there is a relationship between time and the second law of thermodynamics. As Sir Arthur Eddington succinctly expressed it, the second law of thermodynamics is "time's arrow". Implicit in this terse phrase is the idea that this law points the direction of all real events in time.[19]

---

[18] Lincoln Barnett, *The Universe and Dr. Einstein;* New York, Mentor Books, M71, 1957, p. 111.

[19] Harold F. Blum, *Time's Arrow and Evolution;* New York: Harper & Brothers, TB555, 1962, p. 16.

CHAPTER 3
The Need for an Hypothesis

When one thinks of the many writers of that collection of books we call the Bible, one wonders whether we have fully understood their message, whether they themselves ever fully understood it. For, children of their age though they were, pre-philosophic and pre-scientific, their minds were guided by the Creator as their thinking dealt with the basic problems of God's relationship to the world and men. Sometimes the directness of their experience of God frightened them. (Amos 3:8.) Sometimes they besought God for enlightenment and it was denied them. (Jeremiah 12:1-5.) Often their message was contrary to their personal advantage and their desires. (Numbers 23,24; Jeremiah 20:7-9.) But the prophets all believed that they were commissioned by God to give God's messages to the people. The phrase "Thus saith the Lord" reechoes through the teaching of all of them except the last and greatest of their number, and he never uses it, substituting instead another formula, "I say to you," (Matthew 5:18,20,22,26,28,32,34,39,44.) and thereby claiming to be himself the Divine Authority, not merely its proclaimer.

To those in Palestine to whom Jesus spoke, the modern perplexity as to whether the personal God of the Bible exists was a problem which, with the developing science that has made it acute, was as yet a millennium and a half ahead of their intellectual horizon. And yet the practical disbelief in God and his unswerving demands for righteousness flourished then as now when the "cares of the world, and the delight in riches, and the desire for other things, enter in and choke" (Mark 4:19.) the Divine imperative in a man's life. And Jesus knew that there was no way of regaining confidence in the reality of the unseen righteous Creator except through that resubmission to the Divine imperative to righteousness which is available to all. Jesus had been tempted at the beginning of his career (Matthew 4:5-7) to use a spectacular means of gaining popular credence for his power and authority by a physical action of a completely non-moral kind which would impress the intellect while making no

30

righteous demands upon the will. He put this temptation aside as ultimately defeating his long distance purpose. And toward the end of his career, when he thought of the multitudes who had heard him but had been unchanged by his teaching, he was still sure that his early decision was the correct one. When he told the parable of Lazarus and the Rich Man under the shadow of his approaching cross, he describes the rich man as tormented after death and as requesting Father Abraham to send Lazarus back from Paradise to warn the rich man's five brothers to repent in time. "But Abraham said, 'They have Moses and the prophets; let them hear them.' And he said, 'No, father Abraham; but if someone goes to them from the dead, they will repent.' He said to him" in words in which we can hear Jesus thinking out loud of the future of the Church, " 'If they do not hear Moses and the prophets, neither will they be convinced if some one should rise from the dead.' " (Luke 16:29-31.)

There are no accounts of resurrection appearances of Jesus to his enemies, or to the indifferent multitude, only to those who already acknowledged his spiritual authority as seen through the righteousness and love of his life. The great miracle of Christ's resurrection is the keystone of the arch of all specifically Christian thought, for it brings the necessary substantiation to the doctrine of the incarnation. Yet even the historically attested resurrection of Christ would have found few believers through the centuries, were it in turn not corroborated by the righteous love of Christ's perfect life, so completely fulfilling the law that had it been permanently snuffed out the Power behind the universe would have shown itself as callously indifferent to love and righteousness, and as willing to lead on deceitfully and then abandon in extremity his most devoted servant.

Man cannot control God, only obey him and be controlled by him. This is one reason why scientific experiments can never discover God. For science advances by means of the controlled experiment in which men devise schemes to test nature to see how it works. Only one religious controlled experiment was possible by man, and that was the experiment of seeing how the God who had claimed through Moses and the prophets to be righteous would react to a life lived in perfect loving and righteous obedience to himself. When Jesus of Nazareth lived such a life the character and reputation of Almighty God were at stake in the resurrection.

There is another reason why science can never discover the truth of Christianity, which is the truth about the nature of God. Jesus had put from himself as a temptation the strategy of gaining a following by a startling act within the sphere of the physically measurable: a human body of measurable weight leaping from a measurable height in successful defiance of the force of gravity. (Matthew 4:5-7.) For the things physically measurable in themselves reveal nothing of righteous love which is the central characteristic and controlling purpose of the mind of God. Instead it is by following the clue of value, especially moral value, that we get to know the truth about God and his relation to the world, as God through the Bible validates his authority by responding to our feeling for righteousness and by training beyond our comfortable dreams the understanding of it which we already possess. The book of value must remain a closed book to the scientist as scientist, concerned as he is with the physically measurable. When the great scientists tell us that in their scientific work they are haunted by the feeling of the mystery and the beauty of the universe, they are speaking as ordinary men, not in their role as scientists. And when the feeling of the mysterious simplicity of beauty has helped direct them to the hypothesis by which they make a great discovery, the discovery when made will be a technical fact, measurably described, and the aspect of beauty will not itself be an ingredient in the scientific conclusion.

We cannot as Christians, therefore, go to science to construct our religion or prove the truth of our faith. Our knowledge and evidence are gained in another way. Why, then, is it not intellectually permissible for Christianity to present the religious truth it has found while at the same time ignoring the findings of science? The answer is that the good, the beautiful, and the true are not for us bodiless abstractions as they were for Plato, but instead primarily characteristics of the powerful, living God. (The good: Mark 10:18. The beautiful: Psalms 27:4; 29:3; 145:11,12; Exodus 24:10; Isaiah 6:3. The true: John 1:14; 14:6; 15:26. Powerful and living: Exodus 3:14; 19:18-20; Psalms 33:6-10; 145:11-13; Revelation 15:3.) And God and his ways and will for us have been made known to us through the medium of this same physical nature whose dimensions and intricate workings science is engaged in measuring with ever increasing mathematical precision. The physical world is the stage-setting for God's self-revelation to man, not the revelation itself. But Christians must never forget that it genuinely is the stage-setting. The belief that reality is coherent is a presupposition of all scientific, philosophical, and theological thought. Hence if Christianity is true, the stage-setting, if accurately investigated and measured by science independently, will eventually be found to be of such a nature as to be adequate for the use of the self-revelation of the God whose character, will, and activity are known to us through the Bible. The same human mind investigates nature scientifically and thinks religious thoughts in response to God, and that mind must be considered basically trustworthy in both fields or basically untrustworthy in both fields. Thus those people are correct who say that some working interrelation of scientific and theological thought must eventually be found if both science and Christianity are to be believed to be true. This does not rule out the advisability of keeping one's knowledge in the religious and scientific realms tentatively compartmentalized over an uneasily long period of time. Human thought and knowledge are sufficiently inadequate to suggest the wisdom of caution in trying prematurely to bring the two areas of knowledge into a unified intellectual scheme at the expense of denying well attested knowledge in either field. But since there must be coherence in the truth about reality, a science that could be proved true and permanently incompatible with the basic assumptions of Christianity would be genuine (even if not conclusive) evidence against the truth of the latter.

Need we be surprised that in three hundred and fifty years of intellectual struggle theology has not completed its description of Christianity's relation to the swiftly changing scientific thought, when it took Christianity four hundred years to complete its formulation of a working relationship between theology and the static body of Greek philosophy?

The purpose of this book is to attempt to make progress in the interrelation of science and theology. To limit its scope precisely, it is an attempt to use the basic scientific picture of the universe and evolution in constructing an intellectual stage-setting that will not do violence to Christian theology as expressed in the Nicene creed. An intellectual construction that does not do violence to this creedal summary should be found basically related to biblical religion as a whole. For in the end the problem is to relate biblical thought to modern science. Greek philosophy was not part of the Christian revelation, and so ancient and modern European philosophy can be tentatively dropped as impedimenta in order to make our correlation easier. In fact, the thought has grown on me, emotionally, over the years, that Christianity's difficulty in relating science and religion has been partly due to the previous overloading of Christian thought with the static quality of the abstractions of philosophy. The restless, complicated, and specific motion and material power of the macrocosm and the microcosm depicted by science seem somehow less akin to the static wholeness of philosophy than to the Bible's picture of the boundless energy of the Creator God who "made the Pleiades and Orion" (Amos 5:8.), at whose anger "the earth reeled and rocked; the foundations also of the mountains trembled and quaked" (Psalms 18:7), who calls all the stars by name, "and because he is strong in power not one is missing" (Isaiah 40:26), and yet who so watches over the tinier parts of his creation that not a sparrow will fall to the ground without his will. (Matthew 10:29.)

CHAPTER 4

The Second Law of Thermodynamics and the Doctrine of the Creation

It has already been said that the Platonic ideas do not exist for Christianity in eternal isolation, but that the good, the beautiful, and the true are instead thought of as basic characteristics of the powerful, living God. And because God is living, any differentiation of his characteristics into the good, the beautiful, and the true, or into any other classification, would be somewhat arbitrary. Christians are aware, for instance, that there is a beauty of holiness, and they are also aware that holiness is not entirely dissociated from beauty. (Matthew 6:28-30.) The Bible does not use the Platonic formula of the good, the beautiful, and the true. Instead it ascribes to God "the kingdom, and the power, and the glory, forever." (Matthew 6:13.)

Since God is pure spirit the word "power" when ascribed to him includes all that human beings designate by the word intelligence, as well as creation of and control over what we call physical nature and power. The word "kingdom" refers to his righteous sovereignty. It includes his moral goodness because of the Bible's constant description of his rule as righteous. (Deuteronomy 10:17,18; Psalms 67:4; 96:13; 145:8-20; Acts 17:30,31; Revelation 15:3.) The word "glory" refers to the living source of that which on earth we describe as beauty. (Exodus 24:10; Psalms 27:4; 19:1-5; Isaiah 6:3; 28:5; 55:12,13; Matthew 6:28,29; Revelation 21.) Just as his righteousness is righteousness-plus, including the superlative love which we recognize but cannot fathom, so also the ingredient of beauty in the word glory is beauty-plus, it is that for which all earthly beauty awakens hunger and it is that for which we responsively hunger when we create anything beautiful. And likewise the word "intelligence" as an ingredient in our ascription of power to God is not merely the rational intelligence that human beings know, but is rational-intelligence-plus.

This "plus" is extremely important for our thinking. The mistake subjective idealism makes when it tries to flee the materialistic dilemma, is to reduce all things to rational minds and the content of their thought. A beautiful and simple coherence is thus achieved by making the universe the content of the thought of the Absolute Mind, and by making human minds living centers of consciousness within the Divine Mind. The underlying danger in subjective idealism, a danger which makes its philosophy incapable of synthesis with biblical thought, is its basic inability to deal with the problem of evil. This philosophy is a form of pantheism which, by reducing all things, including all evil situations, to the absolute, undercuts the biblical claim that God is unswervingly righteous.

The problem is complicated for us by the fact that our biblical religion does trace all secondary existences back to the mind of God. "In the beginning God .... And God said, 'Let there be' .... And it was so." (Genesis 1:1,3,7) The Mind however, that accounts for all other existence is not just rational mind, but Rational-Mind-Plus. The Bible thinks of the universe as something other than God, having a separate existence on its own. The human mind's closest approximation to the Divine Mind's creative power is the artistic creation of a novelist. But a great novel is at best a vivid static shadow of its author's mind, not a little society with continuing independent dynamic power and freedom of choice which enables the book itself to continue the development of the plot after it has been cast loose from the author's mind by publication.

If we think of the creation as a book that is now leading a separate existence and actively continuing its own story independently, we must think of it as always having the top-flight editorial assistance of the Original Author available, advising here, pruning there, adding a little bit elsewhere, whether or not the "book" enjoys this interference with its self-expression. The Bible thinks of God as doing things constantly to this objectively-other universe which in its basic structure he has previously created, and it unabashedly describes his action in anthropomorphic fashion, under such analogies as a farmer planting a garden, (Genesis 2:8) a potter molding clay, (Jeremiah 18:6) or a teacher teaching a pupil. (Psalms 25:4,5,8,9) The Bible, of course, thinks that God is not limited in the number of places he can be at one time and in the number of things he can do simultaneously.

The modern age is not the first that has been embarrassed by what it considers the primitive naïveté of this picture. It was an

36

embarrassment also to the Christian intellectuals of the second to the fourth centuries who had been trained in Greek philosophy. St. Augustine solved the problem by expressing the basic biblical thought in what the West has always considered intellectually mature terms.

For Augustine and for orthodox Christian thought after him God's constant connection with the created universe is accounted for not by intermittent major and minor intrusions into mundane affairs, but by variations in his mode of working while he continuously sustains it throughout by his power. This sustaining is considered so thoroughgoing and necessary to its being that the universe would not continue to exist if this Divine help should at any time become lacking. Augustine expresses this beautifully in his interpretation of his first great vision of God:

And I looked back on other things; and I saw that they owed their being to Thee; and were all bounded in Thee: but in a different way; not as being in space; but because Thou containest all things in Thine hand in Thy truth . . . . For that all spaces of times, both which have passed, and which shall pass, neither go nor come, but through Thee, working, and abiding. (*Confessions*, Everyman Edition, VII. xv. 21.)

This seems to be close to pantheism, and yet it is not. For God is here still supernatural to his creation, and Augustine's theory has always been harmonized with the essential Hebrew concept of moral evil as involving human wilful misuse of the morally neutral physical world. And yet with our modern knowledge of the intimacy of the human mind's relation to the body we would have to imagine, on Augustine's theory, that God intimately upheld all the neural activity that necessarily accompanied Hitler's planning of his most barbaric strategy. At this point the old pantheistic undercutting of the biblical doctrine of God's righteousness seems to me to emerge to haunt orthodox Christian theology's theory of God's sustaining of the creation.

In the above quoted passage Augustine uses the biblical phrase, "in Thy hand," to refer to God's power sustaining the physical universe, and Christendom has followed Augustine's mistaken interpretation of this Hebraic idiom. In the biblical usage, as we shall see, the phrase means *subject to God's governing control*. Just because the Bible says, "The eternal God is your dwelling place, and underneath are the everlasting arms," (Deuteronomy 33:27) to describe God's sustaining of his faithful followers does not mean that this is the meaning of the biblical idiom, "in his hand." This distinction is not pedantic hair-splitting: a very slight change of wording will alter the meaning of an idiomatic expression. For example, in America, to refer to certain people as "scarlet" is not an emphatic way of saying that they are "in the pink of condition." And no one really conversant with our ways of speaking would think that to say that a man "sees red," that he is financially "in the red," and that he is "politically Red" are statements that all mean about the same thing.

Actually the idea of God "upholding" or "sustaining" the creation at large is not Hebraic. It is not an Old Testament conception. In the New Testament, which is explaining Christianity to a Greek speaking and largely Gentile Church there are a few exceptions to this general rule. The most obvious is a description of Christ as "upholding the universe by his word of power," (Hebrews 1:3.), together with St. Paul's polemic, when he says in trying to convince the Colossians of the cosmic sufficiency of Christ, "In him all things hold together." (Colossians 1:17.) Also St. Paul, in his intellectual appeasement policy in Athens which he afterward regretted (I Corinthians 2:1,2.) says that "In him [God] we live and move and have our being." (Acts 17:28.) Ephesians 4:4-6 need not be considered since it is referring to the Church (compare I Corinthians 12:11-14,27.) rather than to the cosmos. But omitting these few New Testament exceptions *all the biblical references in the Concordance to God "upholding," or "sustaining," or "supporting," or "maintaining," or "giving strength" refer to his relation to men, not to his relation to the structure of the inanimate universe.* (Psalms 37:17,24; 41:12; 51:12; 54:4; 63:8; 119:116; 145:14; Isaiah 41:10; 42:1; Nehemiah 9:21; Psalms 3:5; 55:22; I Kings 8:45,49,59; II Chronicles 6:35,39; Psalms 9:4; 16:5; 140:12; Zechariah 12:5; II Samuel 22:40; Psalms 18:1,32,39; Habakkuk 3:19; Isaiah 40:3[1]; II Samuel 22:33; Psalms 28:8; 31:4; 37:39; 43.2; 52:7; Proverbs 10:29; Isaiah 17:10; 25:4; Joel 3:16; Exodus 15:2; I Samuel 2:10; Psalms 21:1; 28:7,8; 29:11; 46:1; 59:9,17; 62:7; 68:35; 81:1; 84:5; 86:16; 118:14; 138:3; Isaiah 12:2; 45:24; 49:5; Jeremiah 16:19; Micah 5:4.) And as we have said before, the often repeated phrase "in his hand" means *subject to God's governing control,* not *enjoying his sustain-*

ing power. This is obvious from the connotations of the phrase "in his hand" where it has merely human social usage without referring to God. The words are the regular idiom employed to describe a state of capture by military conquest. (Exodus 23:31; Numbers 21:34; Deuteronomy 1:27; 7:24; Joshua 6:2; 10:19.) They are also the regular idiom for the state of a slave in relation to his master. (Genesis 16:6 ARV see Psalms 123:2; Genesis 39:1 ARV; Exodus 3:8.) Some biblical passages with great social realism use the idiom with both the war and the slavery implications. (Judges 3:8; 4:2,9; 10:7; I Samuel 12:9.) David equates the military and religious meaning of the phrase in his reply to the prophet Gad. (v. 14 in II Samuel 24:10-14.)

That the idea of God sustaining the existence of physical nature is not part of the Old Testament view does not mean that the Old Testament ever thinks of God as losing interest in the universe after its creation, or as being in any practical sense its absentee landlord. The important point is that Hebrew belief thought of God as commanding the world into independent being at the creation:

> For he spoke, and it came to be;
> he commanded, and it stood forth.
> (Psalms 33:9.)

God is therefore always supernatural to his creation ("High and lifted up" Isaiah 6:1 compare Genesis 28:12,13.) although he always continues to have a control over it which he exercises at will. God is thought of as continuing to exert his power by an active tinkering with nature in both special and usual ways. But, as in Psalm 29, this is described as God's power *over* nature. In Psalm 147 God's making the grass to grow upon the hills and giving to the beasts their food (vv. 8,9.) is probably, as in the later verses of that Psalm, (vv. 15-18.) the response of nature to the commands of God telling nature to carry out the appropriate activities he has ordained for it. (Genesis 1:11,12,14-16,22,24,26,28-30.) This power over nature, expressed either as a specific individual action or as the establishment of nature's appropriate routines (Job 28:26) is echoed in the Sermon on the Mount. (Matthew 5:45; 6:26.) To say that God continues to tinker with his creation did not imply to the Hebrew mind any haphazard Divine activity. God was always thought of as purposeful, dependable, and self-consistent. So any tinkering that he did would be appropriate to the self-consistent whole of the world ot nature and man in relation to his purposes for it.

The Old Testament belief that the universe exists independently after its original creation without need for God's power to sustain its inanimate matter and structure is essential to the argument of the present book. By giving up as non-Hebraic the theory that God sustains the universe we are enabled to coordinate with theological belief the claim of the second law of thermodynamics that the physical universe is slowly disintegrating and losing its power. Then, by theological appropriation of the doctrine of evolution, which describes a small scale reversal of the second law of thermodynamics within the total cosmic entropy which that law describes, we shall be able to find a scientific parallel to the biblical claim that God does sustain men, especially those who seek to serve him in righteousness.

❂   ❂   ❂   ❂   ❂   ❂

I am suggesting that we tentatively put aside our intellectual sophisticated embarrassment at the so-called naïveté of the Bible and experiment with accepting at face value as genuinely true the over-all picture it is trying to convey of how our world came into being and what God's continuing relation to our world has been.

A widely accepted theory of modern science tells us that the universe began some billions of years ago when all the matter of our present universe was concentrated in one place under extreme pressure. Then in a cosmic explosion in which the elements were formed in two or three hours, the universe started its still continuing career of expansion in all directions. During this process minor eddies of the cosmic dust concentrated to a pressure and consequent heat that caused the fire of atomic fission to take place, and so the stars were formed. Still smaller eddies of dust drawn into a star's gravitational orbit were not sufficiently compressed to ignite and so they became planets. We know that in the case of our planet the right amount of heat is available from our sun to foster the development of life from small relatively uncomplicated organic beginnings to the highly complicated and efficient organism which is man. But the direction of the organic development from the uncomplicated to the highly complicated—when we compare the amount of organic matter that exists with the amount of inorganic matter in the universe—seems to be only a microscopic temporary reversal of the cosmic trend. For biological evolution exists only temporarily within the over-all pattern of the entropy of the universe's slow disintegration of its galaxies and elements toward a motionless homogeneous distribution of the particles of matter throughout space at a low temperature. The universe is supposed to be about midway on this journey to cosmic dissolution.

When the question of a prehistory of the matter of our universe before the cosmic explosion is raised, the answer has to be that if any such prehistory existed all traces of it were wiped out completely by the explosion's intensity. Any theory that the matter of our universe once formed a previous universe is guesswork. The scientific history of the universe begins, then, with the cosmic explosion. If one adopts the hypothesis that the matter in our universe once formed a previous universe the question must be faced of where the matter in *that* universe came from. If one posits the eternity of matter, one then has the insuperable difficulty of showing where conscious mind, which is a very late arrival within our world, came from. To say that *there was a mind factor as a constituent of the chemical inorganic universe from the beginning* is an inadequate explanation, because this original *mind factor* is not consciousness, and from such a *mind factor* to consciousness there still exists the sheer jump that the *mind factor* explanation was invented to explain.

All we have when we are dealing with purely inorganic matter is chemical (or electro-chemical) reactivity within specified limitations. We know that as the process of evolution takes place the subtlety, scope, and complication of the reactivity is increased. *But no degree of subtlety, scope, and complication of reactivity is the equivalent of consciousness.* The pre-conscious heightening of reactivity in protoplasmic matter is not consciousness, it is only "before-consciousness." The super-human scope of reactivity of IBM machines in certain specified computations for which they are designed is not consciousness: it is only super-human scope of reactivity in a limited area. Our human consciousnesses may be sustained and influenced by the chemical (and/or electro-chemical) reactivity of our bodies, and they may make use of the chemical reactivity (and/or electro-chemical reactivity) of our bodies as their basis of operations, but I know from experience that my conscious mind is not chemical reactivity (and/or electro-chemical reactivity)

41

but is conscious mind. When we think back to that original half-hour explosion that formed chemical elements and started the universe on its history of galaxy formation, then protoplasmic formation, and finally man, we know that, infinitely slow and subtle as are the steps by which the present situation has come about, nevertheless my conscious mind is something other than that original stuff: something *new* has been added to our universe whether or not we know how. That *new* is the conscious mind's ability to think, remember, plan, appreciate, love, evaluate ethically and aesthetically, feel pleasure and pain, see, hear, smell, taste, feel hot and cold, etc.

The basic distinction that must be kept in mind is that in the evolution of living protoplasm, so long as one is dealing only with the increasing subtlety and scope of the reactivity of matter—and that probably is the case through a large part of the scale of evolutionary development: throughout the realm of micro-organisms, and the plant world, and in such animals as sea anemones, mud-worms, and oysters—one is dealing with the exclusively objective. We do not know how far backward down the scale of animal evolution conscious mind exists: probably it is considerably below man. *What we do know is that conscious mind does exist in man, and that it is a different kind of reality. It is subjective reality. Objective reality is a fact. Subjective reality is a fact. We consciously know objective reality by means of subjective reality, so the latter cannot be denied without discrediting all beliefs about the former. And the insurmountable mystery is that we do not know the basic relationship between the subjective and the objective.*

In this we encounter an ultimate mystery. Religion has long been accused of claiming for Divine Activity those aspects of the universe as yet unsuccessfully investigated by science, and then of beating a not too dignified retreat before science's advancing discoveries. I personally have come to the conclusion that science may some day successfully synthesize living protoplasm, and if this happens I am thoroughly convinced that science will be no nearer than it is now to solving the ultimate riddle of human life. For science will then only have artificially assembled matter into a pattern in which its subtlety, scope, and complication of reactivity is increased. But science would still be managing only the realm of the objective; it would still be working in the realm in which the first chapter of Genesis says that God told man to have dominion over the earth and subdue it. (Genesis 1:28,29.) In distinction from this, the main theoretical question for human knowledge lies in the problem of the subjective-objective relationship, and this knowledge can only be gained through introspection.

When we are active, mentally or physically, we have a basic awareness at the back of our minds that it is ourselves and not another doing the thing that we are doing. However, as soon as we concentrate on investigating by introspection this mysterious "myself," our motion picture of life halts and we have only a "still." And the content of that "still" turns out to be the content of the previous split-second of consciousness. The "myself" that is now contemplating this previous content of consciousness is never objectifiable to myself although in the act of objectifying my past to myself I have the basic awareness of my existence that I have when I am eating, walking, listening to music, or reading a detective story. By introspection and memory we can rerun a long consecutive portion of the film of our past experience, pausing from time to time to make editorial comments to ourselves. If we try to introspect our present continuing experience, we find that we have a series of "motion bits" and "stills" alternating in rapid succession. But the conscious *thinking I* remains subjective. We can know much of the history of its past activity, but *itself we can never objectively know about. Basically the relation of the subjective to the objective is an insurmountable mystery to the human mind.*

Science, therefore, can only give information useful to a philosophy of existence. It cannot construct that philosophy by itself. For philosophy must try to account for the all. The all we know to contain both the subjective and the objective, and science can analyze only the objective. This holds true even for the science of psychology, which can analyze only the objectified version of the content of men's consciousness and activities.

❋   ❋   ❋   ❋   ❋   ❋

Karl Heim tells us that men cannot think out a philosophy of life without having some fixed point to think *from*. There must be some fundamental stability or absolute to give coherence to the whole. The alternative would be absolute chaos in which no thought was valid. He says that Western scientific thought has tried successively three possible alternatives for this absolute: the absolute object (materialism), absolute space and absolute time, and finally absolute determination of events through an iron law of causality. But modern science and mathematics have proved that none of these alternatives is an absolute. By elimination the only alternative absolute remaining is God, who is absolute creative mind.[1] Since science thus seems to be furnishing us some negative evidence for the existence of God, we are now in a position to try and see whether we can supply a conception of God constructed from biblical materials, which can be integrated with the over-all scientific picture and serve as a complement to it.

Let us start with the implication in the first chapter of Genesis that the Divine Creative Mind was at least Rational-Mind-Plus. The "Plus" includes the ability to think into three dimensional existence. As human beings we have no conception of thought except consecutive thought and hence in trying to describe God as thinking we are forced to discard the—for us—static Greek concept of eternity and instead follow the Hebrew description of the great I AM WHO I AM (Exodus 3:14.) as existing "from everlasting to everlasting," (Psalm 90:2.) always making sure that we remember that God is not subject as we are to time's limiting straitjacket which is on all created activity. There was, then, before our universe was created, a time when it existed only in the mind of God. In his mind he was planning it, planning the chemical elements and all their possible combinations and interactions, and all the laws of chemistry, physics, and mathematics; that is, planning the basic "stuff" of the cosmos and the basic routines within which alone its mechanical activity would be permitted to freely proceed. And all this was still entirely within the mind of God and part of God to the extent that a man's thoughts *while he is thinking them* are part of the man. And yet, as we know introspectively, when we try in vain to capture ourselves thinking, there is always some distinction between the thinker and his thoughts. But this distinction is never so great that there ever is lacking a living connection between the thinker and his thoughts while he is thinking them. God, of course, did not have to think up the universe piecemeal. He can think innumerable thoughts simultaneously.

---

[1] Karl Heim, *The Transformation of the Scientific World View;* New York: Harper & Brothers, 1953, Chapters II, III, and IV.

The basic cosmos, thus already powerfully thought up within his mind, he, by an act of will cast forth from his mind into completely objective independent energy-full four-dimensional (space-time) existence. This correlates with science's picture of that half hour's cosmic explosion in which matter plunged outward in its dizzying career of continuing expansion in all directions. One is reminded of the vision on Patmos when John "saw a great white throne and him who sat upon it; from his presence earth and sky fled away." (Revelation 20:11.) The Plus aspect of the intelligent mind of God is very pronounced. It can do things like that. The universe came forth from the Divine Mind, compacted by that Mind's energy, an energy so great that after the stuff of the universe was released from its confines within the Divine Mind it exploded by means of the pent up energy gained in that original association with the Divine Mind, and so expressed itself in simple powerful action according to Divine expectation. "And God said, 'Let there be light;' and there was light," (Genesis 1:3) the light of that ancient half hour cosmic explosion in which our universe began to take shape. There were now God *and* the universe. God was the original source of all existence and this new universe was an originally derived but now independent existence, completely separated from its Creator, and no longer sustained by him.[2]

This, basically, is the Christian doctrine of the creation. Scientists' objection to believing it will probably be somewhat in the following vein:

(a) The Christian doctrine of creation is a tale entirely spun out of human fancies and there is not the slightest proof of its accuracy that a scientifically trained person would consider good evidence.

(b) The Christian doctrine proceeds entirely by analogy and picture language and has none of the clear-cut mathematical precision that so convincingly articulates complicated relationships as discovered by science.

[2] This theory of creation is not to be confused with the Christian doctrine that from eternity God the Father Almighty begot Christ the Son. The begetting of Christ was a self-projection of the total being of God over against himself. This means that the Father and the Son have always been equally all powerful and have always each been equally able to make the other the object of his own subjective thought and love. In the creation of the world it was not the *being* of God that was projected, only a complicated thought on the part of God, a thought "thought up out of nothing" and not at all essential or necessary to his being.

(c) Furthermore, the doctrine tries to imagine what happened before any human being was there to imagine it.

(d) And lastly, theology's whole argument centers on the belief that a God—whose existence cannot be scientifically proved—thought up the universe as a little thought in his mind, and then changed the little thought in his mind into an objective space-time universe outside his mind, and after making this staggering claim theology freely admits that it has not the foggiest notion of *how* God did this. Therefore no person of intellectual respectability should take this seriously. A person's credence of theology would appear to be in inverse ratio to his intelligence!

Let us take up these objections:

(a) This whole book is not a proof but an hypothesis, and all hypotheses, even scientific ones, are scholarly guesses based on incomplete evidence. They are the scouting expeditions of the intellectual life, upon which strategy is planned for the marshaling of evidence to try to gain new intellectual territory.

(b) There is an unheralded philosophical problem for science itself raised by science's use of the technique of clear-cut mathematical measurement, in that its constant use forces science to omit from consideration all that pertains to duty, beauty, and love, for these three aspects of human experience cannot be reduced to mathematical formulae. But these three aspects of experience bulk large in the religious field which deals with existence at the personal level—not primarily at the level of the mathematical relationships of very unconscious matter. In elucidating human experience at the level involving duty, beauty, and love the employment of analogy is both useful and necessary. Besides, before science condemns the use of analogy in theological discussion it should remember that, in addition to repeated experiment, science itself has two criteria for judging whether or not a scientific hypothesis is true. The first is: Does the hypothesis adequately explain all the facts the scientific problem involves? The second is: Among the possible hypotheses that might fit the facts of a particular problem, does this hypothesis explain the facts most economically? Now if the problem proposed to science is the total explanation of existence, then the relevant factors its scientific explanation must cover include duty, beauty, and love. But in order for science to get her precise mathematical descriptions of matter she has to ignore duty, beauty, and love. So, applying science's own criteria to a philosophy of existence based on science forces science to admit that its vaunted scientific knowledge is incorrect as the answer to the total question of existence, since, in order to seem to cover existence by its theories, it has to ignore such important factors of existence as duty, beauty, and love. One would therefore conclude that in order to get a picture of total existence some technique not involving mathematical measurement would be necessary.

(c) As for science's objecting to theology's spinning a theory of the origin of the universe, on the ground that it involves a pre-human situation of which man can know nothing, one can say very pointedly that science has not hesitated to pretend to scientific knowledge of the pre-human times involved in the studies of geology, early evolution, and the historical aspect of astronomy. Science of course claims that what it does is to project backward with the aid of mathematical calculation directional lines of activity that it discovers in the contemporary situation. But actually the same technique is used by theology. The difference is that theology uses the total man as the starting point—and this is not a method that can be treated contemptuously since man is the instrument through which science is known. This total man that theology starts with includes all the powers of the human being including his intellect, his creative power, and his values in the areas of duty, beauty, and love. Theology's description of the creation involves a projection backward from the known contemporary nature of man into the beginnings before man existed.

(d) Science's uneasiness because God cannot be "scientifically proved" is by no means devastating to theology. We have pointed out that the areas which might be expected to yield some confirmation of the existence of a personal God—namely those areas involving duty, beauty, and love—are deliberately ruled out of scientific consideration. It refuses to consider the evidence in the areas where pertinent evidence might be found. It should also be pointed out that there are, on the positive side, important philosophical arguments for the existence of God which, while not in themselves conclusive, are nevertheless corroborating evidence of appreciable weight. But even more important is the fact that religion's claim that there is a God with whom the worshipper can have personal relations, is a claim that has been tested over the centuries by the experience of millions of people who have served God and experienced a personal relationship to him.

Furthermore, science's claim that religious assertions have to be taken on faith, while scientific assertions are based on proofs that are open to verification by all, needs to be scrutinized carefully. The fundamental "scientific" beliefs of 99 and 44 100ths % of the population are faith pure and simple: How many people have ever seen a pneumococcus under a microscope? And of those who have, how many have personally proved that it is *that* microscopic entity and not something else that is the cause of pneumonia? And it is absurd to think that the scientific proof of relativity and the expanding universe is available to all. To be able really to check these scientific beliefs one would have to have an extraordinarily high I.Q., and that in itself reduces the number who could test the proof to a very small fraction of the world's population. But in the whole world only a tiny fraction of this brilliant fraction has the necessary pre-requisite of a college and graduate school education. And of this fraction of a fraction only those could qualify whose professional training had been extensive in the fields of chemistry, physics, astronomy, and mathematics.

And lastly, for science to object that Christian theology's description of the creation is negligible on the ground that theologians cannot explain *how* it occurred is simply a glaring example of the pot calling the kettle black. The knowledge of the mystery of the creation involves the mystery of the relationship of the subjective to the objective and that is something no human being understands. If scientists, to validate their own discoveries, had to explain *how* non-physical conscious thoughts resulted from physical light rays striking their physical retinas when they looked through a microscope, all scientific discoveries would be discredited as unproved.

CHAPTER 5

The *Second Law of Thermodynamics* and the Doctrine of Evil

In the last chapter we traced the doctrine of creation from the thinking up of the general plan of the inorganic elements and their appropriate modes of activity by the mind of God, to the Divine Mind by divine fiat externalizing elemental nature into objective existence in that half hour's explosion of all the matter in the universe which initiated its still continuing career of expansion in all directions. And science tells us that as the universe expands it is steadily losing power, for by irreversible entropy its energy is slowly passing from the available to the non-available state. We are now midway in that billions of years old process of dissolution that will end in all the matter of the universe being evenly and inertly distributed throughout space at a temperature approaching absolute zero. In the first quarter of this century knowledgeable college undergraduates used to be supercilious about the naive seventeenth century deists who thought of the world as made up and set going by God as a perfect clock might be set going by a perfect clockmaker. We now know that the analogy of the clock is a better one than the deists realized. For if a clockmaker makes and sets going a clock, that clock will some day run down; and correspondingly, *the second law of thermodynamics* makes us aware of the inevitable ticking of the entropy-clock of the universe.

But the Christian is not taken unawares by *the second law of thermodynamics*, for he has already been warned of it in both the Old and New Testaments by the Bible's greatest description of the creation of the cosmos. I say "greatest" advisedly, for the second chapter of Genesis deals exclusively with the creation of the world, (Genesis 2:5-25) and although the heavens, the sun, the moon, and the stars are mentioned in the first chapter of Genesis, the interest of the first chapter also is definitely focused upon the earth. But the book of Hebrews gives us an account of the creation of the cosmos which it quotes from the book of Psalms:

And

'Thou, Lord, didst found the earth in the beginning,
and the heavens are the work of thy hands;
they will perish, but thou remainest;
they will all grow old like a garment,
like a mantle thou wilt roll them up,
and *they will be changed.*
But thou art the same,
and thy years will never end.'

(Hebrews 1:10-12. Italics mine. See Psalms 102:25-27, and see also Isaiah 51:6.) *The great miracle of the creation was the creation of death.* In the beginning there was only Life. "Thou art the same, and thy years will never end." Appalling though the force of explosive power was when the universe's total matter was called into existence and cast forth by the mind of God, that explosive power was only a pale shadow of the Creator's power, and the creation's power from the beginning has been only in the independent state as the fading afterglow of its original intimacy with its Creator as called into being and sustained within his mind. Now, cast forth from him, like a branch cut off from the sustaining vine, (compare John 15:6.) what could it do but wither? And yet, its initial power content was so great that the process of its withering has spanned the billions of years of our universe's existence, and will span the billions of years yet to come. The universe can be compared to an incompetent spendthrift child who has inherited a million dollars from his father and is living on principal. Someday even a fortune will be completely dissipated, but there is a long and pleasant interval until that time comes.

It need only be added that the argument of this book differs from Deism in stressing not only the fact that the clock is running down, but in stressing the fact that the now independently running clock is still subject to the control and purposive action of the clockmaker. The independence of the universe does not mean that it is a Frankenstein's monster that can in any way dispute control with its Maker, and this for four reasons. In the first place, only a small fraction of Deity's limitless power was employed in its creation, so that even in the first of its existence its power was meager as compared to its Maker's. In the second place, since the cosmos owes its existence wholly to his creation, it would be in his power to modify it or annihilate it if he so desired. In the third place, as we have

50

seen, the universe's power is steadily waning, so if a contest of strength were possible—which it is not—time alone would play into the Creator's hands and guarantee his victory. And last and most important of all, the fact of entropy is an indication that the universe, when cast loose from the mind of the Creator, fell away from him and so cannot by its own strength get back to God. The creation has a limited power to hinder the outworking of God's plans *within* the creation, but the universe by its own initiative cannot get back to or contact God directly to struggle against him. Christian piety (as opposed to the pantheistic religions) has abundantly recognized this in regard to the religious life: without the assistance of God's prevenient grace coming to men, men could never get back to God. This present chapter deals with the subject of evil, and to do so has to presuppose the whole account of evolution which will concern us later.

The dying universe was created for a purpose, and the Old Testament stresses the steadiness of God's long distance purposes. Man is assisted by the creation of a relatively stable nature whose routine activities he can count on (Genesis 8:22); and a relatively stable theater of operations assists God's steady planned maneuvering relative to human history in order to bring men freely to everlasting joy in an existence of fellowship with himself which will be forever sustained by his undiminishing power. (Genesis 12:2,3; Exodus 19:4-6; II Samuel 7:11-13; Amos 3:7,8; Isaiah 9:6,7; 53:5,10-12; Jeremiah 31:31-34; I Corinthians 15:20,23; Romans 8:34-39) The purpose of the Trinity in the creation was to enlarge the everlasting joyous loving community which is themself[1] by the permanent adoption (Galatians 4:3-7) of a secondary order of being.

In order to qualify for such an ultimate status man had to be created in the image of God, and this means that he had to be possessed of creative ability, the ability for moral discernment and choice, and the ability to be actively loving. Now the possession of any or all of these abilities involves the possession of freedom, and the possession of freedom involves the unhampered control of power.

So the problem was, how to equip man with the power which was necessary for the freedom which was necessary if man was to

---

[1] I have coined the plural-singular pronoun to indicate the three-one nature of God.

be made in the image of God and at last was to be adopted into the family community which is God. "For there is no power but of God." (Romans 13:1 ARV) Man cannot use God's power but only be used by it, for the power of God is God, and man cannot use God. Hence if the power that is in nature is God himself sustaining nature, then man when he bends nature to his desires would be to some extent using God, which idea is anathema to the whole Jewish-Christian tradition. The theological idea of God sustaining nature is therefore one of the liabilities of the ancient Christian marriage of biblical thought with Western philosophy. Furthermore, it leaves us with the embarrassing problem of how death could ever have come into existence, for what God sustains does not die. *The second law of thermodynamics* proves false the post-biblical claim that God's power constantly sustains the cosmos in being, for God's power is unfailing and what he sustained would not be subject to dissolution. But if the now independent creation had come into existence by being hurled into independent existence by the fiat of the Divine Mind whose thinking combines both idea and power, then it is to be expected that the universe would exhibit both patterns and power. And it is extremely interesting to note that science's analysis of matter is tending to reduce the description of it to energy in patterns. Since the energy in the universe is disconnected from its unfailing source it loses power steadily in the process of releasing it, but the power as it is released by the gradual dissolution of the cosmos is an ample source of genuine independent power available for the human experiment.

Thus the enormous physical cosmos was created that it might die — that was to be its function — in order that a source of power independent of God might be available for the creation of man as well as for man's continuing use. For according to the second chapter of Genesis man was not instantaneously created by Divine fiat, but was instead assembled out of the already independently existing stuff of the cosmos by the tinkering activity of God analogous to a potter's moulding his clay. (Genesis 2:7, 21, 22.) And according to the first chapter of Genesis the lower creation was that over which man was meant to exercise his dominion. (Genesis 1:26, 28, 29.)

*   *   *   *   *   *

Now that our modern minds are furnished with the scientific

knowledge of *the second law of thermodynamics* as a factor to be used in our thinking, a problem that has no clear intellectual solution in the Bible comes closer to a logical solution than it could come in terms of the biblical understanding of nature, and that is the problem of evil. The reason that our intellectual explanation of the problem can be a slight advance upon the solution of the past, is that we have scientific data with which to work which the Old Testament prophets did not have, their Divine inspiration being apparently a miraculous pushing of their minds to an optimum understanding of God's relation to the universe on the basis of the humanly collected knowledge of the universe that they already possessed. Their inspiration does not seem to be a Divinely dictated shortcut to the type of knowledge of the cosmos that would eventually be attainable by unaided human efforts.

The Old Testament insists that God's is the sole Ultimate Creative Power and that he is good, and that therefore all things as he originally created them were good. (Genesis 1:4, 12, 18, 21, 25, 31.) All evil, including death, man's overburdened labor, thorns and thistles, man's domineering over woman, and the pain of childbirth (Genesis 3:16-19.) are traced to sin which is identified with conscious disobedience of the will of God. That this disobedience is basic sin is still correctly held by both Judaism and Christianity, but there are two objections to considering this the complete explanation of the origin of evil. The Old Testament claimed that before the sin of man the lion ate straw like the ox. (Genesis 1:29, 30.) We now know through paleontology's and biology's tracing of evolution that there was considerable evil in the animal world in the form of at least a minimum amount of pain before man came upon the scene. This much evil, therefore, cannot be traced to human sin. Furthermore, in the biblical story of the first human disobedience the question arises of how a perfectly good, perfectly happy, perfectly safe human being could choose to sin. The account of the fall explains it by saying that the woman was tempted by the snake, (Genesis 3:1-5, 13.) which raises the obvious question of how an intelligent talking snake had become sinful. Without taking *the second law of thermodynamics* into consideration there is no explanation of the origin of evil that can explain it fully without in some way smuggling it back as a kind of recessive characteristic of Deity. If, however, we take that scientific law into theological consideration we are enabled to believe the creation of death or dissolution to be a major intended part of the original miracle of creation which was to lay the groundwork for our human life. This gives us a source for evil which is not itself an evil at the time of its creation.

It has often been noticed in science that nature exhibits basic patterns that repeat themselves with innumerable variations. The planets are in orbit about the sun, and the moon is in orbit about the earth. There are also basic patterns that repeat themselves with variations relative to the religious life. One of the indications of the correctness of the hypothesis of this present book's theological use of *the second law of thermodynamics* is that it fits into an already well established Christian pattern relative to death: By the gradual entropy or dissolution of the universe man's freedom was initially made possible; by the death of the Son of God the rescue of man from slavery to sin into the freedom of sonship to God was made possible; by the negating or "dying" of the individual human will's self-centeredness, that person accepts the position of the freedom of God-centered sonship to the heavenly Father which has been freely won for and offered to him by Christ; and by the final death of the physical body the Christian enters into the full and everlasting and joyous fruition of the relationship to the Father, Son, and Holy Spirit which his Christian life on earth has begun to experience.

Originally, then, death or dissolution, as involved in the entropy of the physical universe, was wholly good, since it was essentially useful to God's ultimate purpose. It was part of that which God created and saw "that it was good." (Genesis 1:4.) We do not have to worry over any moral problem involving a raw deal to the stars because the heat of their flaming orbs gradually irreversibly uses up their store of atomic power, so that millions of years in the future they will be merely burnt out cinders disintegrating in the cold blackness of astronomical space.

According to our modern understanding, when man first appeared upon the scene, instead of finding his domicile a safe paradise he found it an environment in which the upward evolutionary thrust of all animate nature was already freely waging a survival struggle against the universe's over-all entropy pattern. The death-pattern involved in entropy is something for whose existence God is fully responsible, and yet it is a contrary-to-God-factor in existence, because the nature of God is deathless life. The animals were already on the scene when man appeared (Genesis 1.), and contact with the higher animals is a semi-social influence for those who live close to nature. To realize this one has only to recall the association with a well loved dog in one's early childhood. (Compare Genesis 2:18, 19.) Thus man, who in his childhood learns by imitation, in his racial childhood was confronted by the example of carnivores that preyed upon other animals in their unrelenting struggle to maintain the living pattern of their existence against the cosmic forces of dissolution. Bloodshed and the infliction of pain was a strategy man learned from his environment, not a vice he invented in a moment of secure leisure.

Again, it is customary for those theologians who take seriously the problem of human sin to fulminate against men for caring for their own interests first of all, and only secondarily for the interests of their fellow men and for the commands of God. Theologians are prone to make this self-centeredness the predisposition to pride and the tap root of moral sinfulness. And yet self-centeredness is partially a result of man's natural endowments and of the learning that inevitably takes place in those first two highly important years of a child's life. For the first learning is immediately through sensation which a child experiences before he has any knowledge of God or any defined knowledge of his fellow man. In sensation, uncorrected by the knowledge that comes from long experience, objects in one's immediate environment do appear larger and more important than comparable objects would appear at a distance, and circumstances which bring immediate pleasure or pain to one's self are at once recognized as being desirable or undesirable, while comparable circumstances bringing pleasure and pain to others are not so recognized. And it must never be forgotten that infancy according to the Bible is part of the Divine program envisaged as part of the "very good" original creation. (Genesis 1:27, 28, 31; and compare Mark 10:14, 15.) In other words — as far as human nature's chance to avoid moral evil and sin is concerned — man was put into the world by God with the cards already stacked against him by the necessity for man to struggle against the over-all cosmic entropy and by the predatory habits which he would learn by observing and dealing with the higher animals, and by the limitations of his understanding which infancy imposes.

This present line of reasoning is not intended to deny the accuracy of the Bible's claim that man ought to love and serve God first of all, that God is served by man's dealing rightly with his fellow man, that man is responsible for his actions and knowingly sins by disobeying God and refusing to carry out his known will to the best of his ability. Furthermore, since all members of the human race who arrive at years of discretion sin by not serving the highest Good to the best of their ability, the whole human race is a "fallen" race. The only point we are engaged in making thus far is that the nature of human sin is more complicated than the basic pride and sensuality under which headings Reinhold Niebuhr, for example, analyzes it.

If we turn from the logical exactness of Christian doctrine's exposition of the nature of sin to the Old Testament's less pretentious, less doctrinaire account of sin as observed in practical human experience, we find an important description of an aspect of human sin that is so undramatic that it is not largely emphasized in Christian discussions of the subject. It is sin as "backsliding." Man's sin is so described in passages in Hosea, Ezekiel, and Proverbs, (Hosea 11:7 ARV; 14:4 ARV; Ezekiel 37:23; Proverbs 14:14 ARV) and the expression becomes prominent in Jeremiah, (Jeremiah 2:19 ARV; 3:6, 8, 11, 12, 14, 22 ARV; 5:6 ARV; 8:5 ARV; 15:6 ARV; 31:22 ARV; 49:4 ARV) whose subtlety in describing the inwardness of individual religious experience and the deceitfulness of the heart (Jeremiah 8:5; 9:6; 17:9; 31:31-34) is a forerunner both of Jesus' constant warnings against hypocrisy, and of the understanding on the part of both Jesus and Paul that sin and righteousness have to do with inner motives. (Matthew 5:3, 4, 5, 6, 8; 6:22; Mark 7:15, 18-23; I Corinthians 8:4, 7-13; 10:25-31; Romans 14:5, 6, 13, 14, 20, 23.)

The expression "backsliding" refers to that state of moral and spiritual slump of which we all are at times painfully aware. I am personally convinced that usually this description of sin is the one that most often directly strikes home to the personal experience of the ordinary inconspicuous citizen. The lack of application to one's self of the denunciations of the sins of sensuality and prideful defiance of God that one hears in the pulpit may be due in part to the hearer's modest estimate of himself: he does not seem to himself a vivid and important enough personality to have the sins which the preacher is denouncing apply to him. Neither his virtues nor his vices nor his accomplishments have appeared colorful or outstanding to himself or his neighbors. But even the most ordinary of us recognize the drab uninteresting sin of backsliding as something with which our own personal life is all too familiar.

A classic modern description of this sin occurs in *The Screwtape Letters*. Here the elder devil in a letter of advice to a younger tempter becomes almost emotional as his description of this type of sin and its usefulness to the purposes of hell reaches its climax:

We know that we have introduced a change of direction in his [the Christian's] course which is already carrying him out of his orbit around the Enemy [God]; but he must be made to imagine that all of the choices which have effected this change of course are trivial and revocable. . . .

As long as he retains externally the habits of a Christian he can still be made to think of himself as one who has adopted a few new friends and amusements but whose spiritual state is much the same as it was six weeks ago. And while he thinks that, we do not have to contend with the explicit repentance of a definite, fully recognized, sin, but only with his vague, though uneasy, feeling that he hasn't been doing very well lately.

This dim uneasiness needs careful handling. . . . If such a feeling is allowed to live, but not allowed to become irresistible and flower into real repentance, it has one invaluable tendency. It increases the patient's reluctance to think about the Enemy [God]. . . .

The Christians describe the Enemy [God] as one 'without whom Nothing is strong.' And Nothing is very strong: strong enough to steal away a man's best years not in sweet sins but in a dreary flickering of the mind over it knows not what and knows not why, in the gratification of curiosities so feeble that the man is only half aware of them. . . .

You will say that these are very small sins; and doubtless, like all young tempters, you are anxious to be able to report spectacular wickedness. But do remember, the only thing that matters is the extent to which you separate the man from the Enemy [God]. It does not matter how small the sins are provided that their cumulative effect is to edge the man away from the Light and out into the Nothing. Murder is no better than

57

cards if cards can do the trick. Indeed the safest road to Hell is the gradual one — the gentle slope, soft underfoot, without sudden turnings, without milestones, without signposts.

Your affectionate uncle

Screwtape.[2]

We have already pointed out the occurrence of basic patterns that repeat themselves with variations in the physical and spiritual realms. We have another parallel in the gradual disintegration of the physical universe when disconnected from the supporting power of God, and in the spiritual disintegration that characterizes "backsliding." Professor Sinnott, in his very suggestive book, *The Biology of the Spirit*,[3] tells us that the impression he has gained from a lifetime of biological study is that the development of organic nature is teleological. He says that an organism has a particular pattern appropriate to it, and that in acquiring nourishment the plant organism seems to be striving to attain and maintain that pattern. Plants even show a wide range of ability to modify their usual growth routine in order to avoid injuries or recuperate from them and so attain and maintain their appropriate pattern in spite of obstacles. This attaining and maintaining of a particular complicated pattern is activity directionally contrary to over-all slow disintegration which characterizes the cosmic entropy. When the plant can no longer maintain its pattern the over-all cosmic pattern of disintegration reasserts itself and the plant dies and decomposes. The same is true of the physical bodies of animals and men.

If the modern scientific theory is correct in claiming that man is a psycho-physical organism that is all of one piece, then one would expect to find parallels between physical and spiritual health. And these parallels exist. Physical health involves the taking in of nourishment from outside the body to help the organism attain and maintain its appropriate pattern. When the organism can no longer do this death and disintegration (or disintegration and death) result. In other words, when the organism relaxes its hold upon its appropriate pattern, the over-all entropy-pattern of the cosmos

---

[2] C. S. Lewis, *The Screwtape Letters;* New York: The Macmillan Company, 1943, Chapter XII.

[3] Edmund W. Sinnott, *The Biology of the Spirit;* New York: The Viking Press, 1959. See especially pp. 15, 17, 22, 31, 32, 49, 50, 57, 65-67, 101, 102, 121-123.

which it has held temporarily at bay gradually or quickly reasserts itself.

But man is more than a living organism with a complicated physical pattern. Men's appropriate pattern includes the intellectual life, creative activity, aesthetic appreciation, love, and a sense of duty. These are the patterns through which human beings appropriately channel the direction of the activity of their living-organism pattern. These spiritual patterns need their own appropriate nourishment which consists of the interchange of ideas, goals to reach, worthwhile tasks to accomplish, people to love, etc. The loss of the nourishment of the psychological side of man's nature makes for psychic ill health, as the loss of physical nourishment makes for organic ill health. Since a man is a psycho-somatic whole, natural man is fully enmeshed in the entropy-pattern of the cosmos. As the book of Isaiah says:

Lift up your eyes to the heavens,
    and look upon the earth beneath;
for the heavens shall vanish away like smoke,
    and the earth shall wax old like a garment;
    and they that dwell therein shall die in like manner:
but my salvation shall be for ever,
    and my righteousness shall not be abolished.
                        (Isaiah 51:6 ARV.)

In as much as the spiritual side of man's nature and its patterns directs the use to which his organic pattern of existence is to be put, one would expect that the impairment of the hold on the spiritual pattern would begin a disintegration-process at the conscious level which would have repercussions at the organic level and tend to accelerate the organism's relaxing grasp upon the organic pattern. And this medicine has found to be the case. Excessive worry or a neurotic state or emotional unhappiness can dull the edge of physical health even in the young. But the importance of the relation of conscious mind to the body can be seen more clearly in those who have passed sixty. All other things being equal, a mature person who is engaged in useful interesting work, and whose social relationships are happy and helpful, stands a better chance of physical health than does a person of the same age whose social relationships are inadequate and unsatisfying, and who has no purpose in his life, no creative outlet for his activity, and no interesting work. It is well known that retirement from business or profession can involve physical hazard, and many wealthy men have died before they could enjoy the fruit of their labor. (Compare Luke 12:16-21) The sudden unaccustomed relaxation of the conscious interests and habits to which the powers of the physical organism have been channelled for a lifetime, seems to trigger the relaxation of the organism's unconscious grip upon the metabolic pattern of the life of the organism itself.

The Jewish-Christian belief about evil and sin being the inappropriate pattern for a human life, and moral goodness and wisdom being man's appropriate pattern, is harmonious with what we know biologically about the organism in health and death. It is instructive that the Old Testament constantly sees a connection between "length of days" and a wise and righteous life. (Exodus 20:12; Deuteronomy 5:32, 33; 6:2; 11:8, 9; 17:18-20; 25:13-16; 30:17, 18; 32:45-47; Psalms 91:14-16; Proverbs 3:1, 2, 13, 16; 16:31) Here again we have an instance of the repetition with variations of the basic idea that the appropriate adjustment to the appropriate pattern fosters integration and health, while lack of such adjustment fosters dissolution and death.

Christianity believes that the saying that man is made in the image of God (Genesis 1:27) means that the pattern appropriate for man to attain and maintain involves not only what might be called human creativity at the physical level — such powers as are needed to master languages and mathematics and build houses and run autos — but also involves spiritual creativity, including the creation and appreciation of beautiful objects but more especially the insight into righteousness and love and the creative orienting of the human life to the service of righteousness and love. For all the creative, intellectual, aesthetic, moral, and loving abilities which man possesses he has because they are reflections of characteristics of God, and in the character of God it is the characteristic of righteous love which is the key to the Divine character, the characteristic around whose purposes all other characteristics are oriented. Therefore for man to fulfill and maintain his appropriate pattern he must serve God by having his own character, like God's, always governed by righteous-love.

According to Christianity, just as the body must feed upon nourishment from the physical world to attain and maintain its appropriate organic pattern, so the higher side of man's nature must feed upon righteous-loving spirit to attain and maintain its specifically human appropriate pattern. (I Corinthians 11:28-30.) But the source of righteous love is not found within the world (Matthew 7:11; Mark 1:14, 15; John 4:10, 13, 14; John 6:41, 48-51, 63; Acts 2:40; Romans 3:10-12.) at the merely inorganic level or the sub-human organic level. The human being to attain and maintain his fully human pattern must feed upon the Spirit of God. (I Corinthians 12:12, 13.) In this feeding the human being cannot capture its sustenance, but only desire it and love and serve God who gives freely to those who seek. (Matthew 5:6; Luke 11:13; John 6:27, 32, 33, 35, 47-51, 54-58, 63.) Sin, or failure to stay in the relationship of obedient love to Deity (Romans 14:23.), means a cutting off of the human spirit's needed nourishment, which eventually has the same disastrous effects at the spiritual level that cutting off the physical food supply has at the organic level. (John 15:4-6, 8.) Therefore "the wages of sin is death," (Romans 6:23.) for "sin when it is full-grown brings forth death," (James 1:15.) and "the soul that sins shall die." (Ezekiel 18:4, 20.)

The Bible attributes the death of the body to the fall of man, that is, to human sin. (Genesis 3:17-19; Romans 5:12; I Corinthians 15:21, 22.) Although we may believe that this is a scientific error, because the entropy of the universe which underlies the biological tendency toward dissolution was functioning long before organic life began, nevertheless our scientific knowledge of *the second law of thermodynamics* and of the uneasy and temporary headway which the process of biological evolution has made against it, makes us realize that as man is a unified psycho-physical being the moral "backsliding" from his appropriate conscious pattern and the entropy-physical backsliding from his merely organic pattern are not wholly unrelated. Thus St. Paul could say both that "the last enemy that shall be abolished is death" and that "the sting of death is sin." (I Corinthians 15:26, 56 ARV.)

If any proof were needed that the long development of Hebrew religious thought was specially fostered by the direct guidance of God, it is furnished by this steady Hebrew insistence that the greatest danger for man to avoid is sin, which is disobedience of God who is disobeyed by all ethically evil action. Compared to the fear of sin, the emphasis on the fear of death does not bulk large in the Old Testament. This is especially remarkable because the ancient Hebrew people were physically and emotionally very sensitive to pain, and because, believing death to be the final end of individuals, they loved life and considered any existence, even when the human lot was painful, a blessing and something to which it was desirable to cling. Judaism has never been defeatist or life-denying like the Oriental pantheistic religions. And yet the Hebrews believed that separation from God caused by sin was the greatest evil, an evil so great that physical death was preferable. But this fear of sin-caused separation from God does not make logical sense, because they believed that, if they suffered martyrdom rather than bring about this separation by sinning, they nevertheless would be permanently separated from God by the grave, which alternative they had freely chosen rather than to disobey him. (Psalms 6:3-5; 88:3-5, 10-13; Isaiah 5:14-16; 14:9-11) Therefore when Ezekiel said, "The soul that sins shall die," (Ezekiel 18:4, 20) he must have been led by God toward a deeper understanding of the entropy of the spirit and the ways of God to men than he understood with his clearcut intellectual knowledge. For he made the statement against the background belief that the grave separated a man forever from God, and he could scarcely have avoided the observation that physical death eventually overtakes the good as well as the bad. Even the great Jeremiah, whose prophetic messages he had probably heard, had pointed out that in many instances wicked men seem particularly well off and prosperous. (Jeremiah 12:1,2).

The cosmic entropy, which bears some resemblance to human "backsliding," is not only a theory for which there are strong preview hints in the Bible, but it is also a theory which in its extra-biblical scientific form provides us with information that we can use in supplying connecting links that have long been needed between certain biblical ideas.

If we take the teaching and actions of Jesus as reported in the synoptic gospels we find more emphasis upon Satan and devils than in all the rest of the Bible put together. There is almost no reference to devils in the Old Testament. But any careful reading of the synoptics shows that Jesus considered his mission as being not only that of leading men to repentance and obedience to God, but also that of being God's champion for men against a common enemy against which both God and man struggle. (Mark 1:23-27, 39; 3:13-19, 22-27; 4:15; 5:8-13; 6:7; 7:25-30; 8:33; 9:25-27, to take only the references in the earliest Gospel.) The problem for Christian theology has always been how to account consistently for the existence of the devil if God is perfectly good and created all things. The standard explanation has been that before the creation of the world the devil was created a good super-angel, and that the devil brought evil into existence by using his God-given freedom to rebel against God.

By means of *the second law of thermodynamics* we can cover somewhat the same ground by describing the cosmic energy originally created by God, as his means of storing power which was other than himself, which energy he so created that it could freely — within prescribed limits — release its power by disintegration. The entropy of the universe was the creation of death, death being part of the great original miracle of creation. We are beginning to believe, according to the quantum theory, that there is a small amount of freedom, within statistical limits, which exists even in inorganic nature. The rate at which radioactive substances lose their radioactivity is statistically known, and therefore the entropy-clock by which the age of the universe is estimated is the proportion of the still existing radioactive material which it contains at present. However, although scientists can tell statistically how long it will take a bit of highly radioactive material to lose nine tenths of its radioactivity, any one atom freely and unpredictably makes the explosive change from the radioactive to the non-radioactive state.

In the preorganic era of the cosmos entropy or dying is entirely good because it is wholly useful to God's purpose to create a source of power which is other than himself. A flaming star is not sinning when, separated from God, it slowly burns itself out by atomic fission, and this gradual dissolution is in no sense a misfortune to the star, since it has no feelings of any sort to take into consideration. The two forms of evil, the evil of misfortune and the evil of sin, are thus originally absent from entropy or death. This corresponds to the biblical belief that matter is morally neutral although it has a certain preciousness as the creation of God. "The earth is the Lord's and the fulness thereof." (Psalms 24:1; and see Psalms 89:11.)

Entropy could only take on the aspect of evil later, after the beginning of the process of evolution. It was only when God tried to "educate" matter into living organisms, and then to the conscious life of the higher animals, and finally into human powers of love, moral choice, aesthetic appreciation, creativity, and abstract reasoning, that the down-grading tendency he had at the creation arranged to have as a characteristic of matter became a hindrance to him, even though a useful hindrance, since it supplied the living creatures with power at their disposal, which was necessary to their increasing freedom. As soon as evolution had progressed to the point at which animals could experience any feeling of satisfaction in their cubs and any feeling of well being in a pleasant nap in the warm sunshine after a comfortable meal, they would also be able to experience the feeling of pain when injured and a slight feeling of bereavement if their cubs were killed. As soon as creatures could experience satisfactions of which they could be deprived, the loss of those satisfactions by pain, bereavement, or death could be considered as evil. Thus the evil of misfortune entered the world. When man reached a point at which he was reflectively able to choose whether or not to increase his own comfort by inflicting unnecessary pain on other human beings and chose to inflict the pain, moral evil came into existence. And when he knew that this choice is contrary to the will of the good God sin came into existence. It is not at all strange that men should bring sin into existence when faced with the alternative of keeping the moral law and suffering an immediate evil of misfortune, or avoiding an immediate evil of misfortune by breaking the moral law and taking chances on the long distance consequences of sin.

At neither the human nor the sub-human levels could sin or misfortune have occurred unless there was a particular law of God for that creature which that creature in a particular situation could fail to embody. In a later chapter, when we discuss evolution as teleological, we will discuss it as the giving by God of increasingly complex pattern, i.e., "law," for the creatures' existence. No evil can attend inorganic matter as inorganic matter. But as soon as any part of matter, such as grass or flowers, has a particular pattern set them by God for them to strive to attain and maintain, then their relaxing grip upon that particular pattern as their constituent matter disintegrates toward the over-all entropy-pattern of the cosmos can be thought of as evil. While plants as unconscious cannot know the evil of death they can experience the evil of death, and man does and God could think wistfully that "the grass withers, the flower fades." (Isaiah 40:8.) If we compare the line of argument we have been developing with St. Paul's famous description in Romans 7:7-24 and 8:5-9, 18-24, we find him as describing nature as groaning until now to be freed from decay. And we find him describing man as recognizing a law in his body that is contrary to the law of his spiritual nature, — that is, to the righteousness and everlasting life God has planned for man — so that if one is carnally oriented he is slumping into the decay that is characteristic of nature. St. Paul even says that sin could not exist apart from the law. In fact, these two chapters in Romans fit so hand in glove with the thesis of this present book that the book might almost be called a modern commentary upon them.

CHAPTER 6

The *Second Law of Thermodynamics* and Jesus' Teaching about Sin and Hell

So far we have made only two drastic divergences from orthodox Christian teaching. One is the claim that God purposely built the death-pattern into the miracle of creation. The other is that by the permission of God man came upon the earthly scene with the cards already heavily stacked against him as regards the probability of man's perseverance in virtue. We must now ask ourselves whether the theory of evil we have elaborated can be fitted to the teaching of Jesus.

Jesus' teaching contains almost no philosophy or history of sin, misfortune, and death, although, as we have said, he does not believe that these evils are entirely man-made. He believes in the existence of Satan as an extra-human force making for evil. This is in line with the present book's argument, although our thought has not personified Satan to the extent to which he is personified in the gospels. (It should be noted, however, that the Satan of the gospels has nowhere near the degree of personification of the Satan of medieval legends.) But on the whole Jesus simply starts with the assumption that man has free will and is genuinely and responsibly a sinner, although to some extent trapped by sin and misfortune. (Mark 2:17; Luke 13:10-16; 15:3-5, 8, 9) Jesus believes that God is wholly good, loving, and powerful and that God is trying to help men. From here on Christ's perfectionist ethics, though so high that none of his followers have been able to live up to them fully, are nevertheless largely couched in terms of the next step for the ordinary devout follower to take. In fact Jesus himself said of his teaching that God had "hidden these things from the wise and understanding and revealed them to babes." (Matthew 11:25.) Jesus' teachings as reported in the gospels have through the centuries served as the spiritual primer for devout Christians of meager education who were bent on following Christ, as well as instruction whose spiritual depth has never been fully plumbed, even by the Church's most learned doctors.

66

Although Jesus assumed that all men are sinners (Mark 1:15; Matthew 7:11.) and in such a predicament that it required the death of the Son of God to arrange a way out of man's difficulties, (Matthew 26:39; Mark 10:45) there is no indication in either incident or parable that Jesus lacked genuine respect and approval and sympathy for the efforts toward faithfulness and goodness that sometimes appear in human lives. (Matthew 5:3-12; 8:8-11; 10:41,42; 11:7-11; Mark 10:19-21; 12:43,44; Luke 7:44-47; 10:33-37; 12:37,42-44; 15:29-31; 19:8-10,16-19.) A doctrinaire denunciation of human nature in general as all bad and entirely responsible for being all bad is lacking from his teaching. "I am a worm," (Psalms 22:6 and see Job 25:5,6.) and "All our righteousnesses are as filthy rags" (Isaiah 64:6 AV.) are types of saying conspicuous by their absence when referring to sinful man as such. Although in Jesus' teaching man is a rebel who needs to repent he is not a total rebel, because he is not sufficiently integrated to be totally anything. However, unless he repents and makes the service of God the overall strategy of his life to which all his powers and interests will increasingly conform, he is rebellious and his life will integrate itself in a direction away from God and become increasingly oriented toward evil and will therefore be doomed.

The sin Jesus lashed out against with a violence born of intense fear is the sin of hypocrisy. This is the human tendency to lie to one's self about one's motives and spiritual state and so, because one pretends to be spiritually in a place where one is not, to effectively block God's guidance to the next appropriate step for one to take from the point at which one actually is. Hypocrisy is not a sin that is in any way forced upon men by evil circumstances that sometimes seem to trap men in desperate moral dilemmas, or to push men by fear into sinful deeds. Although Jesus steadily demands from his followers loyalty to himself even if this involves their martyrdom, (Mark 8:34,35; Matthew 10:16-22,37-39; Luke 9:59-62.) nevertheless many of the particular sins which his teaching singles out to rebuke involve rather obvious shortcomings in which a person neglects to do a good action or follow a good way of life in a situation in which he has sufficient knowledge of what the good is, and in which he is under no especial pressure to do wrong. (Matthew 25:1-13,19-28,41-45; Mark 4:18,19; Luke 7:44-47; 10:31,32,36; 12:15-21,45-48; 14:7-14,15-24; 19:16-23.)

67

In other words, for all practical purposes Jesus' teaching is geared to meet a situation in which the human creature has some real freedom to attempt the next step in the right direction to fulfill the pattern of goodness and love set by God for man, whose characteristics are desired by God to reflect on a small scale the characteristics of God himself. At the same time the teaching takes into consideration that "the spirit indeed is willing but the flesh is weak" (Mark 14:38.) and knows that man on his own is not strong enough to fulfill his prescribed pattern but needs health and strength (nourishment) from God to do it, which assistance Christ constantly reassures men God is only too glad to make available to men if they will turn to him for it. (Matthew 7:11; 11:28-30; 17:20; Luke 11:13; 12:32; 15:17-24.)

If, then, man does not turn to God for the strength beyond human strength, it should follow that, as a creature, man will eventually be subject to the entropy-pattern of death inherent in the cosmos. The question is, can Jesus' teachings on the subject of hell be made to fit this theory? Broadly speaking, I think that they can. In the teaching of Jesus the word for hell is "Gehenna," a Jewish term derived from the name of the city dump under the southwest wall of Jerusalem. Jesus' reference to the ever burning fire and the undying worm (Isaiah 66:24) of Gehenna (Mark 9:47,48.) have this reference in mind. The fire of Gehenna is the fire that destroys or burns up trash. The connotation is not that of endless torture. The same emphasis on fire destroying the wicked is found in John the Baptist's saying, "He will ... gather his wheat into the granary, but the chaff he will burn with unquenchable fire." (Matthew 3:11,12.) Jesus says that it is better to enter into life maimed than with a complete body to be cast into Gehenna. (Matthew 5:29,30; Mark 9:43.) In the parable of the vinedresser the tree will eventually be cut down if it does not bear fruit. (Luke 13: 7-9.) In the discourse in John the branches that do not abide in the vine are withered and cut off and cast into the fire. (John 15:6.) Sometimes the end of the wicked is described simply in terms of exclusion from the Divine Presence. (Matthew 7:21-23; Luke 13:25-28.) Sometimes that state is called "the outer darkness [where] men will weep and gnash their teeth." (Matthew 8:11,12; 22:11-14; 25:28-30) In the parable of the man who went into a far country to get a kingdom we are told that on his return he commanded that those who had not wanted him to rule over them be slain. (Luke 19:27.) All of these references picture the end of the wicked as destruction. It is *finis*, not everlasting torture. These passages can all be made to fit the general pattern of entropy at the spiritual level, which, if left to its own devices, works itself out in the death or disintegration of conscious life.

But it must be admitted that there are three special passages in the gospels that do look more like the doctrinally traditional picture of continuing torture. Of these "the eternal fire prepared for the devil and his angels" (Matthew 25:41) might, however, be claimed to imply that while the fire is eternal, it makes short work of destroying any particular sinner, although the "eternal punishment" of verse 46 does seem antithetically parallel to "eternal life". The fire that torments Dives (Luke 16:23,24) is described as in Hades (not Gehenna, and so not strictly speaking hell). Here the pain is not so intense as to destroy the sinner's ability to do coordinated thinking, and the question of the pain's everlasting continuance or eventual cessation is not discussed. It is only stated that the chasm between Dives and Father Abraham is non-crossable. The final passage (Matthew 13:49,50) does indeed describe the final punishment of the wicked as an extended torment in a "furnace of fire" where "men will weep and gnash their teeth," but it does not say whether or not this suffering is everlasting.[1]

It is difficult to take the teachings of Jesus seriously and at the same time completely to ignore the question of hell. On the other hand, if one is going to take the question seriously, it is well to look at what the eternal torment of any soul in the traditional Protestant or Roman Catholic picture of hell-fire would be like. The priest's sermon describing hell in A *Portrait of the Artist as a Young Man*[2] is not an exaggeration of the implications of this traditional Christian doctrine.

There seem to me to be both moral and psychological and theoretical objections to this traditional orthodox (but post-biblical) theological picture of hell, because of difficulties infused into the conception by the Greek idea of the changelessness of a "frozen" eternity. The logic of the theory of the eternal suffering of the

---

[1] It is to be noticed that exclusion and destruction are the chief elements in the fate of the wicked in II Thessalonians 1:9 and Hebrews 10:26, 27.

[2] James Joyce, A *Portrait of the Artist as a Young Man;* New York: The Modern Library, 1928, Chapter III.

damned is that if time and change are characteristics of this life only, the bent of the soul toward or away from God is made permanent by death. And in Greek fashion the soul is thought of as endowed with eternal life by the mere fact of being a soul. Now, according to the Hebrew conception, God as the great I AM THAT I AM must in some sense enjoy the "complete possession of infinite life all at once" and therefore not be in any way trapped and hindered by time and change as man is. But on Hebrew theory it does not necessarily follow that the damned who have freely separated themselves by "a great chasm" (See Luke 16:26.) from God would experience disassociation from time and change. Although the conscious pattern which is the human individual, which had been evolved through the processes of nature, might be strong enough to survive for a long time the death of the body it would nevertheless be subject to the over-all pattern of decay, which, as *the second law of thermodynamics* is basic law for the created cosmos. Following the spiritual logic of *the second law of thermodynamics* the basic picture of damnation is that portrayed in Michelangelo's painting of the Last Judgment in the Sistine Chapel of the Vatican. It depicts the terror of the wicked, as they fall through space, in their sudden clear realization that in cutting themselves off from God there is no security left and the bottom of their existence has dropped out—forever.

The moral reason for believing that the orthodox theological belief in the eternal suffering of the damned in hell is incorrect is the sheer amount of torture that unending experience of hell would involve. If one imagined that Hitler died unrepentant and went to hell, one might imagine it as just if he suffered *seriatim* a total of all the suffering he caused all German Jews. But if he suffered hell *eternally* it would mean that he suffered one hundred million times the total amount of suffering he caused all German Jews, *and that that would only be the beginning of his suffering*. Hitler's atrocities pale before the fiendishness of this punishment. The defiance of God involved in all human sin is genuine, free, and terrible. But man is too puny to *infinitely* defy the infinite God and so deserve infinite punishment. Man can deserve complete punishment on the human scale by the loss of the infinite good which he has spurned. He cannot deserve positive infinite punishment because he does not sin with infinite knowledge and power.

70

Jesus said that the servant who knew his Lord's will and made not ready would receive a severe (not an infinite) beating. (Luke 12:47.) Heaven and hell in Christian thought have always been correlative doctrines tied up with the belief in the perfect righteousness of God. Christian doctrine has always made it clear that no man is good enough to *merit* the infinite eternal joy of the heavenly relationship with God. There is a real sense in which the afterlife of both St. Paul and the Penitent Thief is equally the free unmerited gift of the Father. If men cannot merit the infinite joy of heaven they could negatively merit the loss of the infinite joy, but not negatively merit the positive experience of superhuman pain infinitely prolonged.[3] Where the orthodox doctrine of hell has been worked out to its logical conclusion the reaction of the "Rubaiyat" is a protest in the name of human decency:

> Oh Thou, who Man of baser Earth didst make,
> And ev'n with Paradise devise the Snake:
> For all the Sin wherewith the Face of Man
> Is blacken'd—Man's forgiveness give—and take!

The theoretical reason for disbelieving the orthodox picture of hell is that human beings would be naturally unable to experience it for an infinite duration or even to experience the intensity of it for very long. The God-caused pain of hell, in the orthodox account, has super-mundane, super-human intensity. In this regard the early Old Testament fear that direct contact with God might be lethal (Exodus 3:6; 19:12,13,21,24; 20:18,19; II Samuel 6:6-8.) is instructive. Man as creature is naturally only able to take experience within a limited range. Exposure to the sheer intensity of God would be destroying, and that is what ought logically to follow an individual's exposure to the infinite wrath of God in the traditional picture of hell. There are limits to the physical and psychological pain that the human being can experience. Where physical pain is felt it means that there is some health left in the body still struggling against the evil that threatens it. When the body finally gives up the struggle just before death the last moments are often characterized by a more or less comatose condition. On the emotional side overwhelming misfortune or grief can produce a kind

---

[3] We can think of a rattlesnake as missing the infinite joy of fellowship with God in the hereafter without thinking of the rattlesnake as being subjected to intense everlasting pain.

of numbness, and in this regard the moral callousness and emotional callousness to fear and scenes of death and suffering on the part of soldiers long engaged in fighting has often been noted. Orthodoxy accounts for the ability of the saints to endure the Beatific Vision by saying that those who are "in Christ" are "a new creation" (II Corinthians 5:17) sustained by the Holy Spirit so that they are able to be at home in the Divine Presence. And the argument that has been used to explain why insensitivity does not progressively characterize souls in hell is in part that in hell the spirit is no longer weakened by the presence of the body. But bodily fatigue is not the only cause of diminished responsiveness on earth. Prolonged acquaintance can lessen one's interest and pleasure in a novelty, and prolonged indulgence in a moral evil which "all the best people do" lessens one's spiritual perceptiveness, and in both instances the body and its neural equipment may be healthy and untired.[4] The theological argument that has been used is that God *sustains* the souls in hell so that they *can* feel its pains with undiminished intensity. This puts God in a class with those barbarians who torture their captives up to the limit of endurance and then carefully nurse them back to health so that they can torture them all over again. Any claim that the soul if unhindered by the body could in its own strength endure either the Beatific Vision or the everlasting pains of hell would have to depend on the Greek theory that the soul like the essences is of itself inherently eternal and indestructible. This is not the biblical belief.

To try to save Deity's reputation orthodoxy has claimed that sin is rebelliousness against God and that those in hell suffer not for the sum total of the sins they have committed in the past but for the continuing rebellion against God in the present. If they would surrender to God they would cease to be in hell. The gates of hell are locked on the inside. There are psychological difficulties to this theory. For human beings, as long as they retain their reason and power of choice, will tend to choose the most advantageous of any two genuine alternatives which they recognize. Thus Christ chose the cross, in spite of its proximate horror, because he be-

---

[4] The instances of the gradual lessening of one's pleasure due to repetition cannot be accounted for in terms of neural, i.e., physical, exhaustion. There are also instances where the same amount of repetition of something good or valuable results in increased, rather than lessened, pleasure.

lieved the choice ultimately advantageous for the Father, men, and himself simultaneously. Christ "for the joy that was set before him endured the cross, despising the shame." (Hebrews 12:2.)

It is possible to surrender voluntarily to God's power or to his righteous love. Hell would involve the feeling of God's power in painful intensity on the part of those who had refused his righteous love. If the suffering of the damned in hell is so intense that they no longer have rational control of their actions, then you have the not very nice picture of God endlessly torturing the hopelessly insane. If men in hell, however, continue to be able to make intelligent choices, they would obviously choose surrender to God with consequent peace, to continuing hopeless rebellion with endless torture. The orthodox doctrine contains the belief that the damned have an accurate knowledge of what their situation really is. They are not being tortured while they are ignorant of the nature of God and his relation to men. The damned soul that under intense torture everlastingly persists freely in hell in rebelliousness out of sheer obstinacy with nothing personally to gain by it is a theological man of straw. The unending rebellion of Satan on the ground that it is "better to reign in hell, than serve in heaven"[5] is psychologically imaginable, because in the traditional picture of hell Satan, although in pain himself, does have some chance to dominate. But the damned souls have no chance whatever to dominate and know it, so they have no positive inducement to rebel and tremendous advantage in ceasing to. To assume that the damned in hell everlastingly rebel out of sheer stubbornness with nothing to gain by it is not true to human nature. Men do not consciously permanently rebel horribly against God, against what they clearly know to be permanently hopeless odds, for the mere desire to rebel. They always think, in any human rebellion we know of in this world, that there is something they can gain by the rebellion. The orthodox picture of eternal torture in hell-fire would at least convince them if they experienced it that rebellion was futile, and drive them in desperation to try any means open to them that offered any chance of even partial relief from pain. If God refused to accept this surrender it would mean that God closed the door to those who desired to surrender to him and this has questionable implications for the character of God. For God to claim that for the surrender to be

---

[5] Milton, *Paradise Lost*, Book I, line 263.

valid the damned must, under the conditions of hell, feel a vivid affectionate love for him would be to add insult to injury. I do not, of course, believe that surrender merely to avoid pain, when no alternative offers *any* positive benefit, is an adequate reason for reversing the doom of the damned and admitting them to eternal joy. I am only trying to point out that the orthodox picture of hell so steps-up the description of the intensity of the torture that it removes the whole situation from the area of ethical choice. And I am certain that the whole Old Testament stands behind the belief that the ethical ingredient is never lost in the relationship between God and man, even when the relationship is the negative relationship of estrangement.

If, instead of taking the orthodox theological picture of hell, we take *the second law of thermodynamics* as a guiding principle in the interpretation of evil and think of hell under the aspect of destruction rather than primarily under the aspect of torture, which Jesus' teaching permits us to do, we get a description of hell both psychologically truer to human nature and morally easier to harmonize with a belief in God's righteousness and love.

We should probably take as the key biblical verse for the understanding of hell-fire the saying concerning Jesus by John the Baptist, where he says, "He will baptize you with the Holy Spirit and with fire. His winnowing fork is in his hand, and he will clear his threshing floor and gather his wheat into the granary, but the chaff he will burn with unquenchable fire." (Matthew 3:11, 12.) The fire that initiates into the life of the kingdom of God and the fire which aids in the destruction of the wicked is the same Holy Spirit. (Hebrews 12:25-29; Deuteronomy 4:24.)

Man is the highest part of the earthly creation, and the God given pattern appropriate to his existence includes righteousness and love by which his nature bears a resemblance to the controlling aspects of the nature of God himself. To find nourishment, i.e., power, to attain and maintain the appropriate pattern of righteousness and love man must draw strength direct from Spiritual Existence, i.e., from God, since all the strength or power he can draw from the creation is that physical power which is released by entropy in the slow dissolution of the cosmos according to *the second law of thermodynamics*. Without strength from God to sustain him man is thoroughly enmeshed in the cosmos and its trend toward self-exhaustion. When a man tries to love and obey God and serves him by attempting to live a righteously loving life, that man cannot in any way save himself; but he has put himself in the appropriate position to take on gradually the intense clarification of the pattern of righteousness and love which is given by close contact with the Holy Spirit of the Father and the Son. (I Corinthians 2:11, 12.) And power to help man attain the pattern and sustain him in it is also given in this same close contact with Deity.

Man is very frail and the righteousness, love, and power characteristic of God are too potent to be safe for much contact with man unless the clarification and power are appropriately received by man, that is, by the man desiring to love and obey God and to serve him by attempting to lead a righteously loving life, in which case God's Spirit assists man and sustains him. If we take air into our bodies appropriately by breathing, we will live. The same air inappropriately let directly into our veins would kill us. The appropriate human position in relation to God is one of surrender to God through Christ, or the desire to surrender to moral goodness which has its source in God and so can be a steppingstone to the desire to surrender to the Source of all Goodness. There must be at least an attempt at welcoming the Divine which one recognizes as divine, in order that God may come into the human life and not merely have a head-on collision with it. (Revelation 3:20; Matthew 12:31, 32). In this life each person is turning into the appropriate position or away from the appropriate position for receiving here and hereafter the spiritual clarification (I Corinthians 2:9-12) and power consequent upon the reception of God's Spirit. (John 10:10). After death the direct contact with God is more intense than it is in this life. Since death changes only the circumstances of spiritual existence, not its basic pattern, the human spirit that has already surrendered on earth to God in an attempted obedience will continue its relationship, now seeing in God directly the radiant source of the pattern of righteous-love he has tried to emulate upon earth. And he will receive from God constantly such an influx of the divine power and strength that his continuing in that state forever is guaranteed.

The incident of death finds the unsurrendered human spirit blocking the influx of God's fortifying power into his life, and therefore finds the man operating solely on his own merely human strength, that is, on the temporary power released by the cosmos in the process of its dissolution and on the psychological power built up in the long process of evolution on the basis of the physical power. So while the psychological power might conceivably outlast temporarily the human body, it is nevertheless subject to the over-all decay[6] that characterizes all created things.

"You are dust, and to dust you shall return," was originally said of the total man. (Genesis 3:19.) It is not that God would not accept the surrender of a soul after death. It is only that the fear and reluctance experienced by a soul on earth as it faces the unknown relationship that will follow upon its surrender, are a fear and reluctance that will be greatly increased by the terrifying quality of the sheer power of the unveiled Deity. Since God forever respects the dignity of man's spiritual freedom, the surrender, if it came after death, would have to be voluntary as it has to be on earth. But if the intensity of the being and the goodness of God are so great as to seem overwhelming and frightening on earth, so that man feels a kind of nervousness at the thought of the establishment of a relationship between man and God, and there tends to be a human shrinking from the establishment of such a relationship, how much more shrinking would there be after death on the part of the unsurrendered soul, at the thought of taking the step of surrender which would be followed by the health-giving vital intercourse between God and man, since in the heavenly situation the physical world would no longer be present to cushion the psychological impact of the immediate presence of the Divine Power.

On earth the great danger of human sin is not that it will harass and stab the human spirit — for that might send it fleeing to God for escape from pain — but rather the danger that sin will numb and anesthetize the human spirit. Jesus feared most the hypocrisy and the successful contented worldliness that enable men to form a temporary pleasing pattern of existence about their own lives and think that they can get on comfortably without God. The persistence in this, as well as the more easily identifiable specific transgressions, lessens a man's ability to be attracted by goodness, and also

---

[6] Plato considers this possibility in the first half of the *Phaedo* and only repudiates it because he believes souls to be eternal in their own right like the essences. The idea of psychic continuation with continuing decay would not be out of line with the world's ghost lore.

lessens his ability to find sin intensely painful. Macbeth is a perfect literary example of the numbing quality of sin. His initial overt crime in the murder of Duncan was followed by emotional horror and a vivid sense of the evil he had committed. As he goes farther and farther into evil each evil deed makes the cost to him of reversal of policy and surrender to goodness greater, so that at each step in his career his going father into evil seems to him a more comfortable and personally advantageous next step than the practical action that he would need to undertake to align his soul with good and not evil. This is the basic difficulty created by the effect of evil on the human soul here and hereafter. In Macbeth's last soliloquy he has almost lost belief in the moral order of existence because he has denied it until he can no longer see it. "Life," he says, "is a tale, told by an idiot, full of sound and fury, signifying nothing." (*Macbeth* Act V. Scene v.) The only thing at the end of the play that indicates any surviving regard for the ethical imperative is Macbeth's short lived attempt, while he still considers himself invulnerable, to avoid personal combat with Macduff. He does this on the ground that "My soul is too much charg'd with blood of thine already." (Act V. Scene viii.)

When we are out of doors for a long time on a cold winter day and our fingers become numbed with the cold, the feeling involves some discomfort. When we go indoors and hold our hands before the fire in the fireplace to re-establish circulation, the initial experience of heat upon our numbed fingers is more painful than the slight unpleasantness of the numbness we are trying to counteract. After the warmth of the fire has readjusted the circulation in our hands to normal, the feeling of the warmth of the fire will be positively pleasant.

This is the situation after death of the soul frozen by sin. It may surrender to God if it so desires and experience an initial stabbing pain of adjustment to the fire of the Divine Love that is temporarily much more painful than the pervasive spiritual malaise that is debilitating its powers. In other words in the life on earth the life lived in moral endeavor is typically described as an "uphill" road involving strenuousness. One does not drift into this life. But one can drift into evil ways and such a life is typically called a "downhill" road. I am suggesting that unless the soul has surrendered to God before death and been "reborn" (John 3:3) i.e., adjusted, strengthened and empowered on earth by God himself for the heavenly life, then the free choice of the "uphill road" or the "downhill road" still awaits the soul after the incident of death, with the initial pain of the surrender greatly intensified, and with the momentum in the downhill direction already long established. (Luke 19:26.)

Furthermore, for souls well established in the evil direction the pain of contact with God would seem real enough, but in many instances it might well be that God's goodness and love would seem positively unattractive because the man had positively centered his well being in evil (not carelessly drifted into it). (See II Thessalonians 2:10-12.) This sin of claiming good to be evil Jesus describes as the unforgivable sin. (Mark 3:28-30. Compare Isaiah 5:20.)

The soul that was unsurrendered to God at death, when faced with the alternative of choosing to undergo the intense pain of surrender to God or to avoid the intense pain by continuing to avoid contact with God, could be expected to choose to prolong its conscious state of mere pervasive spiritual malaise rather than endure the fire of the Love of the Holy Spirit upon its frozen life. This means that the unsurrendered soul after death would continue to operate on its own power and not God's. But all its own power was ultimately drawn from the temporary power released by the cosmos in the process of its dissolution—death having been part of the original miracle of the creation. So the sin-oriented soul after death will proceed farther and farther along the path of "the second death" into "the outer darkness" along with the decay of the created cosmos of which it is still a part. Christ told his disciples to fear him "who can destroy both soul and body in hell." (Matthew 10:28). He did not say God would torture body and soul forever in hell. "For God so loved the world that he gave his only Son, that whoever believes in him *should not perish* but have eternal life. . . . And this is the judgment, that the light has come into the world, and men loved darkness rather than light, because their deeds were evil. For *every one who does evil hates the light, and does not come to the light,* lest his deeds should be exposed." (John 3:16, 19, 20. Italics mine.)

We have seen that when the cosmos was created it had "built-in" to it dying or entropy in order to furnish a source of independent

78

power that life, which God planned to call into being, could use in freedom. In the next chapter we shall clear the ground for a discussion of evolution. After that we shall see that evolution is teleological, and is brought about by the free action of God upon the world he has created, working to reverse at points within the world the overall pattern of entropy. Man by his choice can assist in aiding God to reverse permanently the entropy pattern in the man's own individual life. He can do this by surrendering his own will and so finding his joyous end as *telos* here and hereafter. But he has the inalienable gift of freedom and therefore he can refuse to surrender himself to God and so find his end hereafter as *finis*.

CHAPTER 7

A Chapter of Blind Alleys

In the last chapter we have traced the pervasive influence of *the second law of thermodynamics* not only at the cosmic level but also in its effect of ultimate death to organisms and its effects in relation to pain and sin, projecting the implications of these latter into a reworking of the traditional Christian picture of hell. In doing this we have, however, assumed the appearance of the evolutionary process and the appearance of man on this planet. But no attempt has been made to account for the existence of either evolution or man, and this must now be undertaken. In other words, we must now take up again the doctrine of the creation at the stage of the initial appearance of the immediate precursors of the most primitive organisms. Speaking in other terms, we have described God's creation of something other than himself and separate from himself with which he could have an "I-it" relation. What we must now do is to trace the method by which, within the matrix of the "it" creation, he brought about the transformation of a little of "it" into something with which he could establish an "I-thou" relationship.

If we look back over the history of man's interpretation of his relationship to nature we find that primitive man attributed a kind of aliveness to nature itself. The gods of this and that natural phenomenon which he must take into account in his daily experience seem to merge in an undefined way with the phenomena themselves. Apollo is not wholly dissociated from the flaming sun. The monotheism of the Hebrew religion avoided this. For according to the Old Testament there is only the one God who created nature and is other than nature. Nature may not be deified. However, throughout the Old Testament there is the constant assumption that nature responds to God. On some of the successive days of creation (Genesis 1:3, 6, 14) God is described as saying, "Let there be" such and such. On other days God is described as saying "Let the waters" or "Let the earth" do such and such. (Genesis 1:9, 11, 20, 24.) And in each instance the compliance by the creation produces the appropriate result. Furthermore, throughout the Old Testament there are many statements to the effect that God "commands" nature, and nature "praises" God. That is to say, while nature is not personified, two definitely anthropomorphic terms are applied to nature's ongoing relationship to the Creator. (Psalms 65:12, 13; 69:34; 89:11,12; 96: 11-13; 98:7-9; 103:19-22; 148:3-10; 150:6; Job 36:32; 37:11, 12; 38:8-12; Psalms 78:23; 119:89-91; 148:3-5; Isaiah 44:23; Hosea 2:18; Amos 5:8; 7:4; 9:6; Habakkuk 3:10.) The writers were writing poetry unselfconsciously, and probably would have been embarrassed if asked to explain how the less-than-human can do things that are characteristically human types of activity. Or if it was suggested to them, on the other hand, that they were using the words "praise" and "command" in a merely figurative sense as applied to nature, they would have been equally ill at ease.

The biblical view that ascribes a human-like response on the part of nature carries over into Christian usage. Especially in the literature of the Romantic Movement nature is described as having "moods" — sparkling (vivacious), cold, powerful, sad, haunting, happy, peaceful, depressing, gloomy, serene, violent — paralleling human emotional states. The Romantic writers are of course vague as to whether the moods of nature are not moods at all but simply aspects of nature which tend to foster slightly these moods in the human soul. It is a well known fact that changes in nature do foster changes in human moods. We come across unexpected references to it even in such unlikely authors as John Bunyan, who remarks in *Pilgrim's Progress* that on sunshiny days the ferocious Giant Despair felt a little wobbly. If the "moods" are really thought of as being in nature itself, however, then one is ascribing a quasi-personal existence to nature. Certainly some of the Romantic School really believed that they loved nature, or certain aspects of it, and entered into a quasi-personal relation with it in which their spirits were strengthened by the high mountains and soothed by the babbling brooks.

Science, as it has gained control over popular thinking, has done away with these hints of "unscientific" personification of nature. The universe, according to nineteenth century science, looked increasingly like a perfect self-contained and self-supporting machine which, as part of its own activity, had brought forth the evolutionary process. So completely has this mechanistic view taken hold of the Western imagination that now, far from describing nature in human terms, our current vocabulary uses words appropriate to the activity of inorganic matter to describe man. We say, for example: "A man who has been badly *conditioned* by childhood experiences often does not *contact* others easily or *react* well in social situations and so is with difficulty *integrated* into the group."

But the mechanistic view of science, when carried to an extreme, creates philosophical difficulties for science itself. It finds that it has got a neat picture of existence that somehow completely leaves out of consideration the university trained intellect of the scientific investigator by whose creative thought and investigation the structure of scientific knowledge has been built. The problem for a philosophy of science becomes that of somehow smuggling the scientific investigator himself into the total picture. He could no longer be accounted for as the creation of God, because scientists had long since given the laity to understand that any idea of a supernatural God who could and did tinker miraculously with nature at will was a definitely outmoded belief, because science had made it clear that the cause-and-effect sequences within nature were unbroken and that all effects in the universe were the result of previous causes within the universe.

All this while geology had been pushing back this earth's history into the aeons of the past, so that by now the man-on-the-street knew that science claimed that this earth had existed for countless millions of years before there was any life on it at all, and for many millions more before the appearance of man. Had God miraculously inserted either organic life or human spirit anywhere along the line as distinct entities, there would suddenly have appeared within the world effects, namely organic life and human spirit, for which there would have been no causes within the universe, for their cause would be the direct action of the supernatuaral God who is not part of the universe. Thus effects would have been suddenly fed into the order of nature and that would involve miracle, although these effects, once acclimated to nature, could in turn function as causes for future events within the natural order. But this explanation was not open to the acceptance of science, for science believed that it had ruled out the possibility of a supernatural God miraculously producing effects at will within the natural order.

This left science with the university trained scientist, upon whose creative thought and investigation the whole structure of the scientific picture of the world rested, as an embarrassment to the picture. The philosophy of science had therefore to rethink its position to try to bring the scientist himself within its description of the total scheme of things.

At first it seemed that the theory of evolution would accomplish this. Embryology shows that each human being develops from a one-celled organism, and the study of the history of life on the planet seems to indicate that all the species of plants and animals, including man, developed by a slow process of modification from one-celled organisms in the primeval seas. If I accept these claims to be true — and I do accept them as true — I have to do so on faith, faith in the accuracy and intelligence and integrity of scientists, since in the scientific field I am a layman. The reason the Church fought the theory of evolution was that it seemed to reduce man to the status of the animals and to deny him the dignity of his spirit's special creation in the image of God. To speak autobiographically, I grew up in intellectual and religious circles in which people considered evolution as a description of man's rootage in the more primitive developing forms of organism on this planet, to be an idea firmly established. But neither I nor the exposition of religion I heard in my childhood would have been willing to admit that all the steps in the process of evolution were wholly accounted for by naturalistic explanations. There was admittedly a very fuzzy borderline area in our attempt to combine the theory of evolution with our religious views.

When religion could no longer hold its intellectual line against the theory of the evolution of the human species from lower species of animals, it made a tactical retreat and claimed that the boundary between the organic and inorganic realms was an impassable one and that therefore the origin of life on this planet must have been by miraculous endowment from God. I myself have taught this in past years although without much enthusiasm, basing my argument upon the claim in Lecomte du Noüy's *Human Destiny* that the mathematical improbability of the mere juggling of the inorganic matter of the universe bringing about the existence of organic molecules is so great as to rule out the origin of organisms as being due to mere chance. I am, however, no longer concerned

83

to try to hold a sharp boundary line between the organic and the inorganic, and I think that those religious apologists who are trying to do it are fighting another losing battle.

For in the last few decades science has been erasing this boundary and now, I believe, is claiming that the lowly amoeba is really a very highly developed form, as much more complicated than the first traces of organic life as man is more complicated than the amoeba. *If we define organism as an aggregation of matter that "strives" to maintain a characteristic pattern, that has at least some freedom, that is active rather than inert, and that has the ability to reproduce itself, we can see that all the attributes except that of reproduction are characteristic of inorganic matter.* We now know that the activity within the atom is highly dynamic and follows characteristic patterns, and we are coming to believe that at the subatomic level nature has a slight amount of freedom. Also, simple crystalline substances above the atomic and molecular level sometimes seem to exhibit a "striving" to maintain their appropriate pattern. For example, the appropriate pattern for the crystals of common table salt is a cube. We can destroy this crystalline pattern by dissolving the salt in water. But when we evaporate the water the crystals reform in their characteristic cubic pattern. Some would say that the salt, when freed from solution "strives" to re-attain its characteristic pattern.

We need not concern ourselves with what science considers a partial reconstruction of the steps by which some matter began to become organic. Supposedly the ultraviolet radiation from the sun upon the primordial hydrogen-containing atmosphere of the earth formed amino acid molecules, which drifted down, and became dissolved in the waters of the oceans. I am assuming that science's claim is largely accurate and that science itself in the next few years will correct its minor errors and fill out the description in greater detail. We will suppose that science will, in the not too distant future, also be able to chart in very great detail the steps of gradation between so-called inorganic matter and the lowest forms of organisms, and that science will eventually be able to create synthetically in the laboratory the lowest forms of organisms from inorganic matter. This will mean that science will have succeeded in erasing the hard and fast line of cleavage between organic and inorganic matter, and have shown that man evolved literally "out of the dust of the earth" and that there is no one place in this long process which one can select and say that at this point God breathed into matter the breath of life. This situation poses a tremendous problem for theology.

What may not be at first so obvious is that it also poses a tremendous problem for the philosophy of science. For the philosophy of science has tried to show, first by the doctrine of evolution from the one-celled animalcule to man, and more recently from the evolution of inorganic matter into the animalcule, that man is totally explainable in terms of this evolutionary process *within* nature. Supposedly the erasing of the line at the lower end of the scale between organic and inorganic matter would make it possible to show that man is wholly accounted for by the natural process. The difficulty, however, from the point of view of the scientific explanation, is that this theory still leaves the mind of the university trained scientist, which is resonsible for the whole structure of scientific knowledge and theory, completely unaccounted for. This point needs to be made very clearly, for I have found that most people do not see clearly the lines of demarcation in the issue.

It is true that science may be able to trace the steps by which the process of the evolution of inorganic matter (which under proper conditions will react chemically with other inorganic matter) may come to form complicated compounds in which the scope of reactivity becomes increased and of far wider range and subtlety than matter had hitherto exhibited. Furthermore, aggregates of specific size and shape of these highly complicated compounds may arrive at a stage of subtlety of reactivity in which they are capable of continuing, through spreading their form of organization by reproducing themselves, and so forming what we call organisms. But even if this line of reasoning and investigation could be completely charted all the way to make a complete scientific analysis of the neural activity of the professor of biology, still nothing would have been analyzed except the increasing degree and complexity of reactivity, including the professor's neural reactivity which is an electro-chemical phenomenon capable of objective study and mathematical measurement. The question of mind would not have been investigated at all. For minds are subjective and not capable of objective study and mathematical measurement and hence are beyond the reach of scientific study. By minds we mean minds as thinking, not the preserved product of their thought in spoken and written word, nor the product of the thought as interiorly preserved and available later to the mind as items held in memory. Science can only deal elaborately with brain activity, that is, with the re-activity triggered by the electro-chemical neural activity which is accepted as customarily accompanying the activity of consciousness, and also as functioning to maintain the human organism in many ways that are unaccompanied by consciousness. For example, once food has been swallowed the highly complicated method by which it is digested is governed by neural activity controlling muscles and glands. But it is a process that is unaccompanied by consciousness.

Science has done much to map the physical basis of consciousness and will probably do very much more. But the more thoroughly it substantiates its thesis of the physical explanation of conscious intellectual life, the more completely it shows consciousness to be, scientifically speaking, an unnecessary functionless triviality. For example: the instantaneous withdrawal of my hand in response to a pin-prick is involuntary reflex action not conditioned by consciousness and neurologically not involving the cerebral cortex. The conscious awareness of what I am doing and the accompanying feeling of pain come slightly *after* the initiation of the reflex action.

On the scientific theory *there is no reason why all mind cannot be explained as an unnecessary conscious registering of activity already carried out by the physical organism under neural control. Consciousness would therefore perform no function whatever.*

It is a mistake to think that on scientific theory the conscious experience of the painful pin-prick helps deter one from touching pin-points on a later occasion. For what the theory of the neural determination of consciousness is saying, if ruthlessly pushed to its logical implications, is this: The neurally controlled reflex action of the withdrawal of the hand from the pin-point triggered extensive reaction in another non-motor area of the brain. Bodily memory is the reawakening of faint replicas of previous neural activity made possible by the permanent imprint or track that neural activity leaves upon the nerves themselves. When two or more strong re-actions occur simultaneously, a repetition of a situation that had originally triggered one response, when the new situation again triggers the same response, will serve to set in motion the whole complex of responses. Thus, while I was withdrawing my hand from the pin-point in the first instance, light impressions of the pin-shape were also fixing themselves upon the retina of my eye. When, therefore, a similar object again similarly stimulates the retina of my eye, the reaction connects not only with the remaining traces of the previous eye reaction, but also with the traces of the withdrawal reaction plus the other concomitant reaction in the nonmotor area of the brain. Therefore the body approaches the second pin situation with more complicated maneuvering relative to the preservation of the body than characterized its actions when approaching the first pin situation. Consciousness need not come into the picture at all, for the deterrent influence we usually attribute to the past conscious experience of pain can be wholly accounted for as the *underscoring of the withdrawal reaction by the added neural action which accompanies the feeling of pain, but which is not itself pain or any form of consciousness but is only entirely objective and physical electro-chemical modification within the nerve tissue.*

This line of reasoning can be extended to include all the complexity of modern civilization which can be thought of as originally elaborated and now maintained by the infinite complexity and subtlety of the electro-chemical reactivity of the highly specialized nerve tissue. Consciousness, much less sustained reasoning, is simply not part of any strictly scientific picture of reality. For consciousness can be studied at first hand only by introspection. But, as soon as one tries to look objectively at *himself thinking*, he discovers that he is looking only at the immediate past state of his own mind. The conscious "I", although it is immediately aware of its own existence, is never able to look objectively at itself-thinking. The intelligent consciousness (which has elaborated scientific theory) is itself entirely out of bounds for scientific thought, which investigates the field of objective reality in its mathematically measurable aspects.

A few of the repercussions of the impact of the scientific point of view upon the ordinary citizen's outlook on life should be noted. We have already pointed out that our everyday vocabulary describes men with such words as "condition," "contact," "integrate," "react," and "adjust," all of which would be appropriate words to describe man if he were merely a mechanical robot without consciousness. Thus there is a tendency to think of men as largely "conditioned" by their heredity and environment rather than as the "master of their fate" and the "captain of their souls." The well known fact that twentieth century American psychiatry has been elaborated on a naturalistic basis means just that. And it means that psychology has looked to the influences that have played upon a man in the past rather than to the goals toward which he strives, as the key to the explanation of his conduct. Thus it has followed that psychiatry has described what used to be called moral defects in personality as mental "sickness" due to "poor adjustment." For if all men's actions and thoughts are the result merely of neural action, which in turn is entirely dependent on previous neural action, which is itself governed by the laws of physics and chemistry and is linked with the unbroken cause-and-effect sequences of the re-actions of matter outside of man, then man *is* completely deter-mined by nature and so is not morally responsible for his acts.

The present teen-age generation on the whole is not characterized by a sense of ethical responsibility or by a willingness of individuals to break away from a harmonious adjustment to their group in order to stand alone for what is ethically right. The young have tended to make excuses for their failures by blaming their family or their education. They have not been characterized by the pioneering spirit of gambling their careers on some activity which fascinates them. Rather they have put a premium upon "leader-ship ability." But "leadership" as they use the term is a euphemism for smooth social adjustment plus executive ability which will get a person executive positions in extra-curricular activities in school and college and put him in line for executive positions in the out-side world, so that he will have prestige, affluence, and security. The craving of the young has been for freedom from restrictions and inconveniences rather than freedom to carry out useful and valuable projects in line with goals of great moral and social worth. The young look out on the unsettled conditions of the atomic age and face the possibility of their lives being prematurely cut short. They assume that their conscious life depends for its existence wholly on the life of the body and, when the life of the body ends, the consciousness ends forever. Therefore their practical strategy is, "Let us take for ourselves while we can. When you are dead, you are dead a long time." In all this they are merely living ex-plicitly according to the science-conditioned philosophy of life which the older generation (in spite of its lip service to ideals and religion) has implicitly followed. For ideas considered true by the mind eventually affect conduct.

Of recent years it has been popular to say that this philosophy of science I have been elaborating is not the conclusion of scientists, that genuine scientists themselves are more humble in their personal lives, more open to religion and less dogmatic in the conclusions about life which they draw from their scientific knowledge. While I would not deny this, I would also point out that scientific investigation has become divided into such specialized fields that most scientists concentrate on the particular problem on which they are working and have not thought a great deal about what the essential claims of Christianity are to which Christianity must relate its understanding of science.

The inhospitality of science to Christian belief can be rather easily shown. Suppose you took a poll among scientific experts in the fields of chemistry, physics, and biology, and asked them this question, "Do you believe that telepathic communication between human minds as a matter of fact ever takes place? That is, do you believe that the non-physical consciousness of one man can directly influence the non-physical consciousness of another man at a distance, without employing any physical means of communication?" I think the large majority of scientific experts would answer "no" to that question. Science by and large has not been willing to accept the Duke University investigations as proving telepathy, or to accept the many claims that have been made informally through the centuries by many people who have said that they have had personal experience of telepathic communication. And yet many people who have vouched for personal telepathic experience have been people of as much education and integrity as scientists. For telepathy, if proved true, would not be just one more scientific experiment: it would be a different kind of experiment that would make necessary the rethinking of scientific presuppositions all along the line. For science has been considering consciousness — on an enormous amount of medical evidence — as a mysterious concomitant of neural action in the brain. And the assumption has been that the brain causes the consciousness and not consciousness the brain. (The fetus has a brain but not consciousness.)

Now the claim that telepathy makes is that ordinary, non-physical consciousness, which one thinks of as running, so to speak, on the neural track, can occasionally "jump that track" successfully and by itself — without physical undergirding — influence directly the non-physical consciousness of another person. *But that second person also has a consciousness which normally "runs on a neural track." So that second person's non-physical consciousness, in receiving the non-physical telepathic message must then run it, as part of his memory, on his own "neural track," and his means that his "neural track" must take on the electro-chemical modification normally suited to that memory. And this involves the fact that this particular physical modification of the second person's brain would take place without any physical cause. And science has denied that physical effects take place without physical causes.* It is normal for science to think in terms of the brain influencing consciousness and not of consciousness influencing the brain. Even the recent emphasis on psychosomatic medicine does not invalidate the scientific belief as the establishment of the case for telepathy would do, because all cases of a mind influencing its own body could theoretically be explained in terms of trains of neural power converging to form an unusually great concentration of neural power which would then, with adrenalin-assistance, release more of the whole organism's latent large scale physical energy than is normally available.

I personally have never had what I thought was an experience of a message I believed to be telepathically communicated, and I am open minded as to the Duke University experiments, and undecided as to whether or not the case for telepathy has been conclusively proved. So this present book will make no use of any argument based on human telepathy, although *if* telepathy could be proved, and proved not to employ hitherto unidentified wave lengths, it would be very useful evidence in the direction of substantiating the thesis that this book develops. *I only bring up telepathy to show that science is extremely skeptical of its validity. And this skeptiscism has a distinct bearing upon what scientists on the whole really think about the validity of Christianity.*

For basic Christianity includes the belief in God's revelation of the law to Moses at Mount Sinai, in God's inspiration of the great prophets of Israel, and in the Holy Spirit's guidance of those who love and serve Christ. None of this Divine assistance needs to be thought of as extensive Divine dictation to a human being. For the purposes of our argument all that needs to be assumed is that God can guide and educate men by directly putting pressure upon men to arrest and hold their attention upon particular items, gained from normal experience, as these items flow through the man's stream of consciousness, and that God does this to make the man select as his guide those particular items from his mental equipment which God considers most useful in teaching men about God and his wishes with respect to men's conduct. At least this minimum amount of direct Divine assistance must have characterized the Sinai episode, some of the experience of the great prophets, and the guidance of St. Paul and other great Christians by the Holy Spirit, or Christianity is a well meaning but false religion. *At least this amount of direct Divine assistance to men is essential to Christianity's claims. But if even this minimum amount of direct Divine assistance takes place, then in each instance of it you have the completely non-physical conscious Spirit of God, who is not part of our universe, directly causing an effect to take place in the non-physical consciousness of a man, which effect to be remembered must create an appropriate neural, that is physical, change in the man's brain. For the more adequate "engraving" of these particular ideas upon the man's brain, which is what makes his thought center around these instead of around other ideas, is due directly to the conscious non-physical spirit of God impinging upon the non-physical human consciousness. Thus in God's spiritual guidance of individual men there are involved physical effects in the neural matter of the brain for which there are no physical causes.*

This raises basically the same problem for science that the question of telepathy raises (if telepathy does not make use of wave lengths) with the additional complication that in the case of direct Divine guidance the non-physical cause that brings about the man's neural modification through his consciousness is a power outside the universe, and so the Divine action involves miracle. *For miracle is the direct causing of particualr effects within the universe at non-scheduled times by the direct conscious will of the supernatural God who is not part of the universe but who acts occasionally at points within the universe to further his long distance purposes.* Ask highly trained physicists, chemists, and biologists if they really believe that a supernatural God can and does sporadically act consciously and directly upon the universe to modify it at some point, and the answer you will probably get will be "no."

Most scientists, if they believe in religion, would say that they do not believe in a God who is at all outside of nature, but in a God who is everywhere present in nature, a vital force that assists in the ongoing of all there is. Now the difficulty that makes this description of God an impossible one for Christianity to hold, is that it describes God as having a part in the ongoing of the evil of the world as well as having a part in the ongoing good of the world, for "all there is" includes both good and evil. So this description of God contradicts the fundamental Jewish-Christian claim that God is righteous and hates wickedness. This description of God as part of "all there is" is in fact the Pantheism which is Christianity's most dangerous religious rival. But most earnest scientists who are religiously inclined do not understand enough of what is involved in Christianity to realize that their description of the God they believe in is opposed to Christianity.

So far our argument has made little headway except in charting the nature of the difficulty that science faces when it tries to build a philosophy upon its own findings. It must limit itself to an objective study of the universe in mathematically measurable terms and so must omit from its picture such values as duty, beauty, and love, which are subjectively held by non-material consciousness. And it must omit intelligent consciousness from its sphere of investigation, because the thinking subject cannot objectify himself even to himself, and so cannot be scientifically investigated. But scientists are men as well as scientists, and know from experience that they *are* conscious thinking individuals who *do* take duty, beauty, and love seriously in their personal lives. The problem is how to account for the value-serving intelligent consciousness of individuals.

Scientific theory has itself ruled out the possible positive answers to its question. It cannot say either that the world and intelligent men have always existed by chance, or that this world and intelligent men suddenly came into being at the same time by chance some time in the history of the cosmos. For geology has been at pains to prove that our world existed for many million years before there was any life upon it, and that life when it did appear existed for many millions of years more in only lower, non-intelligent forms. And furthermore, the attempts Christianity has made to account for life, and more especially for value-serving intelligent life, by the hypothesis that the world was created originally by a good God who afterward miraculously inserted first organic life and later intelilgent value-serving life into it, have been elaborately denied by science from two lines of investigation. On the one hand, science has elaborately charted the chemical regularities of nature and declared that nature or the universe is a closed system whose regularities cannot be interfered with by the intrusion of any power from outside the universe. And on the other hand, science has shown through the study of comparative anatomy, of embryology, and of the history of life in the geological record that man appears to have evolved from lower forms of life, and that there is no absolute line of demarcation between human life and the lower forms of life. And finally, recent advanced study of cellular and molecular structure is erasing the fixed line of demarcation between the organic and the inorganic.

Science has been in the habit of assuming that in the beginning there was just matter and then organic life just naturally evolved from matter and later intelligent life just naturally evolved from organic life. But even if all the steps in the process of evolution were charted by science, *science would only have explained the increased structural complication of organisms and the increasing range and subtlety of their reactivity. No explanation at all is given of how consciousness and intelligence should have gradually occurred in conjunction with this increased reactivity and structural complexity. For intelligent consciousness is subjective while reactivity and structural complexity are purely objective. So to explain the appearance of intelligent consciousness by saying that it "evolved" is no more of an explanation than it would be to explain how a man is able to walk by declaring learnedly that it is because he has "ambulatory power."*

Where the philosophy of science has taken full account of science's progress in erasing the line of demarcation between "inanimate" and animate matter, it has tried to get around the difficulty of how mind could have originated from inanimate matter by saying that mind has always been associated with matter, that even what we used to call inanimate matter has always had a latent mind-factor and so the development of intelligence in man is simply an unfolding of what has always been potentially present. When the philosophy of science has found itself forced to adopt this theory it has unwittingly made itself vulnerable to a positive theological offensive. No longer is theology forced to fight a defensive battle of delaying action.

CHAPTER 8
The Constructive Approach

The theological offensive is now in a position to fight on two fronts. It can point out that if this "mind-factor" is simply thought of as a quality inherent in matter, then the explanation is simply a juggling of words and not an explanation. For by mind we mean intelligent consciousness, even if admittedly the borderline between mere living organism and intelligent consciousness is somewhat shadowy. Rudiments of intelligent consciousness seem to appear among such animals as monkeys, dogs, elephants, and porpoises; and in any human life no one can pinpoint the exact moment between conception and kindergarten when intelligent consciousness appears. Nevertheless well developed intelligent consciousness is known to exist, and in its well developed form it is in a different category from the merely self-organizing, self-sustaining, and self-propagating reactivity of those aggregates of matter that are merely organic. Christian theology is in a position to show that if science will accept the biblical claim that the ultimate factor in existence is the highly intelligent, powerful, supernatural mind of God, which caused matter to come into being originally as something other than himself, and that matter so formed was capable of becoming conscious for two reasons, then you have a genuine explanation that science by itself lacks of how any of the original stuff of the universe could "evolve" into highly intelligent men. Christianity's two reasons are first, that "mere matter" as mere matter is amenable to the presence of mind because it was created by Mind, and second, that the Creator's mind is in the habit of associating itself with the created and now independent matter for the purpose of bringing intelligent mind into being within it. Christianity can then claim that these two reasons taken together constitute that "mind factor" which the philosophy of science has been vaguely saying has been associated with matter from the beginning.

The other front upon which Christian theology is now in a position to wage offensive battle is made possible by the philosophy of science's unconscious admission of the validity of argument by analogy. For of course no one *knows* that there is any "mind factor" associated with "mere matter" and with the lower organisms. Men as we know them *are* intelligent consciousness and organic bodies. "Mere matter" and the lower organisms exhibit some of the characteristics of that particular organism-with-which-conscious-intelligence-or-mind-is-associated-which-is-man, and therefore *by analogy* mind is assumed to be a factor of "mere matter" and the lower organisms.

This reverting to argument by analogy on the part of the philosophy of science is really an amazing state of affairs to anyone who knows anything of the history of the two disciplines of theology and science. In the pre-scientific era the attempt to interpret the Bible often made a farfetched use of analogy and so got many fantastic interpretations from passages of scripture. The advent of the scientific era with its emphasis on the mathematically measurable discountenanced the validity of argument by analogy and hence had the indirect salutary effect of causing theology to prune back the luxuriant growth of the use of analogy (which includes allegorizing). The element of austerity thus infused into religious thinking and interpretation has had many decided advantages.

I do not, however, consider argument by analogy necessarily invalid, but only something that should be handled with extreme caution. For it is by analogy that we see relatonships between things, and in the scientific field resemblances that first caught the investigator's eye as analogous have sometimes led to hypotheses capable of scientific proof.

Within mathematics itself there is a type of reasoning which, while not itself analogical, bears some resemblance to it. It is a simple matter in geometry to reconstruct a circle if one is given an arc of it. There is a wholeness and consistency in the circular form which makes it possible to project a knowledge of the unknown part of the circle "on the analogy" of the part already known. (This is not strictly speaking argument by analogy, but it bears a sufficient resemblance to it to be useful for our present purpose.) Now science proceeds upon the assumption that there is a wholeness and consistency and interrelatedness in nature.

A famous instance of scientific deduction based upon this confidence was the finding of the planet Neptune. A peculiar, unexplained variation had been noted in the orbit of the planet Uranus.

By much previous inductive study and research scientists had discovered how much gravitational pull heavenly bodies of certain sizes exerted at certain distances. Now, taking this accumulated knowledge as their starting point, two astronomers argued that, since nature follows uniform laws, the probability was that the present unexplained deviation in the orbit of Uranus was analogous to the variations in the orbits of other heavenly bodies due to the known gravitational influence of particular known bodies. So these astronomers, calculating mathematically *on the analogy of previous astronomical findings, reasoned deductively* that there *ought* to be a planet of particular size at a particular place in the heavens at a particular time to account for the orbital variation of Uranus. They verified this hypothesis by focusing their telescopes at the proper spot in the heavens at the proper time and seeing there the hitherto unknown planet Neptune. After the planet had been experimentally located in 1846 scientific belief about it was no longer based on deductive reasoning based on analogy. But up until the time when the astronomers verified their hypothesis by looking through their telescopes and seeing the planet, their confidence that the planet was there was based on deductive reasoning trusting that this situation would prove analogous to situations with which they were already experimentally familiar.

Now to carry our line of argument a step further: The sciences of chemistry, physics, geology, biology, and astronomy not only claim to describe the natural order as it is at the present time, where their claims would be subject to experimental verification, they also claim to be able to trace the development of life on this planet, to determine the world's geological history, and to describe the activity and in some cases the location of the heavenly bodies before man came upon the earth. But hypotheses about the past are not subject to experimental verification as are those about contemporary phenomena. The best that one can do about establishing as scientific fact something that occurred before human history, is to find converging lines of evidence that very strongly suggest that the hypothesis is correct. We cannot, for example, journey into the past to observe the earth in the first glacial age. What scientists can do is to observe the present effect of modern glaciers upon the terrain, to observe how water erodes rocks and earthbanks, to observe the rate at which rivers deposit silt, etc., and then out of an elaborate knowledge of the present to construct a picture of the past history of our earth, by applying by analogy the knowledge of how nature acts in the present to a reconstruction of the past that will be consistent with the total picture of the earth as we find it at the present. In other words, our knowledge of the early geological ages of this planet is only the type of knowledge the astronomers had of Neptune just before they trained their telescopes on a particular spot in the sky and so were able to verify their hypothesis.

Scientists observe over and over again that certain causes are followed by certain results. Then when scientists later see traces of such results in situations that must have existed long ago, they predicate the conditions in the past that would account for these results *on the assumption that cause and effect functioned in the past as they do in the present.* But that is an assumption. They cannot establish their theories about the past experimentally as the astronomers could do when they first trained their telescopes on the spot in the heavens where they thought an unknown planet ought to be. Even though a scientist may help to substantiate his theory of the world's past by projecting several lines of evidence backward and finding that they seem to interrelate appropriately, he is still arguing by an assumed analogy between the past and the present. There are several lines of evidence, for example, all pointing to approximately the same figure for the age of the cosmos. One of these is the determination of the age of the cosmos by means of radioactivity. The rate at which matter loses its radioactivity can be charted in the present. The percentage of radioactive matter still left in the world is therefore evidence of the age of the matter that composes the world. But this argument is an argument from analogy, for it assumes a similarity between the speed with which matter loses its radioactivity now and the speed at which it lost it millions and billions of years ago.

Take another instance of scientific argument by analogy. We have been told so long and so vividly by scientists that life as we know it began as microscopic one-celled animalcules that in our imaginations we can almost see those wee beasties floating about in the warm primordial oceans. But these original one-celled animalcules are entirely imaginary hypothetical reconstructions on the part of scientists. There are no fossilized remains of these earliest living creatures since they had no skeletons. And no scientist ever looked through a microscopic and saw one of these ancient one-celled creatures, for there were no scientists in that age. No scientist has ever even seen the primeval seas in which these animalcules are said to have floated. The whole thing is an assumption based on detailed studies of embryology and comparative anatomy plus the geological record which shows simpler fossil forms in the earlier rock strata records, and more complicated forms of skeletons appearing for the first time only in later strata. This is cautious and restrained argument from analogy, but it is still argument from analogy.

Let us take another and simpler example of the scientific argument by analogy. By comparing the number of rings in the wood of the cross-section of stumps of trees whose age is already definitely known and falls within the extended present in which scientists can make observations, botanists have discovered that the number of rings is the same as the number of years the tree has lived, and they have therefore arrived at the conclusion that each ring in the cross-section of the wood represents one year in the tree's growth. Using the number of rings as evidence of the tree's age botanists claim that some of the giant sequoias of California are over 3,000 years old. But the conclusion about the sequoias, while probably correct, is not reached by the strictly scientific method of observation and controlled and repeated experiment. *Instead the scientist is arguing to a conclusion about nature in the past, based on the analogy of nature in the present, and this is deductive, not inductive, reasoning.* For of course no scientist has direct access to the situation of the tree growth in the California area during the first millennium B.C. I am not questioning the accuracy of this particular scientific deduction. In fact it seems to me a very reasonable one to make, and I think that in all probabilities it is correct, and does give us accurate information about the past. But when scientists make deductions of this sort on the supposed analogy between the past and the present, they are not using the inductive approach and the controlled and repeated experiment on which the science of the last three centuries has been built. *When science tries to chart the course of nature in the remote past which is non-repeatable, science is making skilled use of the older methods of analogy and deduction which are methods that had long been used by theology, and which science had discountenanced as methods of arriving at the truth.* For in trying to chart the history of nature in times long past, science, on the assumption of the uniformity of nature, has to reason deductively assuming an analogy between nature as it is directly known today and the hypothetical nature of the distant past.

We are now in a position to gauge the importance for theology's relation to science of the explanation given by the philosophy of science to account for the emergence of intelligent consciousness in human life on this planet. For one cannot "discover" mind in inanimate or barely animate nature, because nature at this level can only be studied objectively, and intelligent mind can only be known subjectively. What the philosophy of science is therefore doing is trying to deduce the existence of mind in relation to primitive nature or latent in it on the basis of an analogy based on a similarity of reactivity between inanimate or barely animate matter on the one hand, and the reactivity of the human organism which is intimately associated with the human mind.

This means that the philosophy of science is making use of its knowledge of the fully developed conscious mind as a basis for an analogy between man and the lower forms of nature. To put the matter in different words we can say that a hundred years ago Darwin's theory of the origin of species had the effect of seeming to account for man on the basis of the lower forms of nature and so to eliminate any special Providential activity in man's formation. This seemed to undercut claims of biblical theology. The Church fought this scientific assumption but was unable to make headway against it, and therefore tended steadily to lose intellectual ground as it fought a battle of delaying action against this intellectual threat to its faith. But now the philosophy of science, finding that it cannot account for the intelligent consciousness of man by means of mechanism, has of its own accord, in order to keep its basic assumption of the uniform interrelatedness of nature, resorted to the old theological device of deductive reasoning based on analogy and is now reading back "mind" or a "mind factor" or "latent mind" — which scientists cannot study objectively but only deduce by analogy because they themselves are subjective intelligent consciousnesses — into or into association with the most primitive forms of "inanimate" or barely animate nature. In other words, Darwinism had traced the ascent from primitive organisms to man.

100

Having accomplished this feat evolutionary thought is now forced to trace backward from fully developed man to mere matter in order to account for the presence of intelligent consciousness in the world. The implications of this are revolutionary for the relationship between theological and scientific thought.

For the philosophy of science is unintentionally at this point reversing its standard procedure of accounting for the higher in terms of the lower, and is here partially accounting for the lower in terms of the higher. The only need for any one's thinking that there had to be a "mind factor" or a "striving" applied to amoeba or to inorganic matter is that there are later human minds that need to be accounted for. But to ascribe a "mind factor" to these more primitive forms of matter is to describe them teleologically, or in terms of the thing they are striving to attain. The more primitive forms do not have to consciously "strive," or be intentionally teleological in their activity. But the scientifically minded philosopher, in imputing a "striving" or "mind factor" to them is claiming that their activity is not altogether random but is oriented toward a purpose or purposes, in other words the philosopher is implying that their activity contains as a matter of fact a teleological factor. Obviously no "mind factor" is scientifically discoverable in the lowest organisms and in inanimate matter, for to be scientifically discoverable it would have to be objectively discoverable and only reactivity is objectively discoverable. Each of us knows his own subjective mind and by analogy assumes the minds of those around him by observing their objective reactions, which he interprets on the basis of his knowledge of his own objective reactions that accompany his subjective mind. Science as such was originally quite happy in charting reactivity in nature and scientifically ignoring the presence of mind. But the philosophy of science has eventually had to take mind into consideration.

Now, outside of scientific thought, a great deal is known about the history of the activity of the human mind. Philosophy, religion, ethics, aesthetics, art, literature, history, education, and gossip have for thousands of years been concerned with what men have thought and the activities their thoughts have directed. So, once allow that segment of existence with which we are most intimately familiar — namely human mind — to be used as a basis for deduction with regard to the evolution of mind on this planet, and theology is left free to use as evidence in argument a great deal of important cultural data that was non-available in its discussion with science, as long as science insisted on confining all the evidence it would take into account to that obtainable by an objective study of those aspects of nature that could be mathematically measured and in many cases dealt with by controlled experiments.

We have pointed out at length that science began by analyzing contemporary physical phenomena by observation and mathematical measurements and experiments based on the inductive method. This is the famous scientific method *par excellence.* This is the technique for getting information about existence which science, in its triumphs in the three quarters of a century after 1850, expected would supplant the older deductive reasoning and use of analogy. And it is the investigation by repeatable experiment of the contemporary situation in the physical world that is the basic domain of scientific inquiry.

But, as we have pointed out at length, science did not restrict itself to the contemporary situation in which it could observe nature in action. Instead, one branch of astronomy deals with the history of the universe. Paleontology deals with the history of early life on this planet. Geology deals with the history of the earth's crust. But science can only deduce the past by analogy to the present and by the selection of particular items in the present as giving assistance to this end. For the past is not subject to repetition, and so cannot be investigated by direct observation and controlled experiment. This cannot be said too firmly. For example, it cannot be scientifically proved from our twentieth century position in history that dinosaurs ever lived in the past. Living dinosaurs have never been seen by modern man and can therefore not be made the subject of scientific experiment. What have been found are dinosaur tracks and bones. I am assuming that these bones can be shown to have the same chemical composition as the bones of modern lizards, and that the dinosaur footprints and the dinosaur skeleton resemble the footprints and skeletons of modern lizards. And so reasoning by analogy science deduces that these objects are the skeletons of huge prehistoric lizard-like creatures. But had men been disembodied intellects inhabiting a world in which no animals with physical bodies existed, the most brilliant scientific spirits on earth would never have surmised that these strange objects were the boney structure and footprints of beings that had lived in the past. And no scientific experiment they could have done on the bones would have yielded that information. That science does deduce that these were giant lizards that lived in the distant past is an indication that science has broadened the range of the type of evidence it will accept to include deduction and analogy.

Therefore when the philosophy of science claims that there is a "latent mind" or a "mind factor" associated with matter from the beginning, and claims that this accounts for the evolution of conscious intelligent mind from matter in the course of the ages, then theology is left free to explain the *method* of this evolution of mind in the past by bringing to bear upon the question a judicious use of our accumulation of knowledge about mind gained from introspection, from human goals and ideals, from our knowledge of education and aethetics, from a study of childhood, and from our social knowledge of interpersonal relationships. In the next chapter we shall use this knowledge to reconstruct a theory of evolution.

CHAPTER 9

Aesthetic Experience and Education as Throwing Light on Evolution

At the end of Chapter 4 we concluded our description of a Christian doctrine of creation which takes account of the modern theory that all the matter of the universe was assembled in one place and then, in one half hour of unparalleled explosion in which the chemical elements were formed, it started its still continuing course of expansion outward with a slow but irreversible entropy, or gradual passing of its energy from the available to an unavailable state, with the expectation that the universe is at present about midway in its career from that original explosion to the final situation in which all the particles of matter will be inertly and evenly distributed throughout space at a temperature approching absolute zero. We have fitted the theory of the original explosion into the Christian doctrine of the creation, and we have found a positive doctrinal use for the theory of entropy by describing it as a divinely arranged source of energy made gradually available in the process of its release into the unavailable state, and so constituting a source of energy independent of God which God needed if there was to be any freedom within the universe, for freedom requires some independent control of power. We have also found a second positive theological use for the theory of entropy. For if God created the universe with the intention of having it an independent source of steadily released energy which it steadily releases in the process of running down, then the greatest miracle of the original creation was the creation of the running-down process. For the creation of the universe itself, although it was other than God, was the bringing into being of something that had dynamic physical power that bore a shadowy resemblance to God's spiritual power. But the entropy of the universe is a running down or "dying" of its power and so the entropy or "dying" is the miracle of the existence of something *contrary* to the nature of God who is undiminishing power and endless life. The greatest miracle of the creation was therefore the creation of death. Since this original "death" is death at the inanimate and so non-moral level this creation of entropy in no way contradicts the claim of the first chapter of Genesis that "God saw everything that he had made, and behold, it was very good." On the other hand, because entropy bears no resemblance to the nature of God, a contrary-to-God factor is accounted for from before the time of man, which eases somewhat the theoretical explanation of the beginning of evil, which the Old Testament traces back almost exclusively to human sinfulness, and which the synoptic gospels account for in terms of a personal devil. Not only was the original entropy not evil because it was only a state of modification of inanimate matter and so had no moral implications, but it was, strictly speaking, not created by God. It was desired and planned for by God as useful to his purposes, so he could desire and plan for it without there being any implication of evil in his own nature. And, furthermore, he did not bring it into existence. It was brought into existence inevitably by nature in nature's freedom, as soon as the physical universe had been cast into independent existence. The contrary-to-God factor was therefore planned and arranged for (innocently) by God, but brought into existence by the creation.

In the fourth chapter the doctrine of the creation is carried only through the creation of pre-animate matter. That is, God originally created a universe with which he could have an "I-it" relationship. The doctrine of evolution, theologically interpreted, to which we now turn is the Christian description of how God made possible the shifting of a small fragment of the original creation, from an "I-it" to an "I-thou" relationship to himself.[1]

We have pointed out that Plato heads up all ideas under the static "good, beautiful, and true" while Christianity, which thinks of God as characterized by omnipotent power as well as by ideals, sums up its description of him by ascribing to him the active "kingdom and the power and the glory forever." We have said that the word "kingdom" or sovereignty includes his governing characteristics of righteousness and love, and that the word "power" includes his mind which is intelligently directing power, so that "mind" when it refers to God is not mere rationality, but is rationality-plus. And we have said that his "glory" includes that aspect of

---

[1] This is making use of the famous catchwords of Martin Buber's book, *I and Thou*, with indebtedness to the point of view of his thesis but without copying his argument.

his being which we can designate as "beauty-plus." Thus his "beauty" is not an abstraction but a living power. God of course is not a split personality acting sometimes according to his "kingdom," sometimes according to his "power," and sometimes according to his "glory." All these three characteristics are always present in his action, but from our human point of view now one characteristic and now another seems to be stressed. We have accounted for the original creation by ascribing it to his power (or rationality-plus). We will now account for evolution by ascribing it to the working of his glory.

✻   ✻   ✻   ✻   ✻   ✻

At this point we are not going to analyze the significance of artistic inspiration in the really creative artist, writer, or musician, for that is an extremely complicated matter; we are instead going to confine ourselves to a discussion of artistic appreciation of the beauty of inanimate physical objects by people who are not themselves creative artists.

The beauty of a lovely object can assist in calling up a response of serenity, poise, and delight in a human individual. The Chinese have long surrounded themselves with beautiful ceramics and other art-objects in order to induce serenity of spirit. In aesthetic appreciation, where the craving to dominate is held in abeyance, the person "loves" the beautiful object and quietly opens his spirit to the free unmerited gift of the invasion of his life by its beauty. And this humble, undemanding acceptance becomes a channel through which the object can make available to him still more of its beauty. We have all had this type of experience on occasion, when we have laid our spirits open to the beauty of a landscape, a flower, a sunset, or the interplay of colors in the heart of a perfect diamond, and this appreciative receptivity on our part has been the channel through which more of the beauty of the object offers itself to us. The relationship with the inanimate object in the experience of artistic appreciation is a quasi-interpersonal relationship, something neither a fully "I-thou" relationship nor yet merely an altogether "I-it" relationship. The reason the great tyrants of the world have turned art collectors and art connoisseurs, after their ruthless egotism has gained power and wealth by trampling on those who blocked their paths, is not wholly accounted for by the acquisition of art-

106

objects as a status symbol. By their ruthlessness and selfishness they have isolated themselves from genuine human companionship. For friendship is an interpersonal relationship requiring give-and-take between persons regarding each other with the dignity due to equals. A friend is an end in himself, not a pawn to be manipulated for one's own benefit or played with in one's lighter moments at one's convenience and leisure. If the tyrant admitted the claims of real friendships it would cramp his ruthless freedom to continue his pursuit of selfish power.

But when the summit of selfish power has been reached and the tyrant, having completed the ascent, has leisure to look around him, he becomes dimly aware of the spiritual starvation that accompanies his splendid isolation. He refuses to make the self-surrender required in friendship and yet he is hungry for companionship. In this situation he consoles himself with the semi-interpersonal relationship involved in aesthetic appreciation. He can buy landscapes by Claude Lorrain, and Constable, and Canaletto, and whenever he wishes he can go to them and surrender to the inflowing of their beauty and luminous peace. So he experiences in their presence something of the feeling of security and fulfillment that comes in friendship, for he has entered into a more than I-it relationship. But he will never have to make his appointments to suit the convenience of the canvases, and they will never disapprove of him and demand that he reform his cruel ways. Their beauty will offer itself uncritically to him. He can enjoy them at his leisure and ignore them at his convenience. Their beauty is the Oriental dream-wife of his soul, always at hand to comfort, please, and support, while making no demand to be admitted to full human status with its strenuous ethical and personal demands.

It is this halfway position of the beautiful between the impersonal and the personal that made the Hebrews, who are spiritually the subtlest people who have ever lived, austerely avoid the path of beauty as a path to God. It is not that men should not rejoice in beauty, and it is not that superlative beauty is not a characteristic of God. It is simply that the controlling characteristics of Deity are righteousness and love (or righteous-love inasmuch as the two characteristics coincide in God) and if man is made in God's image and is to fulfill this role that has been assigned to him of reflecting the image of his Maker, then he must enter into relationship with

God at the fully I-thou relationship in order to reflect God's control-ling characteristics of righteousness and love. Helpful though beauty is on some occasions in the spiritual education of all lives, there is always the danger that beauty, because of its high degree of adequacy, will enable its devotees to stop short of the fully interpersonal relationship with God at the strenuous level of his righteousness and love. At this point the insight of Plato is in line with the Hebrew revelation, for Plato also assigned to the beautiful a position below the good in the hierarchy of values.

We have discussed the matter at this length to make clear that in addition to the two relationships into which a man can enter — the "I-it" and the "I-thou" relationships — that there is a third strange intermediate semi-personal relationship of the "I-with-the-beauty-of-the-it."

    *   *   *   *   *   *

Let us now consider another aspect of that segment of mind which we know, namely intelligently conscious human mind, as an aid in hypothetically reconstructing a theory of what may have occurred millions of years ago when life was beginning on this planet. *This procedure is as intellectually legitimate as it is for science to estimate the present rapidity with which substances lose their radioactivity, and projecting that line of evidence into the past to calculate the age of the universe. Both lines of reasoning are reasoning by analogy and both are based on the assumption that the cosmos is coherent and interrelated.*

A new born baby gives evidence of conscious response to sensations, and at least as early as between the second and third birthday gives evidence of some memory, some social responsive-ness, and rudiments of moral awareness (in connection with "Mamma says 'No.'"), some mastery of language, and some dis-crimination in choice. We can say that by the third birthday at least the human young are not merely potentially intelligent human beings, but are already intelligent human beings albeit at a very immature stage.

If we now ask ourselves how this transition to the state of intel-ligent life is accomplished in the space of three years from the state at birth of conscious awareness of sensation, we find that we are confronted with mystery. The same mystery confronts us if we try to understand how a person learns in the latter teen-age years at the threshold of fully adult life. As I look back over more than thirty years of teaching I am well aware that a great deal of learning has taken place in my immediate vicinity. *How* I have had a part in this maturing of young minds I do not know. And the information could not be gained by asking my students. For I am still not able to tell how my mind attained the adult level under the influence of my excellent primary and secondary school teachers. I was even less aware of the nature of their maturing influence during the process than I am in retrospect. And the awareness of this mystery of education is common to experienced teachers of the Liberal Arts.

Apparently immature living mind must feed upon adult living mind in order to mature. Very often the pupil finally outstrips his teachers. But then, it must be remembered that the teacher teaches from great books. And great books (this is not referring to textbooks) are, so to speak, the "canned" minds of the great of the past, preserved and made available to each succeeding generation with the aid of the comparatively mediocre adult minds of the teachers. Occasionally, bright children will go far in the intellectual life with a minimum amount of assistance from living adult minds, if the adults introduce them through books to the records of the great minds of the past. However, books by themselves are not enough. The developing young must have some living contact with living adult minds in order to mature into intelligent adult human beings. From the scanty records we have of children separated from human society and reared with a litter of wolf cubs, we find that the manners and social and mental life of these children who have lacked human relationships do not reach the human level, but only that of the animal foster parents with which they are associated. The rapidity with which leading individuals from the very simple inherited cultures of the historically isolated African tribes, have taken on highly developed intellectual life and civilization, when exposed to the more highly developed culture of intelligent, adult, Western minds, is more widespread but less conclusive evidence in the same direction. In the same way the inhabitants of ancient Britain had remained barbarians for thousands of years, until by social intercourse they were exposed to the more highly developed culture of the Romans.

Another proof of the indispensability of contact of the immature with the mature living mind is the constant desire of graduate students to become the pupils of the outstanding teachers in their particular fields. And learned professors to the end of their days will boast, "I studied under the great so-and-so." It is partly but not entirely academic snobbery that prompts graduate students to try to train directly under the greatest living teachers. The academic world has always proceeded on the assumption that a maturity and power can be acquired by living contact with the living mind of the professor, and this is believed in spite of the fact that the main ideas of these teachers are usually already in print, and of all students the graduate group is best qualified to learn by means of the written word.

It is clear that in that segment of the total development of mind that is directly accessible to our study, namely contemporary human mind, for a child to become a mature intelligent adult it is necessary for his life to start as a one-celled organism which is itself produced by two organisms having intelligent minds (that is, of the race that is characterized by adult intelligent minds), and that the child's organism, after nine months preliminary development, should be educated to the status of an adult intelligent human being by social contact with adult organisms which are governed by adult intelligent minds.

When infants are cared for in a hospital, for the first six weeks of the baby's life its energies are taken up in adjusting to its new post-natal physical environment. In this period if the baby is kept safe and clean and rested and warmed and fed it will thrive even if its care is characterized by laboratory precision ungoverned by human affection and with a minimum of human contact. But a baby two months and more old subjected to merely "scientific" care without human affection and human social environment becomes retarded in its development and even its physical coordination and health suffer. The infant needs to be lovingly handled by an intelligent adult. This is the beginning of his intellectual and social experience. As the experienced hands work with the baby he becomes gradually adjusted by their action to the routines of motion that are the physical concomitant of adult intelligent life. The child is thus becoming educated toward adult human life before his conscious awareness of the world around him is sufficiently developed to be up to human status. A mature intelligent dog has considerably more intelligence and has a wider and more companionable range of social adjustment than a four months old human baby has.

Now if we project the theory of this known course of intellectual development of the contemporary individual into an explanation of the historical development of intelligent mind on this planet, we will only be using the type of argument science has already used in estimating the age of the universe from the rate of decay of radioactivity in matter in the contemporary scene. Or, more exactly, we will be using in the interests of religion the type of argument science has already used, when it used, to reinforce the claims of the theory of biological evolution, the evidence from embryology that the earliest stages of the human embryo seem to resemble some of the simplest species of living things more than they resemble adult mammals.

Thus we are able to pick up our doctrine of creation where we left off with the account of the inanimate creation, and we can claim that the process of evolution began in the primeval seas when "the Spirit of God was moving over the face of the waters" (Genesis 1:2). In other words we can claim that life began because the Creator associated himself intentionally with the otherness of his creation in order to "bring up" or "educate" it. This Divine leading first took the form of the preorganic alignment of certain molecules in the water vapor of the earth's primitive atmosphere, under the influence of sunlight, into a more complicated structure that could later become the constituent of the protein molecule. The protein molecules in turn could be brought to combine into the heightened reactivity of the one-celled animalcule, and thence under the fostering education of the Creator the process could continue until the human organism with intelligent human mind had been brought so far into existence that genuine companionship of part of the creation with God himself was to be within the range of possibility. (Exodus 33:11; Jeremiah 31:33-34; Psalm 139:4,5,10,17,18,23,24; John 14:23; 15:7-11,26; 16:23,24,26,27; Romans 8:14-17; Galatians 4:4-7.)

It is to be noted that in our recent description of present human education the statement was made that for the contemporary "child to become a mature intelligent adult it is necessary for his life to start as a one-celled organism which is itself produced by two

111

organisms having intelligent minds (that is, of the race that is characterized by adult intelligent minds)." This statement purposely leaves open the question of how the adult intelligent organisms that produced the one-celled organism actually produced it. For the purposes of the argument of this book it makes no difference whether the producing organisms with intelligent minds produced the one-celled beginning of the new life by means of the union of two reproductive cells from within their own bodies, which had in turn been produced through the millions of years long process of evolution, or whether the one-celled beginning of the new life was produced synthetically from inanimate matter by biological experts. For the experts who produced the living cell synthetically would themselves be the product of the evolutionary process, producing outside of their own bodies by a technical shortcut the type of cell that by investigation they had discovered to have been produced in the evolutionary process. And whether naturally or synthetically produced this single cell would have to have nine months development into the infant organism, and after that it would need the social environment of adult intelligent organisms in order to bring it to fully adult intelligent human existence.

* * * * *

It has long been urged by science in the interests of establishing the doctrine of evolution that the pre-natal development of the human embryo from a single cell can be used as part of the converging scientific evidence to show that all life on this planet evolved from primeval one-celled organisms. For a long time it has been well known to those who took seriously the question of the relation of Christianity to scientific thought that belief in evolution presents no major problems for Christian faith that are not already presented by embryology. We are now in a position to use the scientific claim that embryology supports the theory of the evolutionary process as a very strong argument against a naturalistic philosophy of evolution.

For using a man's development from a single cell to an adult human being as a support for the theory of the whole evolutionary process—as science uses the present known rate of radioactive decay as furnishing the scale on which the age of the universe can be estimated—Christianity is in a position to show that we have no

112

experience of adult human life that has not been produced and educated by adult intelligent human life. This means that on the individual scale one does not begin with one-celled life and evolve to the more complicated form. One begins with the higher adult intelligent life and organisms, and from them come the one-celled organism that grows, under the fostering care of adult organisms— at first surrounding it bodily and later caring for and educating it —into the adult organism. In other words, in answer to the old riddle, "Which came first the chicken or the egg?" the ultimate philosophic answer, taking the total view of existence into consideration, must reply, "The chicken," in line with the old saying that "The stream does not rise higher than its source." Taking the contemporary fact that now intelligent adult individuals only appear when the original cell of their bodies is produced, and the growing organism nourished, cared for and later educated by adult intelligent individuals, and projecting its description of human life backwards as throwing light on the whole process of evolution, we are able to conclude that the total explanation of human life is not explained by the naturalistic philosophy of the lower to the higher— that is, by inanimate matter eventually by its unaided power evolving one-celled organisms, and one-celled organisms by their unaided power evolving man. Instead we find the contemporary analysis of the beginning and development of each individual more in line with the Christian theological position that in the beginning there was supernatural creative Mind which freely created the world in its inanimate form and gradually "educated" bits of that creation, by planned and willed association of the creative Mind with it, to a point at which rational mind appeared within the creation. Thus the history of the individual from conception to adult life would seem to indicate that the Creator in his supernatural power had always environmented his creation to "educate" it—the Biblical symbol is that of the potter working on the clay (Genesis 2:7; Isaiah 29:16; 64:8; Jeremiah 18:6)—first into self-reproducing patterned aggregates of living matter, then to consciousness, and beyond that to rational consciousness.

Strictly speaking, the scientific doctrine of evolution does not include the growth and development of cultures and civilizations. But the learned disciplines in the cultural group, history, political science, literature, etc., took over long ago the biological theory of evolution as a clue to the interpretation of cultural development, and in the first third of this century "evolution" became a word to conjure with. And the cultural philosophy that took scientific theory into account tended to a wholeness and consistency in the upward thrust of unaided nature from the animate to the barely animate, then to the upward course of biological development on this planet culminating first in man, then in man's cultural development from primitive man to the earliest centuries of written history, culminating in modern man, and in the course of the human development "evolving" values where heretofore values had been completely non-existent.

If we take this learned, but not strictly scientific, projection of the scientific theory of evolution and use it in our theological theory, we can see in the upward development of civilization some traces of the continuing educative power of God. And especially we can compare the special education God gave Israel through the patriarchs, Moses, and the prophets, to a parent's especially careful and concerned rearing of a beloved son from infancy to adult life.

The prenatal human stages are fitted into the evolutionary parallel on Christian theory by seeing the bringing about of the original human cell by a voluntary act of the parents as a rough parallel to God's creation of the world out of nothing. The prenatal stages can be paralleled to God's power environmenting the inanimate matter thus created in order to evolve from mere matter the various forms of life, using the infant's stage of development at birth as parallel to the point of the creation of human beings in the evolutionary series. And then one can compare the social adjustment the infant undergoes in its earliest months, by merely being handled by loving and experienced hands, to God's education of the human species from the threshold of its emergence into humanity to the point at which man's language and thought were sufficiently developed so that he could consciously consider his own education and transmit to his offspring by words what he had learned.

114

CHAPTER 10

Suggestions for a *Modus Operandi* of Evolution

When we ask how God can influence nature if nature is other than God, we have to admit that we are dealing on the grand scale with the mystery that confronts us within our ordinary human life, namely the mystery of how the subjective influences the objective. If we say that the subjective never influences the objective but that the subjective aspect of our lives is nothing but a conscious recognizing of neural action already taken by the body, we are caught in a deterministic naturalistic philosophy that not only has no place in it for the grounding of value in ultimate reality, but also, as we have seen, has no explanation for the need of consciousness to arise at all. If the complicated higher froms of life carry on their activity simply by means of their increased complexity and subtlety of reactivity, then why is not the subtlety and complexity of the physical reactivity sufficient to account for the building of the Empire State Building, and the composition and printing of the *Encyclopaedia Britannica*, without the phenomenon of consciousness ever having occurred? But if one takes human consciousness seriously as a valid clue to the nature of ultimate reality, then one is forced either into the pantheistic-idealistic position typical of Hinduism's Brahman of the *Bhagavad-Gita*, or into the Hebrew explanation of existence which accounts for matter and human consciousness as being created out of nothing by the superintelligent and inherently powerful mind of God. The Hebrew explanation is the necessary one if a person is to take value and especially righteousness and love seriously as clues to the nature of ultimate existence. Materialistic naturalism, idealistic pantheism, or the Hebraic theory of the creator God seem to me to be the three basic alternatives which man is offered as a choice of a life philosophy. Everything else seems to me an elaboration of one of these alternatives, or a phase of thought that is eventually seen to be not fully explanatory and that gradually becomes modified into one of the three basic positions. Thus I think that neither the dualism of Zoroastrianism nor the Platonic trinity of the eternal ideas, matter in motion, and the

115

demiurge will stand up philosophically, for both these explain ultimate reality as consisting of two or more different ultimates, and there is no way of explaining how different ultimates can have any relationship with each other, because as ultimates there would be no common ground beyond them for them exist in, or through which they could interrelate.

If materialistic naturalism is ruled out because it has no real place for the existence of consciousness, one is left with pantheism, which includes the idealistic philosophies, and with the Hebrew belief in the righteous intelligent creator God. Pantheism (which includes idealism) and the Hebraic belief seem to me the two live options for a philosophy of religion. One cannot very well have either a philosophy or a religion that has no integral place in it for consciousness. Pantheism allows one to account for intelligent consciousness in individuals as part of the All, whether or not All includes matter-mind or (as in idealism) reduces all existence to states of consciousness, allowing matter an only seeming existence. But pantheism (including idealism if pushed to its logical conclusion) to attain this consistent simplicity of explanation is forced to dethrone righteousness in the interests of the Oneness of reality. This is what makes the simplicity of pantheism with its ease of adjustability to scientific thought so very dangerous to twentieth century Christianity.

To describe God as unswervingly righteous one has to describe him as supernatural to the universe, because the universe contains evil. This means that his present action within the universe would involve miracle, even if that action required as small an amount of modification of matter as would be involved if God assisted Moses to assemble the ten basic commandments from among the multitude of moral precepts which Moses' mind had already acquired from his own thinking upon the information and precepts furnished by his triple cultural heritage (Hebrew, Egyptian, and Midianite). For miracle is any particular activity of the supernatural God within the creation to further his long-distance purposes. It is this tinkering with the creation from without, what the Bible describes as the work of the potter upon the clay, that is an idea which science's claim to the unbroken cause-and-effect sequences within the natural order has found so unabsorbable to its thought. And this is the thing that has embarrassed theology

116

in its attempt to absorb the scientific description of nature into the Christian description of the world and man in relationship to God.

The first theological attempt to come to terms with science was deism, which got around the problem by concentrating all of the supernatural God's activity with relation to the world to the period of the Creation when he was supposed to have made the world in its present form according to the account in the first chapter of Genesis, and, the deists would add, to have furnished it at that time with a sufficient schedule of scientific and moral law for its continued uninterfered-with ongoing and for man's self-direction. This cleared the present time as a time in which the unbroken sequences of the operation of scientific laws could function. This description of things seemed at first to satisfy the Christian requirement, although on closer inspection deism is seen to make no place for the Old Testament revelation to Moses and the prophets, or for the New Testament's account of the Incarnation, the Resurrection, or the guidance of the Holy Spirit. Deism did, however, make room for rewards and punishments after death, thus completing the picture of God as righteous.

With the discovery of the tremendous age of the world and of the slow process of evolution culminating in man, the deistic picture no longer held. The belief in evolution has created an embarrassment for Christian thought because if inanimate nature entirely unaided produced first one-celled organisms, then the development of species by natural processes, and finally man, then man is simply the intersection of trails which lead nowhere, and is in no sense the special creation of God. If one tries to escape this theory of naturalistic unaided evolution by saying that God intimately upholds all matter at all moments in all its actions, so that what is from one point of view the action of nature is from another point of view the continuing creative act of God, one gets into another kind of difficulty. For if this description of God's sustaining and ongoing creative activity is made co-extensive with physical nature in order to satisfy science's claim for the unbroken cause-and-effect sequences of the natural order, one is really equating the activity of God with that of the natural order and so falling into the trap of pantheism which, by too close an association of God with the world, makes it impossible to sufficiently describe

117

God as opposed to the evil of the world, and so undercuts the basic Jewish-Christian claim that God is unswervingly righteous.

The alternative explanation of evolution would be to say that the evolutionary advances were brought about gradually by small continuing interferences of God with nature. But this is to bring us back to the idea of miracle, and miracle is anathema to the beliefs of most scientists. In spite of all the recent talk about the personal sympathy of scientists with the feeling of religious awe as they are aware of the mystery of the universe, and their feeling that there must be some Power behind the cosmos, their description of this Power is largely in pantheistic terms. The particular scientist in question may be an earnest Christian and churchgoer, but his knowledge of philosophy and Christian doctrine is usually so slight that he does not realize either that his description of God's relation to the world is pantheistic or why it undercuts Christianity.

The physicist, Erwin Schrödinger, is a good example of the religiously concerned scientist, who feels that materialism is an inadequate philosophy. In his book *Mind and Matter*, he says:

The reason why our sentient, percipient and thinking ego is met nowhere within our scientific world picture can be easily indicated in seven words: because it is itself that world picture. [In dealing with the perplexing question of why *many* conscious egos concoct *one* world from their mental experiences he decides that the multiplicity of minds or consciousnesses] is only apparent, in truth there is only one mind. This is the doctrine of the Upanishads . . . . I do believe that this is precisely the point where our present way of thinking does need to be amended, perhaps by a bit of blood-transfusion from Eastern thought.[1]

In other words Professor Schrödinger is frankly recommending a philosophy of idealistic pantheism as a means of tying together in a coherent account individual minds, the apparent world of physical nature, and Ultimate Reality. This coherent philosophy could be used as a background description of existence by some religions, but not by the Jewish or Christian religions.

For if a theologian is interested in a philosophy of religion

---

[1] Erwin Schrödinger, *Mind and Matter;* Cambridge: University Press, 1958, pp. 52, 53, 55.

which allows for not just any idea of divine power, but for the God of the Bible, the theologian must have a philosophy which can describe God as supernatural to the universe in order for his belief to coincide intellectually with the Jewish-Christian belief that God is unswervingly righteous. Some modern thinking on this difficult aspect of the relation of science to the biblical God has made use of physics' recent quantum theory.

According to this theory nature in the large acts according to predictable routines as the older science believed. But the regularity of nature's action at the sub-atomic level has been discovered to be statistical rather than absolute. At the sub-atomic level of quantum mechanics there is built into nature a very small amount of freedom. Thus while the underlying units of motion are free and unpredictable, the enormous number of such movements within even a microscopic bit of matter produces results that, on the law of averages, are in the large measure predictable.

To illustrate statistical regularity and indeterminism: if one throws a die many thousands of times, each of the six numbers will appear on the *average* of one throw in six. However, within the thousands of throws, in a shorter consecutive stretch of one-hundred-eighty throws the number one might appear disproportionately thirty-eight times, and the number five might appear consecutively four times on one occasion, and might appear consecutively three times on each of two occasions. In nature's sub-atomic activity also there can be occasional slight unevennesses and bunchings within the over-all statistical regularity.

What is very much needed in Christian apologetics is some explanation of how there can be sufficient leeway built into nature so that the supernatural God can act providentially with regard to it at the same time that the ongoing of nature, viewed from the scientific perspective, will appear to present an unbroken coherence of nature's dependable sequences of action. The merely statistical uniformity of nature's activity at the sub-atomic level would thus seem to provide the needed theory.

But we must ask the question, is the indeterminacy of sub-atomic action itself always Divine providential action, or does it merely furnish a useful set-up that God can upon occasion make special use of? skillfully forcing action "back-stage", although the result, viewed scientifically, would only look like occasional chance bunching of variant sub-atomic action within the over-all statistical uniformity. The alternative of God's occasional intimate forcing of sub-atomic action is the one Christianity needs.

The other alternative, however, is the one held by Dr. William G. Pollard[2] who, as both a recognized specialist in atomic physics and an Episcopal clergyman, has expert knowledge in both fields. The merely statistical regularity of nature envisaged by the theory of quantum mechanics, he combines with the innumerable occasions of unexpected intersection of widely different cause-and-effect sequences, to account for the unpredictability and enormous variety of history.

But although his identifying providential action with *all* sub-atomic indeterminacy is a theory that offers a partial explanation for the openness and unpredictability of history, it does not explain providence in the biblical sense. For it does not allow for any discrimination in God's activity. There is no place in his theory for evil which God is working against. The theory makes any instance of cancer as much an act of God's providence as the lowering of the waters of the Red Sea to facilitate Israel's escape. Fur-

---

[2] He specifically denies that God applies ". . . suitable pressures in the form of spiritual forces to history in such a way as to make some alternatives more probable and others less. . . . [i.e.,] that God manipulates probabilities. . . . [He says that] it is possible either to assert that all events without exception are subject to the universal laws of nature and to sift out of the profusion of events those which make manifest the universal scope of this assertion, or to assert with equal validity that all events without exception are responsive to the will of Almighty God and to sift out of the profusion of events those which make manifest His universal sovereignty. . . . The Bible . . . is the literary expression of a people whose whole life and history are lived out in a consciously experienced intimate relationship or covenant with the living God. For such a people every event, known or unknown, trivial or important, forgotten or recorded, is an expression of His will. . . . From the Biblical standpoint a miracle is not a special kind of event possessing a quality which common happenings do not share. It is rather an occasion in which the essentially providential character of all events is made manifest in an especially clear and striking manner." (William G. Pollard, *Chance and Providence;* New York: Charles Scribner's Sons, 1958, pp. 95, 96, 114, 111, 112.)

"The essence of the supernatural in Biblical terms is its immediate and intimate contact with the natural at every point and every moment. . . . The ground of existence of every finite being lies beyond itself. Because this is so, the course of the scientific explanation of nature will finally lead beyond nature into supernature. . . . The whole of reality as it is in itself, apart from our experience and knowledge of it, doubtless involves no such division or boundary between nature and supernature." (William G. Pollard, *Physicist and Christian.* Greenwich, Conn.: Seabury Press, 1961, pp. 100, 107, 110.)

thermore, it makes physical action and God's providential action so co-extensive as to blur the conception of man's freedom and the opposition of his sinful actions to God. It is significant that in his two books Dr. Pollard does not really attempt to deal with the problem of evil.

What is needed for the doctrine of providence, as well as for a doctrine of revelation, is a theoretical explanation of how God can perpetrate direct intermittent action at will upon particular situations in the world. It is significant that Dr. Pollard, like other twentieth century divines, has no adequate doctrine of revelation. His book, *Physicist and Christian*, is a brilliant contribution to the understanding of the essential part community plays in revelation, and he shows that God's revelation to Israel was a historical revelation to a covenant community. But this is a looking at the established line of spiritual direction in retrospect as it is shown in the Bible's sifted record. God's original guidance, antedating scripture, could not come to a community without coming to individuals within the community. Upon this aspect of the problem contemporary thought is so silent that a person steeped in it finds it difficult to overcome its atmosphere of pervasive chilliness in order to say his prayers.

For this reason the theory I am developing in this book—which assumes that prayer is consistent with the actual state of existence—embraces the alternative interpretation of the relation of God to the indeterminacy in sub-atomic action. It assumes that some instances of the sub-atomic activity are adroitly forced by God, so that what looks like slightly unusual constellations of random activity within the overall statistical uniformity are in these particular instances not random at all, but directly arranged by God in the interest of furthering his purposes. Human beings, which are "I s", can make selective modifications upon nature's "its", and it is assumed that God, the supernatural "I", can do likewise. The net practical result of either tampering does not *appear from within nature* as any break or irregularity in the action of natural law. We can state the case from the theological point of view by saying that from time to time God forces upon certain parts of nature a tampering with which nature as nature is wholly congenial.

❀   ❀   ❀   ❀   ❀   ❀

121

It is at this point that we gain help from the doctrine of God's glory, which has to do with that powerfully active aspect of his nature which has a shadowy reflection in the creation in what we call beauty. We have seen that with an inanimate object which is beautiful we can enter into a semi-interpersonal relationship, can regard the thing not merely as an "it" for our convenience, but to a small extent almost as a "thou" to be valued and cherished for its own sake, and that as one appreciates the beauty of the beautiful object the appreciation is itself a channel through which the inanimate object "gives" to the beholder more of its beauty.

How can we account for God's beauty progressively domiciling a reflection of itself in the creation and so bringing about what from the human scientific side we call the process of evolution? Perhaps three illustrations drawn from existence as the ordinary man knows it may give us a lead.

When I view an exhibition of paintings of modern non-representational art—about which I am usually not enthusiastic—I tend to complain that the whole thing does not seem to mean anything, that it is only masses of color and straight and curved lines and that only an occasional painting of this type appears to me to be beautiful. I then am carefully told by abstract painting enthusiasts that an abstract painting is not supposed to represent anything. The greatness of the painting is supposed to lie in the fact that the artist has assembled on canvas masses of light and dark and straight and curved lines which, when viewed as a whole, do not convey any particular meaning, but which have the power to make the imagination of the onlooker start working, so that the painting creatively serves as a point of departure to stimulate the creative imagination of the beholder. From the point of view that this book is developing I would suppose that the abstract painting in stimulating the imagination would be initiating that semi-interpersonal relationship between itself and the imagination of the beholder which it is the prerogative of beauty to initiate, and on this ground the abstract painting could be classified as beautiful.

In reply to the claim that non-representational paintings are art because they stimulate the imagination I always say, "If what you claim is true, why could not the ink blots of the Rorschach psychological test be classified as among the greatest artistic productions of the twentieth century?" I have never yet found an advocate of non-representational painting who felt happy about trying to answer this disconcerting question. For of course those ink blots were designed entirely by chance, and are not art at all. But the number of different pictures people imagine that they see in them is extraordinary.

Now for our purposes the remarkable thing about the ink blots constituting the Rorschach test is that the human mind can interact with them and so set up a semi-interpersonal relationship with them as in the appreciation of a work of art, *and these ink blots are at one and the same time entirely due to chance, and yet from another point of view are not due to chance. That is, the patterns of the blots were designed entirely by chance; but it was the psychiatrist's very discriminating mind that selected and preserved those blots most stimulating to the imagination. Thus while each blot separately was formed entirely by chance, the collection taken as a whole is the work of a highly intelligent mind.*

Could this be a clue to the process of evolution? Beginning with the purposeless reshuffling of the groupings of inanimate matter that characterizes the mechanical and chemical activity of the cosmos, did the divine Mind that moved over the face of the waters (Genesis 1:2) select and keep those particular combinations that best suited his purpose? And in the purposeless reshuffling of these selected groupings did the divine Mind make a further selection of the occasional new groupings that appeared that best suited his purpose? If this were the case the process of evolution would appear from God's point of view as the potter moulding the clay, but it would be seen from within nature by scientists simply as the emergence of higher forms from lower.

Before you close the book in disgust at this suggestion and assume it to be mere fantastical romancing, remember that science and the philosophy built upon science have no alternative explanation to offer of how the mere increased complexity and increasingly subtle reactivity of mere unconscious matter could have produced intelligently conscious mind. Remember also that science has no explanation of how inanimate matter itself originally came into existence.

Science traces our universe back to a datable cosmic explosion, but has no way of knowing what came before that or how or when the exploding matter originally came into existence. Scientifically speaking, any pre-explosion history assigned to matter is guesswork, because if there was a previous universe the cosmic explosion wiped out all trace of it, so there is no way of telling whether or not this cosmic explosion was the ultimate beginning of matter or only a phase of its activity. If only a phase, science would still have no answer to the question of the ultimate beginning of matter before the previous phase. If the claim were made that matter is basic and eternal there is the inexplicable question of the origin of intelligent mind which is a late comer in our world.

The biblical belief that God created matter would fit the cosmic explosion theory fully as well as a hypothetical previous universe— itself unaccounted for. And if matter was originally "thought up" into independent existence by the mind of God, we have an explanation of how matter could be constantly amenable to the continuing action of the divine Mind, and how material bodies could in turn be subject to the direction of human mind. If one denies that human bodies are at all subject to the conscious direction of intelligent human minds, one has to hold that human intelligence is merely an inexplicable and useless by-product of human bodies, and that all values are merely illusory subjective estimates and have no grounding in ultimate reality.

Curiously enough, the religious theory of creation we are suggesting as an alternative, according to which the divine Mind thought up the matter of the cosmos and then exploded it into objective independent existence, is analogous to the creative artist's experience, even to the experience of anyone with such slight claims to artistic ability and temperament as myself. When I get ready to write a book, or for that matter while I was getting ready to write an examination or term paper in my college and university days, the time previous to the beginning of the actual writing, in which the mind was storing itself with thought that it wished to express, created a nervous uneasiness intense enough to be felt as a physical malaise. By contrast the actual writing, as soon as it started, is accompanied by a feeling of relaxed well-being. The only physical state I can think of as a comparison to this psychological experience connected with the creative experience of writing, is the not very pretty one of the experience of relief that comes if a physician lances an infection in which pus

124

has been collecting under pressure. If we are using the human analogy seriously, although cautiously, in explaining creation and evolution in terms of the activity of preceding, independent, supercosmic Mind, then a physically explosive beginning as marking the moment of the objectification of the primeval cosmos by the mind of the Maker fits very neatly human psychological experience, as well as both the scientific theory of the beginning of the universe and a Christian theological interpretation of the same. In the biblical account of the creation even the artist's relaxation after the creative act is mentioned: we are told that on the seventh day God rested from the work which he had done. (Genesis 2:2)

Suppose we assume that God's action in bringing about evolution bears some analogy to Dr. Rorschach's selective action relative to his ink blots, can we do any more in imagination to reconstruct the *modus operandi* of God's action upon nature? We have already seen that Dr. Pollard has suggested that the merely statistical regularity of quantum mechanics affords a method of introducing novelty into nature without breaking the regularity of the operation of scientific law.

There is also another possibility of God's mode of action upon nature that science cannot take into consideration and that, contrary to the scientific theory of influence upon an object, which is always the "push" of mechanical causation, is another kind of influence, namely the "pull" that characterizes any teleological explanation. Aristotle called attention to this actionless causation of action on the part of the Divine when he spoke of the Divine as the Unmoved Mover, that which, by virtue of its value-attractiveness, causes other things to attempt voluntarily a conformity to it. Thus God, by his nearness to his creation, can be thought of as having presented constantly to his inanimate creation a lure to conform to the beauty of his glory, a lure to which inanimate nature was from the first equipped to respond, inasmuch as inanimate nature had been thought into existence originally by that selfsame powerful intelligence-plus, which is also characterized by super-beauty, or glory.

Could nature at the unconscious level respond teleologically, by an increase in beauty, to God's super-beauty, or glory? This is a real question, for we tend to think of response to beauty as a characteristic of highly developed consciousness, and we are now

125

asking whether nature — before the rise of organisms — could respond by increased beauty to the super-beauty of the divine glory. This book is suggesting that inanimate nature can make such a response. It is also making this suggestion the other way around. That is to say, it is suggesting that God appreciated the beauty in inanimate nature, and allowed his powerful appreciation (as in all aesthetic contemplation) to be the channel through which the beautiful inanimate object was enabled to give him more of its beauty. Artistic appreciation does not force the object appreciated. But the Divine appreciation may have brought about that semi-personal relationship of God to inanimate nature, which God's continuing relationship gradually fostered into a fully conscious response to God on the part of a tiny fraction of the creation. The Bible claims that "We love, because he first loved us." (I John 4:19). It may be that just as our love is possible as a response to his love, so the life and beauty of the earlier stages of evolution were originally possible because God bestowed upon the original inanimate creation the less full Divine response to it of appreciation of its beauty, and that quite literally in this less complete sense from the beginning "God so loved the world." (John 3:16.)

In trying to deal with the problem of how the origin of life came about we have to make use of two twentieth century developments in scientific investigation. One is the scientific progress toward the erasure of the exact borderline between animate and inanimate nature. This book assumes that science within this century will make good its expectation of being able to produce the lowest forms of life in the laboratory synthetically from inanimate matter. This would indicate that there never was at any one moment a sudden endowment of life upon inanimate matter, but that the evolutionary series is unbroken from inanimate matter (Genesis 3:19; Job 4:19; 10:9; Psalm 103:14; Ecclesiastes 3:19, 20) to man. The other development, this time in theory rather than in research, has been science's own modern tendency to try to trace the history of nature before 10,000 B.C. by deductions from the little segment of nature's history in the present which is available to our study. The total history of the evolutionary development of life on this earth, the early stages of our world's geological history, and the history of the cosmos as a whole are non-repeatable occurrences, so science cannot test them by direct experiment.

If we assume that nature is all of a piece, with no precise moment when life or mind came to it, then since matter can be seen to be of such a sort that conscious mind can associate with it — and this is proved to be the case by the association of our conscious minds with our physical bodies — then since nature is all of a piece some association between primordial matter and conscious mind — in this case the mind of God — must have been possible. And the fact that the social education of the human infant is begun when the baby is as young as two months old and so is unable to think about the education it is undergoing, would lead us to suppose that God has the power to begin "educating" nature while the world was still in the preanimate stage.

CHAPTER 11
Consider the Snowflake

Let us consider the extraordinary case of the ordinary snowflake. Considering the microscopic and sub-microscopic world with which so much scientific investigation deals, a snowflake is a rather large item for study. But since it is so small, and individually so inconspicuous from the perspective of daily human life, it will serve as a useful illustration for us in thinking about God's relationship to pre-organic nature. Furthermore a snowflake is a common bit of chemical substance in a crystalline form that has the advantage of being large enough so that most men know it and have observed it at first hand with the naked eye or with the aid of an ordinary magnifying glass. So when we use the snowflake as an illustration we are using subject matter that the non-scientist is at home with and can easily visualize. Furthermore, since any snowflake is a relatively simple, detached bit of matter that is very beautiful and has highly individual elements in its design, we can use the snowflake in a discussion of freedom in sub-organic matter, of the relation of God to sub-organic matter, of the reflection of the Divine beauty in sub-organic matter, and of the question of the operational method of evolution. We can also use it in discussing the theological questions of the prescience of God and the nature of heaven, and in discussing the philosophical question of scientific determinism. Truly the humble and fragile snowflake becomes a very useful peg upon which to hang an argument.

It is usually noticed that the characteristics of a thing fit normally into its situation and scope of usefulness in interrelated nature. For instance, the fact that snow crystals are normally flat objects about a quarter of an inch in diameter and of a feathery or lacy type of design makes it possible for them as solids to fall upon the earth without injuring what they fall upon. Their six pointed lacy design makes possible the interlocking of the various crystals after they have fallen, so that unless they are trampled upon they form a light airy covering over the earth, which, without crushing small plant and animal life, acts as an insulating blanket against the

128

extreme winter cold and the biting winter winds. Small animals can burrow for warmth into the snow, and it can be used as a much needed water supply for them when the ponds and streams are completely frozen over. So the design of the snowflake has a functional use.

But surely the snowflake's ability to hook on to other snowflakes at odd angles by means of the six-pointed lacy design that characterizes this crystal would be equally well served if there were only two hundred standard patterns for snowflakes. One can imagine two hundred exquisite snowflake patterns endlessly repeated furnishing all the variety needed to make new-fallen snow interlock its crystals to help hold them from settling down heavily by force of gravity upon the earth. There is therefore no physical need to have each of the countless snowflakes different in pattern from all other snowflakes and each one in itself a thing of beauty. When we look out upon new-fallen snow we see it as a white blanket spread upon the earth. We notice its uniformity and are not usually conscious of the endless variety of design of the crystals that compose it.

In the whole problem of the relation of scientific thought to Christian belief one of the difficulties has been that nature has seemed to be a completely interrelated cause-and-effect system upon which no tinkering from outside of nature by a supernatural God would be possible. To the chemistry and physics of the last half of the last century the universe was a vast interrelated machine all of whose parts and their working were completely determined by the nature of the whole. This scientific determinism of the last century still has an emotional hold on the thought of the West, even though science has in the last few decades been more cautious as to its own belief in determinism, and has even, in the quantum theory, established the hypothesis that at the sub-atomic level of the quanta there is individual indeterminacy and only statistical regularity. Nevertheless psychiatry (which is a word to conjure with for the man-on-the-street) still tends to look for the reason for men's actions in their conditioning by past experiences, as if man were a mechanical bit of matter pushed inevitably by past events as causes, in other words as if men were totally caught in a thoroughgoing determinism of nature. Psychiatry has not tended to be teleological, looking toward the goals that lured men consciously into action for an explanation for men's conduct.

And derivative from scholarly thought the art of literature has tended to see man trapped by heredity and environment, completely determined by present surroundings and by the past, so that man is thought of as caught in the determinism of nature and his individual being as fully described in terms of the temporary intersection of roads which lead nowhere. Man's life is thus meaningless. Painting also, as well as the literature of such men as Kafka, and more recently the naturalistic school of writing in general, have reflected this meaninglessness. The sense of meaninglessness has at last reached down to the teenage group of students, and is a problem with which even secondary school teachers must struggle.

Now if determinism is scientifically and philosophically true, then it is true. And if it is really true, then it is fair to put the philosophy or science which holds this belief on the defensive and demand that it shall show all things to be reasonably understood as scientifically determined. If scientific determinism is true, it should have been inevitable, from the factors already in the universe in the opening moments of the cosmic explosion in which our universe got under way, that the exact pattern of leaf in each plant species in the world today would be exactly as it is, and that the characteristic shell pattern of each of the species of the lower forms of ocean life would be exactly as it is. There are thousands and thousands of different patterns of leaves and thousands of different patterns of shells, and each of these plant and animal species propagates according to pattern. We can see that the different patterns of leaf and shell have some functional use, but surely a third of the number of existing patterns would take care of all the different functional necessities in the struggle for existence. Why is there the lavish unneeded display of such various forms of beauty?

The problem becomes even more fantastic for the theory of determinism when we consider the snowflake. For the individual variations in the snowflake's pattern are non-functional (200 standard patterns would serve equally well), and snowflakes being inanimate, do not propagate their patterns as plant and animal life does. And yet if scientific determinism were true the exact pattern of every snowflake that has fallen and will fall in the history of our world was inevitably determined from the beginning. One would have to assume that if any rational mind could have known all about the matter as it was exploding in all directions in unimaginable heat in the first few moments of our universe's existence, he would have to be able to foretell without possibility of error the exact pattern that each particular snowflake in each predetermined snowfall of our world's history must inevitably take. It has always seemed fantastic to me that so many devotees of science have considered people as unduly credulous who took the wonder stories of the Bible as literally true because of biblical authority, and yet the devotees of science expected the unscientific layman to accept as true the theory of determinism — with all its implications as to the snowflake — on the authority of the scientist. Science as science deals with experiments with repeatable events in the area of physical nature. But science cannot deal fully with the snowflake, because each snowflake is an unrepeatable event.

The snowflake does not fit easily into the type of philosophy which optimistically sees the ongoing of existence as bringing value into being and preserving the value it has thus originally created. For an important part of the value of the snowflake is its beauty. Each snowflake's unique pattern of beauty could only be conserved as part of the universe's total value-gains, if the particular pattern of beauty could be observed and appreciated by a conscious mind and so enrich the world by enriching a conscious mind whether human or animal. But only an infinitesimal fraction of the total snowflake patterns are consciously observed. Furthermore in this type of philosophy the preservation of the snowflake's beauty-value in the mind of God would be impossible; because the assumption is that the flux of nature in bringing human consciousness and human values into being is bringing God into being, and so there is no God as an independent center of consciousness, supernatural to man and nature, to appreciate the snowflake's beauty.

The philosophical problem raised by the beauty of a snowflake is somewhat different from that of flowers that are born to blush unseen and waste their sweetness on the desert air. For the beauty of the plant is perpetuated by the species. For example, the individuality of the oak leaf is in the species, and if the beauty of the species is appreciated in the appreciation of a few examples of the species, all oak leaves of that species have to some extent a participation in that appreciation. But in appreciating a few snowflakes one does not appreciate all snowflakes, because, although all snow-flakes share some characteristics in common, each snowflake is a unique unrepeated pattern of beauty.

Now let us take up the problem of the snowflake from the theological angle and discuss it from the viewpoint of the doctrine of the foreordination of God.

❀   ❀   ❀   ❀   ❀   ❀

The Old Testament teaching is that God has some very specific plans for the future, that he "foresees" some future events (Jeremiah 1:4-10) and that his knowledge and power are both so enormous that neither men nor anything else in the creation can act in such a way as to take him by surprise or get out from under his control. The omniscience and omnipotence of God are thought of in their practical, rather than their theoretical, implications. God is thought of as a spirit, a powerful center of creative and governing consciousness, who has all the detailed knowledge and ability that a skillful powerful human ruler has to handle successfully the most difficult situations with which he is confronted. (The analogy is imperfect, because no human ruler has ever had sufficient skill and power to handle all situations, and God's ability is thought of as completely adequate.) God is thought of as having abilities analogous to a human ruler's, but so enormously stepped-up that nothing in the creation can hide from him, thwart him permanently, or suffer neglect due to God's concentrating his attention elsewhere.

When, however, Christianity took its basic scriptures out into a Mediterranean world trained in Greek philosophy and not thinking of life primarily from the practical standpoint, but fascinated by speculation and logical consistency for their own sake, then the doctrines of God's omnipotence and omniscience took on added connotations, and came to involve extreme conclusions which the Hebrew mind did not push through to. For when the doctrines of God's omnipotence and omniscience are pushed to logically neat conclusions they undermine the equally important Hebrew confidence in the freedom and so the moral responsibility of man.

Embarrassment about the so-called naivete of the Bible is no merely modern phenomenon. It was an embarrassment to the Roman intelligentsia as well. (See Augustine's *Confessions* III. v. 9, VII. ix, 13, 14.) And under these circumstances it was very natural that Christian apologists should borrow help from the highly respected Platonic philosophy. Plato had suggested a trinity of eternally existing demiurge (or artificer), chaotic matter in powerful motion, and the eternal forms or essences. This, strictly speaking, does not involve creation, since matter and the ideas are eternal. But the world is thought of as molded into its present shape by the demiurge stamping upon chaotic matter the eternal interrelated pattern of the ideas or essences. What Christian thinkers did was to account for the creation by following the Bible in ascribing all original power and intelligence to God. By his power he created out of nothing mere matter or the dust of the earth. The eternal essences or forms are then not thought of as having an independent existence, as in Plato, but are thought of as part of the content of the mind of the creator God. When a human potter makes a pot, he first has a mental picture of the pot he wishes to make, and then he molds the clay according to that mental pattern. So when God said, "Let birds fly above the earth" (Genesis 1:20), he had a mental picture of the birds that he wished to be brought forth by his creation, and the creation involves a reproducing in the secondary, non-eternal form of existence, that is in matter, of a reflection of this eternal pattern which pre-existed in the mind of God. In the cultural circumstances of those days this method of harmonizing biblical and philosophical thought was of course natural.

Now if we let our minds play with this Platonic conception of the eternal essences or ideas, we begin to ask ourselves how detailed is the pattern that they form from eternity. We know from the *Phaedo* that Plato thought of the essences as including goodness and beauty, tallness and shortness, oddness and evenness, darkness and light, coldness and heat. But there would also have to be a multiple pattern for earthly objects. For example, by partaking of treeness all trees become trees. There would apparently also have to be subdivisions of patterns, such as elm-treeness, palm-treeness, and oak-treeness. This line of reasoning pushed to its farthest extent would imply that the world as a whole is a created copy of an original pattern. (Plato, *Timaeus* pp. 30, 31). When we take this kind of thought and link it up with the first chapter of Genesis considered as authoritative Divine revelation, we see that the divine pattern in the mind of God when he created the sun and moon (Genesis 1:14-16) included not only mental knowledge of

133

such abstractions as roundness, brightness, hotness, coldness, etc., but also these isolated abstractions and other appropriate ones integrated into a full mental pattern-picture in the mind of God. And the complicated non-physical mental pattern-pictures for such physical objects as plants, fruit trees, birds, sea-animals, cattle, beasts, and creeping things must also have pre-existed in the mind of God.

To return to the haunting problem of Plato's interrelated eternal ideas. If all beautiful things become beautiful by participating in beauty or a specific beautiful pattern, would there also have to be a heavenly archetype for each earthly object of beauty that involves a time sequence, such as the waltz, the minuet, and Bach's *B Minor Mass?* And what about goodness, the Platonic essence that is the capstone of Plato's hierarchy of values? Is it a simple abstraction or does it include the complicated abstract patterns of the various forms of social action characterized by goodness? For goodness in the moral sense of righteousness involves choice, and choice involves action, and action involves sequence in time.

If one's mind plays with these questions raised by Platonic thought and takes Platonic thought seriously, and takes the Bible as the authoritative revelation of God, one has to face the Bible's insistent claim that God is almighty, and that means, from the Bible's practical view point, that he is in no way hampered by any lack of knowledge or power. But this practical almightiness, when translated into the terms of abstractions, is described as omnipotence and omniscience. And omniscience means that God knows now in complete detail all that has been, is, or ever will be and that he knew it all in complete detail before the creation of the universe. In other words, using the Platonic way of thinking, the complete pattern of the universe down to the last detail existed in the mind of God before it existed as a creation in space-time. He knows from eternity the complete pattern of all individual objects and the complete pattern of all individual actions. This means that he is — speaking from the practical biblical view point — not unaware of the location of every living mudworm in South America. It also means — speaking from the theoretical Greek point of view — that from before the creation of the world his mind was already possessed with an exact map of all the tunnels through the earth that all the South American mudworms would make during the millions of years of that continent's existence. Omniscience, philosophically speaking, is omniscience.

Now when the theories of omniscience and omnipotence are applied to man's relation to God one gets the theological doctrines of foreordination and predestination. The idea that God foreknew and prearranged for those whom in the course of time he calls to be Christians is a belief which Paul asserts from the religiously practical Jewish viewpoint to cheer the little struggling groups of Christians, dangerously beleaguered by a cruel pagan world, with the assurance of the complete adequacy of the Heavenly Father's care for them. (Romans 8:28-31). The same idea in Augustine's teaching, pushed relentlessly with Greek logic against the background of Greek thought, becomes the doctrine that God foreordains all that comes to pass, and that from before the foundation of the world God has already predestined to heaven or hell each individual soul which is to be born upon earth. It is incorrect to think of these harsh doctrines as a new development of Reformation Calvinism. The doctrine of Divine predestination was held by Thomas Aquinas who is to the present day the most authoritative Roman Catholic theologian. And all people who know the history of theology know the difficulty that both Catholic and Protestant theologians have had in trying to square this austere doctrine with belief both in God's love and in his basic ethical decency, and with the belief that men have sufficient freedom to be morally responsible for their actions, so that those who in the end receive eternal condemnation merit it. Roman Catholicism has tried to avoid the difficulty by the soft-pedaling of the doctrine in its treatises for the laity on the religious life, as well as by some of the saving inconsistencies of its total theology.

The reason the doctrine of predestination is rightly associated with the theology of John Calvin in the minds of those who are not religious specialists is that Calvin did advocate the doctrine openly and popularized it.

There are historical reasons why he did this. The mid-sixteenth century was the century of the great initial vigor and thrust of Protestantism on the continent of Europe. Calvin's lifework had its headquarters in the Protestant city of Geneva. If one looks at the map of Europe one notices that the map of Switzerland is shaped like an ant-eater facing west and thrusting its nose out into the

135

territory of Catholic France. And at the tip of the nose is the Protestant city of Geneva, which, because of the presence of Calvin, was a center of the propagation of Protestant doctrine. In an age when men were put to death for heresy and wars were fought over matters of religious belief, the city of Geneva throughout Calvin's long residence there was in chronic danger of being attacked and destroyed by armies of the adherents of the Roman Catholic faith. Probably the strain of living in West Berlin in the mid-twentieth century is comparable to the strain of living in mid-sixteenth century Geneva. In both cities life would be day by day an emergency situation. In such a situation the doctrine of foreordination was a comfort to Calvin and the little group at Geneva, as the belief in God's foreknowledge and election had been a comfort to the little endangered group of first century Christians.

But the doctrine of God's foreordination also served a vital function both in recommending Protestantism to individuals and in fighting the polemic battle against Roman Catholicism at the intellectual level. When one is carrying on intellectual warfare and trying to convince a group that its belief is wrong at important points, one must take some belief common to both sides and argue, "If this belief is true, as we both hold that it is, then these other beliefs which you hold are untrue, since they are inconsistent with it." Protestantism's basic reason for withdrawal from Roman Catholicism was because the latter had made the Church through the decrees of the councils, the claims of the priesthood, the authority of the pope, and the veneration of the saints and Mary usurp the position of Christ as the sole mediator between God and man. When pushed in practical disputes this meant that the Roman Church retreated to the position: if you want to go to heaven you must obey the dictates of the Roman Catholic Church as expressed in the commands of the Roman Catholic hierarchy. The mutually held doctrine of foreordination undercuts the pretensions of the priesthood: the decision as to who will go to heaven was decided in each individual instance by God before the world began.

The Reformation began in England in the sixteenth century not as a popular religious revival but as a governmental break with the papacy for secular reasons, but the influence of the Continental Protestant thinkers was at that time infiltrating English thought. In England the great creative popular Protestant revival came in the succeeding century. It was during the seventeenth century that the full force of Calvinist thought was felt, and the basic outline of the Calvinist viewpoint was brilliantly summarized for Church direction and popular inculcation in three brief religious classics, *The Westminster Confession* and the *Larger and Shorter Catechism*. The man-on-the-street came to know the doctrine of foreordination.

It has always seemed to me to be significant that the great early formulations of scientific theory in England came in the seventeenth century, the century of the greatest domination of Puritan, i.e., Calvinistic, thought. *For all practical purposes the scientific theory that all things in the universe are determined according to the unbroken sequences of the functioning of the laws of nature is simply the old theological doctrine of foreordination with God omitted.*

The elaborate digression we have made into the thought of the past has been undertaken to point out the intellectual relationship that exists between the theory of strict scientific determinism, which the quantum theory seems to invalidate, and the centuries old formal Chrisian theology that in its intellectual formulation is strongly influenced by the attempt to express biblical teaching in terms that seemed to be philosophically valid to minds trained in Greek thought. I am frankly asking the question of *whether it may not now be advisable for Christian theologians to cease to feel that their Christian thinking must be squared with the requirements of a philosophical tradition inherited from the Greeks, and instead see what can be done by taking the practical picturesque biblical description of God's almightiness and relating it to recent scientific theory, taking advantage of the modern theory of a limited amount of built-in freedom in nature itself in the action of the quanta.* In these two regards let us consider the snowflake.

*   *   *   *   *   *

Any believer in strict scientific or naturalistic determinism could be forced to defend the claim that the pattern of every particular snowflake was already inevitably determined in the first moments of the great explosion that began our universe. We have also seen that the fact of the individual beauty of snowflakes does not harmonize with the philosophy which sees the flux of nature as conserving the values it has originated through the evolutionary process.

137

We have better luck if we compare our snowflake problem with the quantum theory than we have if we compare it with the theory of naturalistic determinism. According to quantum mechanics, sub-atomic activity is not determined, but its component motions exist in such enormous numbers that their free unpredictable action produces a dependable statistical uniformity. The snowflake, in like manner, has freedom of unpredictable pattern within carefully defined limits. That is, a snow crystal does not have freedom to go twenty-two pointed and spherical with a three-hundred foot diameter. The typical dendritic snowflake is restricted to a basic pattern of a flat object roughly a quarter of an inch in diameter, with six spokes of equal length radiating at sixty degree angles from a common center. Within the limits of this general pattern the snowflakes have freedom to construct an apparently endless number of beautiful forms. They might be compared to sonnets which are each an individual variation upon a small, rather rigidly prescribed, literary art form. Within the restrictions prescribed by the sonnet-form the poet has much freedom of self-expression.

We now turn to the theological problem involved in the snowflake in its relation to foreordination, which is the theological counterpart of the problem of naturalistic determinism.

I believe in the powers of God that the doctrine of foreordination tries to guard. I believe that the future never holds the harassing uncertainty for God that it does for us, that God's over-all plan for the future will prevail, that the creation will never get out of hand as far as God is concerned, and that God knows all that is needed to be known about the specific future of each individual to adequately guide and protect that individual in each succeeding present. Now when the doctrine of God's omniscience is pushed to its logical conclusion it involves belief in his foreseeing all our acts now down to the last detail. That is, that the complete lives that we will live are, so to speak, already a kind of Platonic pattern in the mind of God. This raises the question of whether God's foreknowledge allows us any freedom or whether it in effect robs us of freedom and so lessens our moral responsibility. The ingenious answer that Christian doctrine has given is that God is outside of time and characterized by eternity, that therefore he sees our past and future in his everlasting now, and so that he now sees our future as occurring and not as future, and thus his knowledge does not force our action.

This is an excellent explanation but it seems to have one drawback as far as the Christian devotional life is concerned. Everything on earth with which we as human beings are thoroughly familiar which is wholly outside of time or timeless is completely inactive. The multiplication table is an example. Time does not change or deteriorate the multiplication table, and the multiplication table never acts. It is human beings who act when they use or apply the multiplication table. Now the Bible constantly insists that God is righteous. And righteousness is an active virtue. Righteousness as we know it involves the constant choosing of the better alternative and the various acts of choosing involve temporal sequence. The Bible recognizes that God is not bound by time as we are. That is implied in the meaning of the divine name, I AM THAT I AM, and is indicated by such sayings as,

For a thousand years in thy sight
are but as yesterday when it is past,
or as a watch in the night. (Psalm 90:4)

But the typical Hebrew formula for God's unlimited existence is not that of timeless eternity but everlastingness.

From everlasting to everlasting thou art God. (Psalm 90:2)

When the sophisticated Western mind discards the idea of God's everlastingness in favor of an exclusive use of the word eternity, it immediately loses much of the vividness of the Old Testament description of God as constantly and vigorously engaged in carrying out detailed projects as part of his overall plan.

It should be noted that the Greek idea of the static eternity of the Divine fits in with the Greek conception of history as having no ultimate purpose, but as repeating itself in detail endlessly and pointlessly with each revolution of the great cycles of time. To the Hebrew thought time was not circular. Existence was purposeful. There was an important plan which the world was more or less adequately fulfilling. Time was thought of as extending from the past to the present to the future, as a straight line: God is from everlasting to evrlasting. Since science seems to have shown that the overall existence of the cosmos is characterized by irreversible entropy, the Hebrew conception of time as a straight line fits the overall scientific picture better than does the Greek conception that time is circular. This being the case it would be well for theologians to go back to the biblical description of God as "from everlasting to everlasting," being careful as the Bible itself is to qualify and safeguard the use of this formula.

If we think of God as "from everlasting to everlasting" then the doctrine of God's foreordination carries the implication that God, like a great executive, first has a plan and then orders it carried out, that is, a time sequence is involved. And if God is then thought of as omnipotent and omniscient and if he made all things, then his foreordination is as detailed and thorough as naturalism has claimed for the godless mechanical determinism which it advocated.

Let us use the snowflake as a test case. The Calvinistic doctrine of foreordination claims that God foreordains all that comes to pass either directly or by foreordaining all the earliest events with exact knowledge of the secondary causes and the necessary results that these will inevitably give rise to. This corollary doctrine of God's omniscient foreknowledge would mean claiming that before the foundation of the world God already had a complete mental picture of the pattern of each snowflake that would fall in the history of the world, as well as the accurate time-and-place schedule for the falling of each particular snowflake. I am not trying to prove whether God did or did not have this knowledge. I simply want to go on record as saying that I find the doctrine of foreordination, when pushed to this logical conclusion, emotionally revolting. It takes the joy and spontaneity out of life. I do not want to look out on a winter's morning across a field of new fallen snow and think, "The pattern of each of those little snowflakes was already designed by God millions of years before the time of the dinosaurs," as well as a detailed schedule for the "happy landing" of each particular snowflake. Such a thought would take all the freshness out of the scene for me.

I think my reaction must be a not unusual one. For it is curious to notice that the great nature artists and great nature poets have not typically come from those social groups where Calvinist theology has dominated. There is a logical austerity about Calvinism. The curious thing is that this is not due—as is so often claimed—to the fact that Calvinism returned to the austerity of the Old Testament and sloughed off that Greek appreciation of beauty that had been amalgamated to the Catholic synthesis. For the curious fact is that this logical austerity that emanates from Calvinism is not characteristic of the Old Testament. In fact the Old Testament contains some of the world's greatest nature poetry. There are not in the Bible long nature poems centering the attention upon Nature as such, but more characteristically, little jewellike flashes of appreciation of nature's beauty embedded in writing that is God-oriented and not nature-oriented. And yet these little fragments have a freshness and vitality greater than that of the English Romantic poets. The difficulty with Calvinism was that it only partially went back to the Old Testament. It retained the fetters of the Greek mentality that pushed doctrines that the Old Testament had held as a practical description to their strictly logical conclusion, whether or not the logical conclusion violated certain other insights into existence which are basic to the Old Testament.

Now can we take the limited freedom that science is beginning to think is built into nature at the subatomic level, a freedom which, however accounted for, allows nature to produce snowflakes no two of which are alike, and tie it up with the reinterpreted biblical doctrine of creation that this book is outlining? I think that we can.

Suppose that God, when he thought up the universe prior to the original cosmic explosion, not only thought up the general plan of the explosion but also the constituency of matter, so that the chemical elements that would be formed would have the properties that would enable them to be used later in complicated ways. We can suppose, for example, that God prearranged it so that hydrogen and oxygen would have the properties that would enable them to form water, itself a compound of various and curious attributes, among them that of changing from the vaporous to the solid state when the temperature drops to zero degrees centigrade. And we can suppose that God prearranged it so that the characteristic solid form that the water vapor would assume while falling through the air in the lower altitudes would be the well known dendritic crystalline form, that is, the flat, approximately quarter of an inch, six-pointed crystal, the six equal spokes radiating at 60° angles from the center. Imagine for the sake of argument that this much was, so to speak, "on the books" from the original creation, foreordained with complete exactness by the mind of God. This would mean that when conditions in the world brought this part of the plan

141

into play, that the generalized skeleton form of the common snow-flake was already arranged for. Suppose then, when the earth really began to bring forth and actualize snowflakes, that God's command to the snowflakes was, "Little snowflakes, I have given you a standard pattern upon which to build and make yourselves beautiful. Build evenly and independently and freely and crea-tively within and upon this pattern which I have given you, and you cannot go wrong and you will add beauty to my creation."

Again, let me say for the benefit of any scientist or theologian who may read this book that I am purposely talking in pictures and symbols. I do not believe of course that the Almighty literally talks baby-talk to snowflakes! But I am trying to sketch a pic-turesque scheme of things in which it is according to the (literally) conscious Divine foreordination that the general pattern of the snowflake should exhibit scientific determinism, while each particu-lar snowflake should freely embody slight variations upon this basic pattern, and that therefore each snowflake should freely add to the creation its own peculiar beauty.

It must be reiterated and underscored that in accounting for the emergence of consciousness in our world one must either begin with a Consciousness as the ultimate and assume that this Original Consciousness brought matter into being, or begin with Matter as the ultimate and describe matter as the Original which gradually brought consciousness into being. This latter assumption denies the validity of all biblical religion. The Jewish and Christian re-ligions have to believe that Conscious Mind is primary and brought matter into being. Therefore if one still holds the Christian faith to be basically true one must assent to the proposition, "In the beginning, God." And if conscious mind is the creator then we have as much right to use that appropriate segment of reality with which we are very familiar, namely our own conscious minds, to project a hypothetical description of the mind of the Creator, as the right science has to use the little segment of reality to which its discipline has access, namely the contemporary modes of action of matter, to project backward a hypothetical description of the history of life on this planet, and before that the history of the planet itself, and before that the history of the universe. The only difference is that the scientist in dealing with past time assumes that he is dealing with the history of the same old matter that confronts him today. And Christians, on the other hand, when they try to make a hypothetical description of the Divine Mind, have to realize that anything they can imagine is very inadequate. For the quantity and quality of the Divine Mind are indescribably superior to the human, and furthermore the Divine Mind and consciousness would have facets and abilities which human beings know nothing of and so cannot even begin to think about. When we describe God's mind on the analogy of the human pattern, the only pattern to which we have direct access, we can only say that the Creator's mind is in some ways comparable to human mind, and that the Divine Mind in its totality is not inconsistent with human mind. We have already pointed out one ability that the Divine Mind must have which the human mind does not have. The human mind has rationality. The Divine Mind must have rationality-plus, and the "plus" must include the superhuman ability to think into independent three dimensional existence.

The point that this admittedly picture-thinking is building up to is this: We are supposing the general plan of the snowflake to be foreordained by God. We are supposing the material out of which the snowflakes are to be made to have been thought into independent existence by God; but we are not thinking of each particular tiny variation that each snowflake makes on the beautiful general snowflake pattern to have individually been thought up beforehand by God. Therefore as each snowflake crystallizes, something new, something fresh would have been added by way of beauty to total existence. Not of course that any snowflake is more beautiful than the Creator's original thought-pattern, but a fresh variation on the pattern of beauty has been brought about by the creation. The Creator himself made the basic materials and the basic pattern for the snowflake. But part of the design of each particular snowflake is worked out and arranged not by the Creator but by the snowflake. This is one of the marvels of the creation. God not only created out of nothing that which is other than himself. He created out of nothing that which had a slight amount of freedom to collaborate with him in the work of creation. The snowflakes, just be becoming different and beautiful snowflakes, are obeying their Lord and Creator and fulfilling the duty he has assigned to them. God "sends forth his command to the earth; . . . He gives snow like wool." (Psalm 147:15,16) and the "snow and

143

frost" fulfill "his command," (Psalm 148:8) and by so doing they "praise the Lord from the earth." (Psalm 148:7)

We are not being unduly sentimental in these suggestions. The snowflakes do not know that they are obeying God. They have no consciousness of a command and no knowledge of the beautiful patterns they create. Their wholly unconscious creation of these beautiful patterns is due entirely to chance as the forming crystal attaches to itself in its descent the water vapor molecules with which it collides.

Now I have said that this theory appeals to me emotionally, and also that I resent a doctrine of foreordination that would make the divine mind draft—before the world began—the pattern for each particular snowflake. Although genius may be the ability to take infinite pains, an essential characteristic of a great executive is the ability to delegate tasks and power.

I think that the reason that I dislike this doctrine of complete foreordination is that it undercuts any explanation for a purpose in the creation. Certainly if the Almighty set purposively to work to design a snowflake he could make a more beautiful one than those lovely little chance-designed bits of lacy beauty with which we are familiar. Why then bother to have earthly snowflakes exist at all, inasmuch as they would be merely imperfect reproductions of patterns that exist already perfectly in God's mind? Why bother to hang third-rate copies of Gainsborough's paintings on your walls if you happen to possess the originals!

But if we think that his is not only the power and the glory forever but also the kingdom, and that in ascribing to him the kingdom we are ascribing to him that governing righteousness whose heart and summit is love, then we can think of him as wanting and cherishing the less perfect beauty freely created by the creation, and freely offered back by the creation as a gift of praise to the Creator. My dislike for thinking that the blueprint of each snowflake was foreordained by the Creator is not that I think that such enormous attention to detail would strain his powers in the slightest. What I think to be the true state of affairs would require equal capacity on his part. I think that in love he delights with robust joy in each new and beautiful design his creation gives him, so that his unlimited consciousness sees in full detail the design (Luke 12:6,7) of each snowflake that falls to earth, and cherishes (Matthew 10:42) that particular bit of loveliness forever in his memory. With unbounded zest God satisfies his collector's instinct by "taking up what [he] did not lay down, and reaping what [he] did not sow." (Luke 19:22,23)

If this is the case, and if this relation of God's to nature which we have been suggesting in respect to snowflakes is typical of God's relation to all of nature, then we can begin to suggest a guess as to that important aspect of that *modus operandi* of evolution which is outside the range of science's observation.

For if God is conscious intelligent spirit we can project some hypotheses relative to him on the basis of our own experience. We also pointed out previously that science has made us aware of a kind of rhythm in the universe in the sense that basic patterns are repeated with variations in nature as in art. Now we know from our knowledge of the education of the young that they thrive on appreciation. I do not mean undue importance, or flattery, or lack of discipline. I mean that in typical instances, where a small child grows up in a loving and harmonious home, if the parents are appreciatively aware of the child's little constructive accomplishments and beginning attempts to do his duty, that the child will normally respond with more of the activity that gives him a place of approval within the social circle which is his headquarters of safety. We know, too, that part of the educational problem we now face in view of the current social belief that all moral standards are merely relative to the group and that there are no ultimate moral standards, is the intense craving of teenagers for the approval and appreciation of their peer group, no matter what price they pay for this approval in terms of lowering their own moral standards. Also we know that one of the greatest dangers inherent in our over-organization and mechanization of industrial life is the tendency of it to suppress those personal relationships in which alone a person can feel appreciation and approval for a particular action or piece of work to which a person can point as his accomplishment. We are now very much aware that the over-intrusion of machines into social life has tended to dehumanize and depersonalize men, and that men become human only through interpersonal relationships.

Could it be that the Divine appreciation and approval, as in the case of his appreciation and approval of each snowflake's somewhat

145

unique design, was God's method of bringing about evolution, gradually eliciting more and more response to himself from his creation? Is this what his Spirit was doing when so long ago it "was brooding upon the face of the waters?" (Genesis 1:2 ARV alternate translation.) Again, the charge of mere sentimentalism cannot be levied against this proposition on the ground that after all the snowflake is not alive and so cannot respond to appreciation, and that the same is true of all inanimate matter before the process of evolution.

For we have been at pains to show at length in our earlier discussion that philosophic theory based on science has ruled out a miraculous endowment of man by God which distinguished men from beasts, and this theory now feels confident that there is an unbroken natural evolutionary development from inorganic matter, through one-celled organisms, to man. But we have shown that this naturalistic theory, by succeeding in establishing itself so thoroughly, discredits itself by having no explanation for the late appearance on earth of intelligent mind. *To avoid this dilemma, science-based philosophy has to take a step more dangerous for itself than it realizes: it has to assume a "mind factor" inherent in so-called inanimate matter from the beginning. The reason that this is a dangerous step that science is pushed into taking is that it involves a theoretical interpretation of the lower on the basis of analogy to the higher, and an interpretation of the past on the basis of its future goal and not on its own past, instead of following the famed scientific method of interpreting the higher on the basis of the lower which has been understood by means of objective measured experimentation upon it. Christian theologians are now in a position to point out that science is admitting that it can interpret man in terms of his past only by interpreting that past in terms of man's present and so begging the question. And further, Christian theologians are in a position to point out that this philosophical-scientific argument-by-analogy has failed to take all the relevant factors into consideration, for it is making the mistake of taking reactivity as equivalent to mind. So even its capitulation to the previously disdained method of reasoning by analogy cannot establish a naturalistic theory of evolution. For even if an unbroken scale of complexity of reactivity can be shown, beginning with so-called inanimate matter and climaxed by man, this theory still overlooks*

146

the distinction between reactivity which is objective and intelligent consciousness which is subjective, and so this enlargement of the evolutionary theory to include what used to be called inanimate matter does not back up the naturalistic philosophy it was expected to reinforce. Naturalistic philosophy does not, and Christianity does, have an adequate theory to offer for the emergence of intelligent mind on this earth. For by its claim that the universe was originally created out of nothing by supernatural intelligent Mind and then cast into independent existence by that Mind, there are adequate answers possible to the two questions of what the "mind factor" was that was associated with inanimate matter from the beginning, and of how that inanimate matter was enabled to evolve until at last there were intelligent minds on earth.

Modern science has even unintentionally made it easier now than it was a hundred years ago for the educated man-on-the-street to "picture" emotionally a supernatural non-physical Spiritual Being creating matter out of nothing. For "rigid matter has now resolved itself in modern physics into an event, and . . . this event is light, taking the widest sense for that term. For light and electricity tend to coincide."[1] On the other hand, modern science's description of matter in terms of non-visible non-material atomic systems of energy-stresses has made the college-educated man-on-the-street make the mistake of assuming that in the last analysis matter and mind can be equated, and he follows this mistake with the dangerous assumption that mind is an aspect of matter, without realizing that the modern definition of matter still leaves unsolved the insoluble mystery of the distinction between the subjective and the objective.

Christianity says that the "mind factor" associated with matter from the beginning was the supernatural intelligent mind of matter's Creator, and that it was "natural" for matter to be from the first amenable to the influence of supernatural intelligence, because matter had been created by his same supernatural intelligence. If matter was originally thought up and then cast off into independent existence by the Divine Mind, then, if the Divine Mind appreciated a particular snowflake, the matter composing the snowflake would

---

[1] Karl Heim, *The Transformation of the Scientific World View;* New York: Harper & Brothers, 1953, p. 80.

undergo unconsciously the experience of well being by being in some sense "brought back home" to the Mind that had originated it. Since appreciation does not influence in terms of force—as of one billiard ball hitting another billiard ball—but by allurement in terms of an "unmoved mover," this appreciation of the snowflake can be thought of as an external influence upon it which in no way interferes with its freedom of self-determination within the prescribed limitations of its mode of existence.

Again, science cannot claim that unintelligent organism, or pre-organic organizations of matter, could not be gradually "trained" in the direction of intelligent consciousness by supernatural conscious Mind, because we have somewhat of an analogy to this activity taking place which we can observe from our studies of embryology and infancy. The human embryo begins as an unintelligent one-celled organism. We have seen that after the new born baby begins its life in the world, as early as the period when it is six to twelve weeks old, it begins the process of attaining its adult intelligent life by its unknowing response to the care of the intelligent adults who surround it.

If the scientifically minded should claim that the baby, even in its single celled beginning, is nevertheless organic matter, so that Christians still have no theory of how a supernatural Mind could modify inorganic matter, I would point out that we have discussed at length aesthetic appreciation as a peculiar intermediate step between an "I-it" relationship and an "I-thou" relationship. It is a semi-interpersonal relationship to which only one party has to be alive and intelligently conscious. As the conscious intelligence aesthetically appreciates the non-living beautiful object the appreciator lays himself open by an undomineering receptivity to its beauty, and his receptivity becomes a channel by which the appreciated object is enabled to give him more of its beauty. In other words we are imagining the Almighty Creator appreciating the beauty of each individual snowflake and so coming into a semi-personal relationship to it. And we can imagine the matter out of which each individual snowflake is formed (which was made originally by the intelligent mind of God) "striving" unconsciously to produce freely its slightly individual pattern of beauty in response to that appreciation, because, by the circumstances of matter's creation it has a built-in *penchant* for activity relative to the Divine Mind. And it is

148

in this slowly increasing response in nature, which in the religious experience of men is the fully conscious and dedicated desire for conformity to the Creator, that we find the key to the process of evolution. But in this interplay of God and his creation it is only nature's response—not the activity of God—that is observable by science. The all-important off-stage action of the Divine appreciation is forever out-of-bounds to the scientific sphere of investigation.

Edmund W. Sinnott has claimed that a life-long study of plants has convinced him that evolution is teleological, that plants strive to attain and maintain the pattern appropriate to their species. I am going farther than this claim and saying that I think that all embodiment of beauty, even in the inorganic universe, is an unconscious striving on the part of created nature to respond to the appreciation of its Creator who is characterized by ineffable beauty, or glory.

Those advocates of emergent (i.e., unaided) evolution who have tried to keep the naturalistic interpretation of nature and still account for human intelligence and moral values, in attempting to read mind back into inorganic matter, ascribe a kind of life to inorganic matter by saying that it strives and has purposes. The theory I am advocating would explain how inorganic and unconscious matter can be said to strive and have purpose. However, the theory I have been propounding is not what these people mean when they say that matter strives and has purposes.

For their theory of the striving is an integral part of their naturalistic philosophy which says that in the beginning there was just matter in motion characterized by vague unconscious striving. There was not an already existing God as an already existing goal toward which to strive. In this unconscious striving evolution happened to take place and happened to evolve consciousness, which later evolved into intelligent consciousness. After intelligent consciousness appeared it created social, moral, and aesthetic values and goals for itself out of its own imagination and not in response to value already in existence. Thus insofar as man invents value in his imagination and actualizes it in his social experience *he is bringing God into existence*. After this theory had been common knowledge for several decades among the large number of college educated people in America and had been more or less overtly implied in scholarly books in many fields, Sartre came along with a bald statement of the implications of this theory. Look, he has said in effect, values are something a mind has. If there is no God to have values in his mind, there are no eternal values, there are only values as a man happens to have one in his mind. So men cannot cling to values for safety because man is primary as regards value, and insofar as values exist they are wholly dependent on men for safety. Thus man starts with the being of man, and beyond man, as regards a realm of values or a God, there is nothingness. Insofar as man tries to project himself in creating values he is building a bridge out of nothingness, over nothingness, to nothingness. Man is therefore insecure and forlorn. Educators are bemoaning the fact that the young have been attracted to Sartre's atheistic existentialism, and see no values worth striving to attain, and doubt whether there are any moral standards that are grounded in anything beyond group convenience, and so educators lament that the young aim for security, comfort, and group approval rather than devote their lives to far-off goals. But the world has never been a thoroughly good place, and if one climbs the beanstalk of ideals one often has to climb alone. And if one comes to a situation where one must climb alone, then whether or not one believes the beanstalk at the top to be firmly anchored to giant-land makes a great deal of difference as to whether one risks one's self to the practical climb. If the farther up one goes from the dead level of mediocrity the more one's beanstalk of ideals sways dizzily in unlimited emptiness, the greater one's temptation to conform to the mediocre and seek safety in group approval, even if one has to flout some ethical principles in order to make a harmonious group adjustment. The ingredients from which Sartre drew the logical pessimistic conclusion were already being offered in liberal education in my own undergraduate days of the early 1920s. Why do we scold the young for acting on the philosophy that two generations of their elders have implied?

To return to the question of the relation of the snowflake to God and the relation of God to evolution, it may be objected that as the snowflake is inanimate matter and not part of the evolutionary series, that a discussion of it does not help to interpret God's relation to the evolutionary process. But the point we are making is that God utilized the appreciation of beauty which is a semi-interpersonal relationship which an intelligent mind can enter into with a non-living object, as a means of eliciting sufficient response, so that a stage could eventually be reached at which God could have a fully interpersonal relationship with part of his creation. Appreciation is a very strong, non-coercive influence. By this type of influence the small amount of free self-determination open to the snowflake was not interfered with. The snowflake has been used as an illustration because each flake is relatively isolated and uncomplicated, because the diversity within the basic unity of design indicates a slight amount of freedom which our theory needs in combating the popular belief in the natural determination of all physical events, because the snowflake brings into the picture the element of beauty which must be dealt with in any philosophy, and because the snowflake is an illustration of variation within basic unity, and an illustration of a crystal which the non-scientific reader can easily picture. The snowflake serves therefore as a good illustration of our basic theory. God's comparable relationship to the matter involved in the evolutionary theory is assumed. That is, God appreciated ("saw that it was good", Genesis 1) each intimate stage in the process that he desired to keep. This supposes that the changes came about by chance mutations that seem to occur at intervals according to the statistical laws of quantum mechanics. By especial appreciation he strengthened and encouraged that which he desired to keep in what nature had freely produced and so paved the way for the next succeeding step in the evolutionary process. The appreciation of beauty could have been a method that he steadily used. For nature in its healthy aspects is characterized by beauty. Even the lowly slime-mold at the microscopic level is a thing of breathtaking beauty both in its aspect and its functioning. But most readers are better acquainted with snowflakes.

God's appreciation of both snowflakes and slime-mold may enhance their beauty, as a woman becomes more beautiful when she is deeply loved. For the source of all beauty is the glory of God. As Isaiah said, "The whole earth is full of his glory" (Isaiah 6:3). Or as Plato said, "[By participation in] beauty all beautiful things become beautiful." (*Phaedo* p. 100)

As has been said, this influence by appreciation is a variation upon the old idea of God as the Unmoved Mover, moving by alluring. But the biblical picture also assumes that God moves by "push" or "manipulation," that he sometimes directly acts causally in a way that allows no room for freedom in the creature's response, but that upon occasion he forcefully determines the creature's response. For example, I Kings 18:37,38 is a pointless story unless the perfectly natural lightning which struck at that time and place, did so in that instance because God especially desired and arranged that it should, in a way that bears some sort of analogy to the normally present electricity in my room breaking into a flood of illumination at precisely 9:17 P.M., because I willed at exactly that time to turn on my desk light and took the individual, appropriate action of turning the entirely commonplace light switch.

It is, I think, possible to account for God's manipulative action upon portions of his creation at particular times by means of the theory of nature's merely statistical regularity, which allows for a method, built into the creation, by which God can slightly "stack the cards" for a particular physical action that he especially wishes, without causing nature to act in ways contrary to its statistically regular, cause-and-effect routine. Karl Heim, in his book *The Transformation of the Scientific World View* says: "A gene seems to be a single molecule containing somewhere between ten thousand and a million atoms. A particularly clear indication of the molecular character of the gene is the fact that its changes take place in accordance with the laws of quantum mechanics. A gene is capable only of variable changes. Its mutations are quantum jumps of the molecule . . ."[2] If this is true, then the "quantum stacking" that produced any mutation might be due either to chance, or to the manipulative power of God. The action, seen from within nature, would be exactly the same in either case. If it is objected that scientifically it is impossible to think of a completely non-physical spirit changing even slightly the location of matter, the answer has to be that it occurs each time I, by my conscious volition, pick up my pencil, for in some inexplicable way my non-physical thought controls my nerves which move my muscles. If scientists should say that I am mistaken, that the relevant nerve action was only a reaction to previous nerve action, then scientists should be in a position to substantiate the thesis that all the nerve action necessary for carrying on all the activities of the civilizatons of Europe and

---

[2] *Ibid.*, p. 214.

America—including the printing of all the daily papers—could perfectly well be carried on without consciousness ever having arisen on this planet. In this case science would be forced to admit that life "is a tale told by an idiot, full of sound and fury, signifying nothing," and that would make all scientific investigation meaningless. The subjective as well as the objective is essential to the existence of the scientific thinker, but the thinking subject can never be objectively studied, and is therefore wholly outside the domain of scientific research and theory. Religion should never allow the philosophers of science to forget this.

If we assume that the theory we have been elaborating is genuinely what occurred "back stage" while the universe took shape and while life developed on this planet according to the general description of science's attempts to describe these things, can we also believe that the theory we have developed will fit the biblical view of God, the world, and man's relation to God? Obviously the theory this book has been elaborating is not the exact picture that any of the biblical writers had in his mind of how God made the world as we know it, and how God relates himself to the world. It is obvious that the biblical writers did not have the findings of modern science to take into consideration either as a help or a hindrance. But we are not under obligation to follow the details of the biblical scientific view (or views: compare Genesis 7:11 and Job 36:27,28). We are only under obligation to try to find a view which, if true, will allow for the aspect of the world science has investigated, and for the over-all biblical picture of God and his relation to the world and men. To accomplish this coordination of viewpoints some world-picture must be found according to which a God who is other than the world can interact with the world. This is necessary if the basic Hebrew conception of God as purposeful and righteous is to be kept. Deism cannot give us our needed picture of God for it describes him as too aloof to be carrying on righteous purposes within the world. And pantheism which has been so much in vogue in Liberal Protestantism is not usable because any too close equating of God's action with the processes of the world undercuts the claim that God is unswervingly righteous. The theory this book is developing at least makes room for belief in a supernatural intelligent God who is able to interact at will with his creation.

CHAPTER 12
Glory and Nature Poetry

This theory that we have been developing fits also the comparison of the nature poetry of the Bible with the great nature poetry of nineteenth and twentieth century England, especially that of the Romantic poets. The bits of nature appreciation embedded like jewels in the Old Testament have a vitality and freshness lacking in Romantic poetry. This freshness and vitality are due to the glory of the supernatural God shed upon nature. "The whole earth in full of his glory" Isaiah heard the seraphim sing. But the whole earth was not full of God. It was the God who was "sitting upon a throne high and lifted up" whose glory filled the earth. (Isaiah 6:1-3) The glory in the Romantic poets is regarded as a characteristic *of* nature. This is the underlying distinction between the attitude toward nature in Romantic poetry and in the Old Testament. It is Nature itself, or certain aspects of Nature, that comfort and reassure the Romantic Poets, as we see in Shelley's "Ode to the West Wind." But when the Psalmist lifts up his eyes to the hills and asks from whence shall his help come, his answer is that his help comes "from the Lord who made heaven and earth." (Psalm 121:1,2) The Romantic attitude has something of the fertility religions' trust in the vitalities of nature, in its feeling of spiritual reliance upon them.

By contrast the Hebraic attitude is that of the Divine influence *coming to* nature. This is well illustrated in C. S. Lewis' autobiography, *Surprised by Joy.* From childhood and until well into his teens he had from time to time experienced brief elusive hints of the divine vision on lonely walks in the country, when landscape, clouds, and atmospheric conditions seemed to converge in transmitting to him a sense of haunting joy that soon vanished, as Wordsworth had lamented, and left his spirit with the sense of both desolation and longing. Then, just before he was ready for the University, he had the experience that was the beginning for him of the long road back to Christian belief. The scene was one weekend evening in his tutor's house. Lewis was absorbed in a book he had

154

just purchased, *Phantastes, a faerie Romance* by George Mac-Donald. It was a new type of experience for him. The setting of the story was like that of the romantic and chivalrous books of which he was fond. But this book was different. It was not until years later that he identified the new quality as holiness. Lewis said that on reading *Phantastes* it was as if a "bright shadow" had come "out of the book into the real world and [rested] there, transforming all common things and yet itself unchanged. Or, more accurately, [he] saw the common things drawn into the bright shadow."[1] This description seems to me to be distinctly the Hebrew awareness of the earth being full of God's glory, as distinct from the pantheistic impression of the Divine as being immersed in, or as being part of nature. And this spiritual awareness of the "bright shadow" gathering the specific mundane objects into itself fits perfectly with the hypothesis of God's relation to the creation that this present volume is outlining.

Lewis's phrase, "the bright shadow" is a brilliantly accurate description of the experience, and is something quite different from the pantheist's feeling of nature itself as being divine, or as being a carrier or mediator of the Divine. I know this from personal experience. Under this experience one does not feel that nature is transmitting or revealing the Divine to one. It is the other way around. It is nature that is revealed and made intimately available to one by the Divine which is other than nature. The bright shadow does not need to be brought close to the human soul. The moment one is aware of it one recognizes it immediately as pertaining to the soul's Ultimate Fatherland. It is the bright shadow that takes the feeling of strangeness away from the earth in which we live.

There are some people who mistakenly see in St. Francis of Assisi's "Canticle of the Sun," in which he calls the sun and moon and water his "brother" and "sisters," a trace of pantheism. Instead it was the fellowship with the supernatural Creator and with his Son Jesus Christ that brought Francis close to the creation, and that underlies the Christian idea of human brotherhood. According to Christ, loving one's neighbor as one's self is the necessary corollary to the primary law to love God. (Mark 12:29-31) My surmise is that it is the remnants of the biblical belief lingering as a mood

[1] C. S. Lewis, *Surprised by Joy*; New York: Harcourt, Brace and Company, 1955, p. 181.

that enhanced the nature experience reflected in our greatest Western nature poetry.

To speak autobiographically, in my first years out of college in the late 1920s I was much depressed because the extremely liberal biblical education to which I had been exposed was so lacking in a belief in God the Father and in the deity of his Son Jesus Christ, and was further such exclusively technical criticism that my graduate school studies in New Testament in 1926-1927 appeared to me to create a religious vacuum rather than to satisfy a religious need. In the several years that followed I turned to great English novels and poetry for steadiness, and for a regaining of perspective. Great English literature is at least warmly human and with some hints of a perspective beyond the human. I discovered of course the Romantic poets and for a long time the latter part of Shelley's "Adonais" was food for my soul. I liked the Romantic poets' description of nature and its haunting moods because I liked nature and found nature a refreshment in a period of spiritual turmoil. But I never felt any basic inspiration from nature. My own inner religious life was characterized by a steady and cautious fumbling, without loss of confidence in the adherence to the morally good as an aid to the religious pilgrimage, and with an inarticulate sense of direction that I would have been puzzled to explain. Although in retrospect I can see the Divine care throughout my life, my youth was characterized by a conspicuous absence of any periods of religious exhilaration. I was thirty-three years old before I ever had a consciously identifiable experience of the nearness of God. In the preceding years there was only the inexplicable confidence that God could not be described as far away.

As for picturing God the Father to myself, in my middle teens I had a mental picture of the lines of direction of all the virtues—good, better, best—pointing "upward" and at the far away point where I seemed to see all those lines of direction intersecting there was a vague outline of a masculine figure, sufficiently distinct to serve as a pictorial "peg" to hang thought about God's purpose and character and will upon, but not sufficiently distinct so that I could ever see the features or have any particular impression of whether the figure seemed young or old. There has always been a vague impression that the figure was indefinitely clothed. It never, even in my mid teens, seemed an exact visual picture of God, but more a

156

diagram to aid my thought, and as a diagram I find it still largely unchanged and equally useful, and equally unobtrusive as a pictorial image. That is, the diagramatic picture contains the idea that God has individuality, intellect, and personality, that his nature constitutes perfect righteousness and perfect beauty, and that he is supernatural to the creation in the sense of being other than the creation. This general conception of God was based partly on my Church background, and partly on my knowledge of the Bible. By the time I was seventeen I had read the Bible through on my own initiative. With such a conception of God and with so much acquaintance with the Bible it is understandable that the idea of God as a power in nature, or transmitted through nature, or as "the little spark of the divine in each one of us" had no hold on my imagination.

The slightly uncanny feeling of God's influence relative to the subhuman creation by which nature is recognized as being under God's attention, or better, within God's attention, did not come until I was fifty years old, and then only slightly and gradually. When I am conscious of it, I recognize it as a very minor replica of Isaiah's words, "The whole earth is full of his glory," and of C. S. Lewis's description of the "bright shadow" that gathered into itself the coals in the grate, the bread on the table, and his old teacher nodding over his little *Tacitus*.

Accounts of the ecstatic whispers of the Divine about one in nature when one is young, which are in later years eliminated by the inroads of "the light of common day," bear no resemblance to my personal experience, which went steadily from unidentifiable beginnings with an inconspicuous crescendo through periods of happiness but chiefly numbness and long alternating periods of dryness in which I still knew my sense of direction by the elimination of the roads I knew to be blind alleys. The result is that for me the feeling that life is wonderful and new is now, rather than in my chronological youth. And this personal experience is embedded in the doctrinal hypothesis I am elaborating. It is a doctrinal hypothesis which, if true, would fit this religious experience. The glimpses of the "glory" in nature would then be glimpses of nature as it is under the non-coercive impact of God's discriminating appreciation.

I believe that this is a useful idea for Christian thought. It allows for freedom within nature, for appreciation is not coercive, and at

157

the same time it allows for God's constant initiative and activity intimately relative to nature, because appreciation is a very active thing. Thus we make some use of the Classical insight into the Divine as the Unmoved Mover. But we modify the Classical insight to describe the Divine as both personal and active, as befits a religion based on biblical insight.

The theory also enables us to take advantage of the science-based philosophy that has tried to keep naturalism, and then has tried to get an explanation for the emergence of intelligent man by saying that there is a quality of purposive striving in even inanimate nature. For purposive striving is a concerted voluntary movement toward an already existing goal. Any other motion is random or chaotic activity, or coerced action, or action due to gravity, or rhythmical action such as the swinging of a pendulum or the spinning of a top or the motion of the waves of the sea. These classifications are neither philosophic nor scientific. They are simply the ordinary man's practical classification of the types of action around him that are not purposeful and not necessarily significant. But the word "strives" is a goal-seeking, not a scientific word. If there is a "striving" in pre-organic and primitive-organic matter, then even at the base of the evolutionary scale there is a teleological aspect of matter's activity. To deny this and yet to impute to primitive nature a "mind aspect" that "strives," is to connect consciousness with the earliest beginnings of evolution without admitting that this is what one is doing. If matter really "strives," then either the chemical elements are genuinely conscious, or else a Supernatural Consciousness is intimately relating himself to them.

CHAPTER 13

The Prelude to Salvation
from the *Second Law of Thermodynamics*

According to the theory we have been developing nature did not initiate the upward thrust that became the evolutionary development of life on this planet. For the creation, left to itself initiates only entropy or dissolution. But when nature combined and recombined according to the standard procedures for such relationships built into nature itself at the creation, then the divine supernatural Intelligence working upon the completely unconscious inanimate matter, by occasionally stacking the cards by means of the built-in leeway in the regularity of nature's action that comes from the merely statistical subatomic regularity, initiated increasing complication in the activity of matter—first protein molecules, then viruses, then living unicellular forms. As each new step came about, perhaps with a little divine wire-pulling in relation to the changes at first, and also at later stages to form desirable mutations, (not very large scale wire pulling if a mutation is a change in a single gene and a single gene is a single molecule) then the divine appreciation of the change helped make the newly modified pattern for existence something the lowly form of animal life strove to attain and maintain. If most of the mutations were due to chance, with the Divine appreciation concentrating on the mutations God desired to keep, in order to weight the chances in the direction of that mutation's survival, then his appreciation helped cause the lowly animalcules to strive to adjust to his appreciative desire by their attaining and maintaining the new desired pattern. After all, what other *explanation* is there for the rise of the evolutionary process, as distinct from a mere *description* of it? The stock answer of course has been, "The striving for survival." But one can then ask, "Why should the creatures strive for survival before consciousness and the experience of pain had arisen in the course of the evolutionary development?" The answer would be, "They just did strive," and that is a description, not an explanation.

The theory that has been taught for decades is that evolution came about because there were many chance mutations, and that those chance mutations that *adjusted the creature more adequately to his environment won out in the struggle for existence.* But this does not cover the situation *as an explanation.* For it assumes the existence of the full fledged human viewpoint at the very beginning, namely the belief that existence is worth struggling for, and the full fledged human point of view could only have existed in the beginning of the process of evolution if it were consciously held by a supernatural God, while contrary-wise, the science-image has been trying to give a description of evolution leaving a supernatural Creator God entirely out of the picture. But surely the primitive amoeba did not strive to survive because it consciously thought survival a good thing or because it was better adjusted to its environment than the grains of sand and the other inorganic matter around it. (If one claims that the virus preceded the amoeba, one can use this same argument for the virus.)

Try to imagine the world just before the process of evolution got under way. The cosmos was expanding in all directions. Our little planet, Earth, was bare rock and water under the glare of brilliant sunlight. *Every drop of water in the sea and every pebble on the beach is perfectly adjusted to its environment and to the cosmos. For complete and undeviating unanimity of action characterizes the whole show. All the matter of the universe follows the universal custom of entropy.* Dissolution or death is what it is all about: it is the order of the day. Death is what is *done!* The very best matter I can assure you does it! It is the *Cosmic Way!* Why be different!

Now imagine one little amoeba floating about in that warm ocean. Is that little amoeba "adjusted to its environment?" It most certainly is not. *Webster's Dictionary* defines "to adjust" as "to free from differences or discrepancies; . . . to make correspondent or conformable; . . ." That microscopic bit of protoplasm is being a non-conformist. It is *striving* to *maintain its form* by moving about and surrounding nourishing particles and reproducing its form by cell division so that it will not die. But what is wrong with dying? Every clot of earth in the world was doing it. All those cosmic pace-setters, the suns that move in the best circles, were *relaxing.* Eventually they will become so relaxed that they will go all to pieces. That is what entropy is. And here is this microscopic amoeba being unadjusted to the unanimous, thoroughly tested, and workable *mores* of the universe.

After all, *why* should the little amoeba *strive?* What is it going to get out of its exertion? Nothing at all. Why should it struggle to keep its figure? It has no consciousness of its form to think it worth preserving. Of course as long as it keeps its form it will keep death at bay. But why should it want to keep death at bay? It does not even know it has life, and death would cause it no pain. Oh, but, people say, its purposive striving is going to bring about such marvellous evolutionary results in the next billion years! My dear reader! The problem with twentieth century politics is that the highly developed *homo sapiens* is so intent on grabbing what is advantageous for himself at the moment that he refuses to make the sacrifices that would improve the lot of his own great-grand-children. Do not tell me that the amoeba is purposively striving to benefit its descendants a billion years in the future.

The popular notion is that after evolution got started the evolutionary climb of organisms was due to chance mutations, and that those mutations survived that were the "fittest", i.e., those that adjusted the organism best to its environment and so gave it a slight edge over other organisms in the struggle for existence. But this cannot be a fully accurate explanation for evolution, if you mean by environment, environment in the large. Since evolution from the biological point of view is in the direction of more complicated physical organisms and organisms with a wider and more complicated range of reactivity, the direction of the whole is in the direction of unadjustment to the basic nature of the cosmos. For the basic nature of the cosmos is alignment with the principle of entropy.

Scientists should probably therefore account for evolution by saying that:— When chance mutations took place those mutants survived and propagated where the mutation enabled the organism to become more successfully unadjusted to its total environment while at the same time managing to keep alive in its immediate environment. This would certainly hold true for the lowest rungs of the evolutionary ladder. When we consider the higher forms of evolution, if we consider a species of antelope having a mutation that would give it slightly longer legs, we cannot say that the animal was better adjusted to its total immediate environment as far as getting its living was concerned, because it could get water and grass just as well with shorter legs. It would only be better adjusted to the environment in so far as its environment included the lion. But why should we look at life from the antelope's point of view. From the lion's point of view the pre-mutation adjustment was the really adequate one. Considering that the lion is part of the antelope's immediate environment, the mutation *is* a pro-survival adjustment on the part of the antelope as regards to the lion. But why should the antelope strive to survive? Why might it not just as well become lion-fodder? That certainly would be togetherness of a sort.

We get back to the question we asked about the amoeba. Why should the amoeba strive to maintain itself as an independent form unadjusted to its environment which is governed by entropy? The major part of the antelope's environment is also governed by entropy. With the antelope we can give a reason for striving, however, that we could not give with the amoeba. For the antelope has some consciousness and can experience pain. We can say that the antelope strives to survive in order to avoid the pain of being killed by the lion. But, we may ask, why is it that the experience of pain (which as subjective is not objectively studiable by science, only the physiological changes accompanying it being capable of objective study) is an experience that would accompany the antelope's being caught by the lion? The answer is that the experience of pain helps make the antelope avoid that situation, and so the experience of pain in the higher animals is one of the factors that makes their survival possible. Then we are back at the old question that we asked concerning the amoeba: why should a desire or inclination for survival exist in certain aggregates of matter, since this desire is unadjusted to the universe as a whole which in its over-all existence is relaxing into death?

To try to smuggle the late evolved human consciousness back into a naturalistic interpretation of evolution by positing a "purposive striving in all matter" is to fly in the face of the enormous amount of contrary evidence that is available to us to the effect that the over-all tendency of the matter of the universe is not purposive striving, which is a unifying activity, but is a relaxation which is a scattering chaos-directed activity. And no analysis into the mechanism of genetics can explain *why* a purposive striving should appear in a small fraction of nature. The charted activity of DNA particles

162

is not a purposive striving, it is the charted activity of DNA particles in more complicated and more subtly reactive aggregates.

Let us return in argument to that little amoeba moving about in the sunny water of the primeval sea in the midst of a total natural environment that was progressing slowly toward dissolution. Suppose that natural environment (which is all that science can deal with) is not the whole picture. Suppose there is another different coexistent environment. Suppose that quite literally "the Spirit of God was moving over the face of the waters" (Genesis 1:2). Then, howsoever matter got to the state of sufficient complication that characterizes the amoeba (or a more primitive virus, or a still more primitive protein molecule or whatever the first form of life was), it would have been in a state of sufficient complication so that it could make a teensy weensy more response to that other environment which is the Spirit of God than the rest of the creation could make. Even supposing a certain amount of chance in the formation of the simplest protein molecules—chance combined with the action of sunlight on chemicals in solution to form amino acids—nevertheless when this matter (which was originally thought up by the mind of God) *fell into forms of sufficient complication it was capable of responding somewhat to the presence of the Spirit of God, of whose thinking it elements were originally a cast-off product, and therefore for relation to whose mind all matter was characterized by a built-in affinity. The reason this is so is that the nature of the Creator is a many-faceted unity. All matter, even chaotic matter, reflects him somewhat, because all matter is a cast-off product of his thought. But because the unity of his nature is many-faceted, the more complicated the organization of a highly unified aggregate of matter, the more facets of his character it can reflect.*

If this is the case, then literally the "unconscious purpose striving" of the lowly amoeba would be an unconscious attempt to adjust to its environment, to that other environment which is completely out of the range of scientific investigation, i.e., the presence of the supernatural Spirit of God. And this progressive adjustment could be the clue to the whole upward trend of the evolutionary sequence. For this other environment to which a tiny fraction of the world was adjusting was Life itself, deathless and almighty Life. Therefore the unconscious struggle of the little amoeba to maintain its existence was a struggle in its tiny way to conform to

163

the Life that was its coexistent other environment. If one asks, "How could the presence of that supernatural Life assist the little amoeba in its struggle for existence?" the answer is simple, "We do not know." But neither do we know how the proximity of loving intelligent adults assists the unconscious or barely conscious infant to begin successfully its maturing into an adequate human being. But we know that this assistance occurs.

CHAPTER 14

in Response to Human Obedience
God Giving Clarification and Strength

Let us assume the many steps of the evolutionary process to have been taken and man to have arrived finally upon the scene. There may be a shadowy borderline between man and pre-man as we have seen that there was at the bottom of the scale from inorganic to preorganic to barely organic to the one-celled organism. But as organism progressed into greater complexity and wider range of reaction its range of responsiveness to the supernatural Spirit that was near it became greater. For practical purposes, when beings arrived at a degree of development at which they were consciously self-directing, with some sense of beauty, some conscious memory and foresight, some ability for abstract thought, and some ability to make moral choices and to love, there man had come into existence, created in the image of God. (Genesis 1:27) The potter had been nearly a billion years molding the clay (Genesis 2:7).

It is through the Hebrew people that the revelation has come to us that the steering characteristics within God's own nature are his righteousness and love. (Deuteronomy 10:12-22) And so through the Hebrews has also come the revelation that the human adjustment to himself that God demands of men is an adjustment that is beyond the capacity of the sub-human creation, namely an adjustment at the level of God's governing characteristics, righteousness and love. A man who adjusted to God at this level would in a sense be companionable to God himself. In the Old Testament one gets the impression especially in connection with the stories of Abraham and Moses, that these two men walked so faithfully with God that the interpersonal relationship was a friendship as precious to God as it was to the human partner.

Now we come to one of the most remarkable things about the Old Testament. There is a pervasive impression throughout it that when one makes the adjustment to God at the level of righteousness and love, what the Bible calls love and obedience to God, that this is the fear of the Lord and that it turns out to be the beginning of wisdom.

Behold, the fear of the Lord, that is wisdom;
and to depart from evil is understanding.

(Job 28:28)

But clarification of the understanding is not all that comes when one is in right relationship to God at the highest characteristics of righteousness and love. There comes also strength. The mind of God is not mere rationality, as the idealists make the mistake of believing, it is rationality-plus, and the plus includes God's tremendous creative power. As a consequence the appropriate pattern of adjustment to God along the lines of righteousness and love involved for the individual an accession of wisdom and of sustaining strength. Thus the Bible insists that "long life is in [wisdom's] right hand." (Proverbs 3:16) This is because the man who by his choices begins to reflect God's goodness, begins to reflect other characteristics of God as well, including a slightly closer approach to his wisdom and a slightly closer approach to his everlastingness. "With [God] are strength and wisdom." (Job 12:16) This idea of long life being associated with goodness the Old Testament reiterates in spite of what must have been the common knowledge of the many good individuals (as for example Jonathan, I Samuel 31:2) who died young.

The most famous single description in the Old Testament of God's sustaining strength is in the words of Isaiah of Babylon:

The Lord is the everlasting God
the Creator of the ends of the earth.

He does not faint or grow weary,
his understanding is unsearchable.

He gives power to the faint,
and to him who has no might he increases strength.

Even youths shall faint and be weary,
and young men shall fall exhausted;

but they who wait for the Lord shall renew their strength,
they shall mount up with wings like eagles,

they shall run and not be weary,
they shall walk and not faint. (Isaiah 40:28b-31)

But the theme is expressed many times in the Old Testament. (See I Chronicles 16:11; Nehemiah 8:10; Psalms 18:32; 21:1;

166

28:6-9; 29:11; 46:1; 59:17; 68:35; 84:5-7; 86:16; 89:14-17; 105:4; 118:13, 14; 138:3; Isaiah 12:2; 45:24; 49:5; Jeremiah 16:19; Micah 5:4; Habakkuk 3:19.)

In developing the thesis of this book I am following at this point a trail blazed by science. Scientists have taken the known rate of radioactive decay that can be experimentally determined in that little segment of existence to which they have direct access, namely the twentieth century, and, by the assumed analogy of past times to the present, project this knowledge backward to calculate the age of the earth. I am taking the greatest experimental knowledge of God in relation to human life that there is—namely as the account of it is found in the biblical record—and reading its description of the increased strength that comes to human beings in favorable relation to God, back into the account of what happens by way of increased strength to the lowliest organisms at the beginning of the evolutionary process as they adjusted toward life, which was the closest approach that they could make at their level to reflecting the characteristics of the Creator.

Of course this whole theory involves miracle throughout, for it involves the calculated influence of God, who is supernatural to the creation, upon the creation, whether the portion of the creation be a Psalmist or an amoeba. And the idea of a supernatural God *acting upon* the creation is one that the science-image has found hard to accept. But let us try to put the situation clearly again:—

The supernatural Spirit of God influencing the natural creation poses the same kind of theoretical problem for science as that posed by the subjective spirit of man bringing about changes in the location of large pieces of matter, as for example, my subjective desire to pick up my pen resulting in the moving of that object by means of the muscular equipment of my hand. "Oh, but that is different," your modern person usually says, "because when you thought you wanted to pick up the pen there were appropriate changes in the nerve cells of your brain, and these changes, by appropriately modifying the action of the motor nerves, control the muscles." But that dodges the whole point at issue. Because the vital question is, *what caused that particular nerve action that accompanied my conscious thought, "I want to pick up my pen"?* If my conscious thought, which is subjective and so is completely non-material, caused it, then you seem to have a contradiction of

167

the scientific assumption that no physical action takes place unless it follows appropriately from a previous physical action. In that case it looks as if you had miracle, a break in the physical sequences of material nature.

But if my conscious desire to pick up my pen only accompanied a physical change in my nerves, and the physical change in the nerves of my brain which sent the physical stimulation to the nerves controlling the muscles took place as a result of previous physical changes in my nerves which in turn took place as a result of previous physical changes in my nerves which took place as a result of physical influences that entered my body from the outside world by way of the sense organs, then consciousness has no part whatever to play in the action of the world. *It will be noticed that this would mean that the rise of the experience of pain in the evolutionary development would serve no useful function at all. For all the alerting signals that it gives as to what the body needs to avoid have already been completely given the organism in the previous half second by the body's electro-chemical neural activity. And the pain would serve no useful function whatever in impressing the thought of the danger upon the consciousness to assist it in regulating future action. For the consciousness is subjective and non-material, and according to this theory we have seen that the consciousness initiates no action, but its whole existence and function is merely an awareness of action that the body has already taken. Therefore all pain is unnecessary torture because as pain it is an experienced but inactive conscious state, not one of the electro-chemical states that direct all the actions of the body. Why should the subjective experience of pain, therefore, which would on a strictly scientific theory be useless in assisting the organism to survive, have steadily increased in intensity with the development of the higher species?*

Furthermore, if consciousness merely records action the body has already taken, it follows also that no one has any moral responsibility for his actions. For it would mean that all our bodies are really only mechanical robots. And each individual's consciousness is simply a lonely spectator that watches the world's elaborate puppet show from the vantage point of one particular robot. In that case life would be, as Macbeth said, "A tale told by an idiot, full of sound and fury, signifying nothing."

There has been a great deal of very fuzzy thinking about life and its meaning on the part of those who are speaking with a chief concern for the scientific viewpoint. And those who have the Christian viewpoint at heart should constantly needle those who advocate a philosophy based on scientific discoveries, because science, strictly speaking, has to confine its study to the measurable action of matter and/or energy; and therefore to construct a picture of existence out of the findings of science would be to give an account of existence leaving out all consciousness and all purpose, and all values including goodness and beauty. A particular scientist may know a great deal about consciousness and goodness and beauty and purpose, but if he does, he knows it just as the man-on-the-street knows it, he does not know it as a scientist. There is not the slightest *scientific* evidence that consciousness, goodness, beauty, and purpose exist at all. If the scientist really thinks they do exist, then he should be pushed in argument and made to admit that he actually acknowledges another authority besides science for giving him genuine knowledge about the nature of reality, and that practically speaking he does consider the evidence of this other authority to be as valid as scientific evidence. The reason that this admission on the part of scientists would have a salutary effect upon the thinking of the intelligently reading public is that it would help break the dominance of what I have called the "science-image" upon their thinking. If scientists object that my references to science are somewhat dated and that I am not fully abreast of modern discoveries in physics and astronomy and biology, the answer has to be that with scientific theories changing as rapidly as they do it is impossible for a specialist in another field, who has to be very much of a layman in the scientific field, to keep abreast of modern science or to be equipped at all to pass upon its validity in its genuine mathematical form. But the importance of the discoveries of science as reflected in applied science is constantly kept before the layman's notice, and his interest is constantly aroused in it. And general scientific knowledge, in high school and college courses and in popularized accounts in books and in magazine articles is the stuff out of which the educated layman, and that means your novelist, your theologian, your sociologist, your "guidance director" with a master's degree in psychology, your lawyer, your business man, and sometimes your philosopher constructs an integrated whole which we may call the "science image". Whether or not this popular "science image" is wholly accurate or not does not alter the fact that the image does have an almost universal existence in the minds of the educated laymen (laymen as to science), and that the influence of the image has seemed to make it an intellectual authority that cannot be questioned, according to whose picture of existence the basic claims of Christianity just cannot be true. Individually scientists are often very humble people. But this is a situation in which their publicizing their humility by making clear the limited area of existence with which science is competent to deal, namely the measurably objective, would have a very salutary effect. This book of necessity—because in science I am a layman—is really working with the relation of the "science image" to theology. Although of course I hope that my version of the "image" will be as accurately and intelligently done as possible.

There is another argument, not itself scientifically grounded, but one that springs to people's minds when the science-dominated picture of existence seems to them the valid one. This other argument is occasionally stated outright, but more often it is implied. The argument runs like this: Was not all this talk in the Bible about knowing the righteous-loving God just wishful thinking on the part of the Hebrew people? People who want very much to believe something often can make themselves believe it is true. We all have fantasies in which we are much more important people or much more fortunate people than we are in real life. But most of us know they are fantasies and we consciously "turn them off", so to speak, when we are thinking or dealing with the real world. The inability to handle efficiently the transition from fantasy to actual life is a well known neurotic symptom, and we consider people who cannot tell the difference between fact and fantasy in their thinking as mentally unbalanced. Is not that, some people ask, where the idea of God really came from, from fantasy mixed with a misplaced scientific attitude, the kind of belief that would make a primitive tribe believe that the medicine man made the sun rise by beating the tom-tom every morning? The medicine man had beaten the tom-tom and called upon the gods every morning, and in invariable sequence the sun always *had* risen, so it was assumed to be a matter of cause-and-effect.

The last type of argument I once heard elaborated in a very learned paper, given before a group of several hundred Bible professors. The speaker showed that primitive man needed rain for his crops, little lambs in his flocks, and power over his enemies. So he worshipped a Big-Man-Up-In-The-Sky asking for aid to get all these things. But after a while he did not get these benefits, and so he discovered that they came by natural means and that the Big-Man-Up-In-The-Sky could not give them to him, and therefore he stopped worshipping him. The conclusion was that religion would gradually die out in the West with the advance of science.

In the question period afterward one of the Bible professors got up and said, "The speaker's argument is not altogether clear to me. Would he please explain simply and clearly how the Hebrew religion just folded up and came to an end during the Babylonian captivity?" An audible smile went round the assembly and the speaker said nothing.

The idea of the religion of the Hebrews being just wishful fantasy-thinking is preposterous. The theme of almost all the great prophets of Israel was:— God will not accept any ceremonial substitutes for decent behaviour to your fellow man; he demands that you do the morally right thing by your fellow man, and you have not been doing it, and so he is going to punish you and punish you hard! This is not the kind of fantasy-thinking that human nature is prone to indulge in. Even if we admit that the prophets were very unusual people, we still have to account for the fact that their nation came to accept them as prophets of God, and to think their thoughts after them. This influence the prophets have had also eliminates the possibility that they were mentally unbalanced, for the test for insanity has to be a social one, namely whether or not the abnormal individual can get others to agree with him.

The strange thing is that not only has the Old Testament religion persisted for nearly four thousand years, being in fact one of the oldest of the great living religions of the world, but it has also had two daughter religions, Christianity and Islam. And the Jewish people themselves have always been brilliant and hard headed, and in the last hundred years alone have produced three intellectual giants who have changed the civilization of the twentieth century. They are Freud, Einstein, and Karl Marx. All that is good in Communism,

171

the idea that poor laborers should not be mistreated and that a society that does mistreat them is headed for disaster, is simply a secularized version of the teaching of the great Old Testament prophet Amos. So to that extent Communism also goes back to the Old Testament for its inspiration. The atheism of Communism, on the other hand, is derivable from the naturalistic tendencies of the increasingly pervasive theoretical scientism that has characterized ex-Christian European intellectualism. Whatever one thinks about the truth of the biblical teaching, one cannot write it off as "crackpot," because of the sheer amount of influence it has had in the world.

This being the case, the more one thinks about the history of Judaism and the claims of its religion, the stranger they seem from a purely worldly point of view. The Jewish prophets claimed that the gods of the other nations were idols, that their God was the only God and the one who made heaven and earth, and that their land and nation was God's chosen land and nation, and that through them God was going to bless the whole world (Genesis 12:2,3; Isaiah 2:2-4; 49:6; 56:6,7). Yet during the time of some of the greatest prophets, Isaiah of Jerusalem, Jeremiah, Ezekiel, and Isaiah of Babylon, the Hebrew kingdom was politically a poor tiny little domain, only about one third as large as the state of Vermont, and while the last of these four prophets was prophesying, it did not really exist as a kingdom at all, for its constituency were living as displaced persons in a foreign land.

And we can also rule out the idea that the Old Testament religion was fantasy-thinking in the sense of being an opiate for the people and compensating for hard times on earth by dreaming that
> There'll be pie
> By and by
> In the sky.

For it should be made clear that the Hebrew people up until almost the end of the Old Testament period did not believe in life after death. Any relation that they had to God they thought they had in this life only. (For the Old Testament picture of Sheol or the grave see Job 3:11-19; Psalms 6:5; 88:3-12; Ecclesiastes 9:10; Isaiah 14:12-20; 38:18. There are only two clear-cut statements of personal life after death in the Old Testament: Isaiah 26:19-21 and the very late but more explicit Daniel 12:2.)

Furthermore the writers of the Old Testament were candid realistic observers of life around them. There is nothing sentimental about their writings. In fact, there is a sharp vigorous austerity about them that makes them an acquired taste for Westerners. Much of the great Hebrew prophecy came at a time when the international political life was characterized by the more nerve racking phases of the cold war situation, and besides this, armies ravaging the land had been an intermittent normalcy throughout their thousand years of national history.

>The hands of the pitiful women
>have boiled their own children,

wrote the author of Lamentations, (4:10 ARV) describing with grim accuracy the cannibalism in the besieged Jerusalem in the weeks before its fall in 586 B.C. (Compare II Kings 6:24-30) The prophets complain also that the righteous man gets a raw deal in life at the hands of the wicked. (Psalms 11:2,3; 31:17,18; 34:21; 37:14; 54:3; Isaiah 5:22,23; Jeremiah 20:8,10,11; Amos 2:6; 5:10,12; Habakkuk 1:4; and see also Isaiah 1:23; 10:1,2; Jeremiah 5:27,28; Zechariah 7:8-11.) Not only is the whole book of Job an eloquent airing of the problem that the righteous do suffer in this life, but one suspects that the Old Testament's constant harping on the theme of all the misfortune sinners *are going* to get is backhanded testimony of the spiritual perplexity many besides Jeremiah felt (Jeremiah 12:1,2, and compare Psalm 94:3-7) because the wicked seemed to be having a comfortable time of it. If obvious misfortune at the social level invariably and immediately afflicted all evil doers there would have been no need for the prophets' constant warnings: the mere desire for self-preservation would have made the wickedly inclined abstain from evil deeds. The fact that men will take steps to avoid being caught in tidal waves, landslides, floods, and volcanic eruptions is no screening process as to their degree of moral integrity. It seems to have been the righteous rather than the wicked that were firmly convinced that sin brings punishment. Habakkuk stated the spiritual problem this raises when he questioned God saying:

>Why dost thou look on faithless men,
>and art silent when the wicked swallows up
>the man more righteous than he? (Habakkuk 1:13b)

And certainly other ancient Hebrew worthies besides the writer of

Ecclesiastes observed that God's world is so arranged that death makes no distinction between the righteous and the wicked. The writer of Ecclesiastes says quite frankly that "The wise man dies just like the fool! . . . There is a righteous man who perishes in his righteousness, and there is a wicked man who prolongs his life in his evil-doing. . . . For the fate of the sons of men and the fate of beasts is the same; as one dies, so dies the other. They all have the same breath, and man has no advantage over the beasts; for all is vanity. All go to one place; all are from the dust, and all turn to the dust again." (Ecclesiastes 2:16c; 7:15b; 3:19,20)

And yet in spite of the obvious validity of this appraisal of life, the Old Testament—which does not believe in life after death—is constantly asserting that God is righteous, that he demands righteousness of men, that the wicked will be punished, and that those who serve God in righteousness will be rewarded, and that those people who thus serve him, and those only, are secure and guarded and at peace! (Psalm 91) No wonder that to the worldly minded and the uninitiated in the twentieth century the Bible just does not seem to make sense in relation to modern life. The problem of the Bible "making sense" in the practical hurly-burly of the busy life in the world, is a problem that antedates the rise of science.

The only way one can fully make sense of the prophets' teaching is to conclude that they were really aware of another genuinely existing environment of men (namely God) that is other than and different from the practical world that we see around us. This living in a double environment I have speculated on with regard to the amoeba, but the most clear-cut instance of it is the life of St. Paul. Before his conversion to Christianity he was miserable and worried and insecure (Romans 7:9-24), and then Christ came to him and he became a Christian, and the erstwhile brilliant young rabbi with a successful career of scholarship ahead of him became the greatest of the Christian missionaries and his life became characterized by joy and security and permanent deep serenity. As part of this joyous and secure and serene life we know that Paul underwent many imprisonments (II Corinthians 11:23) besides the last four-year stretch recorded at the end of Acts. Also he was officially beaten eight times and he was stoned and left for dead once (II Corinthians 11:24,25; Acts 14:19,20). He survived four shipwrecks (II Corinthians 11:25; Acts 27). He successfully evaded seven attempts

174

to assassinate him (Acts 9:23-25,29-30; 14:5-6; 20:3; 21:31; 23:14-16; 25:2-3) and finally, according to well established Church tradition, he died a martyr's death. Certainly either Paul must have been completely mad or else he must genuinely have been, as he claimed, at home within two types of existence at once, this obvious universe around us, and the all-controlling Power that is supernatural to our universe. (II Corinthians 5:17; Colossians 2:20; 3:1-3) St. Paul's theology is an exposition of the joyous full attaining through Christ of that basic human situation which had haunted the mind of Israel, God's servant, from the first:—

Lord, thou hast been our dwelling place
in all generations. (Psalm 90:1)

The point that it is important to remember here is that the Bible is not a philosophy of life although the writings imply a philosophy. Or to put it the other way around, if the Bible's "findings" about God and man are true, then some philosophical ideas about the nature of man and total existence are false. The Bible gives an experimental account of life as some experts have actually lived it, and what they claim about God is the result of their personal experience of God's direction of their lives and their observance of the light this throws on life around them, correlated with their knowledge of the record of God's dealing with their ancestors. It is not strange that modern science grew up in the part of the world where the culture had been influenced by the Bible, for the knowledge obtained both in science and the Hebrew-Christian religion is experimental knowledge. As the physicist William G. Pollard points out in his book *Physicist and Christian*, physics is not really understood except by the people working experimentally within the group of physicists. And in the same way, he says, Christianity is not really understood except by those practicing Christianity experimentally within the Christian Group.

A basic difference between the scientific and the Hebrew-Christian method of getting experimental knowledge about the nature of existence lies in the "controlled experiment," which religion cannot use. In the controlled experiment scientists artifically set up situations which differ in one factor only. Any difference in the outcome can then be assumed to be connected with the variant factor. For example, if a single batch of tadpoles were divided among three tanks of water differing only in temperature, and a concomi-

175

tant variation was observed between the degree of heat of the water and the rate at which the tadpoles lost their tails, the inference would be that there was some cause-and-effect relationship between the two phenomena.

According to the Bible there is a place for science and religion and the social life of human relationships in the God-given scheme of things, for God intended men to have dominion over the earth and the lower animals (i.e., science, see Genesis 1:26,28), to be obedient to God who is above him (i.e., religion, see Genesis 3:1-3, 11), and to have loving companionship with other human beings who are his equals (i.e., human social life, see Genesis 2:18-22). Man cannot live in intellectual chaos. These three aspects of his life have to be harmoniously related in his thought because in the end our thinking controls our action. Therefore theology, the intellectual discipline whose task it is to formulate the relationship, is necessary. Many college educated Christians do not see this, and they consider theology unnecessary, naively claiming instead that the "simple religion" of loving the loving God who loves and cares for us, and loving and helping others because he wants us to, is sufficient. They do not realize that this simple "practical" statement really is a religious creed that involves large philosophical ideas that run counter to the current pagan secular philosophies of the twentieth century, as well as to much pagan interpretation of science.

But some scientists with equal naivete resent the implication of any antagonism to religion in their work, on the ground that they are not dealing with religion at all but are simply engrossed in investigating particular problems in the scientific field. They seem unaware that what they claim in their field on the basis of their own and other scientists' findings would, if correct, make it difficult for a person to believe that the claims made about Christ and the relation of God to man in Matthew, Mark, and Luke are literally true.

Nature is lower than man and God is higher. Man therefore cannot make up scientifically controlled experiments to learn about God. In this sense no "scientific" knowledge about God would ever be possible. Man's knowledge about God, therefore, has had to be built up, through the trial and error method of trying to allow God to control *him*. So if we want to know whether or not the biblical religion is true we must both read the Bible carefully to learn how

God especially guided the men of his chosen nation in the past— as a scientist starts his independent work on the basis of previous scientific investigation by others—and we must discover by experience how God guides us when we try to obey him by a life lived in line with the record of his previous guidance of others.

The difference between religious experience and the controlled experiments of science is a necessary one. One can see the inevitability of it in lesser matters: a man can prepare experiments that will test the degree of intelligence of a dog because man is more intelligent than a dog. But a dog cannot prepare experiments to subject a man to in order to learn something about the man's intelligence, for the dog as a dog does not have the higher human nature and so cannot comprehend the human intelligence. The only way dogs can begin to comprehend human nature and intelligence is by being "good dogs" and obeying their masters. Then by living close to their human masters their dog nature is enlarged and sometimes seems to be almost human, as if the individual dog were being pushed a little beyond his dogness in an upward direction on the evolutionary scale toward humanity. But this move upward does not take place by biological mutation, and it is not hereditary, and it is not forced upon the dog. Instead it comes about by a voluntary cooperation between the master and dog, the master contributing to the relationship by his association of concerned and responsible governing of the dog, and the dog responding by a loving obedience to his master.

This description of the dog getting to know the higher nature of his master bears some resemblance to the problem of the lower human nature of man getting to know the higher nature of God. In either case attempted obedience to the higher is the first requisite action on the part of the lower partner to the relationship. St. Paul says,

> For who among men knoweth the things of a man, save the spirit of the man which is in him? even so the things of God none knoweth, save the Spirit of God. But we received, not the spirit of the world, but the spirit which is from God; that we might know the things that were freely given to us of God. (I Corinthians 2:11,12. ARV.)

St. Paul is pointing out that human beings understand each other because of similarity. They have human nature in common. So

177

God's Spirit understands God because they both share the Divine nature. How then do we, who are human servants of God, understand God who is above us? God's Spirit, Paul says, who knows God, makes connection with our lives, and so we know somehow by association with God-knowing. Just how this takes place is not really explained. But then, it is a mystery, as is all teaching of the lower by the higher. We do not know how our association with our dogs eventually makes them seem to take on human traits. We just know that this occurs.

The claim that God gives clarification and strength to those who adjust obediently to him is a claim that involves miracle, but not a greater miracle than that of a man's conscious thought directing his own body. For if the mind is thought of as merely the conscious registering of action the body has already undertaken, mind serves no purpose, man has no moral responsibility, and *there is no explanation of why pain should have arisen and increased as organisms evolved. All pain would be functionless torture.*

CHAPTER 15

Western Culture's Greek Orientation
an Obstacle to Bible Reading

Intimacy with another human being is facilitated if there are shared common interests and experiences. So God can increase his intimacy with a man whose rereading of the Bible is constant and extensive. For the Bible is the source-book that shows us God's preferences and dislikes, and tells us how he influenced the Hebrew nation and revealed himself especially in Jesus Christ. As a scientist uses the findings of previous scientists as a guide to the undertaking of his own personal research, so the Christian uses the Bible to guide himself in undertaking his individual life-experiment in relation to God and his fellow man.

There are several reasons why modern people do not read the Bible extensively. One is embarrassment: the book's blunt exposé of human sinfulness can be disconcerting to those not genuinely seeking God. But there are other reasons as well. One is that if a person comes to the Bible initially with a genuine, if unhappy, skepticism as to the existence of the thundering Jehovah of the Old Testament who is also the heavenly Father of the New, he finds the difference in background civilization between ancient Israel and twentieth century America a good deal of an intellectual and emotional handicap.

There is another difficulty that is greater because very few people consciously identify it. Our Western civilization, in so far as it has Christian roots, is biblically based, but its biblical core is heavily embellished, even where it is not somewhat distorted, by selected elements from Greek philosophy, and by the impact of the classical Roman civilization, with its genius for law and administration. The influence of Greek and Roman thought-forms and civilization is almost entirely absent from the Old Testament, and only a little characterizes the thought of the New Testament. Furthermore, the Dead Sea Scrolls are showing us that even that little is largely accounted for by the cautious acclimatization of some Greek ideas

179

by the Jews during the intertestamental period. The New Testament, as well as the Old, is a distinctly Jewish book.

Now one of the great characteristics of Greek thought is its fondness for abstractions. For example, Jesus told men to *love and serve God,* which is specific and concrete. He did not tell men to *take an interest in religion,* which is an abstraction. But the Christian teachers of the early centuries, who often had been trained in philosophy before they became Christians, in trying to explain Christianity in terms other men who had been trained in philosophy could understand, fell into the habit of using the abstract way of talking that is typical of Greek thought. Besides this, after about fourteen hundred years of Christianity Europe rediscovered its classical heritage in the Renaissance period. So for a good four hundred years, even when men believed Christianity to be true, the educated man has been taught a double educational background, a Christian background and a classical background. What all this adds up to is this: There is a general impression widespread in university circles and in books their members write, that ideas are much more profound and impressive if they are expressed in abstract terms. Just because a large vocabulary is a very useful tool in expressing ideas exactly does not mean that a large number of words have to be abstractions and multisyllabled technical expressions. And yet almost all the people who read the books that are written by university professors have the impression that the really important books, the ones that are intellectually "weighty," are written in big abstract terms. People have picked up this impression unconsciously.

There is a curious relation of science to all this abstract type of argument and theorizing that the West has learned from the Greeks. The early scientists had much in common with the biblical way of looking at the world: both talked in terms of specific things rather than in abstractions. Early scientists in effect said, "If two substances combine to make a third substance, let us see if the third substance weighs exactly the same as the sum of the weights of the two substances of which it is composed." Or they said, "Let us look at this drop of pond water under a microscope, and make pictures and describe what we actually see there." For this reason, over the past centuries there has been a simple down-to-earth matter-of-fact quality about science that reminds me more of the biblical point of view than do the arguments of modern philosophers. But more recently a very curious shift has taken place. Science has become mathematically more complicated in its attempts to get an exact picture of the universe about us, and mathematics is par excellence the science of abstract relationships, and as such it greatly appealed long ago to the Greek mind, but not to the Hebrew mind. In fact, the universe as science now describes it is not like anything anyone ever saw or heard or touched or smelled or tasted. In their books for the laymen chemists and physicists show pictures of complicated models of what molecules look like, and then they explain that these pictures are just to help one's thinking, but that molecules do not really look like that, and that when a genuine scientist thinks of those molecules, he thinks of mathematical formulae instead of the models.

The result of all this is that not only does the philosophical conditioning of the educated Western world tend to make the college graduate think that abstract thinking is more important—more valid —than vivid specific thinking about human life, but the influence of modern science also has been in the direction of making the layman believe that communication in abstractions is more valid than simple everyday speech.

All these various factors contribute to making the establishing of the Bible-reading habit difficult, and one that it often takes sheer will-power to start. Also it is a socially lonely habit, not something that one's friends are doing and discussing. Even church-going does not help one much at this point. For most sermons are not examples of the minister weaving his own thought in and out among Bible passages in a fashion that is creatively practical in the modern situation. One of the reasons for this is that extensive and intensive personal Bible reading is not something most clergymen are themselves doing, for ministers, like their parishioners, are children of their generation. But the constant familiarity with the Bible in the receptive mood that can pause to enjoy such nonessential discoveries as the haunting desert twilight in the two great scenes in the marriage of Rebekah story, *is* essential if the Bible is really to assist in teaching a person matters of graver spiritual import.

A particular illustration of how far the educated inclination for big words and abstract thinking can warp a person's spiritual perception has come to my notice when on quite a few occasions I have heard clergymen in sermons on prayer make fun of adults who use the prayer, "Now I lay me down to sleep." But surely an educated and sophisticated adult who knows enough about psychology to know something about all the nasty things that go on in our subconscious minds could very well ask God to take charge while he slept, and so the petition, "I pray thee, Lord, my soul to keep," would be entirely appropriate. "If I should die before I wake, I pray thee, Lord, my soul to take." Certainly any educated person who is alive to the world situation in an atomic age must realize that a moment might unexpectedly come when he needed more adequate rescue than can be afforded by Civil Defense. "And this I ask for Jesus' sake." The creed of the World Council of Churches accepts "our Lord Jesus Christ as God and Saviour," and the prayer of the Church is always through Jesus Christ, the one mediator between men and God. Why, then, is not this little prayer appropriate for an educated adult to pray if he wants to?

The learned clergyman just has not thought the matter through. The real point is that he has the Ph.D. degree and he is very much impressed with the fact. All people who have Ph.D. degrees are. I have one myself, and I know. And so he just unconsciously assumes that a prayer in the language a four year old child can use and understand is somehow not as "spiritual" or "deep" or "earnest" or "valid," in short, that it does not impress God as much as a prayer would that was couched in really adult language. Of course he would see the absurdity of his point of view if he really analyzed it. The whole danger of this kind of assumption on the part of educated people about the importance of impressive language is that it is an unconscious assumption.

If one reads the Bible in order through it to be brought by God's Spirit close to God himself, how does one go about reading? It will help us if we begin with the lesser but allied problem of how one would go about initiating a crude but intelligent boor into the cultivated life of aesthetic appreciation. One would certainly not just have him take notes on lectures on musical counterpoint, poetical techniques, the art of the novel, and the development of European painting from Giotto to Goya. If one did give him these lectures they would be secondary. The thing that would be really important would be for him to have a prolonged time-exposure to great music, poetry, novels, and pictures. It is the great art itself that educates in the course of one's long association with it. But this kind of cultural education, the education of the human spirit, is not a thing that can be acquired overnight. It involves time and the unhurried maturing of the personality. Thus not only has the Christian religion largely gone by default from our great educational institutions, but the Liberal Arts have also suffered. We are a nation eager for "getting ahead" and obtaining quick and tangible results for expenditures of time and energy and money, and unfortunately in this regard the major sciences and other "-ologies" can show so much more immediately noticeable "results."

The method by which works of art train and cultivate the human spirit is a more complicated form of the previously discussed method by which, in the aesthetic appreciation of a beautiful natural object, there is set up a semi-interpersonal realtionship between the conscious spirit and the non-animate object of his contemplation. For in addition to this, where the beautiful object was directly created by a human mind, so that part of the man's total understanding of life itself went into the making of the poem or the painting or the novel or the music, there the aesthetic experience involves for the human spirit intercourse not only with beauty as beauty—and this as direct intercourse—but it also involves a kind of intercourse, at one remove, with the mind of the genius who created the work of art.

This same indirect rapprochement of spirit to spirit takes place when one is intimately open to the Bible's teaching for a long period of time, but here the matter is still further complicated. For here the reader's human spirit is not only in contact at one remove with the great human individuals who wrote the Bible or whose lives are described in it, but one is also in contact, at second remove, with the Spirit of God whose especial guidance of these men was part of his great plan. Furthermore, the Spirit of God, with the record of whose previous activity the Bible thus indirectly brings us into contact, is the still living very active powerful Spirit. God is still working to guide men to himself. And his task of keeping in communication with them is enormously facilitated when he can call their attention, by a changing selective emphasis upon general Bible teaching and upon specific Bible passages, to past evidences of his character and desires. This is precisely how Christ reassured his disciples on the last night of his earthly life that the Holy Spirit

183

would guide them when he was no longer with them in bodily form:

> If you love me, you will keep my commandments. And I will pray the Father, and he will give you another Counselor, to be with you forever, even the Spirit of truth, whom the world can not receive, because it neither sees him nor knows him; you know him, for he dwells with you, and will be in you. . . . These things I have spoken to you, while I am still with you. But the Counselor, the Holy Spirit, whom the Father will send in my name, he will teach you all things, *and bring to your remembrance all that I have said to you.* (John 14:15-17,25,26. Italics mine.)

To those who for a long time have tried to serve God, and whose long standing intimacy with the Bible makes entering into it give them the feeling of coming home, the Bible becomes the means of living fellowship with God, and their merely intellectual absorptive knowledge of its sayings, as they combine and recombine with a strange fluidness in one's stream of consciousness, steers a line of direction that in retrospect is seen to have been traced with more than one's own human ingenuity.

There are many individuals who have claimed that God has made himself and his guidance known to them by means of the Bible, whose intimacy with it is less long and less thorough than the one I have suggested, and without doubt they are correct. I simply have suggested what I believe to be God' normal means of personal guidance by means of Scripture. At least it is fair to say that no one who has not for many years tried to serve God, while at the same time practicing an absorptive knowledge through prolonged intimate association with the Bible's contents, has a right to deny that the Scripture serves as a personal meeting-place between a man and the living Spirit of God.

CHAPTER 16

The Theory of Evolution and Christian Theology

We must now take up the discussion of the evolutionary process, in some of its bearings on Christian theology. God had wanted to call into existence out of nothing a real creation, one that could increase in beauty and wisdom and goodness and love and so respond more and more to him, and reflect more and more of his qualities, so that he could finally joyously possess it as perfected and yet free in its companionable obedience to himself. And as our point of departure we go back to that first little amoeba, or whatever the animalcule was, in the waters of the primeval sea.

Without any consciousness at all, with as yet only the life of protoplasmic reactivity, it was existing in relation to two different environments, the tremendous dying nature of which it was a part, and the far more powerful Creator watching close to it.

The floods have lifted up, O Lord,
    the floods have lifted up their voice,
    the floods lift up their roaring.
Mightier than the thunders of many waters,
    mightier than the waves of the sea,
    the Lord on high is mighty! (Psalm 93:3,4)
The mountains saw thee, and writhed;
    the raging waters swept on;
the deep gave forth its voice,
    it lifted its hands on high. (Habakkuk 3:10)

The little amoeba had been formed partly perhaps by chance, partly through chemical reactions normal to the ancient state of the seas under the action of the sun's rays, and partly also because at the crucial moments when nature itself had moved into a sufficiently adequate concatenation of circumstances, God at a particular point deliberately "stacked the cards," and yet to a degree allowed for by nature's built-in freedom within the prescribed limits of its merely statistical regularity. If this was the case, even to the smallest degree, *there at that one point the sub-atomic action did not have*

185

its usual indeterminacy. It was forced by the conscious powerful will of the Creator.

This is a very important point, and one that I think Dr. Pollard, in his *Chance and Providence*, denies. By equating all sub-atomic indeterminacy with providential action, he makes providential action indiscriminate. But on my interpretation any novel configuration of motions would always be normal chance variation within statistical uniformity from the point of view of science, and might occasionally be the result of direct special action by God from the point of view of religion. For even if miracle actually occurred, the providential action from the scientific point of view would be thoroughly accounted for within the statistical regularities of science. From the point of view of science it does not make any difference whether that slightly unusual grouping of subatomic actions was, as normally, entirely by chance, or whether in this particular case it was not by chance but was deliberately forced by the will of the Creator, who, if he is righteous, *has* to be thought of as a supernatural, powerful, intelligent being. But from the Christian point of view this particular seemingly chance-grouping of motions, if it really is providential action, is not the chance-grouping according to which from the scientific point of view it can be classified, but is in this instance directly forced by the power and desire of God, the supernatural Creator acting miraculously at a specific point upon his creation in order to further his purposes.

We have so far a lifeless world, with the amoeba established as an organism in it. The question arises: how did life come to the amoeba? The answer is relatively simple. All the creation reflects the character of God to some extent, as the work of a skilled craftsman reflects the craftsman, because all matter had been thought into existence originally by God, together with its basic modes of action:

> The heavens declare the glory of God;
> And the firmament showeth his handiwork.
> (Psalm 19:1. ARV)

Now the unity of the character of God is a many faceted simplicity. Nature before the rise of organisms had been relatively simple, but not many faceted. Now, by whatever means the original organism came into existence, once it was in existence it was a unified bit of diverse matter with the highest degree of organization and the most

186

varied and subtle scope of reactivity of any aggregate of matter in the world, *and by the very fact of its high degree of organization and the subtle scope of its reactivity it reflected more facets of the Divine character (in its different earthly fashion) than any other aggregate of matter on earth. Now the Divine Nature is Life, unlimited, deathless, original Life. Therefore the organism, matter moving into a more faceted state, to that extent resembled increasingly its Creator, and so reflected more fully his Life. The shadowy reflection, more or less fully embodied in the physical medium, of the characteristics of God is what we know as life in this world, whether in the amoeba or man.*

Actually the only life in this world that any of us knows directly is our own life which we know subjectively. We attribute life to the amoeba only because there is a resemblance between its cell structure and the structure of the cells in our bodies, and because it moves about and reproduces its kind, and selectively incorporates material from its environment to maintain its form and activity, and discards any material that is no longer useful. Since in these regards it is "more like us" than are oceans and rocks we say that it is alive.

The explanation of "life" on this earth as being matter's increasingly complicated states being an increasingly full reflection in the most closely approximating earthly terms of the many facets of the character of God who is Life Himself (or Themselves, since as Christians we believe God to be Triune), *gives an answer to science for a problem for which science by itself can find no answer. It is the problem of why the general trend of evolution is in the double direction of the greater complexity and greater freedom of the organism. Science can chart in increasing detail this double trend, but it can not give an ultimate explanation of why it should have taken place.*

Science talks as if the evolution of life on this earth had been a developing series of forms from the "lower" to the "higher." And this use of these words is not in their original spatial sense, for man and the higher mammals in general are obviously lower in stature than the giant prehistoric lizards. The words "lower" and "higher," when referring to the evolutionary sequence of the rise of species, are value words. And the scientist has no scientific reason whatever for referring to any species as "higher" than another as to value. He bases his value judgment as to species on his crude everyday-life common sense, the same kind of common sense that an uneducated shepherd might have who would tell you that his fine faithful sheep dog seemed sometimes "almost as intelligent as a human being." And then, if you pressed the shepherd further he would admit that sheep often seemed like rather foolish animals, but even so they were gentle and trusting beasts, and certainly a good deal more companionable than turtles. But even a small turtle, he would admit, would be superior to shellfish for a pet.

If scientists spoke scientifically they would never refer to species as "higher" or "lower," only as species of greater or less complexity of organism and degree of reactivity. What science is able to talk about with authority is the difference in complexity and reactivity. Now what the biologists have noticed is that, by making cross references with the sciences of geology and paleontology, it is obvious that the less physiologically complicated forms existed first on earth, that the more complicated forms gradually came into existence over a period of millions of years, and that the most subtly reactive and physiologically complicated of organisms, that is, man, made his appearance latest in the long line of species. But why there should be any correlation between increased reactivity and organic complexity on the one hand, and the increase on the other hand of the conscious intelligence of the higher mammals and especially man over the other species—for this the scientist has no scientific explanation. This is because, strictly speaking, intelligence is conscious, and therefore subjective, and the relation of the subjective thinker to that which is objective is a mystery. Furthermore, the more scientific theory accounts for evolution in terms of chemistry and physics, and shows mutation to take place by occasional chance variation of single gene molecules, and conscious activity to be accompanied by electro-chemical activity in the nerve tissue, the more irrelevant consciousness becomes from the scientific point of view, for the better picture it makes of a completely unconscious evolution that could have arisen with the increasing complexity of arrangements of matter, an evolution that went all the way from the amoeba to the *homo robot*, including all the latter's twentieth century inventions and international entanglements, without consciousness ever having existed in the world.

On the other hand, the theory I have elaborated allows for the increased material complexity and reactivity to have proceeded exactly as science claims, and does not embarrass the scientific theory by saying that at a certain point God gave life as an added endowment to matter, nor does it say that at the upper end of the scale God suddenly added human spirit as some additional thing to the complicatedly naturally developed organism in order to produce man. If then human consciousness is not a suddenly given miraculous donation from God, breaking into the natural development at a particular point, what becomes of the Bible's claim that "God created man in his own image"? (Genesis 1:27)

On our theory there is a complicated explanation of how this genuinely took place:

(1) The matter of the world, while not consciousness, has a penchant toward consciousness and is amenable to consciousness, because it owes its entire existence to consciousness, having been created out of nothing by the powerfully conscious mind of God.

(2) The coming into existence of free conscious human beings was a purpose God had in mind before he made matter, and therefore the original matter of the creation was so made that it would be useful to this end. Therefore certain things that this matter did naturally, i.e., without any Divine interference, facilitated the formation of protoplasm.

(3) God had arranged, in the original creation of matter and the turning of it loose from himself into free independent existence, to have the merely statistical regularity of matter at the sub-atomic level, give him leeway for slightly but forcibly "pulling the strings" of matter's action whenever it suits his directing purpose to do so. Judaism and Christianity *have* to hold a belief that the supernatural God can interfere in the natural order at will, because the belief that God guides and strengthens men when they pray to him involves the belief in the supernatural God influencing at will man who is part of nature. And Christianity and Judaism both have to hold the belief that God is supernatural to nature, because they have to hold unswervingly to the belief that God is fully righteous and good, which he could not be if he were part of nature which contains unrighteousness and other evil.

(4) By chance configurations of matter and the chemical reactions that are part of matter's ordinary routines, plus perhaps a little strategic "wire pulling" of nature at the sub-atomic level, protoplasmic matter, organized into one-celled animalcules, became a standard arrangement for bits of matter within the world.

(5) When this or later any other arrangement of matter came about that was useful to God's long distance purposes, he "saw that it was good" (Genesis 1:12). Thus by appreciation, which is akin to the semi-interpersonal relationship between a conscious spirit and an unconscious object in aesthetic experience, he could assist those primitive organisms, or later organisms, all the way up the "evolutionary scale," to hold evolutionary advances once achieved, and to "strive" to repair, to its appropriate form, the organism when damaged, and to "strive" to prolong its individual form of its particular type of organism as long as possible against the forces of distintegration. And this assistance by appreciation in no way exerted force upon the organism, for appreciation does not exert force upon the appreciated, but influences it by lure, the Divine in this case acting in the capacity of the Unmoved Mover, rather than the Dominating Force.

(6) Since all the creation reflects to some extent the characteristics of the Creator, and since the simplicity of the Creator's being is a many faceted unity, the more complicated the organization of matter is, the more facets of the Creator's character it will, in its own way and under its own limitations, reflect. Thus one-celled animalcules reflected more facets of the Creator's character than did the other objects comprising the standard stuff of the universe. But the Creator is Life Himself, original, all powerful, undying Life. So to the extent to which matter formed more and more complicated physical organisms, the more it came to reflect the Life characteristic of the Creator. This is how what we call life came to be in this world, and how this life became increasingly more intense as the organisms in the evolutionary scale became more complicated. The life of the creature was never more than a pale reflection of the Life of the Creator, but the fact that it could be reflected at all in the creature is due to matter's owing its entire existence to having been previously formed out of nothing by the Mind of the Creator, and therefore to having within itself potential relatability to the Creator.

(7) But God's Being is not merely Life, it is conscious intelligent Life. Thus consciousness showed itself in the course of the increasing complexity that characterized the evolutionary development, and in the human species the reflection of the Divine characteristics had progressed to such a degree that there is a reflection of

self-consciousness, memory, forethought, and the rudiments even in primitive man of abstract thought.

(8) Furthermore, comparatively early in the evolutionary development sexual reproduction became the method of propagating the organism, and in some of the higher animals, but especially in man, the young require the affectionate care of the parents, thus forming the family, the beginning of social organization. This social organization added a non-biological complexity in the evolutionary development, and as the family proliferated it became the more complicated clan, which is the beginning of civilization. In the family affectionate loyalty appeared for the smooth running of that social "organism", and in the more complicated but less personally intimate clan form of social "organism" moral right and justice appeared which helped to guarantee the loyal consideration of the welfare of others, in a situation where the social relations were sufficiently distant so that spontaneous affection was insufficient to promote the needed assisting action. But in thus "naturally evolving" (from the secular point of view) man was, again, by increasing his complexity in social relations, increasing his "organic" complexity, albeit in a non-biological sense. This insight, that close social relationships can constitute an organic unity, making use of a slightly extended use of the word "organic", is hinted at not only by St. Paul (I Corinthians 12:12-27) but also in the second chapter of Genesis where it says that the man "cleaves to his wife, and they become one flesh." (Genesis 2:24). That this is true in a sense beyond that of both contributing to the physical organism of the offspring is clear from Adam's previous statement about woman, "This at last is bone of my bones and flesh of my flesh" (v. 23), which is said of Eve before the appearance of offspring, in her original social capacity of companionable helper (v. 18).

From the viewpoint of modern secularism, what Christians formerly used to call Natural (or basic Moral) Law is not something— as Christians used to believe—that God had miraculously *planted* in the human heart for man's guidance, but is something—according to secularism—that naturally "evolved" as man became more complex. For much modern thought, therefore, the Moral Law is an entirely man-made phenomenon, and the claim is therefore made that one cannot argue from the world-wide agreement as to basic moral principles to the existence of the Moral Lawgiver.

But in arguing against this secular interpretation the Christian can point out that if man *made up* the basic moral law in order to concoct agreeable social relationships, and if man's contriving was all that there was about it, he would then be able to make different *basic* moral principles and they would work just as well, if everyone agreed upon them. As a matter of fact this cannot be done. If four people sit down to play cards they can, if they want to, change the rules any way they please, and provided they are all agreed on what the new rules are they can have a perfectly good game. That is, they can make, for example, a game in which certain forms of lying and cheating are allowable. This is not true of such things as dishonesty and cheating in the basic rules of the game of life.

There is a complicated reason why the *basic* moral principles cannot be changed at will by man. According to the theory we are developing here, when the organism, man, arrived at a complexity at which it could reflect the intellectual characteristics of the Creator's nature, it did as a matter of fact reflect them. (I am thinking of man's knowledge of intellectual matters at this point, not of the fact that the mathematical exactness of the interrelation of the chemical elements and the motion of the stars in their courses has led some to suggest that whatever else God may be he must at least be the Great Mathematician.) The reason man began to be intellectual, i.e., to reflect God's intellectual characteristics, is because all matter has some penchant toward the divine Mind, and has a relatability to it because it was created by the divine Mind out of nothing, and therefore the divine Mind is its origin. And therefore all matter reflects somewhat the character of its origin. But since the unity of the character of God is a many faceted simplicity, the more complicated the organism becomes the more facets of the Divine character it reflects.

Now according to the biblical idea of God, God is not only intelligent, but his intelligent power is always under the direction of, according to the Old Testament, his loving-righteousness, and, according to the New Testament, his righteous-love. *But love and righteousness are social virtues*, not solitary powers as mere intellectual mathematical competence might be. If, therefore, the nature of God, which is unchanging, is always, and from before the

192

beginning of the creation, characterized by righteousness and love, then God himself must be a Being who can in some sense carry on the social relationship of righteous love *inter se*. The Christian doctrine of the Trinity, that God is Triune (Father, Son, and Holy Spirit), is not a useless bit of unnecessary, mystifying, theological jargon that the Church Fathers added to complicate unnecessarily the "simple" truth of the Christian Gospel. It is an essential doctrine if one asks *how* the Divine Nature could have social characteristics in the beginning, before there was any universe, when there was only God.

The Old Testament does not deal with this question at all. It does not discuss *how* God could be anything. It simply records in a practical manner the way the Hebrew people discovered that God acted toward them, toward the nation as a nation, to devout individuals who served him, and more especially, that is, with a more direct intimacy, to the minds of the prophets. There is, however, a curious suggestion of God's pre-creation "social life" in the first chapter of Genesis (v. 26): "Then God said, 'Let us make man in our image, after our likeness.'" The question is, to whom is God talking? Not to himself, for the Hebrew language is not accustomed to the editorial "we." The Church Fathers saw this passage as an evidence of the doctrine of the Trinity in the Old Testament—the Father, Son, and Holy Spirit having a conference! But although this might be a correct interpretation of what took place, it is certainly not what the writer of the passage understood to be the case, for none of the Old Testament writers believed the doctrine of the Trinity. What the writer thought was happening was that God was speaking to the heavenly host, that army of angelic beings who did God's bidding as earthly rulers have servants to obey them. Angels are not vividly described in the Bible. They efface themselves, and are simply mentioned in reference to the tasks they perform for God. But both the Old and the New Testaments assume their existence. However, the angels also are creations of God's, and if God's eternal characteristics include righteousness and love he must have had a social life *inter se* before the creation of angels.

So when man developed to the place where he was not merely intelligent physical organism but also had become part of a wider social unity—a social "organism" if one extends the meaning of that word—then human life had reached a complication at which it was possible to reflect the governing qualities of God's many faceted nature, his righteousness and his love.

Thus the development of ethical awareness in the human race appears to those who do not believe in God to be something wholly man-created and merely pragmatic when they look at the matter from the outside. This is because man does have social relationships and the basic moral principles can be observed to fit nicely with the well ordering of society. However, to those who already know the righteous God, the basic moral principles seem lines of direction of characteristics that exist in God. If it is only for those who already believe in the righteous God that the basic Moral Law points assuredly to the eternal Moral Lawgiver, while secularists can see other explanations for the rise of the basic moral principles in society, this raises the question of how the basic Moral Law can be used at all as an argument for the existence of the righteous God. The answer is that to the thoroughgoing secularist the basic moral principles may look merely pragmatic and man-made when *viewed from without,* as they are viewed in philosophic discussion and the writing of learned books. But if an individual secularist *made the all-out attempt to live by these basic moral principles* (that is, to follow them to their perfection, not to just what is currently considered a good ethical code) *he would no longer be viewing them from without.* He would have taken them into himself and allowed them a control over himself. When the time comes that allegiance to these principles demands worldly disadvantage to himself and estrangement from society, then the obligation to do right seems to come to him with an absolute authority that is beyond society, and so is evidential of the more than mundane roots of the ethical imperative.

In connection with the doctrine of the Trinity it may be parenthetically pointed out that it is not an accident that Christianity demands that those who set out to serve Christ and to draw near to God through Christ should become members of the Church. The idea of, "I can be just as good a Christian going off by myself without being a Church member" is not in keeping with the Christian idea of God. In a sense the one God is a loving society, and he enjoys a loving society so much that he is extending the loving society which is himself (or themselves) by the adoption of individuals who form a society which is not himself. Heaven will then be a community life for those who love God, and the Church on earth is the little outpost of the great heavenly community of the Church Triumphant. But this is parenthetical to our main argument.

(9) The question arises, in what sense can we really believe the Bible's claim that "God created man in his own image?" For the theory of evolution I have outlined allows for evolution from inanimate matter to the amoeba, to prehistoric man, to Einstein, without any break in the scale of development which science could notice if it were able to chart all the evolutionary steps—which today it certainly is not able to do. The question is, when was it that the two legged animals, our ancestors, became man, human beings in the biblical sense, created in the image of God?

The answer is that as soon as the species of two-legged animals arrived at the point in evolution at which they could make a few artifacts, and their minds had arrived at a state of consciousness that could be capable of memory, forethought, and a small degree of abstract thinking (and this involves having a language in which to communicate ideas) *together with the ability to have affection and appreciation of others* (appreciation is akin to aesthetic ability), *and the ability consciously to make moral decisions, then the species was human, and "made in the image of God." This is because it had reached a stage of development at which it could reflect the governing characteristics of the Deity.*

The reason why the theory of evolution so disturbed the Church when it was advanced a century ago was partly that it seemed to make the earth, and not God, produce man, and this took away the idea of man's human dignity as being specially created by God in God's image. Our theory here makes the dignity of man consist in the fact that God planned the evolutionary process originally, partly with a view to bringing man into existence, that he has guided the "upward" evolutionary trend with this in view, and has brought into existence a species of beings that can reflect the governing characteristics of his nature and so are potentially companionable to God himself. Man's dignity also lies in his preciousness to God, in the care God has taken to reveal himself and his will to men through the Hebrew people, and the personal pain which he undertook in bringing us "the redemption of the world

195

by our Lord Jesus Christ . . . the means of grace, and . . . the hope of glory."[1]

---

[1] If men are human beings because they reflect governing characteristics of God—intelligence, forethought, memory, creative power, moral and aesthetic awareness, love, etc.—can infants be considered human beings? For the status of the embryo or fetus see Exodus 21:22-25. Some at least of the little children whom Jesus blessed saying, "To such belongs the kingdom of God" (Mark 10:14,16), were infants (Luke 18:15). The humanity of the newborn can be accounted for by the human context of their birth, and as an anticipation of their later development of the human traits. It is instructive to note that Christianity has regularly believed that a baptized baby, dying when it was a week old, would go to heaven. But the pious Christian imagination has not pictured these little ones as continuing forever in bliss at the week-old stage of development. Imagination pictures these wee ones as grown up to at least the conscious maturity of an earthly three-year-old, at which mental age a child could in a small way reflect and consciously enjoy the society of Deity. The spiritual salvation of infants would be pointless if they were to continue forever with their consciousness developed only to the seven-day level.

CHAPTER 17

Why Evolution Was Necessary

If one asks why the billion year old evolutionary development was necessary for the creation of man, since this thesis which assumes that God is almighty would also have to assume that he could have created the fully developed whole show instantaneously if he had so desired, the answer, I think, has to do with the question of human freedom. For the sake of argument we can imagine the full creation as taking place instantaneously, and this world beginning its career exactly as it was on the evening after the Battle of Waterloo. At that moment of creation every person, costume, book, dish, house, plant, animal, etc., would exist exactly as they were on that particular early nineteenth century evening. It will be instructive to compare this state of creation with a motion picture film.

When the motion picture industry releases a picture, the situation when the story opens has not been created gradually. When we go to the premiere showing of the film, the scene opens with the commander of the fleet standing on the bridge of his battleship. From the point of view of the participants *within* the story, that moment is the moment of birth for the sea, the battleship, and the commander, in fact for the whole "world" of the picture. The commander lowers the glass that the discovers himself to be looking through, and gives the subordinate officer standing near him the order that will initiate smoothly the complicated fleet maneuver for which neither of them were previously trained either at sea or in the naval academy. And when the fleet returns to the naval base, the commander will go for the first time in his life to his "home," and there quite normally pick up the threads of previous nonexistent conversations with a wife and teenage children he had never seen before that hour.

Granted an all-powerful God, he could have started our world off that way if he had wanted to. After all, omnipotence is omnipotence. Our human situation would then very much resemble that of the hero of the motion picture, whom we found beginning life in mid-career on the bridge of a battleship, and later "continuing" conversational themes that were entirely new to him with a family he had met but a few moments before. And this picture hero will not bungle either his family relationships or the orders that he gives for fleet maneuvers. But the reason there will never be any error is that he has no freedom. Every word, act, and gesture has been "foreordained" by the motion picture industry down to the last detail. Every contributing circumstance in the environment has likewise been "foreordained" down to the last detail.

Now had God started a world going with a complex European and American civilization in full swing as it was, say, on the evening after the Battle of Waterloo, it likewise would have been a puppet civilization saying and acting automatically according to a carefully prepared script. Such a created "civilization," if it were not constantly manipulated by God, would fall apart from lack of inner resources. If you say that it could carry on if God put into all men's minds the ideas of what to do each next succeeding minute, you are really saying that the men would be puppets.

And actually some of this same problem arises if God really started the human race full grown, according to the Garden of Eden story. For the sake of illustrating this point we will take the first three chapters of Genesis together and overlook the fact that the first chapter was probably written several centuries after the second and third chapters.

Now if you will recall the account at the end of the second chapter, you will notice that the creation had been a going concern for only a very short time when God created woman. The Bible describes that event by saying that "the rib which the Lord God had taken from the man he made into a woman and brought her to the man. Then the man said, 'This at last is bone of my bones and flesh of my flesh'." (Genesis 2:22,23)

But accurately speaking, when the lovely lady was brought to Adam he might conceivably have said, " 'This at last is . . . flesh of my flesh.' " But he could not possibly have said, " 'This . . . is . . . bone of my bones'." For he knew nothing about bones. *Bones are on the inside* and he had never seen one. Knowledge that one has bones has to be acquired, and he had had as yet no chance to acquire it. For in that Paradisal situation all the animals were tame

(Genesis 2:18-20) and herbivorous (Genesis 1:30), and no death had yet occurred because no sin had occurred to allow death, the punishment for sin, to enter into the world (Genesis 3:17,19). Furthermore God had performed his surgical operation upon man under complete general anesthesia (Genesis 2:21), and the man did not see God's handiwork until the completed woman was brought to him (Genesis 2:22). The only way Adam could have made the "bone of my bones" remark would have been for God to have dictated it to him and for Adam to have dutifully recited it "for the record." But this ingenious explanation takes all the spontaneity out of the story, and also takes away from the impression that the story makes that man was created with some—and for more —responsible freedom.

If, on the other hand, God chose a method of creation that took billions of years to bring about the existing species of intelligent human beings, he apparently had a reason for doing it that way. The reason I believe lies in his desire to have freedom part of the creation. And scientists have of course noticed the increased freedom that organic life has over inorganic, and the increasing freedom that characterizes the ascending scale of evolutionary development. Even in the differences between individuals in the present human race, the greater the intelligence of a mind the greater its potentiality for intellectual freedom, although the potentiality is often not realized. And we call the general non-technical type of higher education "liberal" education because it liberates the mind by making it free of the knowledge of other civilizations and thinkers and languages. If man is intended to be in the image of God so that he can love God and eventually be companionable to God, then man must be free to love God, for love has to be freely given. If love has to be freely given in order to be love, then man must have the ability to refuse to give it, to "stand up" even his Creator. Furthermore, love in the Jewish-Christian sense is righteous-love, and man must make choices to do this and that, for love is active and must be shown in action, and this involves freedom to manipulate the material world in which he is placed. The need for ability to manipulate the physical world is also present if man is to reflect the creative power of the Creator by his own creativity. Man cannot create out of nothing, as God can. But if man inhabits a world in which there is powerful matter in motion he can express his creativeness by creating arrangements of the God-given matter. And technology and all the arts and crafts exhibit the results of this creativeness. Furthermore, if he is to resemble God, man has to have and use power. (Genesis 1:26,28) This has already been implied if man is to be righteous and creative. But the living God is the only source of power that there is either for man or the universe. If God makes the universe and constantly and intimately upholds its matter in existence by his power, so that it is really God's living power and not matter's power, then the power that men use is God, for the universe by itself would be powerless. This idea of man using God in any way I find spiritually revolting. But if God thinks up and casts free from himself into independent existence a universe, then that universe will have a store of power at its creation because of its origin in the mind of God. When cast free from God, however, it will have no fresh access of energy, but can only live by the slow dissipation of its original store, in accordance with *the second law of thermodynamics*. Evolution then, has to involve the harnessing of this "dying" power as it is released, to create small temporary centers of increasing power, quantitatively insignificant, but qualitatively more important than the fading suns.

Even if men assume that God is evolving life on the unseen planets of many stars besides our sun, there has heretofore been no theory, other than that of the simply exuberant creative power of the Almighty, lavishly disporting himself in the pleasure of the sheer exercise of his ability, to account for the frightening size of the cosmos as modern astronomy is describing it to us. The idea of man's importance has seemed absurd to many in view of the sheer size of the universe. But besides the wholesome humility engendered by the recognition of man's smallness compared to the lavish power of his Creator, plus the cautioning suggestion that our century has always tended to over-value sheer physical size at the expense of things that are unseen and eternal, the theory that this book is elaborating gives some added reason for the enormous size of the universe, if what God especially valued in it was his human experiment. For if he was to give freedom to man God had to "pull the strings" as little as possible. Thus he needed not only a great store of dying energy upon which his evolutionary experiment could draw, but he may have needed also millions of planets to allow the chance reshuffling of matter on a very few to bring about circumstances that would make it possible for him to initiate evolutionary development with the absolute minimum of outside interference from himself.

Furthermore, in order to have genuine freedom man needed to have the prestige of a long family line with strong independent "family backing" from the earthly side, and evolution gives him a family line a billion years old and with with fascinating collateral "poor relations." If we all traced our descent back to just one man we would be related to the whole human race. But now in their properly subordinate place, we do have some connection with monkeys and butterflys and walruses and orchids and oysters and brussels sprouts and lions and chipmunks and sheep and potatoes and hashish and sunflowers and eagles. They all belong to us in a far distant proptoplasmic relationship. God made the earth and saw that it was very good, and we on our own are of the earth earthy, a solidly respectable, if not pre-eminent, family line.

But we are intimately related to all earthly life in another way besides a common ancestry in those primeval unicellular forms. This other relationship consists in the constant borrowing and reborrowing that goes on of the limited amount of material suitable for protoplasmic use. Kipling did not know the half of it when in "L'Envoi" he wrote that he wanted to get away to sea from the city where "The twice-breathed airs blow damp." The air is not twice breathed but millions of times breathed. And all the oxygen of the fresh air of the sea that goes to form our red corpuscles has been in and out of countless creatures, helping to form sabre-tooth tigers and ferns and whales and barley and cave men and Asiatic war lords and olives and lepers and grass and grapes and Roman merchants and coconuts and mice and buttercups and cows and grass and Hebrew prophets and fig trees and pigs and palms and African bushmen and sweet potatoes and New York debutantes and elm trees and alley cats and poison ivy and members of the Gestapo and—temporarily—ourselves. Those who talk in idolatrous terms about "Mother Earth", the genuine rootage of our human family line in something most genuinely *not* God, are speaking of a half truth.

As every teacher knows, sometimes children of high-powered parents need to get away from home in order to develop into strong young men and women, for their unconsciously dominating elders have a smothering influence upon their younger, inexperienced personalities. Man, because of his frailty, needs to pass the three score years and ten of his childhood in a school less intimately charged with immediate Divine power than the ultimate environment of God's presence that God plans for him. Curious corroboration of this spiritual need of man for freedom to be an individual in the worldly sense comes from the rueful comment often made by spiritual directors: that God can often make more use for his own glory of a skillful headstrong man who is positively and actively bent on evil, if he can only be converted to God's service, than he can out of a person who is characterized by a lack of initiative and by tame, undiscriminating conformity, even if the life of the latter has stayed wholly within the major moral bounds.

CHAPTER 18

Why Darwinism Was A Problem for Christianity

Charles Darwin is said not specifically to have rejected the idea of God as original Creator, and not to have foreseen the vigor with which theologians would attack his evolutionary theory. But if man must live in the practical physical world and if reality is coherently interrelated, then there will be some areas of thought and action claimed by both science and religion.

Jesus had said, "Pray then like this: Our Father who art in heaven," (Matthew 6:9) implying that man was in a special position of sonship to the Creator of the universe. Darwinism claimed that man had evolved naturally (with no supernatural assistance mentioned) from very primitive types of organisms. Jesus said, "Blessed are the meek (*i.e.*, the gentle), for they shall inherit the earth. . . . Blessed are the merciful, for they shall obtain mercy. . . . Blessed are the peacemakers. . . ." (Matthew 5:5,7,9) Darwin's well documented thesis as to the origin of species suggested that the most valuable forms of life that had assisted evolution's upward climb to *homo sapiens* had been those best equipped to crowd out competitors and grab for themselves a major share of the limited food supply. The theory seemed to back up impressively what has always been the practical creed of the ruthlessly ambitious. Even without the backing of the Darwinian hypothesis the Church and the Old Testament prophets had always had their hands full fighting the practical preying upon the weak on the part of the strong. And as we have seen, in spite of the ancient prophets' constant declaration that God would punish the ruthless and the unjust, the prophets themselves sometimes complained to God that, practically speaking, the wicked did often seem to have a more comfortable time of it in this life.

The rain is raining all around,
    Upon the just and unjust fellows,
But chiefly on the just, because
    The unjust have the just's umbrellas.

                    (Quoted from memory.)

203

It is entirely probable that Darwin himself had no particular intention that his great books would be an embarrassment to Christianity, because, as a scientist, he was devoting himself to a search for truth *within* the area he had staked out for his investigations, rather than putting much thought on the relation of his theory to biblical teaching. However, neither Darwin nor any modern scientist has had a right to feel that the Church was being obtuse, or meddling in an intellectual matter that was none of its business, when it immediately put up an intellectual battle against the Darwinian hypothesis.

For Darwin's great books set forth a brilliant and well documented thesis which, if correct, at first blush seemed to imply that Jesus Christ did not know what he was talking about. Such a charge strikes adversely at the center of Christianity. There are forms of fitness in the struggle for survival that are not cruelly predatory, as for example the enormous number of eggs laid by fish which serves as a compensation for the large percentage of casualties among the unguarded young. But most people mentally pictured "the survival of the fittest" in terms of supremacy in the battle of tooth and claw. And we should not forget that the German philosopher Nietzsche was an impressionable teenager when Darwin's controversial *Origin of Species* first appeared in print. Nietzsche's philosophy of the dominating superman, which was later to bear such baleful fruits in Nazi ruthlessness of theory and practice, was a philosophy that appeared in the West in the latter decades of the nineteenth century, when the Darwinian theory was gaining widespread acceptance in intellectual circles.

I would be far from suggesting that Darwin, from the Christian point of view, did morally wrong when he published his famous theory. He was a conscientious and painstaking scholar working in the interests of the discovery of truth. Since all theology, science, and philosophy have to believe that reality is interrelated in order to make any thinking at all possible, if Christianity is true, it ought to be relatable to genuine discoveries of secular science. That there would be an intellectual fight between Darwinism and theology was both wholesome and inevitable.

The point I am concerned to make however, is that few educated people today seem aware that there was—and still is—a vital religious issue at stake in the whole Darwinian controversy. Part of the reason educated Christians do not see the vital issue is simply that it is no longer a novelty and so carries no shock. One can get used to almost anything simply by having it around. Another reason is that further biological research has shown that this theory is only a part of the total biological problem. Also the intellectual struggle the Darwinian theory caused led to some genuine insights that enriched our interpretation of Christianity. Christian thought is not necessarily finally a loser by the fact that the general Darwinian thesis has come to be almost universally accepted in educated circles.

Now contrary to the bland assumption of many that there is no longer any disharmony between Christian and scientific thought I want to point out that harmony in all matters is not easily attainable, and there are some possible areas of genuine conflict between Christianity and intelligent and very conscientious secular thought. Some new ideas in science are easier to accommodate than others into the over-all Christian view of existence. It used to be thought that the sun moved round the earth. Then it was discovered that the earth moved round the sun. This took considerable shifting of one's religious pictorial imagination, but the shift can be made. The pious imagination can think of God as creating the situation either one way or the other, and the question of which moves around which can be seen to be a question on the periphery of Christianity. It does not challenge Jesus Christ and the Sermon on the Mount.

But indirectly the Darwinian hypothesis, when it first broke upon the Christian mind, did seem to offer a theory that went directly counter to the teaching of Jesus Christ in the Sermon on the Mount, and to challenge two of the most central passages in that famous statement of his teaching, namely the Lord's Prayer and the Beatitudes. For in the Lord's Prayer Jesus tells men to address God as "Our Father, who art in heaven." Jesus wanted men to think of God as a father, with all the dignity for man that the filial relationship implies. But the doctrine of evolution turned man's attention from the dignity of his relation to God to his relation to the brutes. And man's rise to dominance seemed to have come about by chance and by practicing the very type of activity which Jesus deplored. For if it had happened that there had been chance variations that had given the leopards prehensile paws and vocal cords with a wide and subtle range of tone, then the dominant race on earth might have turned out to be not man, but *leopardus sapiens*.

In the Beatitudes Jesus gives the portrait of the citizen of the Kingdom, man as he was planned by God to be, the kind of character which, since it is a description of the type of person whose life was appropriately in accordance with the will of God, would be the type of character that would enjoy the final triumph. In the Beatitudes Jesus declared the peacemakers and the merciful to be blessed, and he declared that the meek would inherit the earth. This outline for appropriate human character seems directly contrary to the crude grabbing of *lebensraum* upon which the evolutionary theory at first glance seemed to put a premium.

There is another twentieth century problem for Christianity that is emotional rather than scientific. Most Christians are subtly bothered by the fact that they know many things of which Jesus was quite ignorant. He probably had no experience with indoor plumbing. Certainly he never rode in an auto or subway or airplane, and there were no outboard motors on the Sea of Galilee. He never ate a hot-dog or a peanut-butter sandwich, and he was probably not much over five feet tall. He had never been to college. He had never heard of baseball or football, and if he had he would have taken no interest in either. Greco-Roman sports and theaters were fashionable in Palestine in the first century among those who were hospitable to that foreign culture, but the illustrative figures of speech that Jesus used never referred to them. St. Paul was much more consciously aware of the sports of the Greek world. (I Corinthians 9:24,25; Philippians 3:14; II Timothy 4:7,8) Although most of these modern items are quite trivial, they do bulk large in our lives, and it is hard in imagination for sophisticated twentieth century Americans to think of a small town carpenter (who did not even own an electric lathe) as really an authority. For this man lived nineteen-hundred years ago and was woefully ignorant of so much of the impressive triviality that we take for granted. And yet Christianity's claim is that he not only is *an* authority, he is in fact *the* authority for the life of the whole world, the one person with the right—and the power—to demand obedience from all men.

But the devout imagination knows that these twentieth century surroundings are unimportant, and they do not hinder a spiritually earnest person very much in thinking of Christ as the authority for life.

A greater spiritual problem is raised for the devout Christian by the fact that had Jesus been asked, he probably would have said that the sun moves round the earth and not that the earth moves round the sun. Here is a more important fact about the God-planned creation, and one tends to think that if he were "the Son of the Blessed," (Mark 14:61,62) the Second Person of the Trinity incarnate, he really ought to have had "inside" knowledge on this subject. Lack of knowledge here would tend to raise a genuine question of his full divinity. But even here the problem is not insurmountable. For if the Deity was to experience life on human terms some temporary abdication of full divine knowledge and power would have been necessary. And the famous passage in Philippians (2:5-11) suggests that at the incarnation the divine Christ "emptied himself, taking the form of a servant, being born in the likeness of men."

We come in Darwinism, however, to a scientific theory which seemed at first basically at variance with the picture of the relation of man to God which is the central emphasis in Christ's teaching. For Darwinism seemed to make man a chance appearance upon earth with a relationship solely to the brutes, and to advocate a way of life that was in flat contradiction to Christ's ethical teaching, and so the authority of the "Lord Jesus Christ" whom the Christian Church believes to be "God and Saviour" is challenged at its center. If Christ is the Saviour, then he must be able to bring men into ultimate fortunate relation to God. If he was wide the mark both as to God's relation to men, and to the activities appropriate for men if they wished to participate in this ultimate fortunate relationship to God, then Jesus Christ simply did not know what he was talking about when he was talking on his specialty. We could trust our lives to a surgeon who was woefully ignorant about international politics. But I should hate very much to go under the knife of a surgeon who was badly ignorant of the major anatomical structure of the human body. If Jesus Christ was really ignorant on the subject of man's relationship to God and what this involved in the way of human action on earth, then he is no safe spiritual guide to follow and the whole Christian religion is a well meaning mistake.

What worries me personally as I look at my educated contemporaries is not so much the problem that Darwinism raised, and that is in fact raised by the whole new view of this world and the cosmos that the whole range of the sciences taken together has opened up to our attention. Life has always had its problems and the healthy individual makes an effort to deal with them. Most problems that most people deal with most of the time are what are usually called the practical problems of life. But there have always been intellectual problems as well, and it is the duty of the educated person to make thinking a habit of his life and to deal as well as he can steadily and constructively with intellectual problems. For the intellectually educated person to take for granted that the intellectual life involves continuous robust struggle is a good thing; just as it was a good thing for our pioneer ancestors to take for granted that conquering the wilderness in order to get their daily bread involved a life of continuous robust struggle. Service to God by the mind is demanded by Christ of all people, but it holds true especially for the college educated. This demand for the intellectual service of God is made in the two great commandments in which Christ summarized the teaching of the law and prophets. (Matthew 22:34-40) What worries me is the apparent widespread lack of consistent grappling with the religious problems raised by science and other forms of modern thought, undertaken without loss of the biblical perspective.

It bothers me as I talk with my highly educated church affiliated contemporaries that they seem to assume in a rather offhand way that for educated people there is no longer any problem of the relation of science to religion. If pressed a little further they will say glibly and knowingly that science deals with processes and not ultimate causes, and that science deals with facts but not values. The reader will recognize these as presuppositions that this present book uses constantly, but I hope thoughtfully, not as parroted clichés. Then these people say glibly, that after all religion and science are not contradictory, but that they deal with different areas of life. That science deals with the investigation of the physical world and religion deals with values and man's relation to God. After all, they say, the Bible is a religious book and does not claim divine inspiration for its science. Such Christians tend to adopt a condescending attitude towards those who in times past made fools of themselves in their attempt to fight Darwinism.

If these people knew that the difficulty was there, but were so deeply steeped in the teaching of the Bible and so warmly devoted

208

to the service of Christ that the living Saviour was very real to them on experiential grounds and they knew him and his continuing power and existence by their own lives whatever science might say one way or the other, I would not worry so much. But most of these people seem to me to have comparatively little first-hand knowledge of the Bible. And I am even more worried because these people seem completely unenthusiastic on the subject of the supremacy of Christ. It is a subject they seem to want to avoid. The bringing up in intellectual conversation of a reference to Philippians 2:9-11 evokes from them a well bred aura that a social gaucherie has been committed. I cannot help having the feeling that what these people have done—and are afraid to admit even to themselves —is to solve the practical relation between religion and science by making Christianity the beautiful decoration for their lives, and science the authority.

Therefore while I rejoice at the headway that has already been made in relating the scientific picture with basic Christian belief, I think that this work has been incompletely done. In spite of all protestations about the compatibility of the two disciplines I find that the question of the *authority* of Jesus Christ is one from which the majority of educated church members fight very shy. And this shyness is probably only partly due to sinful human nature's dislike of being ordered about—even by God himself. Many years ago a very young pupil put a very large problem in a nutshell when she said one day in class, "Miss King, what I want to know about the teachings of Jesus is this: Are we to take them as the way it would be *nice for us to run the world if we could,* or are we to take them as *the way God runs the universe?*" It is a question that most educated Christians, both laymen and Christian teachers and preachers, seem very anxious to avoid. And yet if Jesus of Nazareth was "the Christ, the Son of the Blessed," then his teaching must give us "inside information" relative to the over-all plans of the Creator of the universe insofar as those plans have a direct bearing on human life. To deny that Jesus Christ was able to do this is to think of him only as the best man who ever lived reaching up toward God, not also God Almighty reaching down to man.

Hence the importance of frankly reopening the question of the compatibility of the scientific image and Christian theory, and of frankly attempting to construct large scale hypotheses to see if one

209

can be found that will harmoniously relate the two without doing basic violence to either.

CHAPTER 19

Pain and Evolutionary Divine Guidance

The incorporation of the *second law of thermodynamics* into the theology of Creation, as we have seen, solves at one point a hitherto insoluble problem for theology, the problem of how, if there is only one God and he is wholly good, evil can come into existence. For in order to bring free, intelligent, powerful, creative beings into existence, which is a great good, he had to provide them for the sake of their free creativity with a source of power other than himself. As he is the only ultimate power, what he created would have by reflection a shadowy resemblance to his power. But even this shadowy resemblance would constantly diminish in created matter cast free from God and not sustained by him. The entropy or "dying" of the universe is itself a great good because it furnishes a source of power which is not God for utilization by the evolutionary process. But as a dissolution, entropy is a dying and so not a reflection of God's nature, but something contrary to God's nature. Thus God had arranged for the creation to bring a contrary-to-himself into existence, whose existence was at once planned by God but created not by God but by the freedom of the original matter God had created. And yet this opposite-to-God in its original form of mere physical entropy entailed no harm to anything that suffered harm and so was not in the beginning an evil.

As soon, however, as we focus our attention on any stage of appreciable advancement in the evolutionary process beyond that of the lowest forms of life, the deathward pull of the over-all entropy of the cosmos upon living organisms does raise the question of God's responsibility for evil.

It should be pointed out for clarity of definition that there are two kinds of evil: the evil of misfortune and the evil of sin. If a thief steals a man's wallet, the theft is the evil of sin on the part of the thief, the deprivation of his money and papers is the evil of misfortune on the part of the man robbed. The evil of sin is not misfortune to the thief, though it may entail misfortune later or immediately, and the evil of misfortune is not a sin for the man stolen from. For example, if the thief were later caught and jailed, his prison sentence would be the evil of misfortune and not the evil of sin, although in this case the misfortune would be the direct consequence of the sin, and in line with the Old Testament teaching that sin brings punishment. Furthermore, by stealing, which is a sin, the thief displeased God and so broke off his relation of friendship with God. The loss of a relation of friendship to God is the consequent evil of misfortune and not the evil of sin, although this particular misfortune never occurs to a person unless it is caused by sin in that person's life, and it is the consequence of sin although there is never any time-lag between the perpetration of the sin and this particular misfortune for the perpetrator. This consequent misfortune can occur even if the perpetrator is not immediately consciously aware of this particular misfortune he is undergoing. Just as a man could be said to suffer the misfortune of financial ruin in a stock market crash on a particular day, even if on that day he was deep in the Canadian woods on a hunting trip, and the news of the disaster only reached him some days later.

This theory of the evil of misfortune and sin underlies the whole biblical point of view, although on the basis of this theory Jesus clarified the Old Testament teaching that sin brings punishment. Job's comforters had argued that sin brings punishment, that Job was obviously suffering greatly, and therefore in the past he must have sinned greatly. This is strictly in line with the Old Testament belief that misfortune is the punishment for sin. Job's whole argument is the insistence that, contrary to this basic Hebrew assumption, although he was suffering almost beyond endurance, he yet had been a good man, obedient to God, and he had not sinned. The Book of Job states the problem clearly and leaves the argument at that point. The religious explanation of Job's suffering is not given. The clarification Jesus' teaching makes to the relation of sin and suffering is the explanation that, while one cannot necessarily argue from a person's present misfortune to his past sin, one can argue from a person's present sin to that person's future misfortune unless he repents. (Luke 13:1-5)[1]

---

[1] For an extended discussion of the part played by the unsynchronized moral tempos of the human life span and the outworking of evil into misfortune on a large social scale, see my book, *God's Boycott of Sin,* (New York: Fellowship Publications, 1947) especially pages 62-91.

Death is the final and greatest earthly evil of misfortune, not only in itself, as the final frustration of life, but also because the recognition of the final frustration works backward, casting the gloom of transiency and futility over all human achievements which likewise will eventually perish. Man needs to be saved from both sin and death, as all thoughtful people know. In Greek thought the emphasis is salvation from death. In the Old Testament the emphasis is almost exclusively on salvation from sin.

The Old Testament preoccupation with salvation from sin is the more remarkable in that for most of the Old Testament period there was no belief in life after death for the individual. (See *ante* page 172.) The confidence that sin or the disobedience of God is the great danger, and that if man just obeyed God, God's watchful interest in man's welfare would take care of the other basic problems, is one of the things that convinces me that the Hebrew people were in closer relationship to God than any other nation has ever been.

Hebrew thought accounted for the misfortune in the world as the penalty for mankind's disobedience to God. This is why the first three chapters of Genesis played an important part in Hebrew thought and have played a still more important part in Christian systematic theology. God as good created everything good according to this biblical explanation. Thorns, thistles, pain in childbirth, daily drudgery, enmity, sinful domination over others, and death itself are all accounted for as the consequence of human sin. (Genesis 3:14-19) Misfortune, according to Hebrew-Christian theory, as a divine punishment of sin and a discourager of future sin, can be a relative good in a situation already characterized by active disobedience to God, and so under these circumstances as a relative good can be approved of and utilized by God with no derogation to his moral perfection. In this sense Isaiah of Babylon can describe God as saying:

I am the Lord, and there is no other.
I form light and create darkness,
I make weal and create woe,
I am the Lord who do all these things.
(Isaiah 45:6c,7.)

The Hebrew answer to the evil of misfortune as coming into the world because of human sin is a brilliant answer to the question of how misfortune could enter a world created wholly good by the good God. Even lions and tigers had been herbivorous originally. (Genesis 1:30) But after the human race sinned by disobeying God (Genesis 3:11), then crime disrupted human interpersonal relationships (Genesis 4:8-10), and as the moral infection spread, society as a whole went to the bad (Genesis 6:5-8). Even the harmony of the lower species became infected as a result of man's sin. This explains why lions and tigers are now carnivorous!

I sympathize deeply with scientists when Christian teachers like myself talk about science as having brought a spiritually unsettling influence into Christian society. These earnest scientists feel that they are being slandered and discriminated against, when really they are decent hard working members of society investigating nature in the interests of truth. Really they have a right to feel very badly used. But the difficulty is that they almost always know so little about genuine Christian belief—this is not because they are scientists but because they are typical twentieth century Western men—that they have almost no idea what distressing problems for Christian thought their innocent little discoveries have caused!

For instance, how many of them realize that such an innocuous study as paleontology, which does not interfere with modern life at all, but contents itself with just digging up the skeletons in nature's ancient closet, has created a major problem for the question of the truth of Christianity. For paleontology discovered that the deeper down one goes in the layers of earth and sedimentary rock, the chronologically earlier the forms of life of which you find evidence. And then there was discovered, in layers antedating the appearance of the human race by millions of years, the skeletons of huge carnivorous lizards. But if they were carnivorous, they caused at least a few very unpleasant moments for the animals they killed and ate. George Gamow says of one of these dinosaurs:

> The most terrifying representative of this group of animals was the so-called *Tyrannosaurus rex*, a huge carnivorous animal up to 20 feet in height and measuring about 45 feet from the tip of its nose to the end of its tail. Compared to this "tyrannous king" of the Cretaceous period, the present king of beasts, His Majesty Lion, is as harmless as a kitten."[2]

---

[2] George Gamow, *Biography of the Earth;* New York: The Viking Press, Compass Books Edition, 1959, pp. 210, 211.

But the *Tyrannosaurus rex* lived about 70,000,000 years ago, millions of years before man appeared upon the earth, and this prehistoric monster perpetrated evil under the permission of God millions of years before man could bring evil into the world as a consequence of and a punishment for his sin. The evil of misfortune, then, has to be thought of as existing on this earth before sin. Sin, because it involves consciously intended moral wrong-doing, requires the intellectual ability to distinguish between moral right and wrong, and the lower animals do not have sufficient intelligence to be morally responsible. But this ancient creature, by leaping upon his enemies or his prospective dinners and tearing them to pieces, caused his victims pain, and pain is a misfortune, and a misfortune is an evil. This holds true even if the animals he killed had more sluggish and less highly developed nervous systems than the present higher mammals, so that the pain of their deaths would not be comparable in intensity to that of a modern fox caught in a steel trap, or of a soldier dying on the battlefield. We are brought back to the problem raised by Job: why is there suffering without previous sin?

Judaism and Christianity have both claimed that God is almighty and perfectly good. The problem of how God can be both is the most difficult intellectual problem for both religious groups. When Archibald MacLeish wrote his modern drama based on the story of the book of Job, he put the problem in a couplet that haunts the thought of the play:

> If God is God He is not good,
> If God is good He is not God.

For of course a good God who was all powerful would want everything that was alive to be happy, and in a state of the highest well being it could attain, and therefore he would not wish unnecessary pain. If then he is all powerful, why should he create a world in which there was pain? For there is obviously a great deal of pain in the world that is due to different species preying upon each other —millions of owls nightly killing millions of field-mice—as well as the pains due to accidents, sickness, and, in the human species in a civilized state, death from the deterioration of old age. The Old Testament had given an answer at once intelligent and deep. God had created everything good and happy. Then came man's freely committed sin of disobedience and so the harmony of man with

God was broken, and that harmony being broken, the harmony of man's control over the beasts was broken also, and cruelty entered into the relationship among the animals as it had previously entered into the human race that was supposed to have dominion over them.

And then came the science of paleontology with the news that animals had fought and preyed upon one another millions of years before man came into existence, and that therefore in the world the evil of misfortune precedes the existence of the evil of sin. That part then of the evil of misfortune which precedes the existence of man must be traced directly to the creation of the Creator, and this reopens the old question: is God, after all, perfectly good?

Many scientists will doubtless think that my argument has been unduly characterized by intellectual hair splitting, and that whether or not prehistoric animals suffered 70,000,000 years ago is not a vitally important question. But it is important, not because the dinosaurs are important for themselves, but for the possible light that they throw on the character of God. For according to Christian belief the God who made and had Eminent Domain over the universe in the time of the dinosaurs is the all powerful intelligent spiritual being who Jesus told his disciples is their Heavenly Father. (Matthew 5:43-48; 6:3-14,31-33; 7:9-12; Luke 15:11-32.) Jesus' characterization of the Ultimate Power is, as a matter of fact, accurate, or as a matter of fact, it is not accurate. This is the reason I may inadvertently seem to be so hard on scientists, who I know are so often deeply spiritual people, and many of whom do believe that there is a God.

But for Christians not just "*a God*" will do. The Christian God has to be as Jesus described him to be. For if Jesus did not know what he was talking about on that subject, then Christianity is a false religion. For to be a Christian is to take Jesus as the authority on the character of God and man's relationship to him. And my impression is that most scientists and those other educated people who have grown up under the shadow of the Science Image do not believe that Jesus' description of God as the Heavenly Father is, as a matter of fact, an accurate description of the really existing Power behind the universe. *If my judgment is at fault here, I hope that the great army of astronomers, physicists, chemists, biologists, psychiatrists, divinity school professors, and university presidents will crush*

me in print by rushing to put themselves on record by signed state-
ments in printed periodicals which say clearly that they as in-
dividuals do really believe that there is a God, and that they really
believe that he truly is of such a nature that Jesus' description of
him as the Heavenly Father, AS JESUS DESCRIBES HIM IN
THE SERMON ON THE MOUNT AND THE FIFTEENTH
CHAPTER OF LUKE IS A NOT INACCURATE DESCRIPTION.

Paleontology's discovery that prehistoric animals preyed upon each other, so that there was widespread incidence of the evil of misfortune in the world millions of years before the existence of the human race and its sin, creates an even more difficult problem for Christian belief than does the modern biological research and the accompanying evolutionary theory that thinks that it will eventually be seen that there is no line of demarcation in the evolutionary sequence between inanimate matter and the lowest animate forms, between the lowest animate forms and the one-celled animalcules, and between the one-celled animalcules and man. We must now see whether, by the theoretical use of the *second law of thermody-namics,* we can hold the Hebrew-Christian belief in God as *at once* all-powerful and all-good, even in view of paleontology's evidence that there was widespread incidence of the evil of misfortune in the world millions of years before human beings and their sin came upon the scene.

❖   ❖   ❖   ❖   ❖   ❖   ❖

It is only fair to admit that there is an old orthodox doctrine about evil that could be stretched to deal with *Tyrannosaurus rex.* That is the belief that before the creation of the world some of the angelic beings rebelled against God and became devils. So as soon as our earth was created it was subject to the malevolent attempts of these cosmic spirits to impede and bring disaster to God's fair purposes. This theory could account for pain and suffering and death on the part of the prehistoric animals. And with some re-course to the belief in the interference of these prior evil spirits it has been standard procedure in Christian doctrine to describe the serpent in the Garden of Eden as the already morally fallen devil who tempts Eve to sin.

Even so paleontology wrecked the old primitive Paradise-picture of Genesis, where God had made a perfect and perfectly happy

217

and secure setting for man, so that human beings had no excuse for disobeying him, and man entirely deserved the pain that overtook his life after the Fall. For the picture, as paleontology paints it for us, shows the human race from its beginning born into a world already bloody with the tooth and claw struggle of the brutes.

But my omitting to use the theory of the pre-fallen devils is partly that it is chiefly the Old Testament that gives us the picture of God the Creator, and so it is largely the Old Testament I am following. The Old Testament has almost no mention of the devil. There is a great deal of mention of Satan and his lesser devils in the teaching of Jesus, however, including the famous but enigmatic saying, "I saw Satan fall like lightning from heaven." (Luke 10:18) A scientist might reasonably retort that I am being unduly and inconsistently eclectic in my selection of Christ's teachings when I insist that scientists are not fully Christian if they refuse to accept the accuracy of Jesus' teachings about the Heavenly Father, while I proceed to ignore his teaching on the subject of the devil. "The Son of the Blessed," being the great expert on the subject of God's righteousness, can be reasonably supposed to be the authority on the subject of evil and its powers, human and superhuman.

I can only plead that this book only attempts to follow the overall trend of biblical teaching, and to make a picture of God's relation to man that will not be inconsistent with the Nicene and Chalcedon Creeds, and with the Trinitarian teaching of the Athanasian Creed. None of these creeds mention the devil. The subject is not *de fide* in any sense approaching the centrality of the doctrine of the Heavenly Father. But it should be further added, that, since this book makes entropy the God-opposing-force, the attempt has later to be made to parallel the New Testament conception of the devil with this law.

* * * * * * *

We will now discuss *the second law of thermodynamics* where its tendency gives rise to the evil of misfortune. For as soon as animals had arisen by the process of evolution that could in any sense as individual animals be considered happier or more content *not to die*, there the working of the over-all dissolution pattern of the universe would be felt as the evil of misfortune. The tooth and claw struggle for survival that was already established on this earth

218

when man appeared upon the scene had arisen in the struggle to get food to sustain life.

Religiously speaking we can, for practical purposes, say that death as regards vegetable life poses no very great religious difficulties. If a plant by dying can fertilize the soil to assist other plants to grow, or can be food for other animals, one can use as regards the plant's death the same argument that was used of the entropy of the cosmos, namely that its dissolution by being a source of power available for more important purposes, and at the same time not being a factor that caused inanimate nature any conscious discomfort, can be regarded as an opposite-to-God activity which at the same time is not an evil.

If our argument returns to the amoeba as an example of one-celled life, it can be noticed that men have pointed out that, since these animalcules reproduce by binary fission, protoplasm at this level is potentially immortal, any destruction of it being accidental —as when it is used by fish for food—but that the amoeba organism does not of itself die after a certain span of life. This means that an amoeba we watch today under a microscope in the laboratory is the same little bon vivant that we met millions of years ago at the beginning of life. When his favorite pastime of eating had induced obesity, he regained his slender figure by dividing himself neatly in two and continued his self-indulgent existence.

But if this little amoeba is to date deathless, of what has his immortality consisted? There is no continuity of memory to make his present self and his past self one, as there is a continuity of memory in a human being, so that St. Augustine could say of this mystery of continuity, "Lo! my infancy died long since, and I live." (*Confessions* I.vi.9.) And neither for the amoeba is there a material immortality, because, by its constant intake of nourishment and subsequent fission, the matter that composes the species has been wholly replaced many times. Its immortality then consists merely in the continuity of form and function, and form and function are neither of them material entities. Even with human beings the complete replacement several times during life of all the matter of the body by the body's processes of intake and discarding, means that even within the three score years and ten the living continuity of the individual is a continuity of form and function and conscious memory, none of which are themselves material, although all three are intimately associated with the material protoplasmic base. This fact of the organism's continuity even in this life being not primarily a physical identity, we shall have reason to return to later in the discussion of the possibility of human immortality.

But the fact of the continuity of even the primitive organisms being a continuity of form and function raises the question of which is primary, the form and function, or the physical organism. Certainly the code for the pattern of the form and function exists in the chromosomes before the organism develops. It was Prof. Sinnott's book, *The Biology of the Spirit*, that called my attention to the fact that any organism, if it were photographed with sufficiently speeded-up photography, would be seen to somewhat resemble a waterfall which, as one sees it from the side, maintains its distinctive shape, although the matter that composes it is constantly replaced.[3]

By the time the evolutionary development had reached *Tyrannosaurus rex*, about 70,000,000 years ago, we can assume that this animal's sluggish and misty consciousness experienced at least a vague sense of relief when it had succeeded in dealing a dangerous adversary a death blow or bite, and of consciously experiencing some diffuse sense of well being when it had had a full meal. This being the case, the animal's inability to obtain dinner we can assume was accompanied by feelings of some discomfort, and the wounds of battle we can assume were accompanied by some pain, and the impulse to prolong its life would be strong enough to make the beast exert all its strength in mortal combat, even at the cost of the pain of its wounds, in order to preserve life itself, i.e., to continue the form-in-function of that aggregate of matter of which the beast had as yet no self-consciousness, in the fully developed human sense.

We come back to the old question we have asked before: why should this creature feel pain when hungry or injured. The answer is to help it prolong its life by alerting it to dangerous situations that would threaten its life. These evils of misfortune, then, have a positive usefulness to the animal and therefore in the over-all scheme of its existence are a good. Therefore *if* the development of the species by the mutation process with the survival of the fittest made pain a tool useful to survival, we can think of God as allowing

---

[3] Edmund W. Sinnott, *The Biology of he Spirit*; New York: Viking Press, 1959, p. 117.

pain to be experienced because it would be a method of directing the animal toward the maintaining of its degree of reflection of the Divine by its vigorous organic life, and yet it would be a method of directing the animal that would allow it more freedom than is allowed to inanimate or barely animate matter. *Pain therefore has an aspect of revelation.*

For in tracing the course of evolution we are trying to trace the course of how a supernatural God could make men and reveal himself to them. In fact it was through the pre-Biblical revelation of God that they became men. Only it should be stated the other way around. As they came to reflect God's characteristics with sufficient well roundedness they became men. In retrospect they realized the existence of God. This follows the pattern of the Christian life as it is lived, in distinction from the Christian life as it is neatly written about. In the Christian life as it is creatively lived I have found that the "growing edge" is almost always a confused, somewhat muddled area of conscious existence, filled with confused and unassorted thoughts and sometimes emotions and giving me no clear picture of where I was going in life. I have also found that the line of direction of the past is increasingly useful in giving a confidence as to the general nature of the line of direction of the future. I have also found that even in the past decades when I had no consciousness of receiving any specific Divine guidance, that I was perfectly sure of some ways that I should not go, and that at any particular time I was quite confident that I was on the right path even though it was a path in a fog. Thus evolution "muddling up" to the great brutes and then finally "muddling up" to man, and then man having attained a point where he did as a matter of fact reflect more of the Divine characteristics, and then man reflecting intellectually on some of the Divine characteristics that he mirrored and finding this a clue to the nature of the God whom he mirrored, all this would seem to me not too unlike the personal religious life-experience of an individual man. Again, the great patterns seem to repeat themselves with variations, like a work of art.

The pain of the dinosaur would then be a divine method of guidance that was positively contributed by the creature, because pain is not a characteristic of God, and yet contributed by God negatively and without the slightest interference on his part with nature, since we have defined pain as the "feel" of the lessening of the animals' reflection of Divine characteristics, and we have defined first organic matter's life and then its first dim consciousness to consist of its increasing ability to reflect the Divine, due to its increased bodily complexity making possible matter's increased ability to reflect more facets of the many faceted unity of the character of God. That the sheer physical complexity of matter made the emergence of life possible is due to the fact that all matter is a product of the Divine mind and so has an affinity for it. We are assuming that God, while never absent from any point in his creation, acts supernaturally now at one point and now at another in the creation. In the course of creating a species he may interfere with subatomic action sufficiently to make a slight change in one gene molecule, and so change the "coding" for the form of the species very slightly in a way that he thinks advantageous. But the animal developing from that particular cell is no more interfered with than his parents had been, for like them he develops within nature according to nature's ways and in reaction to the environment around him.

CHAPTER 20

God's Educational Technique

There is still another standard pattern well known to human life to which there are parallels in the evolutionary process. It is the teacher-pupil relationship. The "teacher" figure is not an inappropriate one for God. For if Jesus is himself the perfect revelation of the heavenly Father, then the highest revelation of God that we have is as a teacher, for Jesus himself was a rabbi. I would suggest that in God's dealing with the world the basic teaching-pattern exists, whether what is being educated is *Tyrannosaurus rex* or a Hebrew prophet. All pupils take the standard pattern of this relationship for granted. The classroom pattern that it forms is the solid social order to which their adolescent lives are adjusted in a world in which they are told that everything is changing. Six points in the pattern may be noted:

(a) God is supernatural to the world, and therefore supernatural to the evolutionary process and not part of it. Teachers also remain a race apart, close to the young's "real", i.e., adolescent, world, but not of it. Once I said in class, "You girls mentally divide all adults into three groups, men, women, and teachers;" and they giggled and said, "Yes, how did you know?"

(b) The human teacher builds upon the past by transferring its accumulated knowledge to the pupil with the assistance of great books of earlier centuries. God builds upon the evolutionary past, as for example by incorporating the primitive attainment of propagation by cell division that characterizes the first animalcules into the production of large many-celled bodies of later organisms, which as total organisms follow a sexual method of reproduction.

(c) Both God and the teacher use pain in disciplining, to steer away from danger and to increase the strength and integration of the one taught. This takes place in many ways. In my own instructing one of the forms was the brief ten minute quiz at the beginning of the class hour, to make sure that the students had prepared their lessons. These quizzes were a nuisance to all concerned and a mild pain to the students, especially if they had neglected to study the night before. These little tests were not among the more creative aspects of teaching. They did, however, help to fence off the evil of ignorance and to hold a kind of structure for knowledge that could serve as a point of departure for the more creative intellectual advances. In a comparable way, when creatures with complicated organisms came into existence, God allowed the experience of pain to become a factor in their lives when the safety of the organism was endangered. In pain's earlier evolutionary uses its value was the negative one of stabilizing advances already made, by helping the animals to avoid danger.

(d) The direction toward freedom is another parallel. In the long evolutionary rise pain, as occurring in the animals, was a freedom-fostering technique. It fenced off a dangerous area of action or passivity, but without dictating what the animal's response would be. Within narrow limits the animal was free in the response it made to pain. Freedom in the classroom involves the coming into existence of an increasing ability to think independently of the current social and intellectual patter.

(e) To teach successfully the good teacher is an independent thinker himself. He cares for his students, knows more than his students, and he enjoys his students. All these characteristics can be paralleled, according to the theory of this book, by God's relationship with the world.

(f) The pupils' minds develop by contact with the more experienced, more learned mind and creative thinking of the teacher, and the emergence of thinking minds in the creation is a response of nature to the society of the Creator. There may even be a parallel between the origin of life on this planet and the fact that sometimes the accumulation of information a student has dutifully acquired suddenly goes into a many faceted unity in his mind, and the student "comes alive" intellectually.

CHAPTER 21

Pain As A Struggle Against A Lack

We have said earlier that science has no way of accounting for the rise of the experience of pain and its increasing intensity in the higher evolutionary species, that science could only account for the nerve action that is pain's physical accompaniment, and that it has no explanation to offer of why this physiological action would not be sufficient to do all the alerting of the body that is needed for the organism's safety, without having this neural action accompanied by the experience of pain. We have also suggested that theology could supply a reason although science could not.

But as yet we have no theological explanation of *how* pain came to exist, because we have accounted for the coming of life into the world by describing it as matter's increasing reflection of the characteristics of the Creator. But the Creator, as perfect, does not have pain as one of his own characteristics for the creation to reflect. Pain, then, has to be accounted for in terms of a contribution of part of the creation to the total of created existence. This is the same line of thinking that led us to realize that God, in order to have a free source of power other than himself, created power-packed matter, and its consequent "dying" or gradual release of its power is entropy, and a contribution to the total creation made freely by the universe.

Now the well-being of the creature, anything from a crystal to a man, consists in doing or conforming to the will of God. (With man of course, active, intelligent, righteous obedience is demanded. But we have not yet got anywhere near man on the ascent of the evolutionary scale.) Whatever pattern is the appropriate one for any form of existence is the pattern which, if held to, constitutes that "creature's" well being. Thus the appropriate form for a drop of water on a smooth surface is a shallow half dome, and the surface tension will hold it in its appropriate form. One can flatten the drop somewhat by mechanical pressure, but once the pressure is removed the drop will "strive" to regain its appropriate shape.

Professor Sinnott, whose specialty has been botany, thinks that all life is teleological and therefore that all life needs to be accounted for in terms of its goals. The genes in the chromosomes are thought to give the coded directions of the form the plant is to take, and the whole life of the plant is an attempt to attain this form by growth, to maintain it after it is attained, to repair it to its appropriate form when it is damaged, to reproduce the form by the production of offspring, and finally to maintain its own form as long as possible against the forces of dissolution.

When animal organisms become sufficiently complicated they reflect the Creator's life sufficiently so that they begin to reflect his characteristic of consciousness. When they thus have consciousness, their total conformity to their appropriate form—which *is* their well being—is accompanied by the feeling of well being, for his "Being" is "well being" at its highest. To fall away from that appropriate form would be to experience the conscious feeling of the lack of well being, which is felt as discomfort, and in more intense instances as pain. This idea of pain being lack of appropriate conformity to God is nothing new in Christian thought. Roman Catholicism defines the pain of hell as basically eternal estrangement from God, the source of all goodness, due to lack of the soul's willingness to attempt conformity to him.

This theory of pain will also cover the higher levels of what we call creative pain. The spiritual pain of the saint when he is striving to be better, and the spiritual pain of the musician trying to compose a musical masterpiece, are both complicated instances of progression within the human life to a closer reflection of the Divine. The lower animals cannot feel this kind of pain. A crocodile is a crocodile, and maintaining the crocodile form is its highest approximation to the blessedness of reflecting God's characteristics of life, activity, consciousness, and power. I am not of course suggesting that God *looks like* a crocodile! A God who could allow snowflakes freedom to create new and beautiful patterns out of material with which he had furnished them, could allow protoplasm to create its beautiful or odd forms to add the joy of variety to the creation to his own glory. But the crocodile, being heavily restricted to bodily ways of reflecting God's characteristics, could feel pain only at bodily lack of conformity, in such situations as when lack of food, bodily injury, or danger of death threatened the existence of the organism itself. In man alone is there a possibility of a great range of reflection of the Divine image, beginning with the minimum basic reflection that constitutes man as man, but with an enormous difference possible in the degree to which any one of God's governing characteristics of intelligence, beauty, righteousness, and love may be reflected.

The pain of the saint or the musician is that each has glimpsed a perfection attainable or partly attainable by the human range of abilities, higher than the attainment that at the time characterizes him. The saint has glimpsed more completely God's righteous-loving perfection and his pain is due to his not yet reflecting the characteristics he has glimpsed. By not yet attaining he has, so to speak, fallen short. The musician also in the creative mood has partially glimpsed, with the hearing of the mind, an aesthetic beauty of which his spirit has not yet attained full sight. In so far as he is aware of the beauty he has not fully glimpsed he also has in a sense the feeling of having fallen short of it, and therefore the desire for this elusive beauty is felt as a lack by his mind and so it is painful. When his mind fully hears the particular beauty that has been on the fringe of his consciousness and yet eluding him, his pain will be over, because his spirit will now adequately conform to this aspect of beauty, which is something he has added to the patterns of his reflection of the eternal Glory (as the snow-flake at its simpler level freely adds endless minute pattern variations to the standard pattern of its crystalline form). After he has fully heard in his mind the music he has begun to hear, the struggle will be over. All he will have to do is to write it down so that others, through the medium of the musical instrument, can hear it also.

If this theory of the origin and basic nature of pain is correct it would account also for three well known experiences of the cessation of pain. At the physical level the body in sustaining lethal injury or sickness is in pain. Pain is an indication of the body's lack of its attaining its appropriate image and its struggle to maintain the image. When the body's struggle becomes hopeless there often occurs a more or less comatose condition just before death.

At the spiritual level the theory would account for two cessations of spiritual pain that are curiously similar and yet at the opposite poles of religious experience. I refer to the spiritual likeness and yet dissimilarity of shamelessness and humility.

In shamelessness a standard of excellence has originally been known and at least approximated. Then there is a realization of transgression of this standard with the spiritual pain which originates in a recognized lack of conformity to the Good. If the predominant desire of the person is self, irrespective of the Good, he will attempt a somewhat lower pattern of excellence to conform to the lesser approximation of the Good that he now embodies. As long as he can keep from noticing the higher standard his spirit will experience some comfort of successful maintaining of an integrated pattern. He feels that his self is holding on to self and avoiding his self's dissolution. It is a warding off of "dying". (Compare Galatians 2:20; Luke 17:33)

There has been a great deal of educational talk at the present time about young people needing to be accepted by their "peer group" in order to have the feeling of emotional security, and much is excused individual young people if they do not live up to the older, accepted standards of right and wrong, because it is said that their urgent need to be accepted by their "peer group" is so strong. This is one of those baleful half-truths, and the fact that adults unquestioningly assume its validity is an indication of how far the older generation is drifting from its Christian moorings, and how reprehensively inadequate is the informal training the older generation has given the younger. The true part of the half-truth is that a person achieves personality only in relationship to other persons. As we have seen, even God, by the very nature of his governing characteristic of righteous-love, has to be in some sense a community, righteously loving *inter se*. So a young person, who has no friends his own age with whom he can carry on community life with some of the equality of interchange of friendship, suffers a great deprivation. The untrue part of this point of view is that it neglects to realize that the human person's nature also craves and needs acceptance by persons higher or better than his peer group. The crude expression of this in "status seeking" in its popular forms or in any form implies in part the craving for the two kinds of acceptance. Where the interrelated friendships of a group are within and subordinated to the desire of each of the members to serve God, there the friendships at the human level minister to both kinds of desires. As each accepts the other there is the "acceptance of the peer group." But inasmuch as each is constantly trying to embody progressively more and more fully the reflection of the Divine, as each strives to adjust to the other he is also pleasingly constrained toward what is higher than his present standard. But where the craving of the members of a group is merely for "group acceptance" or "acceptance by one's peers", "togetherness" tends to be purchased at the expense of progressive lowering of standard.

The person who has done wrong and fallen from the standard he knows he should have followed rightly experiences shame which is a painful feeling of deserved exclusion from the good, for good is of God. If as a result he so centers his attention on himself and his own status that he is uninterested in the "status" of the Good, then he will desire that the idea of his own unacceptability be immediately erased at all costs, and he will seek the companionship of those whose standards are low enough so that they are now his "peers" in his unmodified lower state. A certain amount of the security of community relationship can be gained by him in this way. But if this is the constant strategy of a life for meeting this kind of situation, then a certain kind of freedom from this type of spiritual pain can be attained, but only at the cost of progressively anesthetizing the craving for conformity to the Highest.

On the other hand, if a person has done wrong and feels shame because he has fallen lower than the standard of the good he feels he should follow, if his love is sufficiently set on the Good, he will continue to concentrate his attention and stake his happiness upon the Good. Thus he will be willing to take a lowered position with his "good" friends provided he can still love and have some relation with their goodness.

In relation to God the humble person will still love God and still be glad that God is good, even if it is to the disparagement of himself in his present state. He will still desire to conform to God, but he will be so taken up with his gladness that God is God and God is good that there will be little or no time or energy left for the experience of shame or embarrassment—people being so constituted that they are limited in the number of things upon which they can concentrate simultaneously. This forgetting to worry about one's own status because of one's adoration of God and present desire to be re-conformed to his will is humility.

Thus the dilemma of the spiritual pain caused by the discovery of one's lack of conformity to the Divine can be done away either by giving up loving that aspect of the Divine characteristics to which one has not conformed, or by giving up one's self in order to keep the association with the Divine by continuing at all costs to love the Divine. Complete humility like complete shamelessness would be without pain. It follows, curiously enough, that embarrassment would be an emotion that neither the devil nor Jesus in his own right (except perhaps in Jesus' case through his sympathetic spiritual empathy with other people) could ever experience. The devil could not know embarrassment because by definition he had denied all lordship of the Good. And Jesus could not know it because he was completely devoted to God.

It should be noted that the theory of this book presents an unbroken *religious* view of God's relation to the creation, from inanimate matter through man's redemption. The Divine Teacher of the universe is described as having one consistent method of teaching, consistent with his own perfect nature, which he applies to the inanimate matter of the snowflake and to *Tyrannosaurus rex* and to man. If that great saurian were, in a future state, granted a heightened intelligence and the Beatific Vision, he would then recognize the Divine and his ways, not as something utterly alien to himself, but as "home", as something he had unconsciously been in contact with when he lumbered about in the Cretaceous period, 70,000,000 years ago.

For beginning with the snowflake we showed that God, in his aspect as Unmoved Mover, assisted nature even at the lowest levels toward an interpersonal relationship to himself, by appreciating whatever the creature—in this case the snowflake—had unconsciously done toward adding beautiful or interesting pattern to the creation by means of its leeway of God given freedom, within the basic stuff and under the basic rules God had arranged for the created cosmos. And we also said that in the aesthetic experience one surrenders one's self in undemanding receptivity to the beautiful object, and one's undemanding receptivity becomes the channel through which the inanimate object is enabled to give one more and more of its beauty. Thus the aesthetic experience sets up a semi-interpersonal relationship between a person and an object that is non-personal.

The human strategy of humility as a means of dealing with the experience of the shame that follows wrongdoing is the repetition of the aesthetic pattern of relationship at a level higher than the aesthetic. For the transgressor avoids shamelessness as a way out of his spiritual discomfort by his desire to love or "appreciate" God or the Good that is beyond him. Love and appreciation are closely intertwined in fully interpersonal relationships. And the appreciation in love is like the aesthetic appreciation, the difference in quality between the two lying more in the nature of that which is appreciated than in the activity of the appreciator. With the unconscious snowflake we described God as doing the appreciating. But man is a developed spiritual being capable of reflecting facets of God's character that include the appreciative power. *Thus the contrite sinner is willing to admit his sin and its lack of conformity to God, because he would rather renounce his own status than renounce the privilege of appreciating the Divine.* But his undemanding receptive appreciation of the Divine is the channel through which the Divine, i.e., God, is able to give himself to the man and thus reestablish, by free individual initiative on God's part, that Divine-human interpersonal relationship which was broken off by the man's sin. The insight into this basic structure of the fully interpersonal relationship between God and man is deeply embedded in Jesus' insistence that the two great commands are to *love* God and *love* your neighbor, and it is deeply embedded in Paul's insistence on justification through faith as an interpretation of Jesus' emphasis.

Both Jesus and Paul recognized the importance of the moral law as a revelation of the "structural" quality in God's character at the personal-interpersonal level. For both Jesus and Paul knowledge and approval of the standard of basic moral righteousness constituted a kind of relationship between God and man, an area of shared important knowledge and interest, so to speak. But both Jesus and Paul fought legalism as the ultimate demand of God and as the ultimate human religious strategy, because when legalism is made supreme, it makes it impossible for man to come into his fullest possible relationship to God, and to fulfill the reflection of God by reflecting righteous love, the ultimate governing characteristic of the many faceted unity of the Divine nature.

Thus our definition of pain as the conscious state that corre-

sponds to lack of conformity to the Divine in the degree appropriate to one's immediate level of existence, would hold as an explanation of pain all the way from the prehistoric animals to the highest spiritual reaches of the life of man.

If this definition is correct it should cover even the life of Jesus of Nazareth, whom we believe to be the sinless Son of God and who also suffered. By incarnation Christ became the fusion of the two types of reality, created and uncreated. Like *Tyrannosaurus rex* he had a protoplasmic body. And living protoplasmic bodies—at the merely sentient level—are a reflection at not the highest level of characteristics of God. Therefore an injury done to Christ's physical body or the approaching death of his body was at that level a lessening of his body's attainment of the form that was *its* closest approximation to a reflection of the characteristics of the Creator, and so could be felt by Jesus as physical pain. That this loss of the body's perfection was endured in order that he might fulfill obedience to the highest characteristic of the Father, righteous-love, underscores rather than diminishes Jesus' total perfection. On the question of whether he could feel spiritual pain we have pointed out that in his own right his spirit was always in complete conformity with the Father's and so would feel no spiritually caused pain, although in his own right he could feel intellectual pain and dread at the anticipation of his body's pain. And by the empathy of his spiritual sympathy and love for others he could suffer spiritually to an intense degree vicariously, because of others' lack of spiritual conformity to God. The cry of dereliction on the cross is the most problematic instance of all to fit into our definition. But since Christ had taken on full humanity, and since physical weakness can impair the power of the intellect, it may be that the combination of physical pain and vicarious spiritual suffering, heightened the influence upon his mind that came from his body's almost complete exhaustion, and clouded for a few minutes his intellectual awareness of God's actual nearness. If this were the case, then, as the experience of pain at the physical level was a lack of the body's ability to fulfill the appropriate organism form, so the temporary clouding of the mind would indicate at the human level the temporary lack of ability to fulfill the intellect's function perfectly. Since this deprivation of intellectual insight was undergone in obedience to service to God's highest characteristic of righteous-love, it in no way derogates from his total perfection. This involves the theory that the divine Christ made a full surrender of himself to the Father in order to bring man back to God. The last surrender, before the final surrender to death itself, was the surrender of the governing power of the intellect. Only the complete conformity of his surrendered will, throughout his life fully surrendered to the Father in righteous-love, man's highest possible characteristic, held completely true to conformity with the Creator's governing characteristic of righteous-love, and so accomplished the long planned salvation of the world.

CHAPTER 22
Pain, Sin As *Chata*, and Martyrdom

We must now return to the question of how far there is harmony between the biblical and the evolutionary theory, according to which pain entered the world millions of years before man's sin could occur. For man's sin, according to Genesis, brought about the first introduction of disaster and pain, as retribution for sin, into God's otherwise fair creation. In our basic argument we have only progressed as far as *Tyrannosaurus rex*, and so sin in the strict sense of conscious disobedience to God is as yet impossible. And yet we have accounted for pain in the animals as the conscious state that went with their organism's lack of conformity to the pattern appropriate to it, which was the fullest extent to which it was able to reflect some facets of the many-faceted unity of the character of God.

Now curiously enough the most common Hebrew word meaning "to sin" or "to cause to sin" is some form of *chata*.[1] And it means also "to err" or "to miss the mark." In other words, the use of the word "backsliding" for sin by Hosea but especially by Jeremiah, which we have already tied in as an entropy at the moral level that repeats the pattern of entropy at the material level, is not unrelated in spiritual implication to *chata*, the standard word for sin throughout the Old Testament.

"The idea of sin is the converse of the idea of God." God is strength and his whole action tends only to give strength and life; sin, on the contrary, which assumes the aspect of a hostile force only in the latest Old Testament texts, always produces a state of weakness which is a forerunner of death. . . . If the Yahwist connected sin with the serpent, it is not only because this animal symbolized cunning and mystery more than others: in Semitic religions, the serpent was associated with the representations of chaos and death; hostile to life, it carries within it the poison which kills. . . . There is no contradiction between

---

[1] Transliteration accepted by *Young's Analytical Concordance*.

the external origin of sin and its seat within a man's body. The serpent and man are both taken from the earth, from the 'ada-mah, and though the serpent has a closer link with sin, man also bears within himself, by reason of his creation from the earth, an innate and permanent propensity towards evil. . . . The prophet Jeremiah often speaks of the evil inclinations of the heart (16:12; 17:9; 18:12) and looks on sin as a kind of congenital illness in man stemming from his condition as a created being and not from his fall.[2]

The difference in emphasis is that "back-sliding" connotes especially a declining from a standard once attained, while *chata* carries more implication of missing a mark or erring, in other words has a little more the implication of failure to attain a future goal. I do not think one should put too much weight on this rather fine distinction. However, it should be noticed that a golden age in the past is not the basic orientation of Hebrew thought. The Eden-Paradise and the snake and the disobedience and the fall of man are all *there* in the beginning of Genesis, and *there* in a very important way.

But the purpose is to give an explanation of the nature of sin and the reason for pain, and how it is that a world created wholly good by the good God had as much pain in it as this world now does. However, Hebrew thought typically does not go about lamenting lyrically that it cannot return to Eden. Hebrew thought is forward looking. "The Day of the Lord" and later "The Kingdom of God" are thought of as future.

It has been fashionable theologically in recent years to emphasize how much the prophets were backward looking to the Exodus and Sinai and Israel's experience in the wilderness. Part of this can be accounted for by the fact that socially the prophets were lonely men, using the reference to the Mosaic Age to show that they were in line with what the people already knew to be God's will for them. It is also true that by the nature of the situation the Exodus period was free from some of the worst of the evil practices against which the prophets warned. Before Israel entered Canaan it was not tempted to the worship of other gods or to the morally low

---

[2] Edmond Jacob, Doctor of Theology, Professor of the University of Strasbourg, *Theology of the Old Testament* (New York: Harper & Brothers, 1958), pp. 281-283.

rites of the idolatrous fertility worship of Baalism. Furthermore, when they were all wandering nomads together, the chance was lacking for a concentration of wealth and power in the hands of a few with the resulting widespread injustice to the poor. Elijah, who sets the stage for the great prophets of Israel, lines up firmly for an adherence to the social commands of the Decalogue in the Naboth's Vineyard incident, and with the Decalogue's first commands against graven images and the worship of other gods in the Contest on Mt. Carmel. He does also, it is true, flee to Sinai, as to "home", after the latter incident. Even so, the Sinai-Horeb incident is forward looking. Not only do the commands God gives him there involve three practical tasks for the future, but his complaint to God, in the lowest ebb of his discouragement is, "O Lord, take away my life; for I am no better than my fathers." (I Kings 19:4) The implication is not that the Golden Age was in the past, as it was for the pre-modern Chinese civilization, but that God demands better things in the future. For in spite of the prophets recalling the people's minds to God's care for them at the Exodus, and his making his will known to them through Moses, when the history of the Mosaic time was written down under the impetus of the prophetic movement, the Israelites of that early period are not sentimentally idealized. With the painful clarity of the Hebrew insight into human nature, the fathers of the nation—with the exception of Moses, Joshua, and Caleb—appear on the whole to be a sorry lot of halfhearted muddlers.

The word *chata*, or "missing the mark", as the standard word for sin, is in line with the forward looking orientation in Hebrew spiritual thought. It calls up the mental picture of a man "striving" to shoot an arrow at a target and missing the center. Thus we extend the biblical teaching to harmonize with our teleological evolutionary theory in which all forms of life "strive" in the direction of increasing reflection of characteristics of the Creator. We are not claiming that the interpretation of the origin of pain that this book is making is wholly biblical. We are simply pointing out that we are not altogether out of line with the biblical view when we say: *Sin, or missing the mark of required obedience to God on the part of responsible intelligent creatures, brings punishment (the Old Testament teaching). Injury to conscious organisms, which results in their missing the mark of the God-desired pattern for the bodily form of their species, brings them pain (the extension of the teaching).*

In other words, the evolutionary theory, having pictured the existence of a gradual appearance of life on this planet, with no abrupt breaks between the inorganic and the barely organic, the barely organic and the virus, the virus and the one-celled animalcule, and the one-celled animalcule and man, raises the question of whether this scientific theory can be adjusted to fit Christian belief. We are trying to see if biblical teaching furnishes us with materials so that we can get a picture of God's relation to the world that will not do violence to the findings of science, and will at the same time harmonize with the basic biblical point of view. It seems to me that this theory of pain will fit both points of view with considerable economy.

It should be noticed that our present theory answers a fact about life that evolutionary theory by itself is at a loss to deal with. The basic theory of evolution involves the chance appearance of many species with the struggle for existence weeding out the less competent species and the weaker members within any one species. Quite unknown to the organisms themselves, the struggle for existence and the survival of the fittest are nature's way of practicing selective breeding. If one asks mere evolutionists *why* all living things struggle for continued existence, they would only be able to look puzzled and say, "Well, obviously as a matter of fact, all living organisms do so strive." Which is perfectly accurate as a description of fact, but no explanation at all. Or they may say, "They strive to continue to exist, in order to avoid the pain of injury or death." One may then ask, why should the mere complexity of the arrangement of atoms into highly complex organic molecules, and the organization of these molecules into more complex cells, and the organization of these cells into protoplasm with a cellular structure, and the organization of cells into the highly complex structure of highly developed organisms ever be accompanied by the rise of those organisms' ability to experience pain?" The answer would have to be, "To assist the organism in its struggle for existence." But of course the *why* of the struggle for existence was the original unanswered question. Our theory, does offer an explanation of *how* life came and increased, *why* the creatures struggle to continue to live, *how* pain arose in organisms, and *why* pain arose in organisms.

237

Furthermore, although the development of civilization and the increased sensitivity to intellectual, aesthetic, and moral values is not itself biological evolution, it involves the increased social and spiritual complexity of society in an increasingly "upward" development, and so has been thought of by many persons as in some way a non-biological extension of the "evolutionary trend". (This book agrees with this assumption.) If one asks people who hold the theory about the non-biological social extension of evolution, why it is that the human race, after it had succeeded in becoming dominant, should *strive* for anything more than its physical preservation, the standard answer has been that values give life a fuller *content* than the lower animals have by the mere continuation of their living organisms. And therefore the highly developed man's struggle to attain higher values is part of the struggle for existence, for it is a *struggle to live or exist more fully!*

Now comes the insoluble problem. It is a historical fact that it is typical of the very "highest" specimens of the human race that they will deliberately choose death for themselves if it is the only alternative to doing, or neglecting to do, certain specific things. Some of this, such as the soldier's loyalty to his country, might possibly be explained in terms of group solidarity. And in the same way might be explained also loyalty to one's race or class in a race or class struggle. Cases of isolated heroism can with greater difficulty be fitted into the group solidarity explanation. Examples of this might be the banker who allows himself to be killed by robbers rather than reveal to them the combination of the bank's safe; or the old coastguardman who, when his younger associates remonstrated that they could not get the life boat out to the sinking ship and back in such a storm, replied grimly, "We *have* to go out: we do not *have* to come back."

In all four types of situation, even the last one, it can be argued that a man has so identified himself with his position in society and its duties that the failing to do his duty would have killed him in his own mind by cutting him off from society. Better, therefore, his emotions would reason, to die physically doing his duty, so that his life to the last, and what immortality he would have in the memory of others after his death, would keep him part of the social organism within which he had human life. That is, by dying heroically he would surrender his biological life in order to retain

238

to a slight extent his relationship to the social organism in which he had human life.

I do not personally believe that this is a full explanation for any of the heroic deaths I have mentioned: I am simply giving the suggestion that it might be the explanation because others have sometimes given it. But the point that needs to be made is that there are a few martyrs' deaths which this formula will not cover even by a stretch of the imagination. Of this special group Socrates, Jesus, and Paul are outstanding examples.

None of the three was "well adjusted to society" in the smoothly integrated modern sense of that expression, for all three made enemies constantly throughout the period of their life work. But in each case there was a little group of devoted disciples, and so for the purposes of argument the human personality of each of the three could be thought of as having its human status by adjustment to this inner circle rather than by adjustment to society at large. Now the whole point is that these three did not die to retain status even in the inner group of disciples. The friends of all three were against their pushing on to almost certain death. (Plato, *Crito*; Mark 8:31-33; 14:37, 38, 50, 71; John 11:7-16; Acts 20:22-25, 36, 37; 21:8-14) Each of the three died for something his friends did not really see until his death made it vivid. Socrates died to underscore for men the fact that intellectual integrity is part of moral integrity and that moral-intellectual integrity makes an absolute demand upon each human life. And he set the standard so clearly that to this day when the West asks, "What *is* the integrity the intellectual life demands of the professional man and the scholar?" the answer is, "A character that will stand comparison with that of Socrates." Jesus died claiming to be the Son of God (Mark 14:61-64) and so the person with absolute authority to reassure bewildered humanity of the heavenly Father's unbounded love, and by his sacrificial death and resurrection he fully made clear that he was the Incarnation of the loving God he had proclaimed. And ever since, the Western world has pointed to the character of Jesus when asked to define love. St. Paul saw the Church as the loving society belonging to Christ, which is guided by his continuing influencing to work for him as a man's body is guided by his human will to carry out his purposes; and Paul died, cementing the unity of the Church with his blood.

One cannot get away from the problem these three create for us by saying that they each died for an ideal. For, granted the truth of the modern secularist viewpoint which builds heavily upon the theory that evolution is a natural emergence in an autonomous physical universe, there would be no ideals to die for. For beyond the being of this autonomous physical cosmos of which men are included items, there is only nothingness.

We owe a great debt to Jean-Paul Sartre for clearly defining the implications of the intellectual-West's giving up the idea of God the Creator. He says:

When we conceive God as the Creator, he is generally thought of as a superior sort of artisan. Whatever doctrine we may be considering . . . we always grant that will more or less follows understanding or, at the very least, accompanies it, and that when God creates he knows exactly what he is creating. Thus, the concept of man in the mind of God is comparable to the concept of paper-cutter in the mind of the manufacturer, and, following certain techniques and a conception, God produces man, just as the artisan, following a definition and a technique, makes a paper-cutter. Thus, the individual man is the realization of a certain concept in the divine intelligence. . . .

Atheistic existentialism, which I represent, is . . . coherent . . . When we speak of forlornness, a term Heidegger was fond of, we mean only that God does not exist and that we have to face all the consequences of this. The existentialist is strongly opposed to a certain kind of secular ethics which would like to abolish God with the least possible expense. About 1880, some French teachers tried to set up a secular ethics which went something like this: God is a useless and costly hypothesis; we are discarding it; but, meanwhile, in order for there to be an ethics, a society, a civilization, it is essential that certain values be taken seriously and that they be considered as having an *a priori* existence. It must be obligatory, *a priori*, to be honest, not to lie, not to beat your wife. . . . So we are going to try a little device which will make it possible to show that values exist all the same, inscribed in a heaven of ideas, though otherwise God does not exist. . . .

The existentialist, on the contrary, thinks it very distressing that God does not exist, because all possibility of finding values in a heaven of ideas disappears along with him; there can no longer be an *a priori* Good, since there is no infinite and perfect consciousness to think it. Nowhere is it written that the Good exists, that we must be honest, that we must not lie; because the fact is we are on a plane where there are only men. Dostoievsky said, "If God didn't exist, everything would be possible." That is the very starting point of existentialism. Indeed, everything is permissible if God does not exist. . . .

If God does not exist, we find no values or commands to turn to which legitimize our conduct.[3]

Actually the emotional response to having no values ahead to which to trust one's self does not engender the lonely heroism of martyrdom, it engenders spiritual dizziness. Although without Mr. Sartre's vigorous thinking, the two older generations' belief in God has largely faded, with the resulting undermining of their confidence in values. In spite of their going on, "as if" values had a genuine existence anchored beyond this world, their going on has become more and more a neurotic tendency just to keep moving, faster and faster, over thin ice, to keep from thinking.

The two older generations are confused casualties to the science-image and the naturalistic interpretation of human life. To the thought of the bright contemporary student generation even as young as the secondary school-age group, the pretense of the older generation is seen to have worn so thin that it no longer veils the inner insecurity from the children. With different degrees of intellectual insight and emotional intensity adolescents are consciously facing the void. They are asking the questions: "Is there any purpose to existence?" "Are there any real values or are all values merely relative to changing fashions?" "Who am I?" "Am I a person?" These questions are reflections of a genuine terror of slipping progressively into increasing dehumanization. In view of the theory of entropy, physical and spiritual, that this book has outlined, may not their terror be justified as a true insight into what is actually happening? For if man is made for companionship with God, he is made for an interpersonal relationship that has to be voluntary for both parties concerned. Where man persists in denying his relationship to God, may he not in the end discover

[3] Jean-Paul Sartre, *Existentialism and Human Emotions;* New York: Philosophical Library, 1957, pp. 14, 15, 21-23.

241

that he has denied his own personality, which has come into existence in the course of evolution as a reflection of characteristics of Deity?

The Renaissance glorified the autonomous individual and we think of it as an age of high individualism. But the autonomous individual is a temporary phenomenon like the unsupported cosmos. For all that is not sustained by the power of God perishes. The underlying tendency of created existence is entropy. But just as the created cosmos perishes slowly and releases its power in the process, so a Christian civilization, if it is cut off from God, also perishes slowly, but releases in its perishing the stored power of developed individuality built into it by God in centuries of belief. To use an evolutionary comparison and not a cosmological one: as life during the evolutionary process increased slowly, each new stage profiting by the gains already made in the mundane aspect of the process as well as by the continuing fostering assistance of God, so the devolutionary process is also a slow one, declining gradually from higher positions once held.

George MacDonald told in the beginning of his old story, *The Princess and Curdie*, of how the boy, searching through the castle, found a strange, ancient princess in a tower room. She gave Curdie the power, after he had thrust his hands into her magic fire, of recognizing by the feel of a man's hand the type of animal the degenerating person was turning into. The old woman told Curdie that what was of consequence was not the question of whether men had ascended from the lower animals, but instead it was the danger that men will "go down the hill to the animals' country." In view of the resurgence of barbarism in nations we thought civilized, as well as in view of the other dehumanizing tendencies of the twentieth century, George MacDonald's words have a prophetic ring.

However, the great trio of martyrs we have discussed, Socrates, Jesus, and Paul, did not go about seeking safety by integrating themselves smoothly in society, and they did not go about asking wistfully, "Who am I?" "Am I a person?" And they all died in behalf of ideas to which even their intimate friends were not fully adjusted. So on these three individuals naturalistic evolutionary theory projected to the social level breaks down. For this theory says that the basic motive of life is the struggle for existence.

Creatures struggle in order to keep alive. But these three, all men who had struggled socially and who were competent in the social struggle, and who were thoroughly sane men, voluntarily chose death. And these particular three individuals are too important to be ignored in a theory about life.

The only way an advocate of a naturalistic evolution that includes social evolution, if he believes that truth and the search for it are important, can get out of this dilemma is to say that man's upward evolution toward the fuller and richer life of the intellect and spirit goes on until at last—when he comes to these unavoidable three—the will to live becomes at last the will to die. At this point only a torrent of rhetoric will cover up the fact that he has said something entirely contrary to his evolutionary theory.

But suppose he was wrong in his naturalistic evolutionary theory. Suppose evolution took place but has always had a teleological orientation and has been assisted throughout by a powerful supernatural God whose character is motivated by righteous-love. Then what we call the increasing life of the creatures as evolution progressed would be their increased ability to reflect the Divine who is Life, and their individual struggle to avoid death would be due to their craving, whether conscious or unconscious, to maintain the closest relationship that they can have with God.

But since righteous-love is the motivating characteristic of God the noblest human beings will hold to their reflection of the Divine Life, which is also Power, at the supreme level, even if they are killed for doing it. In other words, the struggle for life exists throughout the whole scale of organic existence. The martyrdom is the affirmation in its highest form of the craving for life. Without this confidence I cannot make sense of the Hebrew insistence, especially during the last six hundred years B.C., that the great danger was sin rather than death, even during the centuries when they had no intellectual belief that there is a life beyond the grave. The belief that martyrdom in loyalty to righteousness is the affirmation of life, not death, is probably almost never a reasoned belief at the time of the martyrdom itself. It represents the final mute clinging of the personality for safety, when arguments are no longer of any avail.

The Greek verb from which the word, martyr, is derived means "to testify", "to bear witness of." The Greek word that the King

James Version translates "witness" in Luke 4:22 and Acts 22:5, it translates "martyr" in Acts 22:20 and Revelation 17:6. The first century world knew just as well as modern evolutionists the intensity of the struggle for life. And the Early Church labeled those who died for the faith "martyrs", that is, those who had given the supreme evidence or witness "that Jesus is the Christ, the Son of God, and that believing [we] may have life [now and forever] in his name." (John 20:31. Compare John 6:47-51, 57, 58.)

CHAPTER 23

The Inadequacies of Modern Theories of Revelation

Since this whole book works from the point of view that God is the divine Teacher, and since there is a type resemblance of all true teachers from the primary grades through graduate school, it will be necessary to describe a theory of revelation that will cover the whole range of God's method of revelation from the beginning of the evolutionary process through the coming of the Holy Spirit at Pentecost. This unified method must be used if we are to consider the whole billion-year old evolutionary process down to the present to be the result of the potter's continuing concerned work upon the clay. The largely fashionable modern view, that "the essence of revelation" is the "intercourse of mind and event,"[1] seems to the present writer to be of some usefulness but to largely emasculate the biblical understanding of the nature of revelation, due to the nervous fear of modern theologians to admit the miraculous activity of a supernatural God upon the creation.

The modern interpretive tendency is to say that the living God acts in history. The basic example of this is God's rescue of Israel from bondage in Egypt and his establishment of his Covenant with the nation at Sinai. The acts of God in history are then interpreted by the human minds of the prophets, and this interpretation is said to constitute the basis of prophetic thought through which God accomplished his progressive self-unveiling. But if one asks scholars who hold this view, whether God's mighty acts in the Exodus period, the plagues and the driving back of the Red Sea, were miracles in the strict sense of the supernatural God's direct specific action intermittently perpetrated upon nature, the answer would be that the plagues were of a type that normally occur from time to time and that the driving back of the Red Sea by the strong east wind is a known natural phenomenon. One may then say to these scholars, "In all probability, yes. But do you believe that the ongoing order of nature produced the intersection of this series of events

---

[1] John Baillie, *The Idea of Revelation in Recent Thought;* New York: Columbia University Press, 1956, p. 110.

with the crucial period in Israelitish history, so that all these plagues and the lowering of the water would have been *produced naturally at that particular time even if Israel had never been enslaved in Egypt?* Or do you believe that a God who is outside of nature ('Our Father, who art in heaven') in any way directly *manipulated nature at the Exodus, so that events ordinary to natural phenomena as we know them were directly maneuvered by God into an extra-ordinary timing to assist Israel's get-away?*" The answer to that question is a profound conspiracy of silence. For the authority of the "Science Image" has made scholars disbelieve or be afraid to say that a supernatural God ever exerts any direct sporadic influence upon nature. But if this were so, and if under these conditions prophetic thought only interpreted God's "mighty acts", then Hebrew prophecy would be entirely a human discovery and not a divine revelation.

I believe that some form of miraculous activity of the supernatural God upon the creation is essential to the Old Testament account of revelation. Although the great revelation in the Old Testament is described as coming especially through Abraham, Moses, and the prophets, not all that is included in the revelation comes through them, that is, through God's influencing their minds and through their interpretation of events as God's actions in history.

Certainly too, in the sense in which the Old Testament understood the word "prophet", it was as a man who delivered a message direct from God to a person or to the community in general. This is clearly shown in Exodus 4:10-16, especially in verse 16. The Bible does not take up the question of how God gets his message across to the prophets, and the Old Testament neither rules out the part played by the thoughtful cooperating intelligence of the prophet, nor God's making use of the prophet's humanly acquired knowledge of God's past dealing with men and nation. But that a message from God was thought to be transmitted to the people is evidenced both by the standard prophetic formula, "Thus saith the Lord," and in such instances as Jeremiah's expression of God's displeasure against the false prophets who prophesy in God's name when God did not "command them or speak to them." (Jeremiah 14:14)

The common fashionable scholarly statement that the prophets were not foretellers of the future (but compare Deuteronomy

18:20-22) but that instead the history of prophetic revelation is that of God's "progressive self-unveiling", is a partial truth, which however as a total conception of prophecy is very inadequate. Again, the reason scholarly thought thus tends to narrow the description of the *content* of prophecy is that modern intellectuals refuse to stick their scholarly necks out by the admission that a supernatural God could directly communicate with a man, because that would be an instance of a supernatural interference within the creation, and therefore miracle. Whatever modern scientists may or may not be saying at the present time about their understanding of nature, the "Science Image" has crippled much top modern scholarly biblical interpretation. The reason why biblical revelation cannot be thought of as merely comprising "the progressive self-revelation of Deity" is that, although the biblical picture is that of a God who is the same yesterday and today and forever, it is also a picture of a God who is always *specifically* active, doing specific thises and thats in a manner that is unscheduled, even though the stability of his character keeps his conduct from being irresponsible or erratic.

There is an often repeated remark that man tends to make a picture of God in his own image. There is a grim truth in that. We live in an era of depersonalized I.Q. tests, depersonalized I.B.M. machine ratings and classifications, the huge manufacturing organizations with the depersonalized assembly-line technique, the increased red tape and bureaucracy in government, and increasing organization and overhead personnel in education. As man becomes depersonalized he tends to think of God as also depersonalized, as a being who like modern men is above all characterized by action on schedule. This is one reason why the Church's thought of God in this century has become so vague, and prayer has come to seem such an irrelevance. What point would there be in praying, "O Super-Cosmic Schedule-Follower"? But perhaps the cause of this picture is the reverse. Perhaps the truth is that the Science-Image, which pressed theologians into believing that the physical cause-and-effect routines of chemical matter were unalterable, made it impossible for them to think of a supernatural God as acting upon nature at will and so, in their effort to continue to describe God as close to human life, made them locate God as a Divine force moving *within* nature, and so with no need to break *into* nature, since he was *there already*. This squares the theological picture

247

with the Science Image at the cost of picturing God as inevitably trapped in matter's invariable cause-and-effect sequences. This theory of Divine immanence brings about a subtle depersonalization of the picture of God on the part of theologians, and takes away from modern man any firm ground to stand on *apart from* the technological system in which he is caught, and so he has no firm *other* ground from which he might fight that system's increasing depersonalization of human life.

It is axiomatic to the development of an individual human personality that we tend to resemble whatever or whomever we persistently love. While it is true that man's description of God is in man's image in the Hebrew-Christian religion because high human personality is the best thing we know in this world, it is also true that a people's image of God eventually has a strongly molding influence upon the character of that people. The leaders who have been molding religious thought in this century have most of them not believed that God genuinely is as Jesus taught—the Father in heaven. For they have not been willing to stand by that belief and the conclusions that are correlative to it when they lectured to their graduate students or wrote articles for their professional equals, for on no account must the all-pervasive authority of the Science-Image be contradicted. God, in upper scholarly circles, where he has been believed in at all by the other scholarly disciplines, has been thought of in terms of a great pervasive power and/or the ideals of righteousness and love. The positive backing-up of these ideals by his power does not connect comfortably with the picture of his immanent power pervading all physical nature indiscriminately, inasmuch as these ideals of righteousness and love would have to discriminate practically against injustice and hate which are part of the natural world. Thus the moral stature of God in modern belief is lowered by the Science Image, which has claimed that matter's non-moral undiscriminating, undeviating, cause-and-effect routines are not subject to modification from without. A God who *merely* "makes his sun rise on the evil and the good, and sends rain on the just and the unjust," (Matthew 5:45) would not be the heavenly Father of whom Jesus taught.

The depersonalization of God, in everything but a "mythical" sense, in highly educated American thought, has accelerated the trend toward the depersonalization of the individual. In the nine-

248

teen-fifties my adolescent pupils were skeptical about whether God the Father in heaven exists. In the nineteen-sixties they have been skeptical about themselves and worried about the questions, "Who am I?" "Am I a person?" It is essential to Christianity that God the Creator be thought of as the Father in heaven, in accord with Jesus' teaching, and this book so thinks of him. Any reader who cannot get it out of his head that in believing this I think of God as a super-grand-old-man with a long white beard sitting on a cloud, will please recall that I have previously said that I think God takes a robust pleasure in consciously remembering the lovely pattern of each individual snowflake that has fallen in the world's history. Such a reader will also please remember that scientists in their books illustrate the structure of atoms with diagrams that look like gum-drops stuck together with toothpicks, and expect all intelligent readers to believe both (a) that atoms as structured activity genuinely exist, and (b) that atoms neither are, nor really look like, gum-drops stuck together with toothpicks.

To interpret all of religious revelation simply as the process of God's progressive "self-unveiling" is to create the impression that God is static, as an abstract ideal is static. The correlative worship of a God so revealed is contemplative adoration. Such an experience resembles the aesthetic, but is spiritually much deeper. As a person's aesthetic sensitiveness is increased he sees more and more deeply into beauty's self-unveiling. But as we pointed out in connection with the semi-interpersonal relationship that characterizes aesthetic experience, the human being has all of the pleasure without having to worry about the appreciated object's suddenly telling him to get busy and do something as his duty, whether or not he happens to want to. Contrary to contemplative religion, the Old Testament thinks that the proper role for men is that of obedient servants of God, as people who exist primarily for their master's use and satisfaction rather than for their own. The steady use of the servant-to-master relationship in many of Jesus' parables is clear evidence that he did not do away with this Old Testament conception when he described God as the Father in heaven.

Now if man is as a servant to God, existing primarily for God's use and satisfaction, then it is characteristic of the relationship that a man should be in the position of taking orders as to how to carry out his divine Master's will. Needless to say, the sum total of all the orders any human executive gives his underlings will constitute a "self-unveiling" of that executive's character. But they will also reveal him as a man of specific action, and his commands, by the very fact that they involve things the underling is to do after he receives them, to a slight extent are foretelling the future. Both the reference to the future and the specific nature of the Divine message are taken for granted by Amos when he says:

> Surely the Lord God does nothing,
> without revealing his secret
> to his servants the prophets. (Amos 3:7)

Our theory of Divine revelation will therefore have to be one that will fit the belief in specific messages with a future reference sometimes being given direct to the prophet's mind by God.

CHAPTER 24

Revelation Throughout Evolution and Salvation Only in the Power of Christ

But our theory of Divine revelation will also have to cover a great deal more than God's personal dealing with a few dozen great religious leaders. It will also have to be a theory that can be fitted to the whole concept of evolution, from the earliest emergence of life to the present. If one asks, "How is the early revelation of the adult human made to the infant human?" we have something that presents interesting points of comparison. Obviously the loving parent arranges for the feeding, bathing, and sleeping of the infant according to a general routine. The infant, then, before it is conscious of what it is doing, adjusts himself organically to the routine his mother has established and to the pervasive security of her love. In a somewhat similar way we have assumed that a real relationship between individual snowflakes or amoeba and God could be established by God's appreciative nearness without their having any consciousness at all. The obvious difference in the two situations is that the mother and infant are both organisms with a very intimate affinity for each other because of the pre-birth relationship. The only point that is being made is that the mother is being a kind of diffuse influence simply as the intimate environment of the newborn infant. The parallel is that God is intimately an environing influence of a diffuse sort for the snowflake and the amoeba. And they too, by their very constitution out of matter have an intimate affinity for the environing presence of God, because of matter's pre-Creation relationship to the mind of God. The infant at birth was cast forth from the mother, another being of her own species. Matter at creation was cast forth from the thought—*not from the being*—of God, as a different type of being altogether, and yet with a continuing affinity for God, because of its antecedent connection with the divine Mind.

When the baby gets a little older he can consciously respond to personally indicated wishes of his parents. By the time the baby is two years old there are two words that he needs to understand, and they are the basis of the child's future education. They are "yes" and "no". The child, just by being a young vigorous organism, is going to try out his physical abilities in a rather random fashion. For example, his rather strong, prehensile hands will pick things up at random and move them about and tear them. He has ears that will hear things and he will pound and drop objects at random to listen to the noise they make. By his parents' "yes" and "no" he gradually learns to sort out which actions to make standard and which to omit. There needs to be a comparable "yes"-"no" method of training applicable to the whole evolutionary sequence. I believe that such a method of Divine teaching can be found.

The one-celled organisms reflect God's character only to the extent that they reflect a little life. Their well-being consists therefore merely in being alive. If they did not incorporate nourishment they would not be alive, therefore they move about and incorporate nourishment. Those who say that there is a "striving" in all matter can say that the one-celled organisms strive to maintain their lives because that constitutes their well-being. (It is to be remembered that the well-being of all creatures is to reflect the character of God to the greatest extent to which they are capable.) Therefore for the amoeba the simple alternative is to maintain its life which is its state of well-being, or to lose its life which is its state of non-well-being. In this striving to hold to one state and avoid the other we do not have to imagine that a one-celled organism has any more consciousness than we normally have of the muscular movements that make our hearts function, or the muscular movements that set up the churning motion of our stomachs in order to digest food. But the simple striving in response to the to-be-or-not-to-be alternative is the one-celled organism's method of following the "yes"-"no" alternative, which is the directive guidance arranged for by God for living creatures at this evolutionary level.

By the time the evolutionary development had produced a creature of the complication of *Tyrannosaurus rex*, we probably have the dim beginnings of consciousness. Therefore the "right adjustment" organic situation would be sensed as a general feeling of comfort and the wrong adjustment would be felt as pain. There is now clearly established the double basic mode of divine direction for the higher living creatures, a mode of direction that continues centrally significant through the highest development of the human race. It is not that an animal will not sometimes willingly undertake pain. To retain to the best of its ability its well being, which is its most adequate reflection of the character of the Creator, an animal will willingly choose actions that bring it immediate discomfort even amounting to pain, if the actions are necessary to get food to sustain life. The height to which the creature has "evolved" can partially be gauged by what it assumes is necessary to sustain its life, and by the degree of pain it is willing to undergo and by the forms of well being it will if necessary discard in order to hold fast its highest reflection—and therefore its appropriate reflection—of the Divine character. For example, some of the higher mammals have a kind of natural affection for their offspring, and have been known to die to protect them from harm. At a far higher level, for St. Paul, and for other Christians after him, the commitment to Christ has meant that, as he said, "It is no longer I who live, but Christ who lives in me; and the life I now live in the flesh I live by faith in the Son of God." (Galatians 2:20) In order to retain conformity to that life, which means allowing that life continuingly to conform him, Paul was willing to undertake death itself. Jesus' words should be interpreted in the context of the same general picture of created living existence: "Whoever would save his life will lose it; and whoever loses his life for my sake and the gospel's will save it." (Mark 8:35) *The socalled Christian paradox would seem paradoxical only from the worldly viewpoint. From the heavenly viewpoint it would seem simply the supreme example, at the highest human level, of the standard technique by which the creature maintains its life.*

❖ ❖ ❖ ❖ ❖ ❖ ❖

Christianity holds that no man ever attains heaven except in the name, i.e., by the power of Jesus Christ. But it does not claim to know of how much of this method of salvation the individual need be personally aware in any one case in order to be rescued by Christ to eternal life. While the eternal salvation through Christ may be effective for all people who have given the last full measure of devotion to the Good as they saw it, there is nothing in the New Testament to encourage a sense of spiritual security in all those worldly-oriented people who have never done anything scandalous and who do not stick pins into babies, but who have never com-

253

mitted themselves to acknowledge Christ's overlordship in their lives.

❖ ❖ ❖ ❖ ❖ ❖ ❖

If the increasing complexity of the creature enables it to reflect more of the many faceted unity of the Divine character, and if righteousness and love are the guiding characteristics of God's nature, then, as man's social life becomes sufficiently developed, the instinctive affection for his mate and young which he shares with some of the higher animals, and which is needed to perpetuate the species, plus his greater intellectual capacity for memory, planning, and foresight, will be the beginning of responsible love; *and what seem to be the needed arrangements for communal living to perpetuate his safety and the safety of the family whom he values will be the rudimentary knowledge of righteousness. If we are right that these qualities are a reflection of the Divine character, then the fact that they may appear to man as something that he thought up as an obvious way to meet a practical situation, does not alter the fact that they are in a way a revelation of God, even if man to some extent appears to himself to come upon these things first, and afterward consciously build some of these characteristics into his idea of God.* (That theory is not out of line with the Bible. Israel first *saw* redeeming love in the life of Moses, in that strange incident of the golden calf in which to us Moses' character looks more like God than God's character does. Compare in Exodus chapter 32 verses 9-13 with verses 30-32. After redeeming love had been seen in human action, Hosea could prophesy that redeeming love is a characteristic of the righteous God. But throughout the Old Testament the first emphasis is on God's righteousness. God may be described as lovingly righteous. The perfect life of Christ seemed to the early Christians more in line with what would be the perfect character of God than the Old Testament picture of God, and therefore in the Christian thought of God the position of the two Old Testament characteristics is reversed, and Christians think of God as righteously loving.) That a divine revelation can take place before it is recognized as such has also previously been implied in the claim that the amoeba to a slight extent reflects God's life simply by being alive. To that extent the amoeba would be to a tiny extent a revelation of a characteristic of God, although it itself has no conscious knowledge of that or of anything else.

254

In the same way a man living in a Stone Age village, and seeing in others some family affection, some cooperation for mutual helpfulness, and some tribal rulings guarding the basic welfare of tribal members from undue encroachment by other tribal members, would be seeing more of the character of God reflected upon earth than he would ever see if he had never in his life seen another human being, but had always lived in an environment inhabited only by salamanders, lobsters, gypsy moths, and hyenas. *The mere fact of intelligent human community existence is in itself a kind of revelation, inasmuch as it exists by being a kind of reflection of God's intelligent community relationship* INTER SE.

This aspect of the self-revelation of the supernatural God must be stressed. It is not that man could have known all that he needed to know about God without the special revelation described in the Bible. It is simply that unless there were some revelation of God already built into mankind as mankind, there would be no way for anyone to recognize the special revelation as revelation when it came. One recalls the tale of the poor woman in an isolated primitive village in India, who ran excitedly into her friend's house exclaiming, "Come quick. There is a strange teacher who has just come to the village. He is telling about a new God who loves all people and who died and rose again so that he could take care of us always! I always said there ought to be a God like that!"

CHAPTER 25
Extra-Biblical Evidence for the Existence of God

There are several ways in which theology has claimed that all men have extra-biblical evidence for the existence of God. These arguments include the belief that one can argue from the consistent intelligible interrelatedness of the whole universe to one intelligent mind behind everything. Also the fact that different human minds can interpret this interrelatedness in the same fashion and communicate with each other by means of the coherent interrelatedness of nature seems to rule out the idea that matter in chance motion is the ultimate reality. This argument fits well the thesis of this present book. Another argument that is also consistent with its theory is the argument that beauty is not merely matter in motion, and therefore cannot be accounted for on the basis of matter as the ultimate factor in existence.

Another argument is the argument from the existence of the basic Moral Law to the Eternal Moral Law Giver. This is a vital argument for the Jewish-Christian religion, and one that makes it essential that Judaism and Christianity avoid all pantheistic and immanent philosophies, which in identifying God with the all of the cosmos make him indiscriminate as to good and evil, both of which this world obviously contains. The Christian argument has been that the existence of the feeling of obligation to do the good to the best of one's ability in so far as one knows the good, is one of the irreducible "givens" that one is forced to include in any attempt to make a total description of existence, and that this experience of the feeling of absolute obligation to do the right no matter at what cost to one's self argues a relationship of man to a righteous God who demands righteousness.

Many attempts on the part of naturalistic philosophy have been made to reduce this basic moral imperative to instinct or social convention, and so give a merely psychological or anthropological account of its origin and thus place it within the structure of a wholly naturalistic philosophy of existence. It can be shown that some animals, governed by instinct and unquestionably sub-moral, endanger themselves to practice a group solidarity. It is argued by a naturalistic interpretation that this solidarity is simply a prolongation of the instinctive tendency to struggle for survival that is the underlying directive influence of the actions of all living beings. In some cases, the argument runs, species that have practiced group solidarity had more safety for the individual in the struggle for existence and so some species that have survived are those that have this instinctive behavior. Therefore the basic moral law in man is reducible to instinctive behavior and there is nothing mysterious about it.

Another method of attempting to reduce the moral imperative to the dimensions of a naturalistic philosophy seems to me to contradict the above naturalistic argument. This argument says that the moral law is entirely a construction of intelligent man in the course of developing civilized life. This theory lays stress on the fact that our word "moral" itself comes from the Latin *mores*, that is, the customs of the community. This theory in supporting itself lays great stress on the great differences in what types of behavior are believed to be right in different centuries and countries. It says that different groups find different ways of acting in different circumstances conducive to human safety and comfort and so make rules accordingly, and what may be thought a virtue in one society may be considered a crime in another. For example, burning trash in the open might in some situations be enjoined as a hygienic measure, and in other situations be prohibited as a fire hazard. There is really no contradiction here, however. It is the same basic moral rule of fostering the physical welfare of the community that is implemented in opposite ways under different circumstances.

The final argument against all merely naturalistic explanations of the moral law is seen if one asks, "Why should I lay down my life in order to do what is right?" Here the naturalistic answer has to be that one ought to do it for the welfare of the community of which one is a part. If the person then asks, "Why ought I to care about increasing the welfare of the community in a situation in which I personally will no longer be in existence to profit by the community's increased welfare?" the answer can only be, simply, "Because you ought." This brings us back to the religious claim that the absolute imperative to try to do the right thing is an irreducible factor in human existence that must be taken into account.

Now the beauty of the theory of this present book is that while it holds firmly to the religiously evidential nature of the presence of the moral imperative in human life, it also ties it in with the theory of evolution and finds a valid place for naturalism's observation that there is a strong resemblance between man's moral sense and the instinctive group solidarity we see in the actions of some species of animals. It also has a place for the other naturalistic theory that the moral law can be accounted for as a social convention.

For our theory of the "living" aspect of evolutionary development being due to the increasingly complicated states of matter being able to reflect more facets of the many faceted simplicity of the Divine character, makes heavy use of the belief that there is a hierarchy of governing traits within the many faceted unity of the Divine character. Inorganic matter reflects God's power. Organic matter reflects his life and increasingly his freedom. The higher organic forms begin to reflect his consciousness and to the extent to which they have any group life they begin to reflect the community aspect of God's Triunity. This rudimentary community life is seen in the custom of buffalos to move in herds, and the custom of both parent birds to build the nest and to assist in the feeding of the helpless young. Since even at this stage the evolutionary reflection has not yet reached the point at which it can reflect intelligence, the animal's actions to promote its own survival and to carry on a minimum of group cooperation have to be governed by inherited neural patterns we call instincts. We cannot call group cooperation "moral" among the lower animals because it lacks the freedom and responsibility that go with the ability to govern one's choices by the intellect. And we cannot call the natural affection many animals show for their helpless young "love" in the fully Christian sense, because it lacks the ingredient of intelligent moral choice that is an essential in the Christian definition of love. Even so, if God were not loving, even this minimum of protective affection for the helpless young would not appear in the animal nature.

Since in many cases what will preserve the individual and help advance the welfare of the herd or flock has some similarity for both animals and humans, it is not strange that some people might confuse the Moral Law with instinctive action. One of the differences, however, is that the moral law only functions where the creature is intelligently self-determining, although both Moral Law and the merely cooperative group action of some species of animals reflect characteristics of Deity.

Where the creature has developed to the point where it can govern its actions by its intelligence, it can substitute free choice for instinctive action, and therefore it has much greater freedom to adapt itself to different environments. However, once a social group has made a successful adaptation either to an environment in which it finds itself or to an environment it has made for itself, it is to the group's advantage to standardize the successful modes of action so that they can be readily taught to the young and take on almost the automatic character of instincts. This is a method by which society consolidates and holds whatever advances it has already made. This reduction of as many gains as possible to automatic action leaves man free time and energy for further activity. Since many of society's standardized modes of behavior have moral connotations it is easy to see why many people think the moral law is merely a social convention.

The reason for saying that the basic moral requirements are the eternal Divine laws written in the hearts of all men is not the belief that at a particular moment when living organism became humanity that God suddenly added basic Moral Law together with a mysterious foreign substance known as soul to the evolved animal organism. We say the basic moral law is God-given because when intelligent animal organisms (which we call people) reflect the community life of God by arranging to live in communities, then, due to the quality of the character of God, which community, to be community, must somewhat reflect, the smooth and happy functioning of community life will be hindered even eventually to the point of destruction, in the degree to which men dishonor their own parents, disrupt other men's family life, murder each other, steal each other's means and fruits of livelihood, and debauch by falsehood man's precious means of communication. That men can discover by trial and error that obedience to these laws is essential to human community life does not lessen their divine character.

The divine imperative to try to carry out the basic divine directive laws for human conduct is at once of Divine origin and the crown of the evolutionary process. This is due to the whole evolutionary process being matter's increasing ability to reflect the character of God. The basic impulse of self-preservation inherent in organisms is due to their life being their means of reflecting God and their highest type of being their fullest reflection of his character. Since he as Creator is the ultimate source of the creation, in that part of it that is sufficiently highly organized to reflect his life (i.e., all organisms) there is a striving of matter, at first unconscious, to conform to its source. In man the reflection can be at the intellectual-moral-loving level. These five basic moral rules for community living (Exodus 20:12-16) turn out to have to do with a minimum standard of assisting community welfare. They turn out therefore to be a minimum standard for love stated in negative and objective terms. All of this, including the various ways in which human nature can reflect the Divine and is therefore under obligation to attempt to do so, is implied in Jesus' summary of the two great commandments. (Matthew 22:36-40; Mark 12:28-31) As we have seen, the willingness to suffer martyrdom in loyalty to God or to righteous-love, turns out to be the highest form of that struggle to hold on to life that we see in the basic direction of the activity of all living matter.

CHAPTER 26

The Primary Mystical and Numinous Experiences

In addition to these "natural" ways of knowing God, that is, ways open to all men who have not heard of the special revelation of God recorded in the Bible, there is still another way of knowing God that people had always been aware of, but which in the nature of the case could not adequately be described in words and so tended to be left out of intellectual discussions of God and his ways with men. It is not what people call the direct mystical approach to God, which is neither part of the Old Testament's understanding of man's approach to God, nor characteristic of the New Testament. My personal belief is that the description of the living union between Christ and the believer, which we find described in Paul's letters and in the fourth Gospel, can only be called "Christ mysticism" by a confusing extension of the word mysticism beyond its usual religious meaning. Mysticism proper is the immediate spiritual awareness of God under the terms for man's relation to God as described by some form of pantheistic thought, which identifies God with the All. The state of spiritual enlightenment which the mystic seeks to cultivate or attain is the intuitive perception that he has no separate existence, but that his whole existence is as a part or aspect of the All. In this mystical experience God is not felt to be supernatural to the creation. Genuine mysticism eventually discards the idea that God is righteously-loving, for that implies a discrimination against evil and so makes it impossible to define God as the All. The Hebrew-Christian God has to be described as thoroughly discriminating against evil, especially moral evil, and therefore he must be described in both personal and supernatural terms.

The direct experience of God, which is other than mystical, and yet can be traced in all ages and cultures, is as a direct experience of the Divine as the Other. This world-wide direct experience of God was identified and defined by Rudolf Otto in 1917, in a book that is now called *The Idea of the Holy*. It is an experience basically without intellectual content, although it may be attached to intellectual content. Otto uses for the Other that causes the experience in men the word *numen* that Latin uses for vaguely defined Divine Power. The experience that the felt presence of the *numen* arouses in a human being is therefore referred to as a *numinous* experience. The characteristics of the experience are the unpredictability of its coming, the length of its duration, the suddenness of its beginning and ending. Many people, even individuals the closeness of whose lives to God can scarcely be questioned, never have had it vividly. Those who do have it vividly may be people of saintly lives, or ordinary conventional lives with no especial emphasis on religion, or even morally bad as well as irreligious lives. Those people who do have the experience may have it only once in a lifetime, or several times. A few people have had it with considerable frequency. Degree of intelligence or education is irrelevant to its occurrence. If one has not had a marked degree of the experience there is no technique by which one can attain it. If one has had the experience there is no way by which it can be prolonged or cultivated. The characteristics of the *numinous* experience as experienced are a feeling of undefined presence that is strongly fascinating at the same time that it arouses in the person the feelings of inadequacy and fear. This is the specific "feel" of the presence of the Divine that we are trying to describe when the experience of the Divine is divorced from any ideational content. There are no words in our vocabulary to describe it adequately. If a person who experienced it said that the total incident was "uncanny," and described the activity of the *numen* by the verb "it spooks," and his own fear as "ghostly dread" he probably would come about as close to a description as our vocabulary will allow. The word *awe* is sometimes used of the numinous feeling. But we have debased "awful" to mean merely *unpleasant,* and "to be in awe of" to mean *to have a strong respect for,* leaving out the element of "dread." But "dread" also has been largely debased to mean *being worried at the thought of future unpleasantness,* as when we say, "I dread going to the dentist." In the numinous experience one does not see a ghost or expect to see a ghost, but the ghostly vocabulary has to be used because the "fear of ghosts" is on the fringes of the uncanny in the numinous sense.

Another peculiarity of the numinous experience is that it cannot be classed as a hallucination. In a hallucination one's senses of touch or sight or hearing react so exactly as they would if the appropriate earthly external stimulus were present that one mistakenly believes the external stimulus to the subjective sensation to be genuinely present, when there is in fact no such external earthly stimulus. However, the response to the *numen* is a total diffuse response without sense impression of sight, sound, touch, taste, smell, hot, cold, dry, wet, or pain. The point Otto makes is that the numinous experience is one of the strands in the compounded knowledge and experience that goes to make up any great religion or any primitive religion. And he stresses the fact that it is from the earthly viewpoint an irreducible ingredient, as the different sense of moral obligation is an irreducible experience. Both experiences have to be accounted for in a total philosophy of life.

I am interested in this description of the numinous experience for two reasons in connection with our present discussion, and both these reasons have to do with what might be called the slight or strong numinous overtones to some experiences that are not primarily numinous, and often are experienced with no trace of the numinous experience. Jesus at times aroused a numinous response in those closest to him. (Mark 4:41; 6:50,51; 9:6,32; Matthew 28:10; Luke 5:7-9.) The fear that the gospels refer to here is obviously no terror in the usual sense of the word. There is a strongly numinous experience of God in Isaiah's vision in the temple, but it is compounded with the experience of beauty (glory) and a tie-up with the moral grandeur of God. (Isaiah 6:1-8). There is one very old incident in which the word "Fear" is used as a title for God, indicating the numinous quality of the religious experience. It is the incident in which Jacob and Laban are at Mizpah. Jacob says that he would have been reduced to poverty "If the God of my father, the God of Abraham and the Fear of Isaac, had not been on my side. . . ." (Genesis 31:42). When the covenant is made we find the statement, " 'The God of Abraham and the God of Nahor, the God of their father, judge between us.' So Jacob swore by the Fear of his father Isaac. . . ." (Genesis 31:53).

We have been positing the idea of a supernatural God bringing influence to bear upon his creation throughout the whole evolutionary process and have said that we need a theory of revelation that will hold true from the amoeba through the Hebrew prophets. This is not to ignore the uniqueness of God's revelation to Israel. But if the *content* of that total revelation is correct, then the Almighty Creator who is also the Father in heaven "so loved the world" (John 3:16) from the very beginning that he related himself to it. It is not irreverent to see a consistency throughout the whole evolutionary process in his *ways* of acting, although the content of what he may reveal may vastly increase. When I became an adult I merely knew my mother better. I did not discard my childhood mother for a more adult one. But then I had known my mother continuously. I cannot help suspecting that those who talk about discarding their childhood God for a greater God when they became adult, in reality went off and left their childhood God when they were nine or ten years old. So when they met him again in different circumstances in adult life they did not recognize him. Had they stayed close to him throughout their lives, after the shock of the adjustment to modern ideas was over, they would realize that the God with whom they were still dealing and the God of their childhood were the same. This awareness is greatly assisted by the practice of constant Bible reading. For even if there were not the problem of modern science and philosophy to which to relate one's thinking, a person who read the Bible constantly throughout life would find his picture of God constantly "growing."

The numinous experience has probably been most illuminating in human history when it has existed in what can be called numinous overtones to other experiences. *For if the numinous experience is, as I think Otto has established, sui generis, then we have in it the "feel" of the direct presence of God. Once granted that this is the case, the way is open for God's slowly educating the human race by attaching overtones of this "feeling" now to one human experience and now to another. To this training, of course, the human race has responded by the trial and error method.*

The whole account of Israel at Sinai is filled with numinous overtones. The description of God descending upon Mt. Sinai (Exodus 19:16-19) reflects the terrifying aspect of the numinous experience, and after the establishment of the covenant, the experience in which Moses and Aaron and the elders of Israel "saw the God of Israel; and there was under his feet as it were a pavement of sapphire stone, like the very heaven for clearness" (Exodus 24:10) has echoes of the aspect of fascination in the numinous experience. The two descriptions taken together contain the characteristic elements of terror and fascination. It is to be noticed that the response of Israel as a whole at the descent of God upon Sinai was that of numinous fear. (Exodus 20:18, 19) The proportion of the elements of fear and fascination may vary in the numinous experience but the combined elements are characteristic of it.

The great revelation of God to Moses at Sinai and through Moses to Israel involved the permanent tie-up in the religion of Israel of several basic ideas: a) The powerful God who had made possible their get-away from Egypt (Exodus 19:4, 5; 20:2) b) demanded their exclusive loyalty (Exodus 20:3-7) and c) he was adopting them as his particular people (Exodus 19:5, 6; 24:3-8). d) His service demanded basically adherence to moral principles that all peoples have recognized as valid (Exodus 20:12-17). e) And therefore their God who had chosen them was at once the God who controls nature, the author of the moral law, and the God whose presence is felt as the numinous experience. It was God's ability to get across this pre-requisite tie-up of ideas in the mind of Israel by means of Moses that gave God a functional starting-point for the revelation that it took him over thirteen hundred years to complete.

Where the numinous experience is an overtone to other experience, or when one comes to the numinous experience with some intellectual knowledge of God, the experience can be associated with particular ideas so that they sometimes seem to be part of the experience. But the numinous experience can exist apart from intellectual ideas. And the experience in an intense form, while sporadic, ranges over human life, modern, ancient, intellectually sophisticated, and unschooled, as well as among the most savage and primitive peoples. This brings us to an important aspect of the experience in relation to our theory of revelation.

The theory has been stated earlier that God acts as the Unmoved Mover luring nature by his appreciation of nature, and so helping nature to hold what evolutionary advances nature to date has made. Of course the whole problem is to give some reasonable explanation of how this can be done, granted very stable cause-and-effect routines in matter as investigated by science. The problem for religion is that religion cannot make as neat and tidy a theory for its position as science can. In facing that problem religion can only retort that science got its original neat and tidy picture by limiting its investigation to that aspect of existence only that can be mathematically measured, thereby eliminating from its province the conscious thinker who does the investigating and also eliminating all of the values that make life worth living, including the investigator's own desire to find out scientific truth.

But having made the negative criticism of the limitation of the province of science, all we have been able so far to offer as to *how* a supernatural God could influence the creation have been the generalized statements that a) the statistical regularity of nature at the sub-atomic level may allow him to slightly modify its action without breaking the over-all scheme of nature's statistical regularity; b) that since all matter was originally brought into existence by Divine thought it has by its very nature a constant relatability to the Divine Thinker; c) that to our human thinking there is a permanently unbridgeable gulf between the thinker and the object of his thought, that the subjective thinker can never be directly known by another and can never even make himself-thinking the object of his thought; and d) that the I-thou relationship differs from the I-it relationship. e) But we have said that the aesthetic or appreciative relationship, where the object is non-conscious, is neither wholly I-it nor altogether I-thou, but is a semi-interpersonal relationship. And therefore perhaps God, by discriminating appreciation of nature, strengthened evolution's direction toward personality.

After man as an intelligent human being with moral and aesthetic abilities appears on the scene, God would have less difficulty communicating with him than with inanimate matter, as we shall later see. But we still have the problem of how a conscious God could influence the non-conscious creation toward consciousness.

Now the numinous experience appears to a human being who has it to involve an intensified or heightened form of his own consciousness during the duration of the experience. So it is barely possible that our knowledge of human numinous experience provides a clue to God's method of strengthening evolution's direction toward personality. We have noticed that it is neither an educated nor an uneducated experience, and that it is characteristic of human experience both among very primitive peoples and in highly advanced societies. *It contains the element of being at-*

tracted by the Divine which is the element needed to complement our theory of God's influencing non-conscious nature by appreciating it. And in itself the numinous experience is non-intellectual and it is not perceived by the senses. Therefore we can at least play with the theory that it sheds light upon the method of influencing matter before the intellect arose, and before highly developed sense organs and consciousness arose.

Scientists say that just as the amoeba can absorb nourishment and discard waste products by the diffused ability of its single cell without the elaborate eating and elimination apparatus such as the higher species have, so primitive protoplasm before the development of the eye has a diffused ability to respond slightly to variations of light and dark. Now it is characteristic of the numinous experience where it occurs in man that it is an intense but diffuse experience. The man with his whole being feels a slight shuddery fascination for the Numen. Perhaps slight traces of this fascination can be exerted upon protoplasm in any stage of biological development, even where the organism is unconscious. This is merely a speculation but it is an interesting one. And it is legitimate as a speculation because naturalistic philosophy, having ruled God out of consideration entirely, started the fashion of reading the present highly developed state of evolution back into its interpretation of the beginning of things in order to account for the existence of conscious intelligence in man in the present. Naturalism has had to suggest a "striving" (a word borrowed from conscious experience) in all matter from the beginning in order to account for the emergence of conscious purpose in the present.

CHAPTER 27

Mysticism *Versus* the Experience of the Numinous

With the claim that science cannot give us religious knowledge comes the necessity for Christianity to define the way in which its specifically religious knowledge is originally acquired, in other words the necessity of defining the method of Divine revelation. This has been discussed at length in connection with the place of miracle in religion. The experience of numinous awe which Otto identified as an irreducible factor in the religious life has also been stressed. What has not been stressed thus far is the mystical experience as another irreducible factor in religion.

The mystical and numinous types of religious experience would seem to be irreducible and—superficially at least—contradictory. Otto does not seem to be aware of their inconsistency. His references to mysticism are approving and non-analytical. Its harmony with his category of "the holy" is obtained by an inadequate definition. He says, "We take Mysticism . . . as meaning the preponderance in religious consciousness, even to the point of one-sided exaggeration, of its non-rational features."[1]

How different mysticism is from the experience of "the holy" as identified by Otto can be seen in the following almost lyric passage in which William James summarizes the religious evidence given us by mysticism:

> This overcoming of all the usual barriers between the individual and the Absolute is the great mystic achievement. In mystic states we both become one with the Absolute and we become aware of our oneness. This is the everlasting and triumphant mystical tradition, hardly altered by differences of clime or creed . . . . so that there is about mystical utterances an eternal unanimity which ought to make a critic stop and think, and which brings it about that the mystical classics have, as has been said, neither birthday nor native land. Perpetually telling

---

[1] Rudolf Otto, *The Idea of the Holy;* London: Humphrey Milford Oxford University Press, 1925, p. 202.

of the unity of man with God, their speech antedates languages, and they do not grow old.[2]

In contrast to this it is the discontinuity between the human and the Divine that Otto stresses in the experience of "the holy." He says:

> We gave to the object to which the numinous consciousness is directed the name 'mysterium tremendum'. (p. 25) . . . . The implications of that aspect of the 'mysterium tremendum' indicated by the adjective . . . so far may be summarized in two words. . . viz. 'absolute unapproachability.' (p. 20) . . . There is, finally, a third element comprised in those of 'tremendum' and 'majestas', awefulness and majesty, and this I venture to call the *urgency* or *energy* of the numinous object. . . . The philosophers have condemned these expressions of the energy of the numen, whenever they are brought on to the scene, as sheer anthropomorphism. (p. 23) . . . It [the numinous experience] lies . . . in a peculiar 'moment' of consciousness, to wit, the *stupor* before something 'wholly other' (p. 27) . . . . something which has no place in our scheme of reality but belongs to an absolutely different one, and which at the same time arouses an irrepressible interest in the mind . . . . The feeling of the 'wholly other' . . . set[s] the numinous object in contrast not only to everything wonted and familiar (i.e., in the end, to nature in general), thereby turning it into the 'supernatural', but finally to the world itself, and thereby exalt[s] it to the 'supermundane', that which is above the whole world-order. (p. 29)[3]

When we come to compare the specific claims made for the numinous and mystical types of experience respectively we discover that there is a ten-point difference between the two. With the numinous the experience is typically (a) brief, with (b) the initiative on the Divine side and (c) man unable to intensify or prolong the visitation by cultivation. With the mystical the initiative can be partly on the human side in that the strength, length, and incidence of the mystical experience can be assisted and intensified by cultivation. In the numinous experience man's reaction is of (d) "fear" and fascination before a Divine that appears (e)

---

[2] William James, *The Varieties of Religious Experience*, Lecture 17.

[3] Otto, *Op. cit.*, pp. 25, 20, 23, 27, 29.

specifically and locally active, (f) "wholly other", and (g) supernatural. But in the mystical experience the typical reaction is one of luminous at-home-ness and love. The Divine seems to be everywhere *there*, the permanent background of existence, immanent in the world and men, and can therefore be looked for by turning the human gaze inward. The numinous experience (h) does not characteristically blend with aesthetic experience, while some of the less advanced forms of mystical experience are a regular ingredient of artistic creativity and aesthetic appreciation. And finally, it is noteworthy that (i) the numinous experience harmonizes easily with an anthropomorphic conception of God and that (j) Rudolf Otto drew much of his illustrative material from the Bible, while mystical experience does not harmonize easily with an anthropomorphic description of God, and Evelyn Underhill drew her examples of mystical experience chiefly from non-Biblical sources.

Although all persons who have strong intuitional experience of the Divine tend to one or the other type of experience, it is not impossible for an individual to experience traces of his non-dominant type of experience. The point is not that the type of religious experience is necessarily limited in any one individual, but rather that there really appear to be two different valid ways of having intuitional contact with the Divine. We must now investigate the question of our description of God and evolution to see whether it may not explain rather neatly why there are these two types of human response, and whether the truth may not be that numinous experience is direct contact with God as powerful and righteously-loving, while the mystical experience is direct or indirect contact with God as glorious or superlatively beautiful and therefore superlatively harmonious.

The words of Evelyn Underhill describe clearly the relation of mysticism to the awareness of beauty. She says:

> Conversion of this sort may be defined as a sudden, intense, and joyous perception of God immanent in the universe; of the divine beauty and unutterable splendour of that larger life in which the individual is immersed, and of a new life to be lived by the self in correspondence with this now dominant fact of existence. . . . For an instant the neophyte sees nature with the eyes of God. In that glorious moment "all is beauty; and know-

ing this is love, and love is duty."[4]

If our theory of evolution is correct and evolution "rises" as nature reflects more and more adequately the traits of the Divine character, then nature reflected the Divine harmonious intelligence (in the mathematical ordering of its ways) and the Divine glory or beauty before the advent of man; and in man it reflected the righteous-love which is the guiding aspect of God's character.

Beauty can be static. Righteous-love has to be active, for constant discriminating choice is of its nature. Embodied beauty can be collected, stock-piled, and stored. This is one of its fascinations. Righteous-love cannot be so collected and stored: it can exist only in present action. For men to keep the righteous gains of the past they have to repeat them constantly by continuing righteous action. This is one of the reasons why there is always a temptation for Christianity to translate and consolidate its spiritual gains into beauty—beautiful churches, beautiful pictures, beautiful vestments, etc. They are to a slight extent spiritual vehicles and they can be stock-piled and stored, giving a sense of spiritual continuity in generations in which the first concern of so-called Christians is not that of serving Christ.

The appropriate response to beauty is loving contemplation, whether the beauty is merely aesthetic or whether it is the deeper Divine beauty realized in the more advanced states of mystical contemplation. The soul empties itself of its desires for this and that and allows itself to be invaded or absorbed by the beauty of the other. Thus the mystics talk a great deal about love, but it is usually union *via* contemplation. One can read Miss Underhill's brilliant *Mysticism* from cover to cover without being aware that the God of mystical "love" is deeply committed to the cause of tough, prosaic, social justice. When the woman in the crowd called out to Jesus, "Blessed is the womb that bore you, and the breasts that you sucked!" he answered, "Blessed rather are those who hear the word of God and keep it!" (Luke 11:27,28). In line with the Old Testament prophets Jesus demanded obedience rather than devoted contemplative admiration. The danger of mysticism is that it attempts to take an inadequate short-cut to the experience of heavenly bliss. The danger of Calvinism has been that in avoiding

---

[4] Evelyn Underhill, *Mysticism;* New York: E. P. Dutton, third edition, 1911, pp. 216, 217.

this danger it has tended to forget the ultimate destiny of enjoying God forever in its preoccupation with the means of obedience.

The feeling of the eerie numinous fear occasionally accompanies the mystical experience but it is not essential to it.[5] It may be that in the approach to the Divine through contemplation in a fashion akin to aesthetic appreciation, that the experience is "cushioned" by the experience's being drawn partly through the assistance of the creation. That is to say, to the extent to which the reflection of God's characteristics has become "built into" the universe it is directly accessible to man through his earthly heritage, something to which he has access simply by being man. This reflected beauty or glory is therefore inherited by men from God then at second or third remove. Some instances of aesthetic appreciation and of the lower ranges of nature-mysticism might be chiefly the human spirit's sudden comprehensive awareness of the traces-of-God-having-been-at-work-upon-the-creation, rather than the revelation by God of his-presence-now-actively-and-specifically-at-work. This theory of luminous awareness of traces of God's past action would explain why some degree of valid mystical experience can often be drug-induced: the mystical state being the result of the expanded and enhanced consciousness's sudden grasp of what is really implied by the material with which the mind is already furnished.

In discussing the borderline region between mystical and aesthetic experience Evelyn Underhill says:

Now the education which tradition has ever prescribed for the mystic, consists in the gradual development of an extraordinary faculty of concentration, a power of spiritual attention . . . . a profound concentration, a self-merging, which operates a real communion between the seer and the seen: in a word in *Contemplation.*

Contemplation, then, is a power which we may — and often must — apply to the perception, not only of Divine Reality, but of anything. It is the condition under which all things give up to us the secret of their life. All artists are of necessity in some measure contemplative. . . .

All that is asked is that we shall look for a little time, in a special and undivided manner, at some simple, concrete, external thing.

---

[5] *Bhagavad-Gita;* New York: New American Library, 1963, Mentor Books, Chapter XI, pp. 92-96.

This object of our contemplation may be almost anything we please: a picture, a statue, a tree, a distant hillside, a growing plant, running water, little living things. . . .

Look, then, at this thing which you have chosen. Willfully refuse the messages which countless other aspects of the world are sending, and so concentrate your whole attention on this one act of sight that all other objects are excluded from the conscious field. . . . First, you will perceive about you a strange and deepening quietness. Next, you will become aware of a heightened significance, an intensified existence in the thing at which you look. As you, with all your consciousness, lean out towards it, an answering current will meet yours. It seems as though the barrier between its life and your own, between subject and object, had melted away. You are merged with it, in an act of true communion. . . .

The contemplative is contented to absorb and be asborbed. . . .

Now this simple experiment exercises on a small scale, and in regard to visible Nature, the faculty by which the mystic apprehends Invisible Reality — enters into communion with the Absolute.[6]

If I have seemed to belittle mysticism by suggesting that the mystic experience can occur when the direct stimulation is not Deity himself but only the reflection of his characteristics built into nature, I would hasten to add that I would believe this to be the case only in some instances of aesthetic appreciation and of the minor forms of drug-induced and nature mysticism. And even here I would assume that if the individual having the experience were at all groping toward God, that God would make use of the experience in his personal effort to draw the man to himself, and that probably combined with the traces of God's past activity there would also be some direct action of God upon the human life. This combination of direct and indirect influence in one experience would be typical of God's strategy for bringing individuals to himself with as little forcing as possible of their natures. On the other hand, in the experiences of deeply committed religious mystics, where the direct hunger for God is intense and the life has sold all that it has to buy the pearl of great price, the probability is that the mystic experience is what the mystic claims it to be: the

6 Underhill, Op. cit., pp. 360-362.

awareness of God directly relating himself to the human spirit.

Furthermore, even in instances in which mystic awareness, as in nature mysticism, may be derived wholly from the traces of God's past action, the experience cannot be written off as a merely scientifically-natural occurrence. For beauty and value are not within the realm of science. To the extent to which the beauty and value recognized in the world exist by a relationship to God's past action nature is not "merely-nature," which science can investigate, but "nature-plus." And yet the plus is not God himself added to nature, because God is supernatural to the creation. Nature-plus is divinely-modified but still nature, still subject to corruption and distintegration.

This analysis offers a practical explanation for that perplexing and ambiguous borderline between the beauty of holiness and the sometimes questionable holiness of beauty. It explains why one might have a slightly aesthetic-mystical experience while looking at Titian's "Venus of Urbino," but avoids claiming that one is therein under the direct inspiration of God, or that Titian himself painted the picture under God's direct inspiration. Cautious of this ambiguity the Bible, while implying that superlative beauty is a characteristic of Deity, and while exhibiting a great sensitiveness to beauty on the part of the men who wrote the Scriptures, consistently avoids suggesting the aesthetic path as a path to God.

But turning now from the aesthetic experience to strictly religious mysticism of an intense type, it is easy to see why the problems of righteousness and active love are in abeyance in mystical experience. For this is a relationship to the Divine which is not at the level of the righteous-love which is the guiding aspect of the personality of God. It is easy also to see why as a consequence a picture of the Divine emerges in mysticism that so stresses Divine immanence as to verge on pantheism, and why the following of the mystical path in the religious life involves "that progressive abolition of self-hood which is of the essence of mystical development."[7] For the selfhood shows itself most strongly in acts of discriminating choice. God is described in the Bible as vigorously personal and as characterized by constant, active, highly discriminating choice of righteousness, and by strong discrimination against unrighteousness. But the mystic strives to attain "Detachment and purity [which] go

---

[7] *Ibid.*, p. 317.

hand in hand, for purity is but detachment of the heart."[8] And "Real detachment means the death of preferences of all kinds: even of those which seem to other men the very proofs of virtue and fine taste."[9] "True mysticism . . . . is in no way concerned with adding to, exploring, re-arranging, or improving anything in the visible universe."[10] The "love" of mysticism is therefore closer to *spiritual-togetherness* than it is to the more highly complicated righteous-love of the Bible. Since "togetherness" of itself implies no line of direction for action, once "togetherness" is attained, the active discriminating choice which righteousness implies and which is an essential characteristic of selfhood fades out of the picture. This is why a religion structurally built along mystical lines tends to be pantheistic. But since righteousness is the guiding characteristic of God's nature, the goal of mere mysticism does not involve the attainment of the full manhood (Ephesians 4:13) which God desires for men who were meant to be in the image of God.

We have here a sympathetic criterion for judging the pantheistic religions of the Orient. In the twentieth century, when all thinking people are very conscious that the world has shrunk and that we are intimately related to people of other religions and cultures, many are asking, "Why is one religion better than another, are they not all ways to the same to God?" "Would God be displeased with men who tried to serve him through other religions?" The theory we have been developing helps to answer these questions, showing *how* there are in these forms of paganism genuine elements of search for and experience of the one true God; and at the same time showing where these forms of paganism are basically inadequate to the full service of God as he wishes men to serve him. Thus Christians can respect and occasionally learn something from the seers of the pantheistic faiths, and can do it while still realizing that the pantheistic mysticisms have a basic inadequacy, so that while they and their adherents can be respected, the Christian must loyally foster and try to spread the biblical religion as the exclusively adequate Divine revelation showing what God is like and the way he wishes men to relate to him and serve him.

No mystic is merely a mystic. He is also a human being. In Christian mysticism the Christian belief is assumed and the mystical

[8] *Ibid.*, p. 248.
[9] *Ibid.*, p. 269.
[10] *Ibid.*, p. 96.

275

insight held in uneasy harmony with it. But Christian mysticism's closer approximation to Christian belief than is characteristic of Oriental mysticism is due to the inheritance of traditional Christianity by the mystic rather than to his mystical experience.

In the last resort, the doctrine of the Incarnation is the only safeguard of the mystics against the pantheism to which they always tend. The Unconditioned Absolute, so soon as it alone becomes the object of their contemplation, is apt to be conceived merely as Divine Essence; the idea of Personality evaporates and loving communion is at an end. This is probably why so many of the greatest contemplatives—Suso and St. Teresa are cases in point – have found that deliberate meditation upon the humanity of Christ, difficult and uncongenial as is this concrete devotion to the mystical temperament, was a necessity if they were to retain a healthy and well-balanced inner life.[11]

The experience of the numinous, on the other hand, which is the other type of direct *feel* of the presence of God, is the inner experience upon which the Hebrew attention was focused as revelatory. In this feeling the Divine presence is realized as uncannily *wholly other*. When this awareness is combined with the discovery that Whatever is conveying this strange feeling to a man conveys it at unpredictable times on its own initiative, – in other words that this strange Something is not just *there*, waiting around for man to practice a regimen to cultivate the feeling – you have an interrelated raw stuff of experience that can be correlated with the belief in an active, personal, righteous God who created the world out of nothing and who has a purpose for his creation and especially for men.

Of course these doctrinal beliefs are not given directly in the numinous experience. As the mystical experience can make use of the stock-piling of the reflection of the Divine characteristics that has been progressively embedded in nature, so the numinous experience can avail itself of the stock-piling of the progressive reflection of the Divine character that has gradually been embedded in human social life: the Being whose presence stimulates the numinous experience in man can be realized to be the author of the moral law. As the Hebrew people decisively made this con-

---

[11] *Ibid.*, p. 144.

nection of ideas, God was able in his dealings with them to relate them — both by harmony and by antagonism — to that aspect of his nature by which his whole Deity is self-guided. This is why "salvation is from the Jews." (John 4:22)

Historically speaking the early Christian Church, as it moved out into the classical world, had to redefine its faith in a way that was relatable to Greek philosophy. The restatement modified somewhat the Old Testament description of a highly personal, specifically active God in the direction of an Omnipotent Omnipresence more in line with the static eternity of Greek philosophy with its emphasis upon the abstract good, beautiful, and true. The mode of immediate Divine awareness to which Catholicism more congenially opened itself theologically was therefore the mystical experience. The institutional inclusion of this type of experience was also unconsciously favored because of mysticism's heavy reliance upon the togetherness aspect of love rather than upon the righteousness aspect. Since "true mysticism . . . . is in no way concerned with adding to, exploring, rearranging, or improving anything in the visible universe,"[12] it is a form of direct religious vitality that can conveniently be given an honorable niche within a highly organized power structure, without causing the discomfort and embarrassment that would be caused by prophetic activity with its uncompromising demands for righteousness and justice reinforced by its numinous awareness of God's specifically active and independent power.

With the coming of the Reformation there was a return to considering the Bible — rather than the institution — as the practical authoritative guide for the Christian. So an increased emphasis upon the numinous type of experience followed. Calvinism especially found highly congenial both the Old Testament emphasis upon God's righteous law and the prophets' independence of established institutions in their direct obedience to the righteous God. Calvinism therefore emphasizes the righteousness aspect of love and fights shy of the mystical approach to God with its heavy emphasis upon love as togetherness. But in being uncongenial to mysticism Calvinism has also been uncongenial to the arts, because of the slightly mystical element in the creative artist's intuitive awareness of the world about him.

---

[12] *Ibid.*, p. 96.

In this regard the austerity of Calvinism differs somewhat from the austerity of the Old Testament. Although both look askance upon graven images, the Old Testament religion was congenial to the arts of music, dancing, and verse, and the tiny gems of nature poetry scattered through the Prophets and Psalms show the heightened awareness of nature in all its freshness and light as it obeys and responds to the Almighty's solicitous activity upon it, which is very close to, but more vigorous than, the artist's slightly mystical awareness of beauty in the objects of the world around him.

The double form of the Old Testament experience of the activity of God upon man and nature is shown in the call of Isaiah. (6:1-8). Here the central vision of the holy and "wholly other" personal God evokes the numinous response of unworthiness and uncleanness with the Hebrew emphasis on God's righteousness: Isaiah knows himself to be in a precarious position because he is "a man of unclean lips, and [he] dwell[s] in the midst of a people of unclean lips." But forming a kind of backdrop of the vision rather than in its central focus are the seraphim chanting, "The whole earth is full of his glory." Thus the account of the call of Isaiah shows clearly the Hebrew understanding of the relationship of the beauty of holiness and the holiness of beauty in their relative importance.

CHAPTER 28

The Problem of How God *Got Across* A Special Content of Ideas to Israel

Since the unspoken assumption characteristic of modern biblical and theological interpretation is disbelief in miracle, some means is searched for to avoid incorporating the miraculous into one's explanation, while at the same time the attempt is made to give the impression of a unique revelation of God to Israel as recorded in the Old Testament. For this reason it is currently fashionable to say that "The Bible is the written witness of that intercourse of mind and event which is the essence of revelation."[1]

In other words, God performed mighty acts in Israel's history, from which the minds of the people of Israel and especially of the prophets deduced God's character, and later prophetic minds gained their insights by meditating upon the past deductions as well as upon the accounts of the mighty acts themselves.

For instance, according to the Bible Hebrew history began when God told Abraham to migrate to a new country and promised to make of him a great nation and said that through him all the families of the earth would be blessed. (Genesis 12:1-3). To avoid the embarrassment of admitting the miracle of a direct message to this effect it is fashionable to claim that Abraham simply migrated in search of pasturage, thus becoming the unwitting tool of God, and that the "call" of Abraham was only a retrospective interpretation by later devout Hebrew thinkers. Thus one seems to avoid admitting that the Hebrew religion was man-created, or at best a man-deduced affair. But one cannot legitimately later account for the revelation to Moses by making it at all dependent on the previous one to Abraham unless that earlier one is established.

Assuming instead, as many do, that the initial revelation came in the period of the Exodus we still run into the same basic difficulty. For to avoid admitting the miracle of the direct transfer-

---

[1] John Baillie, *The Idea of Revelation of Recent Thought;* New York: Columbia University Press, 1956, p. 110.

ences of messages from God to Moses it has to be claimed for the Exodus period that the law was not given by God to Israel at Sinai. Instead what occurred was the rescue of the nation by the mighty acts of the plagues, the driving back of the Red Sea, and the establishment of the covenant. From these great occurrences Israel, "by the intercourse of mind and event which is the essence of revelation," deduced God's love for the nation, and from his love they later deduced his righteousness and his insistence on the moral law, because righteousness is included in love which is the apex and unifying principle for all specific rules for correct interpersonal relationships. These evidential mighty acts of the plagues and the driving back of the Red Sea are further described as wholly natural occurrences, their relation to the Israelitish situation, physically speaking, being entirely coincidental according to modern thought. No claim is made that God did any special background manipulation of nature in order that the time and place of such natural events should be useful to the Hebrew situation. Furthermore, this theory has no real explanation for the establishment of the covenant. How did the Hebrew people know that God wished to establish a covenant with them? Obviously Moses told them so! (Exodus 19:3-6, 10; 24:3-8) But how did Moses know that God wished to establish the covenant? The idea of the covenant would have to be thought of as entirely Moses-invented or Moses-deduced from the mighty, merely coincidental, acts of the exodus, unless it is believed that God conveyed a brief command for its establishment direct to the mind of Moses. The covenant at Sinai cannot be established as revelation if Moses thought it up as a renewal of the covenant with Abraham, because as we have seen, the Divine-human intercourse involved in establishing a covenant with Abraham has not been admitted.

Some people claim that the question of *how* God could reveal the Ten Commandments to Moses at Sinai is irrelevant, because the Decalogue was compiled some centuries later than the exodus period, although it is certain that the belief that God gave the Ten Commandments to Moses at Sinai is at least pre-exilic. (Deuteronomy 10:1-5) But even if the Ten Commandments could be eliminated from the Sinai sojourn the problem of God's revelation of the law still remains. For the Book of the Covenant was read to the people and they accepted it as God-ordained law and agreed

280

to follow it as their part in the covenant. This agreement immediately preceded the blood ceremony at Sinai that ratified the covenant. (Exodus 24:3-8) The Book of the Covenant (Exodus 20:23-23:33) is considered to be one of the oldest extant bits of Hebrew literature, coming from the Mosaic period or very shortly thereafter, and seven of the Ten Commandments are implied by its regulations.

The alternate explanation to believing that the revelation of the law was part of the Sinai experience is the claim that all that was revealed to the people at the time of the covenant was God's love for the nation, with the humanly deduced corollary of the requirement that the nation show responding loyalty to God. Then the claim is made that the Hebrews later deduced the law from the implications of the nature of love.

This explanation when analyzed does not seem to me to be adequate. In the first place, the overall impact of the Old Testament underscores the basic belief in God's justice and righteousness. It took the full New Testament revelation to make clear that the controlling aspect of God's nature is love. A love in which justice and righteousness—i.e., the basic moral law—are not already presupposed is only an affectionate partiality. If it was not made clear to the Hebrews at Sinai that God is a God of basic moral righteousness, his action in rescuing them would have appeared to them more on the analogy of the unpredictable partiality of a prince or wealthy man for a harem favorite, a human situation that does not necessarily imply any moral righteousness at all. On the basis of such an analogy, the deducing of the moral law from the exodus rescue would have been a non sequitur.

The means of Divine contact with the Hebrew people may not have been different from those by which God attempted to guide other nations. But Christianity has believed that God's special relationship to men was never as unhindered by the human medium as it was in the case of the Hebrew people, and that therefore God was able to build up slowly through them a unique content of a long consistently directional revelation of his ways to men, pointing to a full revelation in Jesus Christ, which seals the Old Testament with the New as the unique authoritative revelation of the nature of God and his relation to men and his will for them.

Let us turn now to try and determine what would be a minimum amount of direct (miraculous) Divine guidance of Moses if the exodus period can be thought to contain special Divine revelation. This is not to minimize the already discussed general revelation of God that has come with prehuman and social evolution. All that we have said about evolutionary advances being a reflection of an increasing number of facets of the Divine character holds good here. The development of human intelligence, love, basic sense of moral duty, aesthetic sense, and family and tribal organization, all contain some general reflection of the Divine revelation. *We fully realize all this preliminary training as the work of God only because we see our planet's history in luminous retrospect in the light of special biblical revelation.* The numinous experience with its direct awareness of Divine power is also a well known, even if an intermittent and rather special phenomenon. Furthermore, all nations have known that it makes for the instability of society if a man dishonors his own parents, disrupts the family life of another man, murders, steals from another his means of livelihood or his gains of livelihood by which he supports his family, or if a man debauches by falsehood the precious means we have of communicating with others and of getting close to others by means of language. But only Israel made and firmly insisted on the basic identity between the source of these moral principles and the numinous power. And even the recognition of this identity is insufficient to explain Israel's unique greatness as an assister in the Divine revelation.

Some method of God's direct communication of ideas to the great leaders of Israel needs to be added before a theory of revelation adequate to fit the Old Testament claims is found. This is not meant to detract from the part played by Israel's insight and powers of spiritual deduction—"the intercourse of mind with event." Assuming throughout this book that God can be interpreted as having the attitude of a teacher toward the creation, it is obvious that at the human level those students can be most successfully taught who have a tough intellectual initiative, who have already coherent ideas to which the teacher can relate his teaching, and who do not absorb passively, but who will argue points where they need increased clarification. The most satisfactory pupil is not one whose mind is a *tabula rasa*. The importance of the human being and his intelligent human mind is not played down by the Old Testament. In one particular incident that has a ring to it implied throughout the whole Scripture, we find that the great prophet Ezekiel had an overwhelming vision and says, "When I saw it, I fell on my face, and I heard the voice of one speaking. And he said to me, 'Son of man, stand upon your feet, and I will speak with you.'" (Ezekiel 1:28-2:1)

If one is assuming that the plagues and the driving back of the Red Sea were only coincidental natural occurrences involving no special Divine manipulation of nature, then, to claim that God genuinely "acted" to assist Israel in the exodus period, one would have to try to substantiate the claim that God conveyed sufficient information directly to Moses' mind to indicate to him that the Divine name is Jahweh, that he was commissioning Moses to lead Israel out of Egypt to the land of their forefathers, that he wished with Moses' help to establish a covenant with Israel at Sinai, and that God's covenant relation with Israel involved the duty on the part of Israel of keeping God's law as summarized by the unexpanded form of the Ten Commandments.

Before the burning bush incident (Exodus 3:1-6) we can assume Moses to have been already humanly equipped with a knowledge of Hebrew rules and history from his parents, (Exodus 2:9, 10; 4:14-18) with a knowledge of administrative ways and laws and probably with a formal education through his princess-sponsor, (Exodus 2:10, 11, 14) with a knowledge of Jahweh and desert ways from his father-in-law, (Exodus 2:21, 22; 18:1, 5, 9-12) with a knowledge of the Egyptian situation, and probably with an acquaintance with the monotheistic beliefs of the recent Pharaoh Ikhnaton. At the burning bush incident there is enough Divine assistance to account for God's commission of Moses if, while Moses was in concerned thought about the plight of his people, God "edited" his "stream of consciousness" by causing numinous experience to help him recognize that God is named according to his eternity and to reinforce his questioning thought as to whether he himself ought to try to extricate the Hebrews from injustice. If Divine foreknowledge guided the timing of Moses' attempt to free his people to take advantage of natural phenomena God knew would shortly occur, then God genuinely gave "practical" assistance. Also, if at Sinai God again "edited" Moses' "stream of consciousness" by fixing his attention with numinous overtones

283

upon the basic commands from among the multitude of relevant moral precepts with which Moses was familiar, then there was genuine Divine revelation in the giving of the law. And finally, *if* the covenant with Abraham had been genuinely established by God, then God could use Moses' human knowledge of that previous interference by God in the life of the ancestor, to help convey to Moses the idea that God now wished the covenant relation reaffirmed. Without at least this minimum Divine assistance one cannot truthfully say that God acted at all with any direct help or revelation to Moses. *But even this minimum assistance—I* personally believe there was more—*involves the miraculous action of the Creator upon the creation, i.e., upon Moses.*

Since I have been trying to establish the necessity of miracle in the account of the Old Testament revelation, and since this is a highly unpopular intellectual stand to take, I have purposely tried to advocate the smallest amount of miracle possible, consistent with genuine revelation in the exodus period. It is my personal opinion that large-scale nature miracles cannot be entirely ruled out, although I am not burdening myself with trying to make a theoretical case for their existence. Miracle I believe to be any direct, specific, non-routine action of God upon the creation to further his purposes. My definition of miracle would allow for certain astonishing coincidental events to be caused entirely by nature, and certain other events, which appear normal to men and are unnoticed by them, to contain a factor of direct special Divine action. But unless there is some specific intermittent activity in the world by which God assists his people, the claim that "God acts in history" is spurious (unless all acts are thought of as acts of God, in which case the actions of Hitler and Stalin and all American gangsters would be actions of God, but "God" would then not be the righteous God of biblical religion).

To speak personally, the two nature miracles of Old Testament Hebrew history that I find it hardest to discount are the two crucial incidents of the lowering of the waters of the Red Sea and the descent of the fire on Mt. Carmel. Both incidents were witnessed by multitudes including the leaders of the people, and both were turning points in the nation's history. In both cases the miracle itself probably occurred "off stage." That is, any Divine resetting of the wind currents had probably been done some hours previously and many miles away, so that by the time the "strong east wind" (Exodus 14:21) reached the Red Sea it was a natural wind affecting the water level in a natural fashion. In the same way the lightning that consumed Elijah's sacrifice was ordinary lightning. (I Kings 18:38) The miracle would have had to do with the exact time and place of the bolt. If both these natural occurrences were entirely coincidental their religious significance would be gone. If a woman on her birthday was given a diamond ring by her husband, and had the good fortune on the same day to find another diamond ring in the gutter, both diamonds might be equally perfect one carat bits of compressed carbon. But only the first mentioned diamond would "reveal" anything significant to the woman. God cannot be said to "act in history" without acting specifically. Granted that the Old Testament is the account of the distillation of a slowly accumulating Divine revelation, there still has to be specific Divine revelation to be accumulated and distilled.

CHAPTER 29

God's Initiation of Ideas Into the Mind of Man

Thus far our description of God's method of guidance assumes the existence of the normal human use of human intelligence and the human stream of consciousness, with God both arresting the human being's attention miraculously upon ideas that have entered his mind normally, and perhaps attaching numinous overtones, for emphasis, to certain occasions in a man's thought-life. We now have to ask the question: Does God ever put an idea into a man's consciousness that was not there previously? Three incidents that have been discussed that would have to be so accounted for if they were really Divine revelation would be God's command to Abraham to migrate from Haran to Canaan with its attendant promise, (Genesis 12:1-3) God's command to Moses that he wished to establish a special covenant with Israel by which God adopted Israel as his specially chosen people, (Exodus 3:12; 19:1-6; 24:1-8) and the tremendous linking of the idea of God's power with his righteousness and the insistence that God demands righteousness from men as a basic part of the human relationship of God, and that God backs righteousness and punishes evil. Our previous accounting for these incidents was incomplete. *There has to be made room in a theory of revelation for some initiation of ideas in a man's mind by God.* (Nothing is gained by objecting that we only have the accounts of Abraham and Moses as worked over by later prophetic minds; for this same problem of God's intercourse with men is equally relevant to the prophets.)

Before claiming that God puts ideas into a man's consciousness a certain preliminary discussion to clear the ground is necessary. There are no ideas in a man's mind that do not have their foundation in ordinary human experience, for there are no other ideas that a man has with which to think and with which to communicate. (Thus the numinous experience is non-intellectual and can never be accurately described, because man has nothing in his daily experience in terms of which to describe it.) When an ordinary human teacher teaches, he has to do it by means of sense impression or of knowledge already in the students' minds, for the students' vocabulary is a form of knowledge. For example, if a teacher was trying to tell an immature class something about science, and none of the students had ever heard of a microscope, his use of the word would "reveal" nothing to them. He could then either define the word so that they had an explanation of it in words they already understood, or he could show the students a microscope and allow them to look at something through it and see it functioning. Then he could name the instrument as a microscope and afterward the word as an idea would be in their minds as a tool he could use for further "revealing" of intellectual knowledge to them.

Even such fanciful creatures as centaurs could not exist in the imagination if they were not the patched-up combination of the ideas of a horse and a man, both of which objects are known to ordinary human perception *via* the route of sensation. Thus any idea that God would be able to get across to a man would have to be composed of visual images or of words with which the man was already familiar (or sense impressions such as sounds, tastes, smells, touch, etc.). It does not invalidate our religious knowledge to point out the earthly images of which it is composed. The description of the golden streets and the city gates being each one pearl (Revelation 21:21) only suggests a line of direction for the imagination and is of course inadequate as a description of heaven. But had the vision not come through to the seer in humanly understandable pictorial language it would not have come through to the reader at all. When St. Paul writes to the Corinthians that he was "caught up even to the third heaven . . . . and heard unspeakable words," (II Corinthians 12:2,4 ARV) he means that he was granted in a vision a closer approximation to direct sight of Ultimate Reality than could be put into human terms and so the vision was ineffable. Therefore it conveys nothing whatever to us. What he had heard was of such a nature that it could not be put into words even for his own thought. By contrast when John in his vision sees the martyrs in heaven with harps singing:

Great and marvellous are thy works,
   O Lord God, the Almighty;
righteous and true are thy ways,
   thou King of the ages. (Revelation 15:3 ARV)
he "heard" them singing in Hebrew, Aramaic, or Greek, otherwise

he would not have known what they were singing. That is, the whole form of the vision was conditioned to his understanding. He also saw "the four living creatures, having each of them six wings, [who] are full of eyes round about and within; and they have no rest day and night, saying,

Holy, holy, holy, is the Lord God, the
Almighty, who was and who is and who is to
come." (Revelation 4:8 ARV)

Even these strange supra-earthly creatures, permanent inhabitants of heaven, spoke Hebrew, Aramaic, or Greek in order for the seer to understand them. This is another example of the vision making use of knowledge, in this case words, already in the seer's earthly vocabulary. But Christian piety through the centuries has never thought that we would have to learn one of those three languages in order to be able to converse in heaven!

For the account of God's revelation to man has to be put in terms that build on the earthly knowledge that man already has. The book of Revelation that has just been used by way of illustration is the most extended account in the Bible of visionary experience. The vision not only made use of words already in the seer's mind, but it also draws heavily upon the visions, figures of speech, and quotations from the books of the Old Testament. To the first readers therefore, who knew their Old Testament well, the imagery and sayings in the book would have a depth, or thickness, or foundation and far flung spiritual associations that they do not have for most modern readers who are unfamiliar with the original passages that it echoes. In other words the author of the book of Revelation had acquired a great deal of the information that is recorded in his vision by the perfectly ordinary method of having read and reread books.

If the book of Revelation came to its author originally as a vision, as I believe it did in spite of the claim that is sometimes made that the "vision" is a literary device of its author, then the chances are that the author himself did not know the meaning of all the symbolism that he used, and that the symbolism is important as part of the total impact of the message rather than as isolated items.

If one analyzes Coleridge's poem "Kubla Khan," one loses the poem. This is a visionary poem in which, in a dream induced by opium, the fragments and hints from exotic travel books he had been reading fused themselves in Coleridge's subconscious mind into a poem unrivalled in the haunting witchery of its beauty. The analysis of the poem and its literary sources has been learnedly done from both the literary and psychological viewpoints in a book called *Road to Xanadu* by John Livingston Lowes. My belief is that the book of Revelation was created by the subconscious mind in a comparable way during a dream, trance, or vision of the author. The reason we believe the book of Revelation to be divinely inspired as Coleridge's poem was not, is that we believe John's subconscious mind to have had direct assistance from God in creatively assembling the fragments of his religious knowledge to push the spiritual meaning and insight they convey beyond that contained in the sources incorporated in the vision. The proof that John had thus Divine assistance in composing the book is his claim that he did and the book itself. His conviction that he had been inspired would come to him repeatedly through his memory of his original experience of the vision plus his knowledge after the book was completed that he had produced something beyond his power to produce. After he had written the book he would find his own spirit enlarged and strengthened and brought nearer to God by re-reading the book, which is the same experience by which the inspiration of the book has been tested and retested by devout Christians who have fed upon it in times of persecution and danger.

The book of Revelation is not central to the main line of argument of this present thesis, but in a work of this present kind it is impossible to by-pass it entirely. It is the fitting close of the Christian Bible. For the Bible begins with the account of God's creation of the world, then describes the human fall and the struggle under God's guidance, and man's final redemption, and it ends with Revelation's glorious picture of the final success of God's total plan, when the victory won in principle by Christ is made good on the whole worldly and supra-worldly scale. The book is meant to be read consecutively aloud for the accumulated impact of its picture of the active power of God, triumphantly victorious over the world by his behind-the-scenes activity which will eventually be seen in its triumphant fruition by the entire creation. No book says so well to the emotions of the reader that the most real part of existence is that part which is hidden now from human sight.

The book of Revelation aside, the Bible contains comparatively little visionary experience purporting to pierce the veil of existence beyond this world. There are three famous such visions, however, in the Old Testament. Two of these are very brief. They are the vision of Isaiah in the Temple and the vision in Daniel of the Ancient of Days and the Son of man. (Isaiah 6:1-8; Daniel 7:9-18) Isaiah's is remarkable for the strength of the impression that he saw temporarily into the intersection of two planes of existence, the earthly and the heavenly, simultaneously. Daniel's vision is especially important because it occupies a central place in the teaching of Jesus Christ about himself. The most extensive of the three visions is that of Ezekiel. (Ezekiel 1:1-28; 3:13-15; 9:3-10:22; 11:22-25). It is the most pedestrian of the three visions. Its stage machinery seems to me to creak. But as Scripture and so authoritative its imagery furnishes items that go to make up the far more vivid pictorial aspects of the book of Revelation.

But in all these famous visions of the Beyond, Isaiah's, Ezekiel's, Daniel's, and John's, all the visionary items are originally drawn from human sense experience. *The strange and fantastic figures both in Ezekiel's vision and in the book of Revelation are composed of items known to the mind from its experience of the ordinary everyday world of human knowledge. On the other hand the vision St. Paul had when he was caught up into the third heaven (II Corinthians 12:2-4) could not be expressed in words or images drawn from everyday human experience at all, and therefore his vision, apart from his mere statement that he said he had a vision, constitutes no part of the Divine revelation of which we have the record in the Old and New Testaments.*

We have pointed out at length that God might convey a specific message to a prophet by, so to speak, spotlighting a selection of ideas that were already in the prophet's stream of consciousness. *We are now asking ourselves the question: Could God put ideas into a prophet's consciousness that were not already there? And if God could do it, how could he do it?* Before we attempt to answer this question one flat statement can be made that will help clear the ground for our thinking: *Other than the mere fact of the numinous experience, God is nowhere described in the Bible as*

290

giving a message to a prophet where the message is not composed of items already known as items by the prophet. The items in the prophet's mind include all he has seen and experienced, all he has heard people tell of, all that he knows of the religious teaching of other prophets as they *had responded to God's special guidance, all that the prophet knows of God's past dealing with men and the nation, all the thinking the prophet himself has done, all the prophet's experience of God's special guidance of himself, and finally the whole vocabulary by means of which the prophet thinks. If God is going to put an idea into the prophet's mind that was not there before, God must, in order to do it, make use of items with which the prophet is already acquainted, that is, he must make use of the man's memory, or his immediate sense impressions.* Even supposing Divinely inspired clairvoyance to sometimes take place, the items reported by the seer would all have to be composed of items already familiar to him; because one cannot *imagine* or compose a mental *image* of anything except out of items known by present or past sense impression. (I will admit myself wrong on this point if it can be definitely proved that individuals born totally color blind have "technicolor" dreams.) In the one clearcut description of clairvoyance in the Bible (I Samuel 10:2-6) where Samuel is telling Saul in detail the encounters Saul will have with three groups of people on his journey home, the locations of the encounters were undoubtedly in territory well known to Samuel. And the types of activity, dress, and words of the people involved were not foreign to his everyday knowledge.

In instances where God is described as putting new ideas in a prophet's mind use is made of the prophet's memory far more often than it is made of his present sense impressions. But present sense impression is sometimes used by God, so I will clear the ground by speaking of it first. Perhaps as clear-cut an instance of this as there is in the Bible is the account of Jeremiah watching the potter at work. (Jeremiah 18:1-12; compare 19:1-3, 10-13.)

But an incident I came across some years ago in the *Reader's Digest*[1] will be more useful for purposes of analysis than are the

---

[1] January, 1962. "Message from the Sea" by Arthur Gordon. Condensed from *Guideposts*, 1961. I wish to express special thanks to the *Reader's Digest* for locating this article for me when I could recall neither author nor title.

biblical accounts. The modern account is clear-cut and limited in scope.

According to the story the young man, who had lost everything he had in a business depression, went alone to his seaboard vacation cottage. Early in the morning, when a half-gale was blowing and the sea was wild, he walked down to the beach to commit suicide. His plan was to swim straight out to sea to the limit of his strength and let his exhausted body take care of drowning him. There at the edge of the shore the glint of a little white angel's wing shell caught his attention. He picked it up, and the thought came to him that this fragile thing had survived unhurt when tons of water had thrown it on the hard-packed wet sand. It had survived because it had simply yielded and accepted the storm. Considering this as guidance that he too should accept his situation with faith, he carried the shell back to the cottage and gave up the idea of suicide.

One can count on the healthy young man having at the time he started toward the sea a desire *not* to die that was only less strong than the desire for suicide. One can count also on his being in the state of somewhat heightened total awareness that often accompanies periods of crisis or fear. This being the case, I would say that the incident could probably be accounted for in one of three ways: 1) He may have noticed the shell, his mind attached to it its popular name, angel's wing, and his thoughts by the process of association have made all the necessary mental connections to bring him to the desirable conclusion. 2) God, knowing that this shell lay in his path, may have focused his attention on it, conveying the two words to his thought, "It survived," and then allowing the normal association of ideas working on his heightened state of consciousness, to convey the moral of the lesson to him. 3) The third possibility would be that God, deeply concerned with this man's welfare, and aware that the man was going to pass this shell, did nothing specific at all, but, so to speak, "stood by" to let the man make the connection of ideas without assistance if the man could, but prepared to give the man's thinking the slight push, if necessary, to make him start making the desirable connection of ideas. In this case the whole incident would, in the heightened state of the man's consciousness, have been invested with slightly numinous overtones, overtones so slight that his conscious mind did not recognize them as such, but which nevertheless conveyed to him an unidentified feeling of reassurance. The experience had a directing influence for good on the succeeding decades of the man's life, and as he related the incident he himself implied that he thought it had been not without some extra-human assistance.

Here again, I would interpret the Divine technique in terms of the methods of a human teacher, who likes to let a pupil answer as much of the question as he can on his own. Simply as a matter of personal religious experience I am convinced that God does directly guide an individual; that is, that God does work directly upon a human mind without intermediary. But I am convinced also that God does it with as slight and strategic a contact as will accomplish his purpose. The reason I have found this story, ever since I read it, to be useful to my own religious thinking, is that it clearly points out how slight could be the interference of God with the thought processes of a human being in order to convey an extensive message to that person's mind. Again speaking personally, I would say that there are two aspects of the whole problem in which the divine Teacher is very different from the human counsellor: the divine Teacher is never at all in the dark about any of the total factors involved in a human situation, and never in the slightest degree bungles the job of interfering in a human life. The timing and method of the Divine thrust are perfect, and so swift that I have never "caught" God in the process of acting, only of, as it were, withdrawing after his interference was accomplished. (Compare Exodus 33:20-23.)

Having cleared the ground to a considerable extent, we will now directly deal with the question of a possible method or technique by which God could give a prophet a somewhat extended verbal message on a subject on which the prophet was not already thinking, something slightly comparable to a telephone call that brings a person an unexpected message. This also must be allowed for in the total picture of Hebrew prophecy.

To take as an example a clear-cut directive Divine message in the New Testament, we read in Acts, (8:26) "An angel of the Lord said to Philip, 'Rise and go toward the south to the road that goes down from Jerusalem to Gaza.' This is a desert road." This is not an instance of prophecy, but it is useful as an illustration of the point we are discussing. The word "angel" means "messenger," and the implication is that this is a Divine directive sent to Philip through nonhuman means, and that Philip walked down this desert road without knowing why he had been sent. The reason for using this incident is that Philip apparently obeyed a command that as far as his intelligent consideration was concerned must have seemed to him an irrelevancy. This command, then, is not a case of God's arresting a man's attention upon some thoughts upon which the man's mind was already at work. Here is a thought, disconnected with what the man is thinking, suddenly inserted into his consciousness. The story continues with information that as Philip was walking along there came up an official returning to Ethiopia in his traveling carriage, and the Holy Spirit then commands Philip to join him. Apparently this is the reason for which Philip had originally been told to walk down the Gaza road, a reason that Philip at that time did not know or guess. The question is, in view of modern science, is there any theory possible of a method by which the supernatural God could influence the mind, and this includes the concomitant electro-chemical brain action of Philip, with a command to go down the desert road toward Gaza? The question is important, not so much for this present incident, but because the problem pin-pointed by this incident is the problem of whether any extensive message, initiated by God and not by the intellectual preoccupation of the man, could be given direct by God to Amos, Isaiah, or Jeremiah. The prophetic formula, prefixed to extensive utterances, is, "Thus saith the Lord." Whatever was really the case, the prophets certainly thought their messages were directly given them by God.

Jeremiah, as the most autobiographical of the prophets, gives us most insight into the working of the prophetic mind. He makes it clear that he prophesied against his desire to prophesy, and that the message he delivered was against what he desired to say. He said that because of his message he was derided and made fun of. For he said that as often as he opened his mouth he cried out, "Violence and destruction!" Then he said when he tried to stop his unpleasant prophesying, "There is in my heart as it were a burning fire shut up in my bones, and I am weary with holding it in, and I cannot." (Jeremiah 20:8,9) There is also the very instructive incident in which Jeremiah, after being refused entrance to the Temple court because his prophesying has caused so much disturbance, resorts to having his friend, Baruch the scribe, deliver his prophecies for him. One might think that Jeremiah, in dictating to Baruch, would write a speech appropriate to the immediate occasion. But Jeremiah did not consider all the things he could appropriately have written to be God-given prophecies. Instead he was inspired by God to have Baruch reread to the people the series of prophecies he had given in the past. Apparently Jeremiah had a repertoire of prophecies, many of them in poetic form, that had been given him over the years, and these he dictated to Baruch to read in the Temple court in his stead. (Jeremiah 36:1-8,17,18)

Since therefore the prophets thought that specific messages had been given them by God, we shall try to analyze God's possible *modus operandi* in such a situation. The reason we have taken the non-prophetic directive to Philip to pin-point the problem is that here we have an unusual situation in which it can be rather conclusively shown that God is not making use of what his servant is already thinking.

CHAPTER 30

Trance, Vision, and the Book of Revelation

While I would not belittle the visionary aspect of prophetic thought, visions in the audio-visual sense are not central to it. Elijah at Horeb heard God as a "still small voice." (I Kings 19:12) This was not a new experience for him. There is no indication that the many directives God had given him previously relative to the contest on Mt. Carmel and the events leading up to it were audio-visual. (I Kings 17:1-18:46) Even the medieval Christians, who were predisposed to visions, and tried to cultivate them by fasting and other techniques, distinguished between visions with audio-visual accompaniments and those lacking them, in which God simply spoke directly to the worshiper's heart. And the latter, less spectacular, type of vision was considered the deeper and more advancd.[1] The major emphasis on the non-audio-visual vision is well established centuries before the rise of science. Since the theoretical problems raised by modern thought had not arisen in biblical times, the questions we often raise as to whether an audio-visual vision is "real" or a hallucination just do not arise in that form in the Bible, although it was realized in ancient times that not all visions were from God. Jeremiah speaks of his contemporary prophets as prophesying "lying visions" (14:14, 15) "of their own minds, not from the mouth of the Lord." (23:16; and see Deuteronomy 18:20-22; Ezekiel 13:1-7.)

Probably in biblical times visions with audio-visual accompaniments were thought appropriate to prophetic experience, but when a prophet's intercourse with God was well established in his life the content of the message and not whether or not it had a special "stage setting" was what was important to him and to his hearers. Some of the greatest prophetic passages in Amos, Hosea, I and II Isaiah, and Jeremiah not only are not visionary in the audio-visual sense but they apparently came to the prophets while they were in full contact with the world around them. (See, for example, the

---

[1] Evelyn Underhill, *Mysticism;* New York: E. P. Dutton, 1911, p. 328.

Messianic, Suffering Servant, and New Covenant passages in Isaiah 8:16-9:7; 53; Jeremiah 31:23-34.) There is also very little description of a prophet receiving his message while in a state of trance. Ezekiel and the obscure early prophet Balaam are rather exceptional in the suggestion of a trance state. (See also Daniel 10:8-10 and possibly II Kings 3:15,16.)

The type of direct transfer of a specific message from God to a prophet that I am trying to argue for as "scientifically" possible is the message without either trance or audio-visual accompaniment. This is not because I find either the trance or the audio-visual vision an embarrassment that I think could not be argued for in view of science, or which I am nervous about as "naive" and beneath the level of my intellectual sophistication. It is simply that I am merely interested in substantiating the possibility of God transmitting a message direct to the mind of the prophet, and so I am concentrating on the unspectacular aspect of the problem.

As a matter of fact I am assuming trance to be merely a psychological phenomenon on the part of the religious person, and not part of the Divine activity. There have always been people who purport to be mediums in touch with the spirits of the dead, and these mediums go into trances. While these people are psychologically unusual, their experience is not specifically religious. A person given to trances is not necessarily close to God.

The psychological aspect of the religious trance can be rather easily explained. We suddenly realize how cold the room is after we have finished the exciting detective story. Before that the normal sensation of cold had not reached our consciousness because our minds were wholly concentrated on something else. In direct religious experience of a rather intense sort the concentration of the individual in the experience often causes him to be unheeding of the world around him and confuses also his sense of time. If this type of concentration were very greatly increased there would be the complete or near complete oblivion to the world around and the feeling of timelessness that are characteristic of full religious trance.

But one point needs to be made very clear. There is a very important difference between the trance states of mediums and the trance states of Christian religious experience, or the trance states, in so far as they may have existed, in the Old Testament prophets. The usual explanation given of the trance state of mediums, who try to get in touch with the spirits of the dead, is that the medium, who has unusual powers of detachment, temporarily relinquishes her control of her body to enable the spirits of the dead, who no longer have the physical equipment for mundane communication, to make use of her hands and vocal cords to transmit messages to other human beings. In other words, the spirits of the dead are supposed not primarily to make use of the medium's mind, but of her body. Even where the medium delivers the message consciously, she is at best a mechanical rather than a social go-between. The secretarial voice of a telephone answering service reporting to a physician the calls that have been received in his absence is an occupational example of a human transmitter of messages functioning as a mechanical rather than as a social intermediary. A nurse, caring for a patient under a doctor's orders, performs her task of exact obedience making full use of her training, experience, and insight. She has status as an individual, working intelligently with the physician while working under his direction. These two medical analogies are not exact descriptions of the respective roles of mediums and prophets. But the prophet differs from the medium in the direction of the difference of initiative and previous knowledge involved in the work of the nurse as compared to that of the transmitter of messages in an answering service.

In contrast to the function of a medium, the message from the beyond, from God, is not delivered *through* the prophet, but *to* the prophet. He in turn at a later time delivers the message. It could be weeks or months later, (Amos 7:14,15) or hours later, (I Samuel 3:15-18), or possibly twenty minutes later. (Numbers 23:1-10,13-20) The message always is assumed to go through the prophet's intelligent thinking. It is never mechanical. Even if the whole of the book of Revelation is a vision, there is no indication that when the book was written John was experiencing the vision or trance. The verbs are regularly in the past tense. (See for example Revelation 4:1; 5:1; 6:1; 7:1 etc.) Considering the quickness with which lengthy dreams take place he probably could have had the whole vision in half an hour. Afterwards while the memory of it was still fresh he either wrote or dictated it. The mere mechanics of writing it down would have taken the better part of one day, even if the vision had been verbal throughout, like that of Coleridge's "Kubla Khan." That is, writing down the book of Revelation would have taken one day even if the vision was not merely of the scenes and quoted conversations. But if the visionary scenes were in visual form only, then the seer would later have to think up words to describe accurately what he had seen, and so would have had to do a minimum of editing, polishing, and amplifying to make clear to the reader the vision as it had appeared to him, and this would have taken longer. I am assuming that it would take the better part of one day to dictate the vision even if the vision originally came to him entirely in word form, like a reading accompanied by motion pictures.

I know that there are some people who consider the vision form of the book of Revelation a literary device only. But I doubt whether the possibility of the book being a recording of genuine visionary experience can be altogether ruled out. That "Kubla Khan" is a poem fully composed by the subconscious mind of Coleridge modern sophisticated thinking can believe. And from a study of my own mind I realize that most of my dreams are verbal, with only a slight visual background like the pen and ink sketches in a book. And I myself am almost never a participant in my dreams any more than I am a character in a detective story when I read a detective story. But my dreams typically are not narratives. They seem to be verbal essays, world-shaking in profundity, with all the sentences and paragraphs formed in perfect literary style. I have never, alas, been able to remember even one of the profound sentences I have composed during sleep! But if the subconscious mind is capable of this kind creative writing or composition that concerns ideas, then the possibility of the wording of the book of Revelation being entirely composed by the subconscious during a vision must be at least considered.

The explanation of the inspiration of the book of Revelation would then be that the seer had meditated constantly on Jesus' promises to come again, and upon the verses filled with heavenly imagery and imagery of the end in the apocalyptic passages in the Old Testament—for Revelation to a larger extent than most people realize contains a perfectly fused patchwork of Old Testament quotations—that then his subconscious mind in a visionary or dream state began to fuse all of this into a coherent whole, *and in this process there was miraculous Divine collaboration adding a little to the content of the seer's total thought, and miraculously doing extensive ar-*

ranging and editing of the rest. In other words I think the miraculous Divine collaboration adding somewhat to the total thoughts in the human mind and to a much larger extent editing and arranging the thoughts already in the human mind *is* what we mean when we say the writings of the Old Testament prophets are inspired. If this is the nature of prophetic inspiration it would not matter whether it came to a prophet as collaboration with his subconscious in a dream, or collaboration with his waking thoughts when he was thinking hard about God's relation to the current situation. In either case the question of whether there really had been Divine collaboration, and so the writings could be classed as inspired, would have to be judged on the proof-of-the-pudding-is-the-eating basis, that is, on the basis of whether later generations of God's most loyal servants found that the meditating upon the writings clarified and reinforced their relationship to God. It was human beings, guided by God as they lived in relationship to him, who made the selection of books that form the Old Testament canon.

Leaving aside the question of whether the book of Revelation is a genuine vision or only a book written in visionary form, as C. S. Lewis's *Great Divorce* is written, there are two sets of trance visions reported in the Old Testament. The visions in the first part of the book of Ezekiel form one group. (See especially Ezekiel 8:1-4; 3:26, 27; 33:21,22.) The less famous prophecies of the little known prophet Balaam form the other group. (Numbers 23,24. Notice especially 24:2-4. See also Daniel 10:8-11.) But in these cases the prophecies were not delivered by the prophet to others while the prophet was in trance. And these prophets were very much tangled up in the social situation connected with their prophecies.

Unless I am much mistaken, no great prophetic message in the Old Testament is passed on by the prophet to others while the message is in the process of being originally received by the prophet. This may even hold true of such heated rejoinders as those of Amos and Jeremiah to the religious officials Amaziah and Pashur. (Amos 7:10-17; Jeremiah 20:1-6) But certainly these passages, although they claim to be the word of the Lord, are not among the great prophetic passages in the Old Testament. Certainly I think I am safe in saying that no prophetic message was ever delivered by a prophet to a third party *while* the prophet was in a state of trance. (But see II Kings 3:15-17.) The witch of Endor is not classified as a prophet or a religious leader. She was strictly a medium in the modern sense and her information was obtained in a strictly seance situation. (I Samuel 28:7-20, and compare the Deuteronomic reform II Kings 23:24 and Deuteronomy 18:9-14. See Exodus 22:18.) Whenever a prophet delivered a message the prophet was very much a part of the social situation and very able to view objectively the prophetic message he is giving in relation to the current social situation and to his own intellectual life. This is why "speaking with tongues" was an embarrassment to St. Paul although he himself did it, (I Corinthians 14:1-33) and why he laid down the rule which is in line with all Old Testament prophecy, that "the spirits of prophets are subject to prophets." (I Corinthians 14:29-33) Where God empowers an Old Testament prophet with a particular message, God is in relation to the prophet as a human teacher is to a particularly bright student. Then the prophet, having learned his lesson with God's direct and specific assistance, in turn tries to teach the people God's will.

Before leaving this subject I want to recount the personal experience of a highly respected acquaintance of mine, a woman seventy years old, very intelligent, widely traveled, and a staunch Presbyterian. She told me that in her youth she had been an able, non-professional medium, her specialty being automatic writing. She was convinced that some, at least, of her messages could only be accounted for as the work of discarnate spirits. After a few years she had given up entirely being a medium, she said, because she was convinced that "there was something in it" and she was not sure that it was wholesome. She said that prayer abnegated self-control only in the direction of God and was therefore safe, but that she was afraid to lay herself open spiritually "to the invasion of anything that might be going." Then she added, *"There is an important difference between the experience with the beyond that one has as a medium and the experience with the beyond that one has in prayer. The spirit of a person who habitually prays grows in the slightly mystical experience of prayer. The human spirit does not grow at all through the experience of being a medium."*

CHAPTER 31
God's Method of Conveying Verbal Messages

We now come back to the question of whether God could put into a prophet's mind a somewhat extended thought on a subject on which he was not already thinking. For example, could God have told Philip suddenly and discontinuously from Philip's human thinking that God wanted him to walk down the desert road that goes from Jerusalem in the direction of Gaza, a directive which a man can send in a ten word telegram? In view of science, is it possible to think of God as making even such a brief communication?

Suppose God did it by words that would reach the man as human words do *via* sensation. What would then be involved would be God's miraculous creation of sound waves to reach the human ear. Such sound waves would also reach the ears of any dog or cat or human being that happened to be within their range. This is non-typical of visionary experience. There are three steps in ordinary human communication involving sensation. Mere sensation is insufficient. The mind has to identify the sensation, which is perception, and then classify it and relate it intellectually to other ideas. This third step takes place with the passing of the perception into memory. There are thus three steps in this mental activity, although in familiar circumstances they occur so quickly that we are not conscious of the infinitesimal time-lag between them. The sequence of our sensing and perceiving the salad fork and deducing that we shall have salad for lunch seems to us almost simultaneous. But each of the three steps would occur, and theoretically each of the three would be believed to be accompanied by appropriate electro-chemical changes in the nerve tissue. Since Christianity believes God to be other than the creation, any direct activity of his modifying this sequence at any point would be equally miraculous.

Granted that God is other than his creation and not debarred from acting directly and specifically upon it at will, it follows that it is perfectly easy for God to by-pass *sensation* and begin with *perception* that is shading off into a deduction. If you will listen carefully when people talk you can notice that when a person finishes a sentence there is a split-second in which your mental perception still intellectually "hears" the person speak, although sensation is no longer present, and although the sentence has not yet passed into memory. If God can communicate directly with a human being it would be perfectly possible for God to begin whatever miraculous modification of the human mind and brain was necessary at the post-sensation split-second of mental perception. In the only clear-cut experience I have ever had of "hearing" God speak to me, the incident began at this post-sensation perception that still intellectually heard the fifteen word sentence after it was completed. There was a distinct perception of *having heard* God speak actual words to me, although the sensation to which the perception referred had been completely missing. God seemed outside of me and not in me at all, and yet God seemed completely non-localized. And yet what I was consciously watching throughout the whole incident and watching with objective detachment, was myself as reacting. This was not subjectivism, but as objectively oriented an activity as that of a mariner watching the hands of a compass to determine due-north, which is entirely other than the compass. For one only *knows* God through the human instrument's response to his playing upon it. (This is how all our mundane knowledge, such as the content of the headlines of the newspaper, is obtained by us.) This may sound like a complicated explanation, but the experience was very simple and obvious. I suspect that though such experiences do not usually come many times in a person's life, a very large number of people have some time or other had one or more comparable experiences. During such an experience one is not worried about the mechanics of the Divine intercourse. God always seems quite competent to manage that on short notice. This is why the prophets never really worry about whether God is speaking *in* or *to* them. When God was present to them he identified himself unmistakably and from then on it was the message he was conveying to them that was important.

Even the highly subjective and autobiographical quality of Jeremiah's writings is very different from the present generation's tendency to bog down in subjectivism. Jeremiah's most vivid analysis of his own inner states of consciousness is the passage in which he says that when he decides that he will no longer prophesy for God, there is in his "heart as it were a burning fire shut up in [his] bones,

303

and [he is] weary with holding it in and [he] cannot." (Jeremiah 20:9.) Yet even here we do not really have a focusing of the attention upon Jeremiah. Jeremiah is using his personal experience to focus attention upon God. Temperamentally Jeremiah is a weak timid little man and socially a very lonely person. The power God can exert upon him to bring him to heel is triumphantly asserted as evidence of the strength and nearness of the God who commissioned him and is backing him. Jeremiah may be uncomfortable, but he is at least reassured that he is not alone.

And notice the confused quality of the interior subjective "geography" of the experience. There is nothing really wrong with Jeremiah's bones. If there were, he would feel as if the pain were in his bones. As it is, the fire that he describes as in his bones he does not feel in his bones, but in his heart. There are no words adequate to convey the feel of the presence of God. Jeremiah is getting as close as he can to it by figurative language. And yet one would make a great mistake if he concluded that Jeremiah was merely using poetic and figurative language. He is doing his best to describe exactly a most real feeling that he very literally had.

Of all the direct Divine messages ever given to a Christian the most famous is Christ's message to Paul at his conversion on the road to Damascus. The incident is told on three different occasions in the book of Acts and once by Paul himself in his letter to the Galatians. In Acts 9:3-8 Paul sees a great light and hears the voice of Jesus and falls to the ground. His companions hear a voice, but apparently do not see the light and do not fall to the ground. According to Acts 22:6-11 Paul sees the light and hears the voice and falls to the ground. His companions do not fall to the ground. But contrary to chapter 9, his companions do see the light, but do not hear the voice. However, according to Acts 26:12-18 Paul's companions also fall to the ground, so they apparently do see the light. But Paul seems to be the only one who hears the voice. On the other hand, in Galatians 1:13-18 Paul simply says: "But when it pleased God, who separated me from my mother's womb, and called me by his grace, to reveal his Son in me, that I might preach him among the heathen. . . ." (KJV) no mention is made of either light or voice or of Paul's associates having any experience of being even on the fringes of the vision. A lot of the inconsistencies in these accounts seem to me to be due to the problem of describing the voice that is genuine and yet is not sensation, and the Deity who is *other* and supernatural and yet is known to man only through effects produced within man's spirit, as I have previously described by means of my own very minor experience. For it is only one's own experience that one can describe with certainty. The extent of the audio-visual effects in any contact of man with God is a very minor detail. They do not have to be present at all.

Science assumes that the theory that explains all the relevant facts most economically is the one to go on as a hypothesis. I have never come across a scientific *explanation* of why the simpler useful hypothesis should be supposed to be the correct one. Certainly in social experience it is often not the case: How did Mrs. X learn that Mrs. Y is planning to go to Florida for a month this winter? The simplest hypothesis is that inasmuch as Mrs. X and Mrs. Y are next door neighbors and attend the same bridge club once a week, we can assume that Mrs. X learned it over the bridge table or over the back fence. But of course what may really have happened is that Mrs. Y wrote the news to her son at Amherst, who mentioned it to Mrs. X's daughter whom he was dating at Smith, who in turn repeated the information in her weekly letter home.

When scientists look for the simplest explanation that will account for all the relevant facts one wonders whether they may not be moved thereto by a spiritual hunch that is not itself precisely scientific. One of the things that is very obvious about most individuals of large calibre, is that they are not only very skillful in accomplishing things, but that they also tend to pursue their undertakings with great economy of motion, even when they do not seem to be "efficient" people, with the rather specialized connotations twentieth century America has given to that term. For what America calls "efficiency" is not always beautiful, and if one watches in mental slow motion the directness of these large calibre persons' actions, one finds that the simplicity of the directness of their activity satisfies a craving that is akin to aesthetic craving.

Similarly, although I cannot prove it to be true, I believe as a matter of faith that God acts with the greatest directness and simplicity and with the minimum of interference in his world that is compatible with his achieving his proximate and long distance purposes, taking all the relevant factors into consideration. The simplicity merely seems to be aesthetically appropriate, just as the simplicity of truthfulness, in a really truthful nature, may have an almost aesthetic attractiveness. I find the idea of God's performing an unnecessary miracle spiritually embarrassing. An unnecessary miracle would be one in which God directly intervened in nature where the natural ongoing of the world and of society would have achieved the result he wanted without his interference. This hunch about the economy of means in the spiritual world is purely a hunch, and yet I find it a strong one.

It is partly this hunch that makes me believe that the major part of the Divine guidance of God's servants, whether Old Testament prophets or present day Christians, consists in God's arresting the man's attention upon certain God-selected items that are already normally within the man's stream of consciousness. Such action on the part of God would interfere least with the man's freedom of activity and would probably involve the least possible Divine interference with nature at the physical level, and so would seem to me appropriate. This is not said because of doubts about Almighty God's ability to act on a large scale within his creation when and how he pleases.

St. Augustine was not conditioned by modern man's obsession with the Science Image, and Augustine did not doubt God's ability to control his creation as he pleased. And yet the powerful direct action of God upon Augustine, which even in its reflected form throughout the *Confessions* is exhausting to the reader, is accomplished with a minimum of Divine interference. God fascinated Augustine as the ultimate explanation and the ultimate stability and then simply boycotted him when he went astray, by allowing him to discover the destructive power of time and the lassitude and boredom of the human spirit which eventually render unsatisfying all pleasures that are not grounded in God. When Augustine had been sufficiently educated in this negative manner and God acts with positive initiative to modify Augustine's thoughts directly and to reveal himself directly to Augustine, God "speaks" to Augustine by illumining and making available to him in a new way a series of items with which Augustine's mind is already intellectually furnished.[1]

---

[1] *Confessions*, Bk. VII, Chap. X. For an extended discussion of this incident see my book, *The Omission of the Holy Spirit From Reinhold Niebuhr's Theology;* New York: Philosophical Library, 1964, pp. 102-106.

Even in the scene in the garden in the most important conversion incident in Christian history since St. Paul's vision on the road to Damascus, God largely leaves Augustine to wear himself out by the civil war of the two opposing desires of his spirit. The "outside" influence that marks the watershed moment in his life is his hearing the voice of a child in the neighboring garden chant, "Take up and read." He noticed the words and was at once struck by the fact that they were unusual on the lips of a child, and he took them for a Divine directive to himself which they undoubtedly were. However, Augustine never knew—or cared—whether it was a child simply and normally at play, or a child at play who had been miraculously steered by God for God's own purposes into incorporating those words into his play, or whether it was a miraculous angelic voice in the garden masquerading as a child's voice to assist Augustine, or whether it was God himself speaking to Augustine wholly within Augustine's mind. If the last alternative was the true one, then in-so-far as the voice seemed to come from the neighboring garden the effect was one of hallucination, although in-so-far as the content of the message was concerned it was not hallucination at all, because the content of the message was instigated by the really present power of God for Augustine's benefit, and Augustine's mind did not on its own conjure up an idea that was so vivid that it attached to itself the sensation of heard words. Again, God's activity that finally completes the conversion of Augustine is one of those instances in which God's activity is recognized only after it is accomplished. Augustine can only describe the result: "All the darkness of doubt vanished away." [*Confessions* Bk. VIII, chaps. vii-xii]

There are parallels to this incident in the story of the would-be suicide who saw the angel's wing shell. In the case of the sight of the shell and in the case of the words, "Take up and read," we are left with the possibility that the whole incident might be merely natural, or with the possibility that God is using a natural occurrence and miraculously calling a man's attention to it. In both incidents the man is left to do as much as he can by his human powers, and both instances give the strong impression of the power of God close at hand watching and prepared to assist if necessary.

The problem of whether God ever actually transmits ideas directly to a man involves the question of how our ordinary thinking is initiated. Secular learning has assumed that all thinking is

307

initiated originally by sensation and perception, and the mind's cross-reference system dealing with what it has received in this way. Although thoughts can also be initiated by previous thoughts, which in turn are called up by still previous thoughts, ultimately they all depend on information the mind has received through sensation and the innate ability of the mind to deal with sensation. Supposedly there is no other source for human thoughts. The modern theory of the subconscious mind claims that thinking goes on continuously in the subconscious mind during sleep, and thus conveniently explains why sleep does not render the human personality discontinuous. The theory also explains our experience of sudden ideas "popping into our minds" as unexpected emergences into consciousness of bits of the thinking being constantly carried on by the subconscious mind. Thus there would seem to be no exception to the rule that any thinking that we do—where not initiated directly by sensation and perception—makes use of other thoughts which depend ultimately on sensation and perception.

If this theory explains all our thinking, it looks as if there were no way open for God's direct initiation of ideas in a man's mind. The question now is, can any third method be found of initiating ideas in a person's consciousness that will be in line with information we have obtained through science? I believe that it can be found, and that this third method very possibly has light to throw on the method of God's direct communication with men. A recent scientific discovery may suggest what that third way is. A contemporary brain surgeon[2] has recently discovered that when he had cut away the skull and exposed the brain during an operation, that he was helped in locating the exact portion of the brain upon which he needed to operate and in avoiding those portions with which it was wise not to tamper, if he touched one point and then another of the brain with a delicate instrument that conveyed a very slight electrical stimulus to the brain tissue. When he touched certain areas he discovered that the patient recalled in extraordinarily vivid detail incidents and conversations from her past. Later experimentation with other patients yielded the same results. This seems to be clinical corroboration for the long held hypothesis that the brain acts as a tape-recorder, recording all our experience, and then that our brain

---

[2] I am basing this on an article by Dr. Wilder Penfield, "The Uncommitted Cortex," which appeared in *The Atlantic Monthly*, July, 1964, pp. 77-81.

replays parts of our experience to us, and that that is the physiological basis of memory. But these memories are usually not called up with such vividness that we seem to be reliving the experience. However the subjects of this clinical electrical brain stimulus recalled the events with almost the vividness of their original experience of them, although from the description in the article I gather that the intensity was not full hallucination, for during it they were still aware of where they were and that they were undergoing surgical treatment.

My own deduction from the article is that the increased vividness of recall that these patients experienced was due to the electrical stimulus employed by the doctor being slightly greater than the electro-chemical stimulus the brain usually furnishes to recall past events.

The peculiar thing about this stimulation the surgeon used is that it was purely mechanical stimulation, using neither immediate sensation nor the association of ideas currently in the patients' minds to trigger the mind's reawakening of memories. And the same mechanical stimulation produced qualitatively different results at the conscious level depending upon the part of the brain that was stimulated. Touching different parts of the brain reawakened different memories. One really gets here something roughly corresponding to the qualitatively different response given by the various harp strings to the same mechanical plucking on the part of the harpist. If the person who is plucking the harp strings is not experimenting in a hit or miss fashion, but is an experienced harpist who really understands the range of the instrument, then the sounds that result may be arranged in the sequence of highly artistic music, and the harp may give forth a tune that it has never before given forth.

I would like to suggest the tentative hypothesis that by some such mechanical means God can convey if he wishes a new and detailed message to a human mind.

We have already made heavy use of the theory that God's ability to use the merely statistical regularity of matter to effect very slight changes at the sub-atomic level may account for the method by which he brings about effects in nature, effects that are very strategic to his plan and usually very small as to the amount of matter involved. We have also stated as a basic hypothesis that all matter, being originally the creation of mind, is relatable to mind. So it would be hypothetically possible for God either to deflect electric currents already existing in a human mind, or to create *ex nihilo* sufficient electrical stimulus to stimulate a human mind. In either case genuine miracle in a small area of matter would take place. The stimulation as applied by God would also differ from that of the surgeon in that God would know in absolute detail the human instrument upon which his power was playing so that he would be able to combine at will both complex and very simple memories to compose a new message he wished to convey. (Remember that our vocabulary itself is part of the tape recorded message that is held for us by our brains.) God could also in doing this, allow much or little of the cooperation of the normal human association of ideas to play into the construction of the message in the human being's consciousness. The important thing, for direct Divine guidance to occur, is that the human being shall end up with an idea God wishes him to get, and that the process of the man's getting it shall involve some specific direct off-schedule activity of God upon the man's consciousness, in which God does something to the man with the immediate purpose of assisting him to gain this idea. Needless to say, God has probably guided most those whom he could guide with the least direct interference, as in human education the human teacher can convey ideas and directions more economically to bright mature students than to youngsters.

If this fantastic-appearing hypothesis of mine is correct it would explain several things that have very much needed explaining. It would explain why the "word of the Lord" came through in such various literary styles to the various prophets. The same prophetic thread of ideas runs through all Hebrew prophecy, but the styles of Amos, Hosea, Nahum, and Jeremiah differ markedly from each other. After all, one could play the same tune on a guitar, mandolin, harp, violin, or base viol, but the music in each case would take on the characteristic sound of the instrument. The theory also accounts for the element of progressive revelation. A superb musician can play more adequately upon a five manual organ than upon a two manual organ. Granted equal devotion to God on the part of the prophets, and equal Divine assistance to each prophet, the more extensive the prophet's personal and social experience and the greater his knowledge at the intellectual level with the history of the nation and the teachings of other prophets, the greater the range of latent ideas from which God could make a selection in formulating a message to a prophet. This does not necessarily mean that the more highly schooled in a technical sense a person is the more potentially useful he is to God. A great deal of education can be picked up in an informal way, and furthermore, sometimes the informal type of education leaves the mind less cluttered by pedantic minutiae and so more sensitive to God and more free for Divine guidance and creative thought. However, part of the usefulness of St. Paul to Christ and to the Church lay in the fact that he combined an uncluttered mind with great learning.

This explanation of God's method of directly inspiring a prophet also accounts for something in the Old Testament attitude toward Scripture that is very hard for the great majority of twentieth century Americans to grasp. If one points out that there are ancient beliefs embedded in the Old Testament to which later Old Testament writers would not subscribe, as when God was thought to be the kind of God who would knock Uzzah down dead when the latter inadvertently touched the ark of the covenant to steady it on the cart that was transporting it, (II Samuel 6:1-11) they tend to think of the Old Testament as sociologically primitive and not authoritative for our modern lives. On the other hand, where the Fundamentalist groups have tried to fight the admitted dangers of this modern viewpoint they have done so by claiming verbal inspiration in a sense approaching Divine dictation.

The Old Testament attitude toward Scripture is different from either. In the first place Genesis and Exodus were not *written up* from previous source material. They were an edited verbatim patchwork of previous source material. J., E., and P. strands were carefully preserved and dovetailed together with a minimum amount of editing to make a consecutive narrative. The writer or writers who did this felt responsible for accurate transmission of the sources. But they also felt free to do a minimum amount of necessary editing under God's guidance.

CHAPTER 32

Miracle Involved in the Biblical Revelation As the Special Revelation of God

God's self-imposed task was that of bringing the creation back in freedom to himself. As the overall picture of matter is that of dissolution, so the overall picture of evolution is that of increasing life and freedom. With the earliest living forms the divine pattern for their existence, which the creatures strove to hold, was that of life against death. Later, when animals had definite means of locomotion, pain appeared to assist them to keep away from inimical situations. The animal now had reached the level at which it strove not only to hold its being in pattern appropriate to its species, but also to hold its *well*-being. The further development of the animals includes the increase of consciousness, the rudiments of affection, and some organized social life. Throughout the course of evolution, when it is seen in its over-all pattern, the increasing complexity of the organisms enables them to reflect more and more facets of God's nature.

With the attainment of what we think of as the specifically human abilities, culminating in the ability to recognize and choose between moral right and wrong and in the ability to love, man is thought of as reflecting the guiding characteristics and activity of the Godhead and so as being made in the image of Deity. Man has now reached a point at which he is potentially capable of a social relationship with God himself. The question arises of how God could carry on social relationships with men, for social relationships at the human level involve the give-and-take of ideas. It is therefore necessary to find some theoretical possibility in the theory of evolution for the give-and-take of ideas between men and God.

At this point the major collision has come between Christian and scientific thought. For the plants and animals throughout the whole evolutionary sequence, and man because he is also an animal, are complicated organized systems of matter, which as they increase in complication exhibit life in an increasingly intense and many faceted form. But even human organisms are composed of matter, and matter moves in an interrelated fashion according to the standard patterns of chemistry and physics. Even the conscious mind of man seems to act with concomitant changes in the physical brain. Now, from the point of view of physical science there is no problem in the social give-and-take between man and God on the side of God's receiving from man—deism can envisage this—but only on the side of man's receiving from God. Theoretically, if God were thought of in entirely deistic fashion as supernatural to the world, but not in any way acting upon it, then scientists would have no difficulty with the Christian claim that God hears men's prayers. Science would merely point out that the reasons for men's praying could be found in events in the natural world and that the prayers they mentally offer are accompanied by physiological changes in the brain. If God is conscious of these prayers the problem of whether he exists and if so how he becomes conscious of these prayers is of no concern whatever to science, because science deals only with the universe in its objectively measurable aspects, and a deistic God is by definition completely outside the universe. How or whether he acts at all completely outside the universe does not intersect with the domain of scientific thought.

If, however, there is a social relationship in which a God, who is not part of the universe, speaks to a man who is part of the universe, then, since man is a psycho-physical organism, the repercussions of the supernatural God's speaking to the man initiate changes at the material level, and science has thought of nature as an interacting interrelated whole, and has allowed no place in its theory for a breaking of nature's pattern by interaction from outside of nature.

Now it is the thesis of this book that the pattern of nature, when left entirely to its own devices, is an overall entropy. It follows then that the whole evolutionary sequence reflects God's specific dealings with specific portions of his creation at specific times and places. A considerable amount of space was devoted to suggesting how, by means of the leeway allowed by the merely statistical regularity of subatomic action, he could adequately manipulate nature in the direction of desirable mutations, and/or the mutations having taken place (possibly by chance) he could assist the desired organisms in their struggle for existence by appreciation, experience that is a half-way point between the "I-it" and the "I-thou" relationship.

Certainly one must think of God's continuing with members of religions outside of Judaism and Christianity *at least* the kinds of intimacy and care and encouragement that our theory posits of his relation in the course of evolution with the sub-human creation.

But when we come to Christianity we come to a religion that claims that in the case of the Hebrew people there has been a tiny nation which God especially chose and with which he entered into full social intercourse, and that the Christian Church inherits its position of being the true religion which God wishes to have universally accepted, because Christianity is the inheritor of and continuing cooperator with the full Hebrew revelation. The problem of substantiating the possibility of this in relation to science is much more difficult.

The Christian claim of revelation involves the claim that God especially called Abraham to found a special nation, that God rescued the clans of his descendants from slavery in Egypt, showed them at Sinai that he wished them to worship him alone and that his basic service consisted in following basic moral principles, and then that he officially adopted the nation. All this is involved in the exodus, the giving of the Ten Commandments, and the establishment of the covenant. In the thousand years that followed men arose within this nation who are thought by Judaism and Christianity to be mouthpieces of the Lord through whom he directly warned and guided and illuminated his people, and prepared them for the path ahead. The problem is, can any method of God's direct social intercourse in which messages of specific content were conveyed from God to the mind of Moses and the great prophets be theoretically accounted for? The conveying of messages to this handful of great individuals is not all that is meant by Hebrew prophecy, not the only way in which God related himself to the nation. Yet it is fair to say that if all direct messages to Abraham, Moses, and the great prophets were ruled out, that the Hebrew religion's claim to direct revelation from God is disastrously refuted. Our long account of the possible methods of direct contact of God with the human soul has been intended to clear the way for the acceptance of the Hebrew religion's claim to be revealed by God.

314

Now salvation, according to Christianity, is supposed to be salvation from sin and death, which involves salvation to harmony with God and to the permanent joy that is the opposite of all ennui and frustration. The emphasis we have put upon the *second law of thermodynamics* links those two aspects of salvation. Christ, by dying to save man from sin, overcame death itself on man's behalf to God's glory. In doing this Jesus Christ was the culmination and completion of the prophetic revelation. Let us see how the work of Christ fits into the picture of human existence we have been outlining.

CHAPTER 33

Augustinianism, Pelagianism, and the Cultural Lag

In the first place our theory eases the theoretical problem of original sin and the Augustinian-Pelagian dilemma. To put those positions in extreme opposition the Augustinian says: "If men by their own efforts can please God, Christ's death for our sins was unnecessary. But Christ's death was necessary because all men are trapped in original sin, which all men inherit from Adam by natural generation. Thus all men are sinners, deserving death, and can only be saved through Christ by God's grace." The Pelagian position counters by saying: "If man can do nothing toward saving himself, and can make no effort toward his salvation that is not due to the grace of God, then man has no freedom of choice and so no moral responsibility. Therefore God would not be a righteous God because he would be arbitrarily giving his saving grace to some and arbitrarily damning others by not giving them his saving grace. But God is as a matter of fact righteous, and man as a matter of fact has moral responsibility. Therefore man must have freedom to turn or not to turn to God." A third position as to sin that has been popular in recent times is that it is the evolutionary lag man has not yet overcome but which he will eventually overcome by his own efforts in his ever upward social climb to bigger and better things. This third theory has been less popular since World War II has shown that men increase evil by means of their increased knowledge. Modern men have become more discouraged about man's ability to perfect man. The third theory, although shallow, does take evolution into account in spite of the theory's inadequacy in dealing with the problem of sin and salvation.

If, however, we take the entropy of the universe into account we are able to say that there is a sense in which the old theologians were correct when they said that the only thing man contributes toward his salvation is his sin! For all the power man has control of to use follows the entropy tendency. The slump toward patternless inaction or entropy or "death" is the great miracle of creation. The miracle was not the creation of something other-than-God, but the creation of something other-than-God that contained a contrary-to-God aspect, because diminution, dissipation, exhaustion, or death has no counterpart in the experience of God as God. Because God is the only self-sufficient source of strength, the matter which was created by God, when left to move on its own without his support, inevitably manifested entropy. God was responsible for this inevitability but not for the entropy which did not set in until matter was "on its own." And furthermore, since the original entropy or "death factor," was not an evil—there being no living things in the universe for the entropy to be an evil *for*—God cannot be said to be the Creator of evil.

It is only when God interfered with the "comfortable slump" of inorganic matter to try gradually to get matter to freely reverse the entropy trend in the direction of free conformity to matter's Creator, that the entropy trend, in pulling against the increasing organization of matter into higher and higher organisms, became an evil. We have sketched the possible way in which God brought evolution about and described the possibility that once a valuable mutation was established the power of God by his appreciation and by his presence as "lure" may have assisted the organism to struggle to hold its appropriate pattern as long as possible. The "striving" that is being predicated now of all organisms, even beneath the level of consciousness, may be the creaturely response to this Divine activity. But even so no organism could hold out long against exhaustion due to the entropy tendency of the matter of which it was formed. And God could not counteract the entropy tendency by force, by the "push from behind" which he would have been entirely capable of administering. For to *force* the organism's continuation in life would have taken away freedom, and the whole daring plan of God involved having the free return of the creation to himself in surrendering love. So the ingenious device of reproduction was utilized by which new fresh organisms were formed to hold the line of the organism's characteristic pattern when the parent organism was at length forced by entropy to lose the struggle of holding matter in highly organized form against the force of dissolution. And reproduction also made possible increasing complication of organisms by mutations which became standardized species forms. Thus far we are talking about evolution in the early stages, that is, pre-vertebrate evolution.

Now the point that must be made is this: Each creature if left to its own devices will inevitably perish, because the creature is composed of matter which is characterized by dissolution or entropy. But in its upward course the evolutionary rise consolidates and passes on to later generations and species the help against entropy to which it has been assisted by God. And so, by the time the higher mammals appeared, they appeared as creatures that had inherited considerable anti-entropy power from their predecessors, which they now had on their own, in addition to the contemporary assistance they were receiving in terms of the "lure" of "appreciation" of God's presence. Of course, even with this inherited anti-entropy power the mammals, too, eventually succumb to death.

That evolution is a process in which organisms build upon and consolidate the hard-won strength and freedom so that what originally came from God is now the property of the creatures, from the immediate point of view their earthly inheritance, can be observed by considering the progress in the method of nourishment. The plants transmute inorganic to organic matter. Animals feed upon plants and so have part of their work done for them. Some of the higher animals are carnivores, increasing their own freedom by adopting the labor-saving device of feeding directly on animal protoplasm. When we come to social and intellectual evolution in man, we find education and then writing the means by which the race's hard won cultural attainments can be neatly "packaged" and "fed" to each succeeding generation, to equip them as expeditiously as possible with power for further social advances.[1]

For the repetition of this accumulative process of strength in evolution has its counterpart in the accumulating inherited power of the creature, man, in the social evolution that we are thinking of as continuing in another form of development after man reached the organic species' physical maturity. Until man appeared in the evolutionary sequence the trend was toward increased complexity to increase the creatures' hold upon life. With human social development the evolutionary struggle to hold on to life came to include the holding on to increasingly valuable life, the attempt not only to live but to live well. The evolutionary technique of consolidating

---

[1] It should be noted parenthetically that Christianity describes the ultimate well-being of men in terms of lives turned voluntarily to direct feeding upon God himself. John 6:47-51.

the gains of the past (all of which were originally made by the fostering assistance of God) can be seen in the history of the Hebrew religion also. It has been pointed out that all of the prophets had their own serious thinking and their human knowledge of their nation's past to build upon, and that then God seems to have "pulled the strings" of their spiritual insight, but to have done so with the minimum violence to the creature's mental life that it was possible for him to employ if he was to make them bearers of prophetic messages from himself.

If we project our evolutionary theory upon the moral insight that novelists, teachers, and the theological man-on-the-street have always had, we get a theoretical interpretation of man's freedom, power, and yet ultimate impotence that seems reasonable. (Neither Pelagianism nor Augustinianism has ever seemed really reasonable to me.) Because God has assisted the human race, each generation to some extent stands on the shoulders of previous generations. We at least have records of various methods of government and how they work. We know that some things are favorable to human health and some are not. We have the accumulated spiritual experience of the past to guide us including that recorded in the Bible that came through God's special revelation, and we have the insight of non-biblical thinkers, and we are all trained in early childhood by a generation steeped in the heritage of the past so that much of our inheritance we absorbed unconsciously, and we follow its pattern almost unconsciously. Now the direction of biological evolution and of socio-cultural evolution which has followed it has been in the direction of increased freedom and power, and this accumulated freedom and power is part of our heritage. We therefore as individuals have some genuine freedom and ability to know and do the right, that are part of our earthly heritage now, derived from our human and pre-human ancestors, and which are not now *directly* derived from the grace of God. We have therefore some real freedom and moral insight now apart from God, and we have therefore a corresponding responsibility.

So far Pelagian common sense is correct, and it in no way derogates from the prestige and over-ruling authority of God. Many a high powered family has sent its children to boarding school with the express intention of giving the young a chance to be self-determining away from the smothering influence of the too close proximity of their dominating parents. God wanted his children to have real freedom, and that means some real freedom on their own to do what is good as well as freedom to do what is evil.

But of course man cannot save himself, because he holds his pattern for living—not just life as the animals have it but the morally good life—within the overall pattern of the entropy of the cosmos of which he is a part. By himself, therefore, he cannot hold constantly and continuously to the pattern he should follow, but slumps into his tendency to "backslide" which is his inherited entropy and is a fatal defect with which he is born, the "original" quasi-sin over which man has no control, and which, when it inevitably sometimes includes moral backsliding, is his spiritual sickness rather than his vice, but is still sin in that it is a drawing of the personality away from God. The free positive voluntary linkage of the personality with this tendency to backslide is positive sin in the culpable sense, and earns a man death as part of the total dissolution of the creation. (Romans 6:20,21,23) The assistance God gives to help man in this predicament is supernatural assistance and therefore has to be the free—and miraculous—gift of God's grace and nothing man is able to do or get on his own. This explains the seeming ambiguity of Jesus' teaching: the shepherd had to go and get the lost sheep and the woman had to search for the lost coin, but the Prodigal Son had to say, "I will arise and go to my father." (Luke 15) The inanimate and subhuman creation has almost no accumulated ability to take the initiative in returning to God, and man as he is linked to the lower creation shares some of its impotence; but in so far as he is human he has some conscious freedom and power on his own to attempt the return to his Maker and is therefore morally culpable if he does not make the effort. But even if the Prodigal Son did make the effort and return on his own two feet, it was only an attempted return and would not have accomplished its purpose had not his father taken the initiative and received him back into the family. Salvation has to be always God's free gift.

We are not yet discussing how God attempts to assist all men all along the path of life, both pagans who have never heard of Christ and those who have grown up in the Christian tradition but are not yet converted to Christ. The assistance he can give these people is genuine, but limited by his own decision to respect his creation, and especially man, without interfering with the creature's freedom.

320

It may be that the randomness of sub-atomic nature is the randomness of undisciplined (i.e., untrained) nature at its very beginning. In that case the existence of the atomic elements themselves would be due to God's acting upon the basic stuff of the creation to assist the basic stuff of creation to hold itself in primitive constellations or aggregates which in their turn could be usable in the future evolutionary process.

If, then, man has some real freedom and power to turn to God and to try and do what is right, what becomes of the demand of Christian teaching that man has nothing by himself of which to boast, but that it is his duty to attribute his sin to himself and to attribute his salvation and any efforts he may make thereto and any good he may accomplish before or after his conversion wholly to the prevenient grace of God? The answer can be made in story form, but the story can be only a parable, and not fully an allegory.

Suppose there was a boy who went away to college, his father paying his full board and room and tuition to enable him to do so. It so happened that independently of his father he had a small income from a trust fund that had been left him in the will of his paternal grandfather. This small income was sufficient to cover comfortably but not lavishly his expenses for books, clothes, and incidentals. This small independent income which was his legally would give him some genuine independence from his father, and a degree of financial independence greater than that enjoyed by those of his classmates who were entirely dependent on the monthly allowance from home. But it would be the height of foolishness for this student to pride himself on being a "self-made man" because of this independent income, and this for two reasons. In the first place the basic factor of his continuing in college is dependent upon the loving gift, or charity, of his father, in paying his board, room, and tuition. In the second place, this inherited income, which is now legally his own and not now dependent upon the giving of another, is nothing he himself has earned. It was made possible by the loving gift, or charity, of his grandfather, and represents wealth earned by the years of labor of his grandfather and father, and all those who under them labored in the family business. This income that is now his by right, and is not a contemporary gift, is an inheriting of the charity of the past.

In the same way man is completely dependent upon God for

321

the initial gift of the universe itself that man is now free to use, as well as completely dependent upon God for his salvation, and not to acknowledge thankfully God's gifts by attempting to serve him devotedly is both sinful ingratitude and foolishness. For no one can escape the ultimate power of physical death except by the power of God. And no one can escape the power of moral evil, sin as moral slump, without the charity of God's present power upholding him.

But it is possible for man, entirely on his own, to retard both the physical and moral forms of degeneration a little. A man who treats his body with respect and lives according to a regime that is conducive to health may live a few years longer than he would had he done otherwise. And a man whose life is not personally committed to God, but who has an intelligent appreciation of the advantages of the general comfort of a morally stable society, may rather steadily make arrangements where he conveniently can in life that are in line with the basic dictates of righteousness, and do this on the motivation of enlightened self-interest and diffuse altruism. This type of life has some positive goodness in it which should not be belittled. Many times such men have conferred some benefits upon the human race, although the benefits may not have been as unadulterated as the donors believed and the recipients hoped. For since it is true that he who pays the piper tends to call the tune, these benefits tend to have built into them more selfish worldliness than the donors pictured to themselves, although not more than actually governed their lives and the lives of the recipients who played-up to them. Nevertheless there are apparently a few people in the world whose lot in life has been such that they are able to pursue the strategy of enlightened self-interest and diffuse altruism for the three score years and ten without doing any one thing that flagrantly transgresses the basic rules of the moral law. But this type of life usually compromises a little if it has to "hold its own" in competition, and even if it largely escapes personal compromise it lacks a "living" quality, and does not increase, but at best transmits, society's built-in heritage of moral strength.

It is true, however, that within limits merely self-centered worldly life has power to foster its bodily health and to organize its conduct in a good direction in both the moral and aesthetic areas, and this without any present help from God. Practically speaking, each individual does have a certain amount of autonomous power which he is responsible for using wisely. This is the great insight that becomes dangerous when elevated by secularism's individualism to a basic life-strategy. For secularism's individualism confuses this small degree of human God-entrusted autonomous *power* with the idea of human autonomous *law*, and assumes that mankind is a law unto itself. This is sinful denial of the overlordship of God. The distinction made here between autonomous power and autonomous law is a major emphasis of the Old Testament: man is to have power and dominion over the earth (Genesis 1:26), but he is responsible for freely using his power and dominion in obedience to God (Genesis 2:16, 17).

The Christian has a right to know that he has this autonomous power and therefore the responsibility for its right use, just as the college student had a right to know that he had an independent control over and a right to the income from his grandfather's inheritance. But the Christian or non-Christian should recognize, like the college student, that the extent of his autonomous power, in the total life situation in which he finds himself, is comparatively small. He should also realize, with respectful conscientious gratitude for it, that it is a charitable gift to him from the past.

Gratitude is a virtue and ingratitude is a sin. A person who does not believe in the existence of God can still rightfully be held guilty if his life is not at least characterized by gratitude for benefits conferred upon him by present and past society. For all that we have came to us through the blood and tears of the long upward struggle, the struggle of the prehuman creatures who made possible the evolutionary development of our highly developed bodies, the struggle at the human level of primitive man who with great labor learned to make earthenware pots and flint knives, and to domesticate cattle and to make rules for primitive tribal organization. Then there was the whole hard process by which knowledge was consolidated and writing invented for its transmission. The labors of unknown people lie behind the more spectacular legacy to us of the great lawgivers, philosophers, literary men, historians, artists, musicians, scientists, physicians, and inventors of the age of recorded history.

The Christian, however, has a double gratitude. He is grateful to the past creation, human and pre-human, for the inheritance it has bequeathed to him. But he is also aware that evolution, biological and cultural, could only have arisen and have made headway against the powerful tendency of entropy by means of the lure and appreciation of Deity, forever watching over the creation with loving concern, and assisting the creation in embodying at last high values, and in holding tenaciously to them and transmitting them. Thus what comes to the Christian from the nature it is his province to dominate is indirectly charity from God. Therefore, like the college student whose independence is brought about by family charity, the Christian knows that all good things that he is or possesses come originally from God, and so he is grateful to God for all good things that he possesses or is or does, even though he knows that much of the good came to him from nature. For it was the wise and careful preparation of the creation by God in the past that now makes it possible for man to have access to physical power and embodied values that are made available to him in ways that will not interfere with his free will.

Incidentally this is one of the reasons why the completion of the revelation of God had to be by the Incarnation. People often wonder why God could not accomplish the revelation of himself directly to each human soul. But to complete the revelation of himself directly to our human consciousness would overpower us by the intensity of the Divine presence and take away our freedom. By the Incarnation God made the completion of his self-revelation part of the world with which we could deal without loss of our freedom.

CHAPTER 34

The Reason and Need for the Incarnation

But the great difficulty is that nature and man at the physical level, and man at the moral level, can only hold out for a little while against the forces of dissolution. The death of physical organisms was always obvious and the human tendency to moral backsliding had been made obvious by the Old Testament prophets. They had also made clear that God is a God of righteousness and steadfast love who wanted human beings to serve him and find their well-being in his service, and that he is actively engaged in trying to promote this.

But something more was needed than an increasing reflection of the Divine, for the reflection was made upon a human medium that was itself impermanent. The matter of which the universe and man were originally made could only have autonomous power by releasing it by "dying". The addition of God's own deathless life was needed within the created universe to anchor it to deathlessness by anchoring it to himself. But true to God's custom of avoiding doing violence to the creation that would destroy its freedom, the ground had to be carefully prepared for the Incarnation of God.

The brief earthly life of the Son of God had to be placed in a human environment that sufficiently understood it to make it possible for Christ to act with significance toward it, and for it to make his significance intelligible to the world at large afterwards. An easy-going nation that took with tolerance Jesus' claim to be the Son of God would have been less useful to him in making the world understand his mission than a nation that was so aware of the predicament of human sin and the moral difference between man and his Maker that they would execute him for blasphemy for making the claim to be the "Christ, the Son of the Blessed." (Mark 14:61-64)

The violence with which Jesus spoke against the Pharisees makes us tend to caricature them and to be blind to the amount of similarity between his religious views and theirs. What Jesus lashed out against was often the standard ordinary Pharisee. In any great intellectual movement that has popularity and prestige many who are attracted to it lack the subtlety of insight and the purity of devotion of the movement's great leaders. But even Pharisaism at its best was off-center in Jesus' estimation, because it seemed to make man's salvation dependent on what man did, rather than upon God's charity to man; and Pharisaism's attempt to serve God by keeping the law made the mistake of thinking that keeping the exact details of the ceremonial law are essential to man's right relationship with God. Thus the mind of the devotee was drawn away from the realization that righteousness and especially love are the central characteristics of God himself, and of his motives regarding men. To the best Hebrew thought the giving of the law had been a favor conferred by God upon his people, because in the law he had shadowed forth to them a portrait of his own nature. The attempt to keep the law therefore had in it at its best an element of spontaneous gratitude. It was the eager attempt of the beloved to conform to the Lover.

The genius of Pharisaism at its best recognized that the nation, trapped by the power of Rome, could not save itself nationally in a political fashion. The Pharisees realized that their only safety depended upon the good pleasure and activity of the supernatural God who is the Lord of history. He had founded the nation in an original rescue of his people from slavery and he would rescue the nation again and reestablish it in triumph. But by the first century well over a thousand years of training in the law and the prophets had intervened since the original exodus. The Hebrew nation was now far more intensely aware of the ingredient of righteousness in the holy otherness of God.

This created a predicament. The nation needed God's help to insure its safety. But God, as himself perfectly righteous, could only show himself favorably inclined to righteous men. (Exodus 19:5, 6). There would, as it were, have to be a welcoming committee, even if it were a minority of the nation, with whom God could make favorable rapport with no derogation of his own righteousness. For since God is against wickedness, if he drew near and found men unrighteous his reaction to them would have to be the reverse of pleasant because of the consistency of the Divine character. Amos had pointed out this basic fact long before and struck a key note in Hebrew prophecy when he said,

Woe to you who desire the day of the Lord!
Why would you have the day of the Lord!
It is darkness, and not light. (Amos 5:18.)
In this difficulty the passion of the best of the Pharisees for keeping themselves scrupulously pure and separate from evil, even in all the details of the ceremonial law, was not just a contempt for others and a selfish interest in their own salvation. They were attempting by their purity to do something that would aid the nation as a whole. They were making their lives the red carpet appropriate for Divine approach: the landing-strip was being prepared for heavenly traffic. As devout Pharisees undoubtedly realized, and as the Pharisee Saul of Tarsus realized with intense torment in his own life, human nature could not make this preparation perfectly. It is against the background of this understanding of the human situation that the first Jewish exponents of Christianity proclaimed joyously that Jesus Christ had "fulfilled the law." In one instance a human life had been completely obedient to God. (Galatians 4:4; Matthew 5:17; Romans 13:10).

Thus far in this book I have fought the modern theory that Old Testament prophecy can be defined in terms of God's self-unveiling. My reason for doing this is that by thus reducing Hebrew prophecy modern theologians have a plausible excuse for making a static picture of God's self-revelation, and so are able to avoid the embarrassment of describing God as active in specific instances in relation to particular men. For this activity, even if it were only that of conveying a particular brief message to a particular prophet, would involve the taboo question of miracle.

However, in spite of the fact that God revealed himself by his activity, the *goal* of revelation is not specific thises and thats of a subordinate variety, but the self-revelation of God himself to man to take men into intimate companionship with himself.

The reason the Pharisees' legalistic strategy for assisting in the coming of the kingdom of God seems foolish to us in the twentieth century is not that we are characterized as Jesus was by the flaming love of God and one's neighbor that fulfills the law (Galatians 5:14; Romans 13:10), but rather that the currently admired characteristic that is generally assumed to be a great virtue is a harmony-fostering genial broadmindedness, and a mis-definition of humility to mean that everybody should be treated alike because every-

327

body is as good as everybody else, and any obvious moral discrimination is therefore an indication of the sin of pride. The idea that one partakes of moral evil or sin by condoning it in others, and that not to stand against moral evil is to be guilty of it one's self, (Leviticus 5:1) is not an idea that is congenial to the modern mind. To be an acquiescing accessory to moral evil before, during, or after the fact is to partake of it. This position the Bible makes very clear. One is warned not to entangle one's self by accepting favors from wicked men: "Let me not eat of their dainties!" (Psalm 141:4)[1]

God's setting up his Kingdom involved his revealing himself in more intimate relationship to his nation. But although the Old Testament says God forgives sins and God loves men, its great emphasis is nevertheless on his uncompromising righteousness. Were God to interfere miraculously to set up the hoped-for Kingdom, if his further self-unveiling were to show his graciousness, the nation, or a minority within the nation, would have to be in fact righteous, otherwise God's graciousness would imply a compromise of his own ethical integrity. And man, as St. Paul very well knew, could not be perfectly righteous, and so merit the graciousness of the perfectly righteous God.

A partial answer to the difficulty, that God hates the sinner's sin rather than the sinner, which eases somewhat the problem of God's compromising himself by loving the sinner, only seems obvious to us because we are Christians. We do not realize that the problem was a Gordian knot that could only be cut by the Incarnation, that is, by God coming to the human level, and permanently entangling himself with human life. Jesus Christ as the God-man could welcome sinners and unveil his, and the Father's love for us without compromising the Divine Righteousness. In this he was able to do what the Father by himself could not do, because of the Father's refusal to interfere with men's freedom. Although Christ consorted with sinners and showed his love for them he could make it clear that he could not allow himself to be a party to their sinfulness. He drew this distinction by avoiding sin entirely for himself and struggling so hard for righteousness and against sin in others that the evil in men brought about his violent

---

[1] See also Proverbs 17:15; 22:24, 25; 23:1-3; 23:20, 21; 24:1, 2, 24, 25; 28:4, 17; 29:24, 27; and I Corinthians 5:11, 13.

death after a brief three year ministry.

But God the Father could not make this distinction clear to men. For God as God does not have to struggle for personal righteousness, and maintain his personal righteousness at the cost of severe injury inflicted upon his person by evil. The Father does not have to struggle for personal righteousness because he is himself its living source. And the Father as Supreme Power does not have to stand for righteousness at the cost of personal danger and injury to himself. For by definition God in his supreme power cannot be injured by men or by any other part of his creation. The most that men can do by their sins is to sadden God since by his choice he allows men's sins to sadden him. (Ephesians 4:30). But since Jesus Christ was human as well as divine he could in his humanity experience in himself the struggle against evil in maintaining his own righteousness, and he could experience injury of body and enforced nervous strain at the hands of those whom he opposed. He was thus by his life, which was crowned by his death, able to unveil God's character as loving the sinner and being willing to take the initiative to assist him graciously, while at the same time hating and fighting against the sinner's sin. In this sense at least the old theology was correct in its claim that God needed Christ's death in order to be gracious to sinners.

There is another reason why the Incarnation, suffering, and death of the Son of God were necessary if God was to establish his favorable connection with men for which the Pharisees hoped. We have seen how the first three chapters of Genesis claim that God created man in his own image and gave him dominion over the earth and animals but demanded of man obedience to himself, and that man sinned by refusing to be obedient to God. Putting it theologically we can say that man resembles God in having power, intelligence, the moral ability to discern and choose, and the ability to love. In God's completely unified character the divine power and intelligence are always under the guidance of the righteous-love. The same subordination of characteristics should also characterize men. But when men use their intelligent power primarily for themselves (instead of lovingly serving God and seeking through justice the welfare of their neighbors), this misuse of their power defaces their likeness to God and breaks off the harmonious relationship between God and man. The reason the way back to God now involves suffering is that since men originally tried to get power without righteous-love, God has had to present them with the choice of righteous-love without power in order to make it clear that they really want to obey God.

If a charming, aged, pious Christian has a host of friends, and he also happens to be a very generous person and a bachelor with a private fortune of twenty-five million dollars, it may be that all his host of friends are devoted to him because they love and admire his saintly Christian life. On the other hand, the combination of his age, charm, generosity, and fortune does not by itself provide a screening process to test the unselfish devotion to him and the devotion to Christ and the right on the part of the people who enthusiastically claim his friendship. In the same way, God as God cannot offer himself with pleasant attractiveness to sinful man, because God as God includes desirable power as well as righteous-love. Evilly ambitious men will put themselves to great pains to adjust pleasantly to others in order to attain power. God could not therefore offer himself in a loving and unterrifying way with his attractive power to men, for as he is in himself he contains the highly desirable attribute of power which ambitious men, who care little for him or his righteous love, would crave to possess. For this reason also God had to incarnate himself to offer himself to men who are sinful. For as incarnate he could strip himself of the forms of power that selfish men would covet. (Philippians 2:6-8). At least in this sense also it is accurate to say that God could not have reconciled sinful man to himself without the Incarnation and the crucifixion.

In line with this type of interpretation it is interesting to note that although the Church was built upon the Resurrection, the great vividness of Christ's character and his great teachings do not come in the Resurrection experiences. But when one thinks of it, this is what one would expect. Christ could no longer exhibit the depth of his courageous love to men when his love and righteousness could no longer endanger him personally, and when his love could no longer entail action that drove almost past endurance the flagging powers of an overworked body.

In this regard it is also significant that none of the Resurrection appearances were to Jesus' enemies. This generalization holds true even of the appearance to Paul on the road to Damascus. For although Paul was persecuting the Christians he was doing it under an honest misapprehension. He genuinely believed that Jesus was not the Son of God who had risen from the dead. He therefore believed that persecuting this sect was a duty God required of him. (Deuteronomy 13:1-18). He was persecuting entirely as an act of allegiance to God, with no inmixture of selfish professional fear for the popular prestige of the accepted religious leaders of Judaism of which he was one. That this is the correct interpretation is proved by the fact that the only conversion needed was that of the intellect. There was no question of a need to bring the will of Paul to submission to God. Jesus could therefore appear in favorable aspect to Paul throughout the incident. The man-handling that the gentle Jesus gave Paul on that occasion was merely for purposes of identification, and was in no way punitive or antagonistic.

But had Jesus appeared to his enemies after his Resurrection, to those who promoted his death because of personal spite or to protect their stake in the *status quo*, he would have had either to accept or reject them *in toto* on their terms of opposition to him. The Son was now in the same position relative to mankind as a whole as the position the Father had always occupied, in regard to the difficulty of revealing himself adequately to men. *For now Jesus himself did not have to struggle and exhaust himself to do the right in the human scene, or run the risk that his enemies might injure or kill him. He therefore could no longer make the distinction clear of loving the sinner while hating the sin. This is why Christ cannot now reveal himself to men without the assistance of the historical revelation that he made in his Incarnation.*

This is not contradicted by the fact that many people now who know intimately the risen Christ first came to know him as sinners when he showed himself gracious to them and forgave their sin and accepted them as his followers. But in such instances the sinner is not a successful contented sinner. For public or private reasons the sinner is aware that his wrongdoing has put him in a bad way. His sins are a burden to him. Here the man does not want to side with his sins but against them, and yet he is too entangled in them to help himself. A man in such a situation can be desperate, for life in his present state can be distressing to him. In such

331

a situation if he has heard only a little of Christ but knows that he hates sin but loves sinners he can turn to him and Christ can show him favor without more ado. For the man wants the Divine favor on the terms on which Christ can offer it. But Christ could not have appeared favorably to Macbeth while he was planning the murder of Banquo and Fleance. Jesus could, however, in Gethsemane, heal the ear of the slave who was assisting in his arrest (Luke 22:50, 51) without compromising his moral integrity. It is also possible for Jesus now to accept directly those who want to follow him just because they find his love and helpfulness attractive, without being particularly aware of their own sinfulness. This is especially true with regard to little children. But it also holds true of some older people who have really tried conscientiously all their lives to do the right, and who have not been guilty of any flagrant social misdemeanor. Provided all these people take on Christ as a Master, because they want to be dominated by him because of his goodness, their vivid awareness of their sin and death from which they need to be rescued by him can come later, in the course of their discipleship. Their knowledge of their sin can come as their continuing association with him shows them their spiritual inadequacy and their hankering after their own way when obedience is difficult, and their knowledge of the hold of death upon them is easily learned from the vicissitudes of life and its frustrations and brevity.

The incarnation, crucifixion, and resurrection of Jesus Christ upon which the Christian Church—as distinct from Judaism—has been built can fit very neatly into the science-adjusted interpretation of our religion which this book is tentatively suggesting. By means of entropy there existed a source of power that was not God for the creation to use. This made possible God's working upon the creation to assist it to bring forth that which could reflect his beauty and creative power and in the end his intelligence, righteousness, and love. And this reflection of God was to be a creation brought forth freely—not under constraint—and freely offered back as a gift to the Creator, so that the God who was in himself complete could receive his "own with interest." (Matthew 25:26, 27) The method by which God carried out his plan was by the means of evolution.

Now, taking the evolutionary theory as a whole, if we say "evolution develops" or "has progressed" we are implying that it is getting somewhere. That means that the process itself must have a goal. And this is what Christianity claims Jesus of Nazareth to be, namely creation's goal. (Philippians 2:9-11) For if God has been all along striving to bring the creation to reflect his characteristics more and more adequately, it would be reasonable to suppose that God would want to bring nature to the point at which it would reflect perfectly his governing characteristic of righteous-love functioning intelligently. And Christianity claims that the human being, Jesus of Nazareth, did this, and therefore in this sense is the goal of creation from the evolutionary standpoint. As biological advances in evolution have incorporated and built upon previous advances, so he could not appear until the fullness of time had come, the first century Mediterranean civilization had been prepared to facilitate the spread of his message, and the Jewish religious situation brought through the law, the prophets, and the Pharisees to the point at which he found it. So far we have described merely the human Jesus, the greatest of the long line of prophets and their completion.

But it has been pointed out that the slow upward trend of evolution has been a battle against the force of entropy or dissolution. Even the plants, according to Professor Sinnott, seem each of them to "strive" to maintain the pattern appropriate to its species, and each plant and animal and human being wages a losing battle, but by the strategy of reproduction fresh reserves are brought up to take the front line positions in the battle in which the previous generation has died. But a species is an abstraction. It is individuals who die, and certainly in the case of the human species, it is individuals who are valuable. And if God cherishes his creation, especially men, it is individual men whom he wishes to preserve.

CHAPTER 35
Christ, the Devil and Sin

The fastidiously genial but spiritually shallow modern religious outlook discreetly overlooks the fact that more is said about the devil by Jesus in the synoptic gospels than in all the rest of the Bible put together. We moderns have tried to cover up for Jesus his naive uneducated provincialism in accepting the popular superstition of an angelic power of evil! On the contrary, the devil and the struggle against him are not on the periphery of Jesus' teaching, but are an important part of what he considered was concerned with his mission. Anyone who reads the gospels through with open-minded attention notices that this is one of the essential differences between Jesus and the prophets in their fight against evil. The prophets saw evil and suffering as the result of men's sin, and called men to repent so that God would be favorable to them. The opening chapters of Genesis seem to ascribe even such inconveniences as thorns and thistles and the carnivorousness of lions to the fall of man. Job voices the skeptical reaction against this theory that all evil and suffering are attributable to men's sin.

Jesus does not deal theoretically with the problem. Like the prophets he calls men to repent that they may be found by the Father in heaven and come safely under his care. There is no question but what he considered the human plight desperate: he went to the cross to alleviate it. But the sins which he scored were sins of omission or hypocrisy, almost without exception situations in which men were under no cruel pressure to do an evil deed at another's behest, but where they had some scope for social freedom and could have exerted themselves to try to serve God and work for the welfare of their neighbors. The inveighing against men because they were evil through and through due to original sin is absent from Jesus' teaching.

This is because original sin is deviation from God's will for us at the point at which we have no control over it. We are trapped in it, and it is part of our desperate awayness from God, and yet it is sin as suffered. It is a tendency, rather than an act. We are

334

guilty of it only when we amalgamate our actions to it. Its nature can be seen when we think of the controversy that has raged in times past about the salvation of unbaptized infants. Augustine was right: if original or root sin is characteristic of the human race as human, and unbaptized babies are part of the human race, then original sin is characteristic of unbaptized babies, and if so they are in a perishing state if they do not have Divine assistance. Augustine's mistake lay in assuming that God could not make arrangements for infants without the aid of the ceremony of baptism, and also the mistake of assuming that this original sin as it applied to babies was something that put God in a position of "wrath" or antagonism toward them.

I wish to make the rather bold suggestion that there was a tie-up in Jesus' mind between what he referred to as Satan, or the devil, and the predicament that later theologians refer to under the aspect of original sin. In so far as Jesus stresses the devil, he certainly shows that he considered that there is a power of evil for which men are not responsible, but which is nevertheless part of the human difficulty. Not only did he in his earthly ministry try to get men to repent and to try to serve God as prerequisite to their right relationship to God, but he also gave the distinct impression that he and the Father were standing shoulder to shoulder fighting *for* men, against a common adversary that was other than human nature although troubling human nature.

We will not be far wrong if we identify this hostile power as entropy. The devil may include more than the pervasive, non-personal entropy tendency, but his nature is certainly allied to it. For it has been typical of theological discussion of the devil to claim that he is parasitic and cannot create. All creation has its ultimate source in the power of God. Evil can and does proliferate of course, but it is only to "create" a destruction, as war, which is due to the snowballing of sin and evil until it bursts the steady framework of society, very clearly indicates. It is an instance of "sin when it is full-grown [bringing] forth death." (James 1:15)

If we ask the old question of whether God, since he is all-powerful, is responsible for evil, the answer must be that evil is in no way part of himself or his purpose, but that the entropy factor in evil he is responsible for, (Isaiah 45:6, 7) since he created matter pre-knowing that it would originate entropy. But this original

335

entropy of the cosmos is not as such evil, because it made possible an energy independent of God that God could use in building freedom into his creation. However, as matter in evolution became sentient and then conscious, entropy became a factor fraught with evil for sentient beings which were attempting to reflect in their appropriate degree the characteristics of their Creator. Although God did not create evil, he certainly "let man in for it" in the interests of man's ultimate good. It is only our familiarity with the Lord's Prayer that makes us unaware of one of its petitions. (Matthew 6:13) It should be said, however, that from the point of view of Christian theology God took his responsibility to men seriously enough to entangle himself in the human mess and to die by torture for men.

The theory of this book, taking the scientific world-view into account, reverses the biblical order of sin and evil. According to the Bible, first came the sin of conscious intelligent disobedience of God, and the evil of misfortune and pain and death followed as a consequence. According to our theory, first came entropy or dissolution which had a baleful or evil effect upon sentient organisms, including man, when man appeared in the evolutionary sequence. (There is a slight Old Testament suggestion of our view of evil as pre-existing man in the account of the snake in the Garden of Eden.) Furthermore, since the "duty" of each species is to hold to the pattern which is its characteristic reflection of aspects of God's complex nature, and since in man this requires that he hold consciously and undeviatingly to God's governing characteristic of righteous-love, the entropy or death-factor in his bodily existence serves as a deterrent to his choice to attempt to hold the higher pattern prescribed for him at the intelligent social level, namely the pattern of righteous-love. For there will be times when the comfort and safety of his physical organism would urge him to a line of conduct that contradicted the priority demand that he reflect God's governing characteristic of righteous-love. If we take entropy as the irreducible factor in our human life that makes sin possible, we can call it original sin, the sin-fostering tendency. It is at least original-quasi-sin. Then we can say that when man gives way to the urge to save his organic self at the expense of ceasing to hold even if need be unto death the pattern of righteous-love that God has given for his life, then the man attaches himself for his safety to his own organism which must eventually die, instead of to God who is deathless, and so he consciously disobeys God and by choice makes original-quasi-sin or the dissolution tendency his own. This is sin in the form of antagonism to God, sin proper, the thing upon which God's wrath rests.

In this whole discussion we are making use of Reinhold Niebuhr's brilliant analysis of human sin. Sin, he says, has two basic types, pride and sensuality. Sensuality is man's trying to "[lose] himself in some aspect of the world's vitalities."[1] Pride, he says, is man's defiance of God, when man tries to counteract his own insecurity by making himself the center of creation and seizing power for himself instead of keeping his use of power obedient to God. Probably the sin of backsliding as I have described it Niebuhr would say combined to some extent both types of sin. Certainly the sin of backsliding, while it contains an element of pride, is not sinful pride in its most concentrated and virulent form. But the sin of backsliding I would say fits in well with the general Old Testament word for sin which means "to miss the mark." Anyhow, Niebuhr claims that while man's insecurity is not sin, the inborn tendency that he has, due to his insecurity, to make himself his security rather than God, is original sin. The argument of this book uses this analysis in slightly modified form, making the entropy-tendency original-quasi-sin, and man's choosing disobedience to God in order to avoid entropy, and so being further trapped in the entropy-tendency, the description of sin in its positive and culpable form. "The wages of sin is death." (Romans 6:23)

Jesus of Nazareth was thus God's champion, not only fighting against positive sin in individual lives, but also fighting in league with God on man's behalf against the devil or entropy which is the common enemy of God and man. The sin of backsliding connects with physical entropy because it dissolves the higher-patterned life of righteous-love for a lower and less complicated pattern of intelligent, comfortable organism-oriented existence.

Thus the Hebrews were right as against the Greeks, for the Hebrews made positive sin and not death the basic evil from which man needed to be saved. For disobedience to God was the aspect of the problem in which man had some choice: if man did his

---

[1] Reinhold Niebuhr, *The Nature and Destiny of Man;* New York: Charles Scribner's Sons, 1941, Vol. I, p. 179.

part and obeyed God, God could look after the problem of organic death which is beyond man's control because it is part of the dissolution of the universe of which he is a part. The Hebrews also saw that in the subtlety of the life and career of an individual human being, sin and death are connected, and that sin causes death. (I Corinthians 15:22, 26, 56)

We now come to the theory of how Christ conquered sin-death as this relates to the theory we have been developing. It is needless to worry about how Jesus could have been born completely free from the taint of original sin. For in a sense this inheritance was necessary to his mission, and therefore God "for our sake . . . made [Christ] to be sin who knew no sin" (II Corinthians 5:21) so that he might conquer it for us. Christ had to come to grips—in his own person—with the "original sin" of entropy in order to conquer it, that is, to conquer death. In this sense also it is correct to say that the death of Christ was necessary for man's salvation.

The New Testament writers did not feel any nervousness about describing Christ as fully tangled up in the world's sin and misery, in spite of his own sustained spotless innocence in relation to God and man. Any over-scrupulous attempt to disconnect Jesus completely from original sin ends by making his human life not quite fully genuine, that is, it inserts the slight suggestion of play-acting into his humanity. Its tendencies, therefore, are docetic.

But with our redefinition of original sin as the entropy-force in human life one can say frankly both that Christ was born subject to original sin and that his life was entirely sinless. This of course is a dangerous thing to say and it can only be said without blasphemy where the term *original sin* is reexplained and redefined as entropy in relation to the whole evolutionary process, as I think must be done if we are to rework our theological interpretation of the faith to include a picture of the universe as having existed for billions of years, and of man as the most highly developed of an unbroken series of living things, the earliest members of this sequence being microscopic bits of matter in a state of organization only sufficiently high to exhibit a reactivity we define as sentience.

We define original sin as entropy when applied to any living organism which had a characteristic pattern to hold by its physiologically poised, but highly unstable complicated aggregate of matter which is itself. In the organic world, including man, original sin expresses itself actively as death, that is, as something in the creature that God is working against and yet has permitted in the interests of the larger good.

> [It is] the law of sin and death. . . . The creation was subjected to vanity, not of its own will, but by reason of him who subjected it, in hope that the creation itself also shall be delivered from the bondage of corruption. . . . The whole creation groaneth and travaileth in pain together until now. . . . [For] the last enemy to be destroyed is death. (Romans 8:2b, 20, 21a, 22. ARV; I Corinthians 15:26)

The description of the creation groaning and travailing in pain is using the imagery of childbirth, imagery which fits better than Paul knew organic nature's long hard upward struggle toward the goal which it blindly felt but did not understand in the course of an evolutionary process of which Paul had never heard. At the very primitive pre-human evolutionary level sin (i.e., the opposition that is done with reference to God) and evil (i.e., the resulting misfortune to living creatures) are for all practical purposes the same.

In spite of Jesus' resolute putting behind him the temptation to put the emphasis of his ministry upon caring for men's physical needs, (Matthew 4:4) he spent a great deal of time and energy in healing the sick. His ministry was one of driving back the forces of sin on all fronts, both on the front in which men consciously choose to disobey God, which is the point at which sin proliferates virulently, and at the point of bodily disability, which is the territory occupied from pre-history by the force of dissolution. And when Jesus during his ministry sent his disciples out to preach and teach, he likewise gave them instructions to cast out evil spirits and to heal. When the seventy returned and said, "'Even the demons are subject to us in your name,'" he replied, "'I saw Satan fall as lightning from heaven. Behold, I have given you authority . . . over all the power of the enemy.'" (Luke 10:17-19) Here he seems to imply that the war he is waging against evil is of cosmic proportions. One gets the same impression from his claim that he is able to cast minor devils out of people because he has got the better of Satan himself. (Mark 3:22-27) It has been fashionable in recent decades to explain Jesus' casting out of demons as stabilizing the psychological outlook of the menally disturbed, i.e., Mary Magdalene (Luke 8:2) and the Gerasene demoniac (Mark 5:1-20) did not really have devils in them: they just needed to go to a psychiatrist! Without discussing the merits of either the ancient or modern theory of insanity, I want to point out that Jesus classes as the work of Satan two instances of illness that we would class as physical ailments, namely epilepsy and arthritis. (Mark 9:17-29 and Luke 13:10-17) Paul also saw the Christian struggle as one in which the Christian works with Christ against cosmic forces of evil. He says that "We are not contending against flesh and blood, but against the principalities, against the powers, against the world rulers of this present darkness, against the spiritual hosts of wickedness in the heavenly places." (Ephesians 6:12)

What would Jesus of Nazareth have had to do to save man, i.e., in some way to connect God permanently in a favorable fashion with the earth (and the whole creation) and with men? In other words what would Jesus have had to do to be the personal bridge for men between man and God? Well, obviously, as Pharasaic thought emphasized, God could not ally himself with moral evil. God as righteous-loving cannot ally himself with the moral opposite of righteous-love, and its moral opposite was characteristic of all mankind, since all people are culpable sinners in the sense of being willfully disobedient to God. Only in a human life that perfectly kept the law could God permanently ally himself with earth. (Deuteronomy 7:9-15). Jesus believed that his was the task of furnishing this perfect life that would make it possible for God to inaugurate the New Covenant (I Corinthians 11:25) prophesied by Jeremiah. (Jeremiah 31:31-34). This is the significance of Jesus' saying, "Think not that I have come to abolish the law and the prophets; I have come not to abolish them but to fulfil them." (Matthew 5:17.). The statement occurs in the Sermon on the Mount where it prefaces that amazing series of statements in which Jesus keeps repeating, "You have heard that it was said . . . . But I say to you," indicating that his extension of the Mosaic legislation has precedence over the Torah. In this regard Jesus' saying that he came to fulfil the law does not just mean that he came to make it clear that all the law and the prophets are detailed commentaries on the two great commandments to love God and one's neighbor. Some of the best Jewish thought in Jesus' day had already independently reached that conclusion about the summary of the law. (Luke 10:25-28; Mark 12:28-33). Jesus was saying that he had come to fulfil in the sense of perfectly embodying that law in its full implication of love.

CHAPTER 36

The Incarnation

So far we have spoken of Jesus only in terms of the human being, Jesus of Nazareth. But he himself thought of himself as more than a prophet, as being in fact the divine Son of God in a unique sense. There are six ways in which this is implied in the synoptic gospels: (a) Jesus acted on his own authority without asking the Father's assistance when he healed the sick and cast out demons, when he gave his disciples authority to do likewise, (Matthew 10:1) and when he rebuked the wind and the waves. (Mark 4:39). He never gives God the Father credit or thanks for any of the healings or exorcisms he performs. (Compare Numbers 20:10, 11; 27:14, 15; Deuteronomy 32:48-52).

(b) He uses the title, Son of man, for himself, and this usage implies a unique relationship to God when it is combined with his use of the expression in other passages. (Matthew 5:11, 12; 7:21-23; 16:19; 25:31-33; Luke 22:28-30; Mark 2:19, 20; 10:29, 37, 40; 13:9, 26, 32; 14:61, 62. And see Daniel 7:13, 14.) (c) His status is also implied in certain parables. (Matthew 22:1-10; Mark 12:1-12; Luke 19:11-27) (d) Jesus never refers to God as "our Father." He refers to him as "my Father" and "your Father." He tells his disciples to pray "Our Father," but he never prays *with* them, only *for* them. His only prayer *with* others is in taking part in the routine synagogue service, where he (presumably) joined others in prayer as part of his fulfilling of the routine demands of Judaism.

(e) He forgives sin, that is, he takes men back into the friendship of God. But only God can take men back into the friendship of God. (f) He substitutes "I say unto you" for the standard prophetic formula, "Thus saith the Lord," which he avoids.

The opening chapters of the gospels of Matthew and Luke explain the method by which the divine Son of God became incarnate by saying that the woman of whom Jesus was born was a virgin, the Holy Spirit (instead of a human male parent) providing the cooperation in the production of the offspring. Jesus' own

342

lack of reference to the Virgin Birth is to be expected. To have used it as evidence for his unique Sonship would have been to base his claim to his special status upon what would have been for him, historically speaking, hearsay evidence. But since the doctrine of the Virgin Birth is extremely important, it will be well to summarize here the intellectual corroboration for the claim.

There is partial precedent for the Virgin Birth story in the accounts of the God-assisted births of other important biblical leaders; (Genesis 18:10, 14 and 21:1, 2; 25:19-23; 30:22-24; Exodus 2:3-10; Judges 13:2-5; I Samuel 1:9-20; Jeremiah 1:4-6; Luke 1:13-15; Galatians 1:15, 16) and the Lukan account of Christ's birth seems to have originated in a Jewish community as the included hymns are in the Hebrew-type poetry.

What is essential to Christianity is the permanent amalgamation of the created human and the uncreated Divine Being in Jesus of Nazareth. The Virgin Birth account, with the Divine intrusion at conception, involves the least extensive interference with the natural order of any of the possible methods. Theoretically the formation of a Divine sperm within Mary's body could be accepted by anyone who could accept the original miracle of creation *ex nihilo*. The other alternative of the non-physical Spirit amalgamating with the ovum would be a miracle not beyond the credibility of anyone who believed it possible for the non-physical human mind to influence sometimes the physical brain.

That virgin birth is statistically highly improbable is no complete disproof of its occurrence. All historical incidents are statistically improbable before they occur. When the Pyramids were built it was statistically improbable that Columbus would discover America in 1492. Both the Virgin Birth event and the Columbus' discovery event have had large scale repercussions in history. It is easier to think the Columbus' discovery credible because it is composed of incidents that resemble many other incidents that have occurred and can be duplicated. However, in connection with this aspect of the problem it should be noticed that modern biology has induced parthenogenesis in rabbits, which is sufficiently high up the evolutionary scale to ease the credibility of a sound organism being produced without a human father. The "fatherless" aspect of the virgin birth of Jesus is not, however, what is important. What is essential in this doctrine is the supernatural co-

343

operation and amalgamation of the Being of Deity with that which was of Mary in the production of Jesus.

The alternatives to the Virgin Birth story would be either the amalgamation of Deity with a fetus normally conceived, or a later amalgamation, probably at the Baptism. This last alternative would be equally miraculous and involves the added wonder of the thirty sinless years of Christ's life *before* this special Divine undergirding. No direct physiological check-up on the Virgin Birth belief has ever been possible. Mary could only have affirmed that to the best of her knowledge she had never had intercourse with a man before Jesus' birth. But even she would have had to take the Divine Paternity on faith.

The only experiment man could ever make upon God would be to obey God *perfectly* and observe how God responded. Jesus is the only man who obeyed God perfectly, and the Divine response was the Resurrection upon which Christianity is built and which—together with the power of the Holy Spirit in the Church—is the strongest argument for the Incarnation.

The incarnation of the Being of God would be a fitting climax to an evolutionary sequence in which a reflection of Deity's characteristics had been incarnated with progressively increasing adequacy. The Virgin Birth story makes a claim that fitted in neatly as a variation upon the theme of species modification long before anyone knew about evolution and mutation. For Christianity said that when God wanted to give the dying human race a fresh, deathless start (I Corinthians 15:22, 45, 46) he brought forth the new type of being on earth by affecting a single cell in a woman's body. Then he made use of the non-biological social supplement to the evolutionary process to propagate the effects of the changes wrought by the Incarnation in a way that would make use of, rather than over-rule, the human freedom that he had been carefully preparing for and nurturing in the whole evolutionary process.

For however the method of the Incarnation is accounted for one thing is clear: from the Christian viewpoint any explanation is completely ruled out that ends up by describing the Incarnation as the perfect reflection of God's *characteristics*. For *characteristics* are an abstraction, and men in the particular need to be saved from sin and death. If Jesus were merely a perfectly good man, then the divine characteristics of righteousness and love would have been perfectly imprinted only temporarily upon a human being, because Jesus of Nazareth as a merely human organism would have been, like the rest of the world, firmly trapped in the universe's overall pattern of death, which is the basic, in the sense of being the first, contrary-to-God factor. "The perishable" does not "inherit the imperishable," (I Corinthians 15:50) and "The last enemy to be destroyed is death." (I Corinthians 15:26). For ultimate salvation from the all-destroying entropy, there was needed by the dying creation the cross-fertilization of the Original Imperishable Life.

CHAPTER 37

Both Original and Culpable Sin Attacked by the Incarnation

Assuming, then, the occurrence of the Incarnation of Deity, so that Jesus Christ was literally the God-man living upon earth centuries ago, how can we describe Jesus Christ as sinless if he was truly human as well as truly Divine, inasmuch as the entire human race is entangled in original sin? The answer must involve an analysis of the constituent factors of the total problem of evil.

Below man in the evolutionary scale self-preservation and the preservation of the species is the highest law. That is, the organism serves God simply by trying to keep the functioning pattern of the organism intact. But in addition to the animal body and its preservation, man is supposed also to reflect the governing characteristics of God's nature, especially righteous-love, and to hold to the pattern of righteous-love even where it conflicts with self-preservation. Man is required to obey God at the social level at which he, uniquely among the animals, is capable of resembling God. Rebellion or disobedience in this regard is culpable sin, sin in its most basic anti-God state, committed by means of the intelligence and freedom by which human beings especially resemble God. Toward sin in this sense God is always actively and vigorously an enemy. Jesus Christ never disobeyed God, that is, he in no way connected himself with this sin either by being guilty of it himself or condoning it in others. He, with the Father, always struggled against committed culpable sin in others. Not only was he fully Divine in his heavenly nature, but the image of God's governing characteristics, as reflected in his human nature, was perfect. His human nature, however, included a human body which was subject to the vicissitudes of the flesh. (Mark 14:38).

Men are trapped because their prehuman evolutionary history has been one in which organic self-preservation or the preservation of the species was the highest law of life. It is hard to force one's self to forego this strategy for action in the situations in which it conflicts with the over-all devotion to God's higher law of righ-

346

teous-love. But even though the cards are stacked against man he does have free choice and so sins culpably when he follows the lower law at the expense of obeying God in his demand for adherence to the higher law, and of trusting his self-preservation to God. (Mark 8:35). The sin of self-centeredness, of putting one's safety ahead of serving God in righteous-love, is, like all specific sins, a perversion. It destroys the characteristic of man most precious to God. One of the great proofs of God's inspiration of the Hebrew people is the witness they gave that they believed that if men obeyed God and lived righteously, it would be well with them. They held out for this in the face of its apparent refutation by disaster and death centuries before they believed that man had anything to look forward to beyond the grave. The Old Testament shows its Divine inspiration by the fact that it constantly fears sin more than death.

The evolutionary gearing of the organism to bodily self-preservation and the human being's struggle under this handicap to maintain obedience to God's law of righteous-love, which men, as beings in his image, ought to follow, have been most perfectly expressed by St. Paul:

For I delight in the law of God, in my inmost self, but I see in my members another law at war with the law of my mind and making me captive to the law of sin which dwells in my members. Wretched man that I am! Who will deliver me from this body of death? . . . So then, I of myself serve the law of God with my mind, but with my flesh I serve the law of sin. (Romans 7:22-25).

The "body of death" from which man needs to be delivered has to do with another constituent in the total problem of evil, namely, entropy-death. If sin is defined in its broadest terms as free action contrary to the nature of God it includes the entropy of the cosmos or death as well as man's consciously disobedient actions which we have already discussed. We have already identified entropy-death as original-quasi-sin. The cosmos freely initiated it inevitably by its lack of power, not by its power. So physical entropy-death and pain (which is the conscious creature's awareness of a lack of well being and the third constituent of evil) are evils that are endured rather than perpetrated, and as being merely endured are not culpable. Entropy-death can, however, be called quasi-sin, because

347

it does fulfill the role traditionally ascribed to original sin: (a) it is a disability inherited by all men by the mere fact of their being men; (b) it is an aspect of all men that is not in the image of God; and (c) by the insecurity that it fosters in human life it is a direct goad to human disobedience and faithlessness which is sin proper, or culpable spiritual sin.

After making this analysis and definition, to say that Jesus Christ was born subject to original sin while completely free of sin as disloyalty to God, is not contrary to New Testament teaching. Jesus himself claimed that it was only what comes "from within, out of the heart [i.e., volitional energies] of man" that can "defile a man." (Mark 7:21, 23). St. Paul and the book of Hebrews are even more explicit:

> God has done what the law, weakened by the flesh could not do: sending his own Son in the likeness of sinful flesh and for sin, he condemned sin in the flesh. (Romans 8:3).
>
> For our sake he [God] made him [Christ] to be sin who knew no sin. (II Corinthians 5:21).
>
> Since therefore the children share in flesh and blood, he himself [Christ] likewise partook of the same nature, that through death he might destroy him who has the power of death, that is, the devil. (Hebrews 2:14).

Intimate assimilation into our human life can have different effects, depending upon whether what we assimilate is physical or spiritual. If we take food, which is physical, into ourselves, we destroy the bread or apple as such in the course of making use of it. If we take spiritual things such as learning, music, or hate into our hearts [our volitional energies] we become learned, or musical, or hateful. Spiritual things are increased by being taken into one's heart and can only be destroyed or lessened by being avoided.

Jesus's ministry shows the double strategy necessary in dealing with this complex problem of evil. Sin as disobedience to God he overcame by completely avoiding it in his own life (Matthew 4:1-10; Mark 3:27) and never condoning it in the lives of others, but trying instead to lead others from it. But the evils of death and pain which men merely suffer and which do not come out of the volitional energies but are related to matter's entropy-slump, these he could only come adequately to grips with by taking them into himself—swallowing them up by Uncreated Life—to break their

348

stranglehold on the human race. In this regard also it was necessary for Christ to suffer and die for man's salvation.

The "original sin" of entropy could be permanently overcome only by being cancelled by the return of the creation to the sustaining power of the Creator. The opportunity came for God to initiate this new state of things without moral compromise to himself when at Calvary, in Jesus Christ's body and humanity, the creation at last at one point fully returned as a loving gift, freely and obediently given, to the Creator, thus establishing a permanent bridge betwen the creation and Uncreated Life. In the Father's acceptance of the gift the stranglehold of entropy was at last broken in the Resurrection, and the way opened (John 14:6) to bring the creation at large back to everlasting fellowship with God.

The theory of "original" and positive sin that we have been describing takes into account both the biblical idea of the origin of sin and the modern theory of sin as the evolutionary lag in human life. Just as our bodies incorporate earlier evolutionary developments, so our conscious life and neural reflexes incorporate the strategy for the organic preservation of the self and the species which is the highest law for subhuman life, but which has disastrous consequences when made the dominant factor in human lives. On the other hand, sin in the positive sense only entered the creation when in man creatures were evolved who could reflect God's guiding characteristic of intelligent righteous-love and man became made in the image of God. With intelligence came the requirement for conscious obedience or conformity to the God whose governing characteristic is righteous-love, and there followed the human initiation of positive sin when man refused that obedience in favor of the more primitive strategy.

While our present theory is not exactly that held by the biblical writers, who know nothing of the modern theory of biological evolution, we can, I think, hold that it is a theory they might have held had evolutionary knowledge been a factor in their worldview. They might have seen in "the serpent" who "was more subtle than any other wild creature that the Lord God had made," (Genesis 3:1) the lower creation at its highest development throwing the weight of its influence against man's adherence to his newly attained ability of intelligently conscious obedience to God. Whether or not this would have been the case, I think our working sketch of the nature and origin of sin will fit Jesus' estimate of the complicated human predicament as it is portrayed in the synoptic gospels.

There are indications that Jesus thought of himself as working with God in a fight against man and God's common enemy, Satan, and that his healings and exorcisms, though less central to his mission than his teaching, were part of his attempt to drive back the forces of evil on all fronts. (Mark 1:23-25, 34; 9:17-25; Luke 10:17-20; 13:16, 17; 22:31, 32; Matthew 25:41). There is even in his teaching a double focus on sin itself. On the one hand he recognizes an element of sinfulness in which man is simply trapped, and needs rescue. (Mark 2:17; Luke 15:8-10). For this reason he never tells men that they need to repent and be forgiven for their total sinful natures, because part of what is wrong with their natures is not under human control and so is not culpable sin for which they are responsible. Men are to pray for forgiveness of their sins, in the plural. (Matthew 6:12,14,15) He rejoices when men turn from specific sins (Luke 19:8-10) and tells the rich young ruler to keep the commandments if he would have eternal life. (Matthew 19:16-19) He tells men that their sins—in the plural—have been forgiven. (Mark 2:5; Luke 7:47) The general repentance that he calls for is to a service of God and a reliance upon him, and to a turning from particular sins that one recognizes. Repentance in Jesus' teaching is not meditation upon one's sinfulness as such, it is turning to God obediently to be helped to take the next practical step with God's assistance.

This is not to imply that he considered the problem of human culpable sin a minor one (Matthew 7:11) or that he advocated spiritual complacency. (Luke 18:9-14) He wanted men to do what they can and emphasized the assistance God is eager and powerful to give, and he thought of himself as part of that assistance. He knew that men are in a desperate situation because of their responsible sin, so desperate that he went to the cross to help us in this emergency. In fact, the question might be raised of whether he did not think almost exclusively in terms of salvation from sin, assuming, in line with Jewish thought, that if a man's situation with respect to sin could be put right, that the problem of death could be safely left in the hands of God.

The prayer in Gethsemane, "Remove this cup from me," (Mark

14:36) would scarcely be logical if Christ thought of his mission as chiefly involving a direct fight with death. However, the prayer in Gethsemane does not have to be strictly logical. It probably contained an element of simply telling God how he felt about it all, even though at the back of his mind he never deviated from his expectation of going through with the crucifixion. The prayer is in part a taking God into his confidence in the desolate emergency of the situation. One can see this aspect of the Gethsemane prayer more clearly if one asks one's self how God would have felt about it if Jesus had not gone to him with the problem of how much he dreaded what was ahead of him. If Jesus had not gone to God with that prayer it would have put the Almighty Creator in the position of a human father who is dutifully obeyed but not confided in by his child, a poignantly distressing position for a parent, although one of which he has no right to complain.

CHAPTER 38

The Death and Resurrection of Jesus Christ

The passage in which Jesus implies that the conquest of death is part of his agenda comes in the strange prediction of his death and resurrection in Matthew where he says that no sign shall be given "except the sign of the prophet Jonah. For as Jonah was three days and three nights in the belly of the whale"—the Greek word is a great sea-monster—"so will the Son of man be three days and three nights in the heart of the earth." (Matthew 12:39,40) The whale's belly is already associated with Sheol or the grave in the book of Jonah itself. (Jonah 1:17-2:2) Sheol is also pictured in a famous passage in Isaiah as a great monster that swallows up men:

Therefore Sheol has enlarged its appetite
and opened its mouth beyond measure,
and the nobility of Jerusalem and her multitude go down,
her throng and he who exults in her.
Man is bowed down, and men are brought low,
and the eyes of the haughty are humbled.

(Isaiah 5:14,15)

The figure of a monster associated with God's destruction of death is further found in the book of Isaiah in one of the Old Testament's earliest suggestions of the idea of resurrection:

Thy dead shall live, their bodies shall rise.
O dwellers in the dust, awake and sing for joy!
For thy dew is a dew of light,
and on the land of the shades thou wilt let it fall.
Come, my people, enter your chambers,
and shut your doors behind you;
hide yourselves for a little while
until the wrath is past.
For behold, the Lord is coming forth out of his place
to punish the inhabitants of the earth for their iniquity,
and the earth will disclose the blood shed upon her,
and will no more cover her slain.

In that day the Lord with his hard and great and strong sword will punish Leviathan the fleeing serpent, Leviathan the twisting serpent, and he will slay the dragon that is in the sea.

(Isaiah 26:19-27:1)

The remark about the "sign of the prophet Jonah" is a very important indication that Jesus predicted his own resurrection as well as his own death. The inaccuracy of the prediction—Jesus was not three nights in the tomb—is very strong evidence against those who think the prediction was made up by the disciples *ex post facto*. Jesus was in the tomb only two nights. After his death at three P.M. Friday (Mark 15:34,36) permission had to be obtained that evening from Pilate to bury the body (Matthew 27:57-59; Mark 15:42-46) before the work of taking it down from the cross could begin; and the Resurrection was already an accomplished fact by the very early dawn of Sunday. (Mark 16:2; Matthew 28:1,2; Luke 24:1; John 20:1,14,15) Jesus' body could therefore have been in the tomb thirty-six hours at the longest, and probably several hours under that estimate.

All the gospels, considered as biographies, give a disproportionately large amount of space to the period from Palm Sunday through Easter. Although they think of Christ's whole ministry as significant, they think of it as leading up to this week which, as they looked back upon it, was the week which consummated in triumph what he did for men. It looks very much as if this week was meant to signify the work of the new creation. As God labored according to Genesis for six days to create the world and rested on the seventh or sabbath, so the Son of God travailed especially for six days to save the lost creation, and rested from his successful accomplishment in the grave over the sabbath.

Just how soon after sundown on Saturday he arose we have no way of knowing. The tomb had been sealed by the authorities on Saturday. (Matthew 27:62-66) We do not know when the Resurrection took place after that, except that it had to have taken place before the women discovered the empty tomb. There is only one further bit of evidence. The early Church used Psalm 16:9-11 as a prophecy of the Resurrection of Christ:

Therefore my heart is glad,
and my glory rejoiceth:
My flesh also shall dwell in safety.

For thou wilt not leave my soul to Sheol;
Neither wilt thou suffer thy
   holy one to see corruption.
Thou wilt show me the path of life:
In thy presence is fulness of joy;
In thy right hand there are
   pleasures for evermore. (ARV)

(And see Acts 2:27 and 13:35-37.) The implication is that the rest in the tomb over the sabbath was fitting, but that the transmuting of the physical into the deathless state into another existence than our space-time universe probably was accomplished quite early afterwards.

We now come back to the question of Jesus' own interpretation of the significance of his death. In some sense he died on behalf of our (committed) sins and of our original sin (entropy). And he died as a consequence of both types of sin. That he was able to do this is due to entropy; that he died a violent death at an early age is due to the sins for which men are responsible. That he considered his death a sacrificial substitute because of men's sins is highly probable, for the idea of a sacrificial substitute was deeply ingrained in Hebrew religious thought. There was a type of sacrifice that was especially a sin offering, (Leviticus 4:13-35) and there was also the type of offering or payment that redeemed the first born, (Exodus 13:1,11-16; 34:19,20; Numbers 18:15-17) and finally there was the spiritualizing of sacrifice in the vicarious death of the Suffering Servant. (Isaiah 53:1-12)

Another common form of worship in which the worshipper ate of the sacrifice was one in which is reflected the social custom of forging or reaffirming ties of kinship or alliance by "breaking bread" together. (Exodus 18:12; Deuteronomy 12:5-7; I Samuel 9:11-14) This form of sacrifice would be sacramental of a community relationship between the people and God. That Jesus also viewed his death in terms of this type of sacrifice is obvious from his institution of the Lord's Supper. (I Corinthians 11:23-26)

But beyond all this, Jesus believed his death to be efficacious in still another way in uniting men to God. He believed that it established the new covenant (I Corinthians 11:25) prophesied by Jeremiah. (Jeremiah 31:31-34) The old covenant had established by a blood ceremony the relationship between God and the people. At

354

the ceremony at Sinai to ratify the covenant Moses had thrown the blood of the sacrificial animals on the altar and on the worshippers. (Exodus 24:3-8) The life of animals was thought to reside in their blood, (Genesis 9:4) and all blood was therefore holy to God. Politically the nation was organized by clans or families and this ceremony symbolized dramatically God tying the nation to himself and becoming the head of their clans in a living relationship. The symbolism of Sinai recurs in a greatly enhanced form when Jesus said in establishing the Lord's Supper, "This cup is the new covenant in my blood." (I Corinthians 11:25)

There remains the idea of the efficacy of Jesus' death expressed in his words, "The Son of man . . . came not to be served but to serve, and to give his life as a ransom for many." (Mark 10:45) A ransom is a price paid for the release of someone from the power of another hostile person or nation, such as a kidnapped person or a prisoner of war. Now if Christ gave his life as a ransom, from whom was he ransoming men? Certainly not from the baleful power of God! If he speaks of his life as a ransom, it must mean ransom from some sort of evil entrapment of man that could be personified. We know that he believed in the existence of the devil, which means that he believed in a superhuman power of evil inimical to man against which the Father and he were fighting on man's behalf. Paul's later saying is in line with this attitude of Christ's: "For we are not contending against flesh and blood, but against the principalities, against the powers, against the world rulers of this present darkness, against the spiritual hosts of wickedness in the heavenly places." (Ephesians 6:12) Both Paul and Christ believed in demonic powers which they spoke of in personified but not in highly personalized terms.

If we assume that Jesus did believe in demonic power, and that he thought of his death as in some sense ransoming man from its clutches, then, since he compared his death to the Jonah and the sea monster story, with the probability of the linkage between that story as an apologetic for resurrection and Isaiah's picture of death under the figure of a monster that swallows men up, (Isaiah 5:14,15 and see 26:19-27:1 and Jonah 1:17-2:2) then it is more than likely that Christ believed that his death would save men from death itself. This is implied in his claim that his death would bring in the new age of the kingdom so soon that some of his immediate followers would not taste of death before its coming, (Mark 9:1) a statement which proved to be embarrassingly inaccurate, and therefore would not have been preserved unless known to be authentic.

If we think of Christ as the resolver of spiritual dilemmas increasingly recognized by the Old Testament, then his thinking *ought* to have included, subsidiary to the main idea of salvation from sin, the idea of salvation from death itself. The death of the Maccabean martyrs had made acute the question of whether God genuinely cares for those who serve him faithfully, and had been the occasion of the Old Testament's clearest expression of the resurrection hope. (Daniel 12:2,3) Also, negatively, even the life most blessed by worldly benefits had been shown by Ecclesiastes to have the nerve of its optimism, happiness, and incentive cut by the backward working of death's frustration. Furthermore, the suggestion of a "ransom" from death had been broached by the forty-ninth Psalm. There may have been an echo of this Psalm in Jesus' mind when he said he had come "to give his life as a ransom for many." (Mark 10:45)

Truly no man can ransom himself,
    or give to God the price of his life,
for the ransom of his life is costly,
    and can never suffice,
that he should continue to live on forever,
    and never see the Pit.
Yea, he shall see that even the wise die. . . .
Man cannot abide his pomp,
    he is like the beasts that perish. . . .
Like sheep they are appointed for Sheol;
    Death shall be their shepherd;
straight to the grave they descend . . . .
    Sheol shall be their home.
But God will ransom my soul from the power of Sheol,
    for he will receive me.

(Psalm 49:7-10a,12,14,15)

CHAPTER 39

Self-Preservation and the Power-Shift Appropriate to Man

We are now in a position to take the modern scientific observation that the process of evolution has increasingly, but only temporarily, reversed the process of entropy, and tie this scientific datum in with the Christian teaching that Jesus Christ was truly God incarnate who died for men and by his death and resurrection broke the stranglehold of death.

If we account for evolution as the supernatural God's fostering the complication of organism so that it could progressively reflect more and more of his characteristics, until man had become capable of reflecting God's righteous-love and was reflecting his deathlessness a little by a civilization which could pass on in writing to succeeding generations the attainments of the past, then we can think of Deity culminating the program by inserting himself, not just a reflection of himself, into his creation in the person of his Son.

Since Jesus Christ was a man and as a man perfectly obedient to God, he is the climax of the evolutionary process, the human being perfectly reflecting the righteous-love of the Creator. But inasmuch as Jesus Christ was God incarnate he was also the Deity which his human nature perfectly reflected. Thus the two natures, Divine and human, coincided in the one Lord Jesus Christ without detriment to either, in accordance with the teaching of the Creed of Chalcedon. But although the incarnation was not detrimental to the deity, it did restrict the scope of the deity's activity in two ways. One was that Jesus Christ, as also human, was subject to physical entropy or dissolution or death which the cosmos causes and in which all things in it participate. Evolution had been a struggle against dissolution, with the good men and the prophets trying desperately to obey the highest part of the human duty, the insight into righteous-love, as the pattern for men to follow in their reflection of God. But just as the body eventually slumped into disintegration by reason of the entropy of the cosmos, so this entropy of the cosmos, or original-quasi-sin, by making man insecure, triggered the other

357

entropy of his conscious life from its God-given pattern of righteous-love. So man back-slid spiritually and thus wickedly disobeyed God, and the snowballing of the wickedness as its effects became embedded in human society increased the predicament of man.

But it was man's spiritual backsliding and not his physical entropy that caused his dangerous alienation from God. God could receive to himself that which was weak, but not that which with full conscious responsibility disobeyed the governing characteristic of the Divine nature, the characteristic of righteous-love. For the whole purpose of the creation had been to give nature freedom so that nature or the creation could freely give itself back to God. The mere inorganic nature and the nature of the lower organisms did not have sufficient freedom and consciousness to surrender to God on their own behalf. And man who did have sufficient freedom and consciousness found he could not do it because of his moral "entropy" or culpable sin of backsliding, due to his self-centeredness, which had brought him into a state of active disobedience to God.

If the creation at any point gave itself back fully to God it had to be done by the agency of man. When men proved unable to do it God genuinely incarnated himself in the person of his Son. The task of the Son was to fulfill completely the God-given human pattern of righteous-love under the handicap of a human-life-organism subject to entropy and the fear of entropy, (Mark 14:36-38) and at the same time throughout his human life to hold unwaveringly to the required pattern of righteous-love. In other words, Christ became incarnate *to fulfill the law.* This Jesus saw as his task (Matthew 5:17) and this he accomplished. (John 16:33) Although subject to original-quasi-sin (physical entropy) he refused to sin by backsliding into disobedience to God. Thus for his own life he experienced physical evil and did not yield to spiritual evil. (Matthew 4:1-11) Instead he conquered it for his own life and thus was in a position to make inroads into the evil around him. (Mark 3:27)

Jesus Christ's task would have been fairly simple if the evil he had had to fight had been largely due to original-quasi-sin (or physical entropy) and to the ensuing precariousness it caused in his own life. He could then have fought it successfully and when in the course of time he died a natural death he could have given his life, and the creation in his life, back to the Father.

But the situation was much more complicated than that. The

power of positive sinning had so snowballed in the world that its destructive nature was a greater danger and threat to Jesus Christ than was the power of original-quasi-sin. For man in his insecurity had originally craved power for himself apart from his obedience to God's righteous-love. Since man is supposed to reflect the nature of God and God's nature includes power there is nothing wrong in itself for man to desire power. (Genesis 1:26,28) The only thing that is wrong is that man wants it selfishly, without being willing to hold it under an obedient reflection of God's governing characteristic of righteous-love. God therefore had to deal with the situation by demanding that insecure man first be obedient to God's righteous-love (and so reflect it). After he had become obedient to the righteous-love of God first, it would be safe to trust him with power. But the point is that men, because of their insecurity, were trying without righteous-love to grab power. Thus if any man tried now to serve God in righteous-love without grabbing power, the people who were grabbing power would crush him because their desire to grab power would invade the area of his existence, and they would furthermore see the good man's attempt to follow righteous-love as a threat to the moral status of their own life-strategy. To act vigorously, governed by righteous-love without recourse to power, (Matthew 4:3,9; 26:53; 27:42) was to court attack from men. The seeking for power—although it had originally been morally harmless (Genesis 1:28)—was now, in man's state of rebellion against God's righteous-love, a line of human endeavor that was largely under the control of the "devil." (Matthew 4:8,9) The reason that the death-tendency and the power-seeking combination formed such a vicious circle was that men were haunted by the fear of death and this forced them to try to grab power. The seizing of power was a convulsive grasping toward self-preservation. But as all people were grabbing at the limited amount of power available their interests conflicted and brought about violent clashes—seen most conspicuously in war—that brought about on a large scale the very death and destruction which they feared.

And yet in the earlier stages of evolution to attempt to grab for one's "self" to stave off death was always the appropriate pattern for activity. A tree "strives" to ward off death by grabbing and fortifying its "self" with the power of the sunlight, the rain, and the chemicals of the earth. The strategy only became inappropriate

359

at the points at which it conflicted in man with what should be the controlling pattern of righteous-love in obedient relation to God. At the points at which the decisions had to be made that righteous-love necessitated, man was not planned by God to be powerless, but instead to shift to another kind of power, namely the direct power of God.

We must reemphasize the importance of pattern in evolution. Let us take again Sinnott's important saying that an organism is like a waterfall that holds its form by means of a constantly changing stream of matter that flows through it. We know also that organisms are selective of the matter they will take into themselves and of the use they make of it once they have allowed its invasion. In fact, an organism is described as dead when it can no longer practice selectivity as to what invades it or the use to which what invades it shall be put. In spite of the fact that all organisms are composed of matter, it is also true that the higher up the evolutionary scale one goes the more the organism appears *to be* its pattern. If we see a dead flower, a dead fish, a dead fox, and a dead man, we are increasingly aware of death, that is, of something missing that appropriately should be present. A dead man seems to us much more unlike a man than a dead fish seems unlike a fish.

Earlier in this book we suggested that in the whole evolutionary struggle God's appreciation of the emerging and struggling forms of life was a rudimentary semi-interpersonal relationship with his creation and as such lent a slight amount of the Divine power to assist the organisms to hold their appropriate patterns against the force of entropy. In other words, the whole theory of this book assumes that evolution is teleological, and that the goal is not only the thing for which the creature is striving, but also an assistance in the struggle, an assistance that is an appreciation and so a transmitter of slightly more steadying power to the organism than would be possible if the Divine were merely the Unmoved Mover. The more the creature can reflect the characteristics of the Divine, the more the Divine power relates to it. When we come to man, who can reflect the highest characteristic, that is, the righteous-love of God, we come to a creature to which God can relate himself personally and directly, through the strengthening power of the Holy Spirit.

The word "love" has become so debased in this century that I have felt it necessary to use the hyphenated form, righteous-love, to indicate that for the Christian *love* always has the structural quality of *righteousness* built into it. This love is the guiding motive in the mind of God. When the relation of man to God through Christ is also one of love, there the interpersonal relationship is at its greatest and the power of the Holy Spirit most available to man. The relation to God through law and righteousness is less completely the interpersonal relationship. This is because righteousness is less the top guiding characteristic than it is the technique for bringing about love's desired outcome. (Men cared for the welfare of their fellow men, which is love. As a governmental technique to aid men's welfare they tried to establish just law courts and enforce the equality of all men before the law. The interest in legal justice is unthinkable, if there is no caring for the welfare of people.) So in the Old Testament, which emphasizes righteousness there is by no means a complete absence of the Holy Spirit. The work of the Holy Spirit in men's lives can be seen in the writings of the psalmists and prophets. Both of these types of writing underscore the claim that

They who wait for the Lord shall renew their strength,
    they shall mount up with wings like eagles,
they shall run and not be weary,
    they shall walk and not faint. (Isaiah 40:31)

The whole Old Testament is a testimony to the reality of the Divine Power, and God's dependability in undergirding with it the lives of those who serve him.

When, then, man had had the law of righteous-love superimposed upon the law of self-preservation, (which is part of the characteristic pattern for all organisms) God also made available to man another kind of power, God's own direct Spiritual Power to undergird and strengthen men, when they tried to obey the law of righteous-love in situations in which such obedience involved giving up their natural attempts at self-preservation. If God has "no pleasure in the death of the wicked" (Ezekiel 33:11) still less would he have pleasure in the death of his faithful servants. (Compare Luke 12:37) If the Bible's claim throughout is not basically false then a realistic appraisal of the human situation must include the belief that God loves and strengthens his faithful servants, and also that all men eventually die. But if the power of God can especially undergird those who faithfully serve him, we will raise the question in a later chapter of whether eventually the specifically-worked-out-pattern which *is* the person, may not be totally shifted by God at death to a non-physical undergirding. This involves the question of the resurrection body. (I Corinthians 15:42-50)

In the state into which the world had fallen, if the Son of God wanted to live a perfect human life on earth he must follow righteous-love without worldly power. Thus, whatever the final denouement might involve, in the immediate short-range situation he would be injured not only by entropy, but also by the culpable sin of men. The incarnate God, therefore, could not in his life on earth exhibit all the God-like qualities, for in social relationships he had to exhibit righteous-love fully, but with power curtailed. Or, if he exhibited power on earth it must be some other type of power than that which ambitious men normally exert to get and hold positions of authority. All these conditions the earthly career of Jesus of Nazareth fulfilled. "He humbled himself and became obedient unto death, even death on a cross." (Philippians 2:8)

We think of Christ's death as paying the price of securing man's salvation from sin. This salvation includes adequacy to rescue from the power of culpable sins already committed and from the alienation from God caused by these sins. And together with the Resurrection it includes the adequacy to break the stranglehold of sin on human life and to assist man to avoid sins in the future. That is, it is an aid toward the positive sanctification of the Christian. The epistle to the Hebrews says:

> Since therefore the children share in flesh and blood, he himself likewise partook of the same nature, that through death he might destroy him who has the power of death, that is, the devil, and deliver all those who through fear of death were subject to lifelong bondage.
>
> (Hebrews 2:14,15)

This statement is in line with the thesis of this book. Here you have the devil associated with the power of death or dissolution, which we said originated in the creation with its early originating and manifestation of entropy. The Son of God took on the full organic-spiritual life of man that had evolved slowly over the millennia as God had assisted his creation in its struggle to overcome entropy in a small fragment of itself by the evolutionary process. This passage in Hebrews sees the death of Christ (and his Resurrection) as the means of breaking the stranglehold of death as such: that is, of breaking completely at one point the power of entropy in the creation. In other words, in the terms that we are using we would say that the defeat of death broke the stranglehold of original sin. Another way of saying it is that by his life, death, and resurrection Jesus Christ remedied the original defect the creation had originated and continued, due to its combination of freedom and separation from the sustaining power of God.

But this passage from Hebrews suggests that by breaking the power of death or original sin Jesus lessened the power of the devil in the more dangerous area of men's specific sins in which men consciously put worldly advantage ahead of obedience to God and so become culpably guilty and alienate themselves from God. For when men are confronted with particular choices involving service of God, or themselves, the devil's trump card is always the insinuation of the thought: "If you take the way of obedience to God you will neglect your own security. Your life will go to pieces as to its social competence when compared with your peers, and if matters get pushed to extremes you court real specific disaster and probably injury and death for yourself." But if Jesus lived the perfect life and so took humanity back to God beyond the grave, then the proof has been given that obedience to God is the *successful* way to act, not the way of *defeat*, whatever misfortune or undue abbreviation of life on earth one may suffer.

This needs to be elaborated because many modern religious writers have spoken as if man should just normally do the right and think nothing of the consequences. That is not how people plan their lives in matters about which they really care, and a person would either be a person who was so sure of God's love and Christ's victory that he could take the welcome beyond the grave for granted, or a saintly agnostic whose life clung blindly to the hope that moral righteousness is a guiding clue to Ultimate Reality, if he could with integrity give this advice. But most of the many people I have heard give this advice have appeared to me so shallow, or spiritually dishonest, or spiritually inexperienced that they seemed never to have faced the choice between obeying God and acting for their own advantage in a situation in which they were called upon to sacrifice heavily to obey God.

For we must never underestimate the fact that what we call the law of self-preservation is the highest law for the whole organic world to obey from the first far off original protein molecules through the course of evolution up to the one-celled animals such as the amoeba and then up the long evolutionary climb to the animals just below man. For it was the increasing complication of organisms that made the higher organisms able to reflect more and more characteristics of God. To do its unconscious part in serving God the organism strove to attain and maintain the living organic pattern appropriate to its species. In the lower organisms therefore their being in existence *is* their service to him. So in them "duty to God" and the law of self-preservation always coincide. But when the human stage is reached the law for humans is not only to live, but to live the good life. That is to live intelligently following the law of righteous-love. But in the circumstances in which human life must be lived the law of righteous-love often goes counter to the law of self-preservation of the organism. Here is the devil's trump card, the pressure upon the human being in his insecurity to fall back to the strategy of following the highest law of the sub-human species. Here too is the bafflement of any naturalistic interpretation of human existence which, by interpreting man on the basis of his evolutionary past, *must* follow worldly self-preservation as the key to understanding human conduct. The organizing of society with legal codes, the development of art, music, literature, science, technology, and medicine can by a stretch of the imagination be assumed to be a refinement upon the law of self-preservation, the enhanced existence that these things bring by enabling man to live more deeply being thought of as fully underscoring the natural passion for the preservation of the self. But the naturalistic theory of self-preservation breaks down entirely in the face of the most revered men of history who have died rather than betray an ideal they saw making demands upon their allegiance, an ideal that was beyond that of the accepted *mores* of their group.

Now if the Christian claim is true, if Jesus Christ rose from the dead, then evidence is available that the beckoning Goal that the great martyrs struggled toward through death is no mirage, and that in them nature's pattern of self-preservation was more complicated but did not contradict itself. In other words, a point can be reached in which the surrender of one's human life in the last full measure of devotion to obedience to the law of righteous-love accomplishes the final preservation of the individual by preserving

364

the apropriate living human pattern intact to the point at which it can be detached from its physical organism and equipped with another body for a life beyond death. If Christianity is true, Jesus was speaking literally, not paradoxically, when he gave as the prescription for the ultimate technique for the preservation of the individual, "Whoever would save his life will lose it; and whoever loses his life for my sake and the gospel's will save it." (Mark 8:35)

The early Christians were inconspicuous ordinary men turned powerful heroes, for in them the stranglehold that death has upon human activity through fear had been broken. Peter who had been frightened after Gethsemane by the High Priest's maidservant (Mark 14:66-72) was in a matter of weeks as bold as a lion and telling the High Priest himself what to do to be saved. (Acts 4:6-12) The resurrection of Jesus Christ was the source of Peter's new boldness. The worst the High Priest could do to Peter was to kill him. But Peter was no longer afraid, because if he died all necessary arrangements to take care of him would be made by Peter's best friend who was now a Very Important Person on the other side of death.

CHAPTER 40

"Credo in . . . Carnis Resurrectionem"

Thus the Resurrection of Jesus Christ can be seen to fit logically into an evolutionary interpretation in which God first began by assisting the creation to bring forth life, then assisted its development, then assisted its human enhancement, and then assisted powerfully its ultimate salvation. This brings us to the question of how the Resurrection can be thought to have taken place.

The Resurrection of Christ is underlined by the statement in the Apostles' Creed: *"Credo in . . . carnis resurrectionem,"* "I believe in the resurrection of the flesh." The empty tomb stories and the two quotations in Acts that his flesh saw no corruption (Acts 2:31,32; 13:34-37) indicate that the thought of the early Church was that Jesus' entire body "evaporated" out of his grave clothes into a new state of being that is not part of our universe, that the matter composing the physical body of Jesus Christ together with his full continuity of memory of his earthly life was taken out of our universe entirely. For this reason the word "evaporate" can only be figuratively used in this connection, for literally it means the transformation of matter from the solid or liquid state to the gaseous state *within our universe.*

What is indicated in the Resurrection stories is straight miracle. Of course it is not to be believed that the body of Jesus became gaseous or that it took a new form enmeshed within the cause-and-effect sequences of matter within our universe. Instead, there was a complete interruption at this point of the cyclical processes of nature by which a body that has maintained its life by "refuelling" its strength through eating other organic matter finally dies, decays, and fertilizes the plant life which will serve as food for other animal organisms. This particular poundage of flesh and bones was transmuted and taken entirely out of the regular cause-and-effect sequences within our universe into another kind of existence entirely. The word "evaporate" is the closest word we have to describe this although strictly speaking it is inaccurate.

If the Resurrection did not occur, the foundation upon which

Christianity is built is undercut. If it did occur, it is straight miracle, uncongenial as the thought of miracle is to the modern mind. It may make the belief in this miracle easier to the modern mind if one remembers that modern physics does not think of matter as composed of solid particles, but thinks of matter simply as patterned energy. It also may make it easier to accept the claim that Jesus Christ rose from the dead if one realizes that the miraculous aspect of the Resurrection involves something similar to a reversal of the miracle of the Creation. One can accept the credibility of the Resurrection of Christ's body (or transmutation into an extra-universe state), if one accepts the miracle of Creation. The biblical belief is that there is one God and that he is all-powerful and righteous. Therefore he could exist if there were no physical universe; he is not part of it (or he would partake of its evil), and yet it owes its existence entirely to him (or he would not be all powerful). He therefore in the beginning must have created it out of nothing (creation *ex nihilo*). This theory has been dealt with at length earlier in this book. The universe is not God-thinking, which is pantheism or philosophical idealism, but instead is the product of his thought. The matter of which it is composed—which according to modern physics is simply patterned energy—owes what power it has entirely to the vigor of that Mind which thought it originally into independent existence. Jesus Christ's earthly life was lived so perfectly that God could, without derogation to his own moral perfection, draw it wholly back into himself. The matter composing Jesus' earthly body had been created originally by the mind of God and cast forth from the mind of God into independent existence. Now this same matter, having perfectly served God, was gathered back by God into God. Christians say that God was from the beginning Triune, Father, Son, and Holy Spirit. After Easter the Triune God is the Father, the God-man-Son, and the Holy Spirit.[1] The crea-

---

[1] This is to be understood in the sense meant by the Athanasian Creed:
. . . . our Lord Jesus Christ, the Son of God, is God and Man;
God, of the Substance of the Father, begotten before the worlds: and Man, of the Substance of his Mother, born in the world;
Perfect God, and Perfect Man: of a reasonable soul and human flesh subsisting;
Equal to the Father, as touching his Godhead: and inferior to the Father, as touching his Manhood.
Who although he be God and Man: yet he is not two, but one Christ;
One, not by conversion of the Godhead into flesh: but by taking of the

tion, after Easter, is permanently anchored to the Creator.

In the resurrection stories in the Gospels Luke says that Peter "ran unto the tomb; and stooping and looking in, he seeth the linen cloths by themselves." (Luke 24:12 ARV) John says that Peter and the disciple Jesus loved ran together to the tomb, the beloved disciple reaching it first.

Then Simon Peter came, following him, and he went into the tomb; he saw the linen cloths lying, and the napkin, which had been on his head, not lying with the linen cloths but rolled up in a place by itself. Then the other disciple, who reached the tomb first, also went in, and he saw and believed. (John 20:6-8)

The method of burial in first century Palestine can be clearly seen from the story of the raising of Lazarus. Here the processes of death are said to have been reversed so that Lazarus' flesh took on its aforetime quality. According to the account, the stone of the tomb had been rolled back to let Lazarus out, for Lazarus came out with the same earthly body functioning in the normal human way. When Jesus said,

"Lazarus, come out." The dead man came out, his hands and feet bound with bandages, and his face wrapped with a cloth. Jesus said to them, "Unbind him, and let him go." (John 11:43,44)

What is important to notice is that Lazarus' body was wound with grave clothes. He must have been somewhat hobbled by them and so got rather clumsily out of the tomb. But his head covering was not part of the funeral bandages that swathed his body. The head was covered by a separate piece of cloth. One can imagine the bystanders hastily untying or cutting the funeral wrappings and undoing the face cloth in their excited haste to get Lazarus free. So in the first moments after Lazarus had been raised one pictures the man standing there alive and well, and the face cloth and the rumpled grave clothes in a confused heap together on the ground about his feet.

But this is not the picture that is given us of the grave clothes in the tomb of Jesus. Luke says Peter saw "the linen cloths by them-

---

Manhood into God;
   One altogether, not by confusion of Substance: but by unity of Person.
   For as the reasonable soul and flesh is one man: so God and Man is one Christ . . . .
   He ascended into heaven . . . .

selves." The Gospel of John says that Peter "saw the linen cloths lying, and the napkin, which had been on his head, not lying with the linen cloths but rolled up in a place by itself." The impression is given that the body had been wrapped and laid at full length on a stone slab in a heretofore unused tomb, and that the disciples found the grave clothes collapsed but still in the exact position in which they had been left when the entombment was completed. And this was all that they found. Since there was no included body making a unified whole of the wrappings, the napkin that had been carefully folded around the head would of course be seen neatly collapsed (folded) "by itself," that is, separated by perhaps half an inch from the linen cloths that had swathed the body. The enveloping grave clothes had not been the slightest hindrance at the Resurrection, and had not been at all disarranged by it. This is why the misleading and inadequate expression "evaporate out" has to be used.

From the large scale amount of physical matter involved in the Resurrection this miracle is harder for the modern mind to "swallow" than is the miracle of the Incarnation which needed to involve only a microscopic amount of matter. In fact, what took place deep within the body of Mary had to be taken on faith—even by Mary. Even if the account of the annunciation and birth as told by Luke is literally accurate in each of its statements, even Mary herself could only have known that she believed that she had seen an angel who told her that she would have a child who would have God for a father instead of a human father, and that after the appropriate time interval she had given birth to Jesus, and that to the best of her knowledge she had never before that time had sex relations with a man. But she was not a witness to the all-important miracle of conception that took place within her own body.

As a matter of fact it is the miracle of the Resurrection that substantiates the miracle of the conception.

Actually the Resurrection evidence is not just the empty tomb stories although they are vital to it. There is the corroborating logical evidence that the Resurrection was needed to fulfill the Old Testament claim that God is righteous and loving. Jesus had perfectly obeyed God, and thus perfectly fulfilled the human requirements for the relationship of God's favor, as the conditions of the covenant were given at Sinai. (Exodus 19:4-6; Deuteonomy 4:39-40; 5:33;

369

30:15,16) A God who discarded Jesus at the crucifixion would not be righteous-loving. The character and reputation of Almighty God are at stake in the Resurrection.

The arrangement of the grave clothes when Jesus' friends found the tomb empty is an indication that the body had not been stolen. Avid readers of detective stories may imagine an involved situation in which the body *was* stolen and the clothes carefully rearranged in their original position to mislead those who visited the tomb. But a theft involving such details would have required considerable time, and the tomb is said to have been guarded by the authorities to exclude the possibility of theft. (Matthew 27:62-28:4) The Jewish idea of resurrection was the resurrection of the organism, not the continuing life of a soul that had shed its earthly body. But among the current ideas of resurrection there were differences of opinion ranging all the way from the idea that the resurrected body was of solid protoplasm as in our present existence, (compare Ezekiel 37:1-14) to the idea of a modified body with angelic characteristics. (Mark 12:18-27) Jesus' followers therefore would not have believed in the Resurrection had they known the earthly body of Jesus to be extant. They would have considered his Easter to Pentecost appearances to have been ghostly visitations. They believed in ghosts, (Mark 6:49,50) but that belief was not connected with their belief that God would annul the power of dissolution and bring about a resurrection. (Luke 24:36-43) The traditional ghost is the shadowy impotent remaining débris of its earthly existence. The resurrection to which the Pharisaic party of Judaism looked forward was a life of increased vitality and joy. Without the belief in Christ's genuine Resurrection, there is no way of explaining the sudden change from the mood of defeat to victory on the part of Christ's disciples. There was nothing in the tomb to tempt mercenary robbers. Robbing the tomb as a practical joke seems out of the question. And Jesus' enemies, Jewish or Roman, would be the last people to want to steal and hide the body. For the disciples were soon claiming that the Resurrection had occurred, and to have been able to have produced the body would have convinced Jerusalem that the Resurrection had not taken place, and would have undermined the disciples' own confidence in Jesus' continued powerful existence. The body of Jesus would have been "exhibit A" for the Sadducean and Roman authorities who wished to discredit the Christian movement at the outset. It is for this reason that they had taken the precaution of having the tomb guarded. (Matthew 27:62-66)

The Resurrection of Christ is the hardest one of all the important miracle stories of the Bible for the scientifically trained person to believe. Such stories as Balaam's ass speaking (Numbers 22:21-30) and Moses' walking-stick turning into a snake (Exodus 4:2-5) and Elisha causing the iron axe-head to float (II Kings 6:4-7) could all be assumed to be apocryphal fictional stories having their origin in the pious popular imagination, and the validity of the Christian religion and its parent Judaism would not be discredited. But Christianity is founded on the belief in the Resurrection. The Resurrection story is essential to Christianity.

If Jesus Christ was incarnate Deity, the Resurrection was inevitable if Deity wished not to slough off the body, for Deity is all controlling and deathless by definition. But the whole account of the Incarnation needs the heavy use of the Resurrection for its validation. (Romans 1:3,4)

If all off-schedule manipulation of the world by God is considered miracle—such as the "stacking" of the activity within a single molecule to produce a gene mutation, or the direct guiding or strengthening of the soul of a man—there are still three miracles that are in a class by themselves. They are the original Creation ex nihilo, and the Incarnation and Resurrection of Jesus Christ. Since belief in the Incarnation makes use of the Resurrection for its validation, the Resurrection needs to be classed with the original Creation. That is, both are unique, large scale, and unexplainable except by reference to the character and power of God, and believed in by circumstantial evidence. The evidence for the Creation is the existent universe. The evidence for the Resurrection is its necessity to complete the line of direction of Old Testament experience and thought, especially of the character of God as righteous and the source of basic moral law which at its apex is love, (Deuteronomy 10:17-19) together with the stories of the Resurrection, the disciples' belief in it, and the power of the Spirit of the risen Christ in their lives and in the life of the Church.

When I was attempting to suggest a possible way in which God could bring about desirable mutations and so advance evolutionary development, I suggested that he might by "stacking" the activity in a gene molecule cause a change and so effect an evolutionary modi-

371

fication without a wrench to the order of nature, because he would be making use of a built-in leeway in nature itself afforded by the merely statistical regularity at the sub-atomic level. But after the Divine tinkering with nature the result was still nature, still within the cause-and-effect sequences of the universe. No appeal to quantum mechanics will be made in connection with the Resurrection, for here the question is not one of rearranging the pattern of matter within the universe, but—to put it crudely—the removing from our universe entirely of a particular aggregate of matter approximately 60 x 6 x 12 inches in bulk, and the accomplishing of this in probably a very few minutes of time. I fully realize that in saying this I sound "medieval" and intellectually unsophisticated. But it must be frankly pointed out that this is what the empty tomb story implies. It would claim that there is not the slightest possibility of an archaeologist ever coming across the skull of Jesus, because beginning with Easter morning there was no body of Jesus within our universe for an archaeologist to find. The empty tomb stories, the two statements in Acts, (2:31; 13:36,37), and the *"carnis resurrectionem"* of the Apostles' Creed, are all definite on this point. (See also I Thessalonians 4:15-17; Philippians 3:20,21.) And based on biblical teaching Article IV of the Thirty-Nine Articles of the Church of England and of the Episcopal Church in the United States still reads:

> Christ did truly rise again from death, and took again his body, with flesh, bones and all things appertaining to the perfection of Man's nature; wherewith he ascended into Heaven, and there sitteth, until he return to judge all Men at the last day.

The point needs to be stressed that the question of whether miracle, that is, the direct action of the supernatural God upon the creation, can occur, is the key problem that science in the last three centuries has posed for the Christian faith. It needs also to be stressed that if one admits that God can at will "stack" the activity in a particular molecule and so bring about a mutation that furthered his plan for evolution, one is admitting miracle in principle. A Creator God who would be able to do this could interfere in any way he wished with his creation, could, for example, miraculously and instantaneously multiply five loaves and two fishes to an amount sufficient to give an adequate meal to five thousand people. (Mark 6:35-44) If there *is* an all powerful Creator-God outside of nature, there is no limit other than this own desire to what he could do to nature. This is why those who deny miracle out of deference to science, if they are consistent thinkers, have to describe God's relation to nature as being always *in* nature in a way that actually is pantheistic, and they end up by denying altogether that God genuinely is, as Jesus taught, "Our Father who art in heaven." Then, to be consistent, they are forced to deny that Jesus Christ was really the supernatural God incarnate, and that he literally rose from the dead. But if one denies that Jesus Christ was genuinely the Son of God, and that he genuinely rose from the dead, and that he knew what God is like when he told his followers that he is "Our Father who art in heaven," then one has given up Christianity. This path of denial is the one Liberalism has progressively taken, and its final open denial of God in the mid-twentieth century claim of some theologians that "God is dead" is no surprise to those who have really understood the implications of Liberalism, but is a healthy bringing into the open of a point of view that has long been implicit but covered up when ministers and divinity professors speak to laymen. The "God is dead" movement in theology at last makes clear to laymen the presence of an anti-Christian intellectual belief in the thinking of many of the clergy, most of whom have not the courage to state their lack of Christian belief as baldly as the "God is dead" advocates have done.

It has often been said that Judaism and Christianity, in contrast to the world-denying religions of the Orient, are the most materialistic of all the great religions. The basic doctrine of the Resurrection of Jesus Christ is a case in point. I have stated the problem of the Resurrection bluntly, because it needs to be pointed out that the doctrine of Christ's Resurrection is the key log in the log-jam of modern theology.

Here as the cornerstone of the Christian Church is a doctrine in which the claims of science and religion—each speaking within the realm in which it claims to be the authority—inevitably cross. There are aspects of existence where the domains of the two disciplines can be more or less separated. One can say that the conscious and thinking subject and the I-thou relationship and all the ultimate explanations of why, and all purposes, ideals, and values are outside the domain of science. This means that these areas offer genuine other-than-scientific evidence about the nature of ultimate reality.

The evidence of these other areas I have heartily welcomed all my adult life, as enabling me to hold and teach the Christian faith with intellectual integrity, even though the intellectual integration of Christian teaching and scientific thought has not been adequately made. But it is upon belief in the Resurrection of Jesus Christ that the Christian Church was built under the power of the Holy Spirit. And the belief in the resurrection of the total Jesus Christ includes the *carnis resurrectionem*. This *carnis resurrectionem* is not a conscious thinking subject or an I-thou relationship, or a purpose, or an ideal, or a value, or an explanation of why. It involves instead the transformation of objective, measurable, weighable matter composed of the chemical elements with which science deals. This matter, shut away from all human sight within a tomb is claimed by Christianity to have undergone a unique process that may have been instantaneous, or may have continued for a few seconds, or may have involved a matter of minutes.

In other words, the resurrection of Jesus Christ is a religious matter of the first importance that is directly related to the realm of science and scientific theory. At this point the questions and the claims of science are distinctly relevant even though Christianity may have adequate reason for claiming that in this unique situation matter acted in a unique way, and that therefore the ordinary routines by which matter acts ceased to apply in this particular instance, and that no pronouncement of science as to the possibility of the *"carnis resurrectionem"* would be authoritative.

The basic Christian belief in the Resurrection, including as it does the account of the empty tomb, has been for a century the key log in the doctrinal log jam of Christianity. It is such an embarrassment to Christianity that theological discussion avoids openly admitting that the problem exists. Liberalism in its more conservative form has thought in terms of the living soul or personal consciousness of Jesus Christ living on in joy with the Father, and by cautious use of words when dealing with the Resurrection stories has by-passed in Easter sermons the question of what became of the body of Jesus.

Full-fledged Liberalism tries to sound Christian but leaves God sufficiently undefined to make possible its carrying on in established Christian institutions without subscribing to Jesus' belief that we can with accuracy describe God as "Our Father who art

374

in heaven." As far as the Resurrection of Jesus Christ is concerned, full-fledged Liberalism by-passes the empty tomb stories, and at Easter by a careful use of words does not make it too clear that its conception of the Resurrection is merely the resurgence in Jesus' followers of their human memory of him, not the continuation of Jesus' personal consciousness and memory in enhanced joy and power. Full-fledged Liberalism is not Christian. Less than full-fledged Liberalism is intellectually inconsistent. The clearly Fundamentalist group that is thoroughgoing in its belief in the verbal inspiration of the Scriptures, finds them sufficient and closes its mind to the problems raised by science, and so keeps the Christian heritage at the price of trying to ignore the world of the twentieth century. The combination of radio, television, space travel, advances in medicine, magazines, automation, and our increasing contact with foreign cultures makes this position increasingly difficult.

Much more hope for the future of theology is to be placed in an important group of conservatives that would be roughly labeled as Fundamentalists by Full-Fledged Liberals, men who have either come out of the Thoroughgoing Fundamentalist Group or have moved toward Conservatism through disillusion with the bankruptcy of Liberalism. These men sympathize with what the Thoroughgoing Fundamentalists are trying to do, and like the Fundamentalists believe the Apostles', Nicene, and Chalcedon Creeds and the full Trinitarianism of the Athanasian Creed. But they do not subscribe wholeheartedly to all the intellectual techniques Fundamentalism has used to protect this orthodoxy, and they are aware of the cultural and scientific changes in the last hundred years and are awake to the need of some intellectual method of getting on in an intellectual working arrangement with the development of scientific knowledge. In this situation they are fortunate in having some corroboration from an increasing number of scientists who have a direct spiritual awareness of life's mystery and science's incompleteness, scientists who are willing to go on record as believing in a God who is beyond the range of science and scientific inquiry, and some of whom are willing to go on record as believing that through the divine Christ man has remission of his sins. Possibly the greatest hope for renewed Christian belief in America at large comes from these intelligently conservative religious leaders and the spiritually oriented scientists.

But when I come to the statements of both these religious specialists and these scientific specialists, I find that the statements they make have great vagueness at such points as those at which their specialties interrelate. Both groups hurry on to areas in which they can speak more safely in generalizations.[2] Discussion by both groups on the implications of the Resurrection is sorely needed. I shall attempt to throw light on this most difficult problem. If some light is thrown on it, it will be a great gain.

[2] William G. Pollard, in his *Chance and Providence,* is an exception to this, in that he tries to come to intimate scientific grips with the question of the personal God's relation to the world as seen by science.

CHAPTER 41

The *Carnis Resurrectio* and the Completion of God's Task

As to the *how* of the Resurrection three suggestions are made by the New Testament. One is that Jesus Christ rose from the dead by his own power. One is that God raised him from the dead. The third alternative is the simple statement that he rose from the dead or would rise from the dead with no indication specified as to whether this would be by his own power or by the power of God (the Father).

We now come to the question of a hypothetical method of Divine action in bringing about the frankly miraculous Resurrection. What we have to do is to see if an explanation can be made that will harmonize with the total theory this book has been developing. I think that such an explanation can be made, and it will fit the theory that Jesus was a perfect man upon whom the Spirit of God came at his baptism, (Mark 1:10, 11) who served God with perfect goodness throughout his sacrificial ministry and death, and who was raised from the dead by God the Father. (Acts 2:22-24). It will also fit the belief that Jesus of Nazareth was the preexistent Christ who within Mary had taken on full human life, (Philippians 2:5-8; John 1:1, 2, 14) and after the task of redemption was completed rose from the dead by his own power inasmuch as, being the eternal Son of God, he was by his own nature Deity. (John 10:17, 18; 16:27, 28.)

The explanation of the Resurrection is a corollary of the hypothesis of the Creation and of the theory of evolution as this book has been developing it. It also includes in it the biblical belief in the Ascension of Christ, (Acts 1:9-11; Mark 16:19, 20; Matthew 28:16-20) for the Ascension is the completion of the Resurrection. Jesus did not rise from the dead just "to be about" and to enjoy continued conscious existence. He rose from the dead to return to the Father and from his strategic position with the Father to continue the work he had begun on earth. The Resurrection appearances were a special interim manifestation of him to convince the

377

disciples that he really was alive and powerful, so that they would have intellectual preparation for his continuing work with them through the Holy Spirit.

There never was anything to physical matter as such that did not have its original existence in the mind of God. Matter originally was in no way a projection of God's being as the Second and Third Persons of the Trinity are, but matter was originated as a product of God's thought which he disassociated from himself and cast loose into objective independent existence. The terrific power still inherent in matter is a lingering far-off echo of its Divine source. The fact that that power slowly but steadily diminishes is due to its present independent status unsustained by that source. The fact that the mind of God, by appreciation and by the maneuvering of matter in the area of quantum mechanics, especially in mutations, has been able to maneuver a small portion of matter through evolution into aggregates of increasing complexity and reactivity culminating in intelligent consciousness, is due to matter's normal affinity for mind, because it is itself a product of the divine Mind. We have seen that in the highest evolutionary species, man, the complexity and reactivity have risen to such an extent that man is capable of reflecting the righteous-love which is the supreme, policy-determining characteristic of the Godhead.

This means that if a man were freely to live a life of perfect righteous-love, in him the creature's independent existence would be brought to a perfection that would enable it to be gathered back again to God by God who was its ultimate origin, without any derogation to the Creator's spiritual perfection. This is the "fulfilling of the law" that Jesus Christ perfectly accomplished. And so, the perfect voluntary surrender of the creature to God having been completed at Calvary, God gathered the creature back to himself—forever. It was not just the consciousness of Jesus that returned to the Father, but the whole Jesus. This is why *credo in . . . carnis resurrectionem* is one of the statements in the Apostles' Creed. One can free from their pantheistic implications three lines from Shelley's "Adonais" and apply them to the status of Jesus of Nazareth after the Resurrection.

> He is a presence to be felt and known . . .
> Spreading itself where'er that Power may move
> Which has withdrawn his being to its own.

378

The flesh of Jesus of Nazareth was human flesh, made up like ours of protoplasm containing atoms that had been used and reused for millions of years in the organic material of plants and men and animals and birds and fish and animalcules back in the primeval seas. And through all the millions of years of struggle the creatures had fought for survival, fought with more and more complicated strategies against the inevitable dissolution by which nature disintegrates in accordance with the *second law of thermodynamics*. And now at last a bridgehead to victory had been achieved. In the body of Jesus of Nazareth the *second law of thermodynamics* had at last been cancelled. "The last enemy to be destroyed is death," said St. Paul. (I Corinthians 15:26). And in the earthly career of Jesus of Nazareth that crucial battle had been won. "Be of good cheer;" he said on the last night to his disciples, "I have overcome the world." (John 16:33). In him Nature, in its obedient but independent status, went home, deathless at last, to the Father. The Eternal Mind, that could cast free its thought into the patterned energy of independent existence (matter), could joyously recall it into free companionship with himself.

According to the doctrine of the Trinity God is a Three-One God from all eternity: the Father having from eternity begotten the Son from his own being as a sharer of his perfections and power, and having loved him eternally with perfect, active, outgoing love. The Son reciprocates, loving the Father with the same perfect, active, outgoing love, which shared perfect love is the Holy Spirit proceeding from the Father and the Son. God therefore from eternity is the Trinity, Father, Son, and Holy Spirit. But if the Chalcedon Creed is followed which steers officially between the heresies of docetism and adoptionism in defining the relation of the Divine and human in Jesus Christ, then the Triune God is now God the Father, the God-man Son, and the Holy Spirit who proceeds from the God-man Son and from the Father. This explains why it was that the Holy Spirit could not be poured out until Christ was raised from the dead. It is not that the Holy Spirit had never before been active in the world. The work of the Old Testament prophets had been carried on under the inspiration of the Holy Spirit. In fact, according to the thesis of this book, the slow, upward thrust of the evolutionary process has been due to the activity of God's Spirit, or the Holy Spirit, from the earliest

379

stages when, according to Genesis, "The Spirit of God was brooding upon the face of the waters." (Genesis 1:2 ARV alternate reading).

But God is God and the creation is other than God and the problem has always been how God could get his guidance and power across to his creation without interfering with its status as free. But this is greatly facilitated now that man can accept the Divine through the human in Jesus Christ who as human is "one of us" although as Divine he is also Deity. The Divine power was put into the human type in order that it might more adequately transfuse our lives.

> In the beginning was the Word [Christ], and the Word was with God, and the Word was God. . . . And the Word became flesh and dwelt among us. . . . Jesus said to them. . . . "I am the living bread which came down from heaven; if any one eats of this bread, he will live forever. . . ." "I am the vine, you are the branches. . . ." "As the branch cannot bear fruit by itself, unless it abides in the vine, neither can you, unless you abide in me." (John 1:1, 14; 6:35, 51; 15:5, 4).

One word of caution needs to be given. We have spoken as if the Resurrection effected a bridgehead in the connecting of man with God. It would be more accurate to say that it completed the bridgehead. Human nature on its own would never have been able to effect the return to God. The original bridgehead had been made on God's initiative. It was the Incarnation of God as Man. The Resurrection made the Incarnation permanent, thus anchoring God firmly forever to his creation.

CHAPTER 42

Evolution and the Biblical Idea of the Life to Come

There are people who suggest that man does not know very much about either "the furniture of heaven or the temperature of hell" and conclude that the less people try to talk knowingly about heaven and hell the better. But such a statement caricatures the subject to belittle it. It is true that the New Testament exhibits a wise reticence in its remarks about the life after death. But it is also true that what is beyond this present life bulks large in New Testament thought, even if its thought on the subject is still somewhat fluid. We find the old idea of the dead waiting in their graves until a final resurrection in what was thought to be the very near future, competing with the growing confidence that death for the Christian would involve an immediate transition to the Divine presence. (Compare I Thessalonians 4:16 with Philippians 1:23.) Throughout the New Testament the description of heaven (excepting in the Book of Revelation) is lightly sketched in by scattered hints. We are given the lines of direction for composing the picture rather than the picture itself. But the lines of direction are definitely there. The emphasis is not on a description of the beyond for its own sake. Any picture of the beyond serves only as a backdrop for the great Christian affirmation that the Christian will be forever with Christ. (Philippians 1:23; I Thessalonians 4:17; Acts 7:55, 56, 59; Luke 23:43; John 14:3-6; Revelation 19:9).

But the New Testament idea of heaven, or the everlasting final fulfillment beyond this present life, contains a great deal more than the idea that the naked soul or consciousness somehow lives on. It should be emphasized that some elaboration of the picture of heaven is not an indication of a selfish or a "materialistic" or an unsophisticated or unintelligent mind, not something for the knowing to wink at as necessary for the piety of the simple minded who are unable to dispense with such crutches. Quite the contrary, the elaboration of the picture of heaven is a theological corollary of our belief about God. One of the structural ideas of this book is the belief that the nature of God is a many faceted unity. The upward thrust of the evolutionary process we have attributed to the increasing complication of organisms making it possible for them to reflect more and more aspects of the many-faceted unity of the Divine nature. It is obvious that if we think of mudworms at the lower end of the scale and twentieth century civilized man at the higher end, that if the difference is due to man's higher degree of reflection of the nature of God, then any sophisticated picturing of heaven as "a great white blur" can be dismissed at the outset as inadequate. For the basic fact of heaven is the presence of God. When in the life to come we no longer "see in a mirror dimly, but . . . face to face," (I Corinthians 13:12) we shall see a simple yet involved and complicated beauty (glory) beyond anything that we can imagine. God himself will environ his servants. A conception of the life to come including that to which design, color, structure, and music are only inadequate symbols, would be closer to the reality than our usual tendency to think of heaven as "a great white blur."

We are, however, primarily creatures of earth and therefore not adjusted to the environment simply of Deity as such. But this problem has been cared for. In the Resurrection, Christ took some of our earth (his body) into the beyond, where he went "to prepare a place" for us, (John 14:2) a non-cosmic dimension of existence suited to our needs. He himself, the God-man, will form our environment, and he himself is now both heavenly and earthly.

God will "make all things new;" (Revelation 21:5) there will be "a new heaven and a new earth." (Revelation 21:1). By the resurrection of his body Christ anchored our universe safely to God and is himself the carry-over of the universe which is our original home into the glorious new and renewed dimension of existence that is to be. It is this that made the empty tomb and the Ascension of the complete Jesus Christ, the God-man, with the organism through which he had expressed himself, necessary to the Divine plan of salvation. It is why the creed's old statement, "*Credo in . . . carnis resurrectionem*", is of such great importance to the Christian faith. God in Christ came to redeem his creation, not just certain souls selected out of the creation, although man is the most important part of the world to God:

For God so loved the world, that he gave his only begotten Son . . . (John 3:16 ARV)

382

For as in Adam all die, so also in Christ shall all be made alive. (I Corinthians 15:22)

When anyone is united to Christ, there is a new world; the old order has gone, and a new order has already begun. . . . God was in Christ reconciling the world to himself. (II Corinthians 5:17, 19 NEB)

But we have his promise, and look forward to new heavens and a new earth, the home of justice. (II Peter 3:13 NEB)

'There are many dwelling-places in my Father's house; if it were not so I should have told you; for I am going there on purpose to prepare a place for you. And if I go and prepare a place for you, I shall come again and receive you to myself, so that where I am you may be also; and my way there is known to you.' Thomas said, 'Lord, we do not know where you are going, so how can we know the way?' Jesus replied, 'I am the way; I am the truth and I am life; no one comes to the Father except by me.' (John 14:2-6 NEB)

CHAPTER 43

The Conquest of Death
and the Direction of the Evolutionary Trend

We will now see if we can construct a picture of the life to come in line with the picture of the creation and the subsequent picture of evolution that we have been drawing, and then we shall see how this will fit the hints and the lines of direction in the biblical picture of the life to come.

A guiding thread we have followed has been the separation of the creation from God in order to insure its freedom. For freedom and love are characteristics of the Creator. Freedom is necessary for both love and moral responsibility and, since God is righteous-loving, men must have freedom and love and moral responsibility if they are to be in the image of God and eventually come into a community of fellowship with him. This seems to have been God's purpose in the creation, to make out of nothing that which could eventually become companionable to himself. (Exodus 19:3-6; 33:11; Isaiah 41:8; 54:5; Jeremiah 31:32-34; Hosea 2:14-20; Matthew 6:8, 9; 7:9-11; Mark 3:34, 35; John 14:23; 15:15; 17:22-24). But the problem was that, because the creation was separated from the Creator, there was involved entropy at the inanimate level, death at the animate level, and sin or "backsliding" at the human level. All these three disabilities were conquered—in reverse order—by the life, death, Resurrection, and Ascension of Jesus Christ, the incarnate Son of God, in whose person the creation was permanently re-linked with the Creator. We miss much of the thrill of the Christmas story if we fail to see in the "multitude of the heavenly host" who appeared with the angel to the shepherds (Luke 2:13) the fierce joy of the heavenly armies on the universe's "D-day", when their great leader opened the offensive in which he was to win single-handed and incognito the strategic battle that would break the stranglehold of entropy, death, and sin and restore the "lost" creation to the Creator. (I Corinthians 15:22, 24-28). The New Testament idea is that Christ's victory is applied in some way to other men and affects the creation as a whole. And Christ's victory enables the Father to deal more intimately with men and therefore with the creation.

The whole rise of evolution had been made possible by God's "brooding upon" (Genesis 1:2 ARV alternate reading) the creation, as has been discussed in detail. Thus biological evolution and man's social struggle toward the good, as well as especially the historical and spiritual struggle of Israel as recorded in the Old Testament, all reflect the redemptive power of God and have a part in the whole plan of the redemption of the world. In this sense God is the Redeemer even in Old Testament times. (Psalms 19:14; 25:22; 26:11; 31:5; 34:22; 44:26; 49:15; 69:18; 71:23; 72:14; 78:35; 103:4; 106:10; 107:2; 130:8; Isaiah 29:22; 35:9; 41:14; 43:1; 44:6, 22-24; 48:17; 49:7; 51:11; 54:5,8; 59:20; 62:12; 63:4, 9, 16; Hosea 7:13; 13:14; Micah 6:4). And of course the whole prophetic movement in the Old Testament has little meaning unless it is evidence of the special activity of the Holy Spirit assisting Israel through the prophets. If the activity of the Holy Spirit is seen in the Old Testament, why then was the Incarnation and Ascension of Jesus Christ necessary for the coming of Holy Spirit in the Christian sense at Pentecost, in the fuller sense in which the prophet Joel looked forward to it when he said, " 'In the last days it shall be, God declares, that I will pour out my Spirit upon all flesh?' " (Acts 2:17, quoted from Joel 2:28)

The answer is that God's eternity is to be thought of in the Old Testament sense: although God is not bound by time it is not irrelevant to him. Therefore before the Incarnation the Holy Spirit proceeded from the Father and Christ. After Pentecost the Holy Spirit proceeds from the Father and Jesus Christ. That is, the eternal Son is now the God-man. This means that the uncreated God-Life, whose undergirding is essential to us if we are to escape the otherwise inevitable clutch of entropy, is now more intimately available to us because it can be filtered to us through God's acquired human nature. Its transfusion can strengthen us more adequately by being already in the human type.

Before you put down the book in disgust at this fantastic sounding claim, which sounds like sheer romancing of the imagination, remember that none of the things that make life worth living are within the realm of science. Color, light, sound, odors, beauty, ethics, ideals, thought, purpose, and love are all outside the realm of science. But if on extra-scientific grounds one can believe in an intelligent Creator-God, then this theory of the conquest of death in our lives as due to the transfusion of power through the risen God-man is a theory far more relatable to the over-all scientific picture than is the more typically used Christian picture of man as consisting of an immortal soul and a physical body mysteriously "glued" together in this life and separated at death, which is a picture taken over from Plato (*Phaedo*). For the whole course of evolution is accounted for on our theory by God's interest in and intimate working with his material creation to enable it to take on aspects increasingly less like mere matter, which aspects are available for it to acquire by reflection from association with the Creator. We unconsciously acquire characteristics of those with whom we associate even within human society, especially the traits of those we love and admire. Dogs are more nearly human than wolves because dogs acquire some human characteristics by association with human beings. It therefore does not need to seem altogether strange that man should acquire some divine characteristics (which of course he can sinfully misuse) by association with God. And it is to be noticed that the course of evolution studied as history indicates that the line of evolutionary development has been in the dual direction of increasing freedom for the organism while it lives, and increasingly adequate strategies for fighting against death. If the development of civilization is seen as a kind of non-biological evolutionary development, then the development of language, writing, recorded history, stores of learning, and the fine and applied arts is seen as a way of increasing the permanence of the enriched attainments of man's conscious life. And of course the great modern advances in medicine are conscious attempts to improve and prolong the life of the human body.

We are now in a position to dovetail the Johannine and Pauline teaching with our Christian-evolutionary theory to get a continuous picture of how God by his grace ultimately defeats the stranglehold of entropy in and upon the creation, which he has "manifested through the appearing of our Saviour Christ Jesus, who abolished death and brought life and immortality to light . . ." (II Timothy 1:10)

386

The new creation and the new age that Judaism looked forward to have been initiated by Jesus Christ. He is the Second Adam (I Corinthians 15:22, 45) initiating a new, changed human race. He *is* the source of the new creation. Its specifications lie coded within his being with—figuratively speaking—a similarity to the coding for the life of a new organism within its original cell. Using a more biblical figure, he in his Resurrection and Ascension is the yeast of the old creation carried over into the life of God to form out of the old creation a new creation which will be untroubled by entropy and its correlative ills. (II Peter 3:13). This "place" which he has gone to prepare for us (John 14:2) is formed by means of that fragment of the old creation which he amalgamated to himself and which can now assume new dimensions when his divine Life has reassumed its supracosmic proportions from which it had to restrict itself temporarily for the purpose of the Incarnation. (Philippians 2:7) God is now in the position of being able to environ us in the life beyond with a created and human environment suited to our needs, because he took it with him for us when he rose from the dead. (John 14:3)

This is why Christ is thought of as having risen and "ascended" bodily, and therefore as having "risen from the dead, and become the firstfruits of them that slept." (I Corinthians 15:30 KJV) And yet the Church has not found as an insuperable difficulty the obvious fact that the bodies of his followers decay after death in the same old way that they did before the Incarnation. For Paul the doctrine that the Christian in this life is "in Christ" is fully as important as his doctrine of justification by faith. The doctrine of being "in Christ" while still in this present life means that from the time when the individual surrenders himself to Christ he lives a dual existence. He lives the old human life as usual in the world. But the new supracosmic life is also in the process of formation within him. The Gospel of John in the vine and the branches and the bread of life passages (15:1, 2, 4, 5; 6:33-35, 40, 47-51, 58, 63) uses more easily picturable language for this than the terms in which Paul expresses it. But both John and Paul mean something far more than just the idea that we become morally better and so reflect God's righteousness more adequately. Both mean that our lives already in this life partake of the existence which is not of this universe. The reason why science finds no difference between

Christians and non-Christians is that this new life is not of our universe, and science is by definition restricted to what is of this universe. Had a modern physician done a complete blood-count on Jesus he would have found his hemoglobin to be merely normal human hemoglobin: Jesus Christ had full humanity. His full deity was not of the universe and so would not have shown up in scientific investigation.

❉　❉　❉　❉　❉　❉

We now come to the point where it is necessary to see whether a plausible account of heaven can be given, plausible to twentieth century minds which, even if they are Christian, unconsciously take for granted the science-conditioned mind-set. In order to fight the almost complete stranglehold scientism has upon the modern intellect and imagination one must begin by realizing at the outset what science cannot do. Science, strictly speaking, describes for us a world without color, sound, light, beauty, values, courage, morals, purpose, and love. And science cannot deal with the thinking thinker. There is no place for either the scientist or the poet within the strictly scientific picture of the world. It is illogical to conclude that there can be no Christian heaven merely because the authoritative scientific data have no place for it. For the authoritative scientific data have no place for the beauties, values, virtues and purposes that constitute human life as we know it in this world. If one rules out heaven because it is not part of the scientific picture one would have to rule out beauty, color, purpose, love, pain, and hunger for the same reason; for if one knows only science one could not deduce the existence of any of these. That is, all these are subjective responses, and as such science is not equipped to deal with them, but only to deal with the physiological action that apparently accompanies these subjective states. That is something different. The gap between the thinking subject and the objective world seems unbridgeable, due to the nature of the human mind.

Furthermore, it cannot be ruled out *a priori* that there are forms of existence other than our universe. By this is not meant a platform in the sky billions of miles from the earth, for that would still be our universe. What is meant is a form of existence in a different space-time from our universe and not normally interlock-

388

ing with it. Imagine tiny creatures to whom dampness of any description was so completely foreign that they could know nothing whatever about it. If they lived intelligently all their lives in a sponge that was wholly immersed in water they would be able to describe accurately their sponge universe but they would know nothing whatever of the water, and it would not figure at all in their descriptions of their own lives or of the sponge.

It must also be remembered that mathematicians can make valid equations with the 5th, 6th, and 7th dimensions of which they have no immediate awareness of any kind such as we have of length, breadth, thickness, and time. This does not prove that universes in other dimensions do exist, but it does mean that their possible existence cannot be categorically denied.

There are certain Biblical specifications that must be met if the Christian heaven does exist. For one thing it must be a place which we cannot now see but from which the activity of our world can be seen. (Luke 2:13, 14; 9:30, 31; Acts 7:59; Hebrews 12:1?; Revelation 6:9-11?; 8:3, 4; 19:1, 2). Its existence and character must be related in some way to the personality and presence of Christ and the Father. (John 14:1-6; I Thessalonians 4:17; Philippians 1:23; Revelation 21:22, 23) It must also be a situation to which lives, begun on this earth, can some day be transplanted. (Matthew 5:11, 12; Mark 12:24, 25; Romans 6:5-8, 22; I Corinthians 3:12-15; 15:17-19). And finally it must be a state of things from which evil is excluded and only what is good remains. (Matthew 25:31-46; 7:21-23; Luke 16:19-31; I Corinthians 3:11-15; Galatians 5:19-21; Revelation 21:27; 22:14, 15). Do we have any experiences within our present life in this world that resemble that imagined state of things sufficiently so that they seem to serve as pointers towards its existence, to establish lines of spiritual direction which, if they could be projected beyond our earthly existence, would be in accord with the traditional picture of heaven?

I think that we do have such experiences. Even at the mechanical level we now have screens and mirrors which are transparent from one side and opaque from the other. And at the intellectual level it is typical for the higher to understand the lower better than the lower understands the higher. An adult can know more about a pre-school child than a pre-school child can know about an adult. A human being can know more about an oyster than an

389

oyster can know about a human being.

That the existence and character of heaven must be related to the personality of Deity is true by definition, otherwise it would not be heaven. For the experience of heaven must be a state of ultimate satisfaction and nothing short of relationship to Deity would provide this. Apart from Deity no supramundane stage-setting could be permanently attractive. To a large extent things are attractive by relationship to personality even at the purely human level. Elegant houses impersonally furnished by an interior decorator seem less adequate as homes than those that reflect the life and interests and good taste of their occupants. Those people who feel the urge to collect beautiful antiques are motivated in part by the desire to strengthen the feeling of the aliveness of their own personalities by relation to objects freighted with a long association with human history. And we know of objects and localities, not beautiful in themselves, which have a deep permanent attraction for us by association with some moment in which they were shared by someone dear to us.

Traces of experience in line with the belief that heaven includes the good and excludes evil occur even in this life. The "great chasm . . . fixed" between Lazarus and Dives (Luke 16:26) is not arranged by arbitrary fiat by an omnipotent autocrat. Although the basic orientation toward good or evil cannot be easily recognized in childhood or early youth, as lives develop according to their basic orientation (Matthew 13:24-30) the tendency of like to gravitate to like tends to make spiritual communication between those of diverse spiritual orientation increasingly difficult. If Adolf Hitler and Albert Schweitzer had been exactly contemporaneous, we could have imagined them playing happily together in their kindergarten days. It is impossible to think of them as enjoying each other's society during their full maturity.

The other human experience that has given men the feeling of the greater strength and permanence of the good is the discovery as one grows older that the mind constantly reassesses one's own past experience, and in retrospect its pain and misfortune seem more shadowy, less "real" than the good.

Being transplanted for growth is another experience normal to us. We find such standard examples of it as a young person being sent away to college, or a young woman leaving her family for a new home with her husband. The experience of being transplanted occurs in a much subtler and slightly uncanny fashion in some social relationships. We all have known a few individuals whose relation to space was rather odd. They all occupied a certain amount of ordinary space. They also gave the impression of carrying their own space—of a different sort—with them. This space seemed a wide and satisfying domain to which they might or might not give us access. With such people one seems to one's self to be more real, to have increased in stature and status. Knowing them seems a kind of initiation.

This experience of the different and larger "space", of another realm of reality, comes even more definitely from prolonged religious experience. William G. Pollard, who was an experienced physicist before he became a Christian, dedicated his book, *Chance and Providence,* to his wife, "Through whom", he said, "by the providence of God, this previously inaccessible range of reality has been opened to me." The testimony is noteworthy, not because it is unusual, but because it is given by a man whose knowledge of the physical realm was so profound, subtle, and exact before his spiritual initiation into Christianity. The initiation through another human personality into a wider range of reality has points of similarity with St. Paul's description of what takes place more fully in the Christian's relation to the Holy Spirit:

No one comprehends the thoughts of God except the Spirit of God. Now we have received not the spirit of the world, but the Spirit which is from God, that we might understand the gifts bestowed on us by God. . . . The unspiritual man does not receive the gifts of the Spirit of God, for they are folly to him, and he is not able to understand them because they are spiritually discerned. (I Corinthians 2:11, 12, 14)

Those who have had Christian experience know that they are initiated into an aspect of everyday life that some individuals are and other individuals are not aware of, depending upon whether or not the person has had this initiation. To some extent the fringes of the other realm of reality, the "other spaces" of the "other dimensions", or heaven, apparently are beginning to be accessible to the Christian in this life (John 5:24; 8:51, 52; 11:26; II Corinthians 5:17; Ephesians 2:4-6) through the assistance of the Holy Spirit. It may not at first seem vivid to the Christian that he is beginning to live close to the fringes of the life of heaven. He may seem to himself to be very much living in this world and trying to serve God here. The startling realization that he is living in more than this world may come to him suddenly when he discovers that the radiance and preciousness and purposiveness of the world around him and the permanent importance of working well in it, which he takes for granted as a normal experience of *this* world, may be something that many about him cannot see or understand.

Furthermore, this human experience, together with St. Paul's saying about our understanding about "the gifts bestowed on us by God" through "the Spirit which is from God," fits in well with the evolutionary theory as this book has outlined it. For the claim has been made that God's "appreciation" of his creation in each of its advances assists the creatures, empowering them to some extent to hold the patterns appropriate to their existence as well as helping in the emergence and identification of the patterns themselves. The process of sanctification, in the Christian theological sense, is the final and crowning form of what God has been doing in evolution from the beginning. Sanctification is another example of God's habit of repeating great themes, with variations, within his creation. From the first dawn of evolution until the final sanctification of his saints it is the same God at work. This accounts for the similarities in the method.

CHAPTER 44

Problems Created for God
by Nature's Coming of Age in Man

The differences in the method of sanctification from God's ways of working with the lower creation are modifications due to the degree of previous attainment of *homo sapiens* and the need for rushing the work with human lives. For God had brought the creation in man to the point of reflecting the governing aspects of God's nature, his intelligent righteous-love. Man was made in the image of God. Therefore it was individual men who were precious and needed to be saved. With the lower animals where the perpetuation of a species was the most important factor God could take a million years to accomplish a particular task. By comparison the threescore years and ten to which he was limited by the human life-span necessitated a new, rapid technique for dealing with men.

The difference in the situation with which he was now faced lay in man's greater accumulation of earthly-background-strength, and in his possession of greater intelligence and freedom than that which characterized the lower creation. As at the beginning God had cast physical nature into independent existence, furnished with power which it could use independently by expending, so each hard-won gain in the evolutionary climb, although won with the help of God, became to a certain extent a precarious and unstable possession of the creature in its own right. This was necessary if the freedom of the creatures was to increase. Thus when historical development continued the evolutionary process in man in a modified non-biological form, the transmittable gains made by the race in terms of artifacts, mores, language, literature, art, philosophy, technology, and science became a transmittable heritage within man's control for which he did not have to depend directly upon his Maker. Given health, education, and equally high native intelligence, a man who serves God and a man who rebels against God are each capable of planting corn, building houses, solving geometry problems, playing the guitar, and organizing political states.

For these abilities men owe direct gratitude to their ancestors, and indirect gratitude to God. Over the millennia the heavenly Father assisted his children to earn, but to keep and accumulate their earnings. What he had wanted from each generation of men was not their possessions but themselves, the loving obedience of strong lives freighted with the power of the possession of the heritage of the past. Man was made of the dust of the earth and the dust had become glorious in man.

Several disadvantages followed this stockpiling of the attainments of human power. One is that with genuine increase in human adequacy came an erroneous confidence in complete human self-sufficiency. The dust which man has ennobled is still dust and subject to the over-all entropy. Man simply tires out holding on to his attainments once the drive to attain has spent itself, and man is left to keep, on his own strength, and merely for the sake of holding, attainments which have lost the charm of novelty merely by long possession. Since he has cut himself off from God by his claim to autonomous self-sufficiency, he no longer is receiving that power by which men mount up with wings as eagles, and run without being weary, and walk without fainting.

Although the autonomous individual is a phenomenon that has characterized Western culture since the Renaissance, it is only in the past generation that the inadequacies of autonomous individualism have been made unmistakably evident in the breakdown of culture from within and the loss of men's ability to keep the situation under control, because the nerve of their endeavor has been cut by their discovery that their sense of ultimate coherence and ultimate purpose in life has evaporated. The built-in strength of the Christian heritage in the West was so great that it has taken four hundred years of men cutting themselves off from the life-giving power of God before the social and cultural fabric as a whole showed its bankruptcy, and left the godless individuals, who in their imagined self-sufficiency had not realized how much they had depended for spiritual sustenance upon the cultural fabric, trapped in poverty and chaos.

Without the God-given power to run and not to weary and to walk and not faint, man in his exhaustion and lack of purpose often turns to drunkenness and sexual misconduct to appease the healthy craving for accomplishment and variety without the task of assembling and disciplining his energies, for which task he feels that he has somehow lost his grip. The degenerative vices have always been an embarrassment because man has always had the vague awareness that through them he was reverting to the subhuman type, that he was indulging in a form of devolution. And yet sexual misconduct in these circumstances is not healthily "natural" as he claims. For sex is not used appropriately within an overall pattern of obedience to God and the morally good. Neither is it simply the healthy sexual excitement and release of the animals, which is non-moral but a good approved by God. For human sex misused as an antidote to purposelessness and spiritual poverty is not just an attempt to find physical release. It is an attempt to find a spiritual feeling of free achievement, "of getting somewhere," of covering spiritual distance without the expenditure of creative energy. All "naughty" art, literature, and drama makes a covert reference to the moral law it is flouting. Without that reference, there would be no sense of accomplishment in the deviation from the standard. But since the lowered standard, once it is accepted as normative, palls in turn through habitual association, a still further deviation from the standard of righteousness is needed to revive the sense of accomplishment, of getting somewhere, of covering spiritual distance. No thoughtful and honest life can continue in this way for long without being aware that the sexual interest is being used to plot a non-sexual line of direction, or without being able to foresee that the outcome, if projected far enough, is the dissipation or scattering of the human aspect of the human being. The moral slump, as long as man can continue the active process of it, does carry a slight sense of accomplishment, as in the pre-sentient pattern of the cosmos energy is released by dissolution.

There is an alternative strategy the human life can adopt that is an assembling and disciplining of its energies to act in a way that does not fall back to the subhuman level, but perverts the human pattern man is supposed to follow. This is usually referred to as the sin of pride. Pride follows the Divine injunction to have dominion over the earth, but does it without the other aspect of man's required activity, which is obedience to God. The attempt is made to make one's self the center of one's security, to secure the continuation of the human civilized pattern by merely human strength, without reference to God. Among the competent godless, the question of which individuals are motivated by sinful pride is one the answer to which only God knows. I strongly suspect that the dividing line may come between those who are trying to follow goodness obediently, because righteousness, justice, and love seem to the person to make authoritative demands upon him, and those who also find these values attractive, and want to find *a use for them in a convenient place* within the house of life *they are constructing for themselves*. The second group is man-centered and unsurrendered. To this group belong all those who at the back of their minds believe in the existence of the Christian God, but who are trying to embody *values* without reference to him. Those whose lives try to follow goodness obediently rather than follow the Christian God because they do not believe that the Christian God exists, are probably not governed by pride and are not wholly cut off from him since he is the ultimate source of all goodness, and they are following the closest approximation to it that they know of.

It is of the essence of pride that it is the state of a spiritual nature voluntarily cutting itself off from God. Since all human natures are part of the created universe they are subject to the over-all law of dissolution. Where they attempt to defy this law in their own strength, they must do so by sucking strength into themselves from the world around them. This is the evolutionary pattern. The plants suck up energy from the sun and from the inanimate chemicals of the earth. The herbivorous animals eat plants. The carnivores take their nourishment more fully prepared by eating other animals. At the intellectual level, man packages the knowledge attained by previous generations and feeds it to his young in a process that we call education.

Sometimes the feeding upon others is harmless and mutually beneficial, as in the transfer of intellectual knowledge. Intellectual knowledge held by the rational mind can be held in detachment from the total personal life of an individual, as a person of my age and learning holds the alphabet and the multiplication table. The growing edge of my personal life is far beyond these items of knowledge. To gain rational knowledge man can feed upon the rational knowledge in the minds of his fellows without injuring them. To this extent human beings can feed themselves appropriately on knowledge gained from the rational minds of others. But where the food that an unsurrendered person tries to take is for the enhancement of his own psychological strength, the increase of his selfhood at the expense of others to combat his subtle perception that he as a person is weak and impermanent, there the feeding upon others tends to follow the old carnivorous strategy at the spiritual level and becomes a refined psychological and social cannibalism. The medieval superstition of the vampire continues to fascinate us because of its analogy to this typical perversion of the human spirit. This spiritual cannibalism destroys intimate social intercourse and finally pulls apart the structure of society itself. For it is pride; and though pride seems to create, it creates structures in the world that only temporarily stave off but eventually accelerate the forces of dissolution. War, in its causes and consequences, is the supreme example of this on the large social scale.

Although men were not meant to prey upon one another they do need strength other than their own and this they were meant to derive from God, the one direction in which their cannibalistic tendency can be safely practiced. The central rite of the Christian Church is cannibalistic: we eat our God. The reason this form of cannibalism is morally good, while preying upon other people is morally bad, is simply due to two practical differences. One is that God's strength is so limitless that all men's drafts upon him cannot exhaust or inconvenience him. The other is that God is so much more powerful than men that they cannot invade and take from him. If they draw sustenance at all from him it has to be because he freely gives it. A man, when he is consciously very hungry for God, learns quickly that his proper activity to attain his end is simply humble surrender. From God he cannot take, he can only receive charity.

All people, religious and non-religious, the good and the bad alike, know that they ought not to destroy other human lives. What is needed is not that men should be told this, but that they should have strength given them from God, so that having it they will not try to grab it convulsively from other lives in order to save themselves, and thus inadvertently destroy other lives. Historically there is an accumulation of evidence to show that where human love is genuinely Christian it can intimately enhance the life of the person loved without preying upon it. This is because the person who is loved is not the primary source of strength to the other. The

397

person who loves has strength amply in God. Therefore he can freely give to the one he loves and rejoice in what is freely given him in return, but without grasping at it, and so without violating the integrity of the other's personality. Divine strength is so needed to sustain this type of human love that where this human love exists it is evidence of the background presence of the power of God. (I John 4:7, 8)

This pragmatic test of the Christian life would indicate that in the course of living such a life actual strength is given direct to the individual by the uncreated life of God. As we have seen, any direct guidance given by God to the Christian involves miracle, even if the "wire-pulling" that the Almighty does were nothing more than focusing a man's attention upon certain passages of Scripture that he would not otherwise have noticed. We hesitate to admit miracle, and guidance seems to us to involve a less extensive form of it than would be involved in the transfer of strength. For the transfer of strength to a man would involve the transfer of an endowment to man, or at least the transfer of a loan which was subject to God's withdrawal but which he hoped he would have reason to allow to be permanent. The modern mind, conditioned by the point of view of contemporary scientism, hesitates to admit any genuine direct traffic between God and man. How often have we heard modern Christian apologists say, "All men have untapped energy that their lives are not using. I believe that when a man prays he becomes so properly oriented to God that some of this energy becomes available to the man in a measure to which it would not otherwise be available."

There is undoubtedly some truth in this statement, but it dodges the whole point at issue. It is well known that a worried depressed mental state lessens a person's normal energy and that some emergencies release energies not normally available to the individual. It is also known that when a life seems to be as we say "at loose ends" that if the person becomes absorbed by a consuming purpose or interest in something, even in something bad, that his energies will increase and he will become more coordinated. All these are a purely human phenomenon and do not necessarily involve Divine aid. Jesus said, "No one can serve two masters." (Matthew 6:24) So if the unified devotion of a man's life is toward something evil, the singleness of purpose will still increase the human strength at least temporarily, even if it increases the eventual disaster.

Now when a person prays to God for strength, some of the strength that results is doubtless his own human strength made available to him. This availability might be brought about by God directly—and miraculously—or it might be humanly induced because the person had unified his life about God. There are some instances in which it does not much matter to the man *how* the strength comes. If a frightened Christian prayed mentally, "God, save me," and then managed to get over the fence in time away from an angry bull, he would simply give thanks to God. He would not much bother about whether the needed strength came through miracle, or through the emotion of fear releasing adrenalin into his blood.

But in the over-all emergency of life merely a man's human strength made fully available to him will not suffice. For that strength is of the creation and the whole creation is subject to death. What the Christian craves for strength is the strength of God. He longs to know that "The eternal [and supernatural] God is [his] dwelling place, and underneath are the everlasting arms." (Deuteronomy 33:27) Or as St. Paul prayed for the Ephesians "to be strengthened with might through his Spirit in the inner man." (Ephesians 3:16) And of himself he said, "I can do all things through him [the Lord] who strengthens me," (Philippians 4:13) for "Though our outward man is decaying, yet our inward man is renewed day by day." (II Corinthians 4:16 ARV) The infiltration of uncreated Power into the human life is pictured definitely but cautiously in the communion service according to *The Book of Common Prayer*:

Grant us . . . gracious Lord, so to eat the flesh of thy dear Son Jesus Christ, and to drink his blood . . . that we may evermore dwell in him, and he in us. . . . The Body of our Lord Jesus Christ, which was given for thee, preserve thy body and soul unto everlasting life . . . The Blood of our Lord Jesus Christ, which was shed for thee, preserve thy body and soul unto everlasting life.

Christ's words of institution of the Lord's Supper imply that these words of the prayerbook are not just later theological interpretation but are implied as not foreign to Christ's own thinking. For his giving his disciples bread and wine as symbols of his body and

399

blood must be seen against the background of the original covenant at Sinai, where the blood symbolized a uniting of God and the nation, and against the ancient belief that conditioned the specific laws of hospitality, namely the belief that if two strangers ate together they became temporarily blood brothers, and against the Old Testament blood taboo, according to which blood was sacred to God, and might not be touched or eaten, because the life of a person or animal was thought to reside in its blood. (Genesis 9:4). That feeding upon Christ completes at the spiritual level the method of gaining strength against entropy which is characteristic of organisms throughout the whole evolutionary process, is a corroboration of what Christians have always claimed, namely that in spiritual union with Christ there is a genuine and miraculous infiltration of Uncreated Power into the worshiper's life, preparing him for the permanent and more intense existence of the life to come.

CHAPTER 45

The Transfer of a Strong Acting-Pattern

It is customary for theologians at the present time to claim that there are two conflicting theories of *how* the Christian is able to survive death. One is the idea that the inherently immortal soul is glued to the body in this life (Plato, *Phaedo*) and is separated from the body at death. This is a Greek idea and not biblical. It is also an idea that is farther from the understanding of man that science has given us than is the biblical idea which is that man is a unified soul-body organism. When the man dies, the whole man dies: "You are dust," said God to Adam, "and to dust you shall return." (Genesis 3:19) When Hebrew thought came to believe in a glorious hereafter it was in terms of resurrection, a more or less literal rendering of what was originally figurative in Ezekiel's vision of the Valley of Dry Bones where "the bones came together, bone to its bone." And "Thus says the Lord God: 'Behold, I will open your graves, and raise you from your graves.'" (Ezekiel 37:7, 12). Resurrection would be strictly miraculous and would occur at some future time at the Day of the Lord, the Day of Judgment.

Modern divines, who on the whole do not seem personally very confident in the life everlasting, tend to talk as if these were the only alternatives. The first they easily discredit as being non-biblical, and the second, bluntly stated, seems so contrary to the teaching of science that they can assume that its impossibility will be taken for granted by the modern mind. I submit that there is a third alternative which has been at least vaguely implied by Christian piety and thought through the centuries, to which the theory of this present book is easily adjusted.

As we have noted earlier, in practical human experience it has often seemed that it is the pattern and purpose of life that have held a weakened organism together. (See *ante* pp. 58-60). When the pattern of life is broken after the person has become old, and where the person no longer strives to fulfil a purpose, the grip upon the physical coordination relaxes and the disintegration and death of the organism results. Sinnott raises the question of whether, even at the low level of plant existence, life may not be teleological, and the pattern may not be instrumental in producing the organism, rather than being merely its product.

Although the idea of reincarnation is doctrinally abhorrent to Christianity, it is useful to mention at this point that such astute people as the Hindu and Buddhist thinkers have emphasized the strength of this acting-pattern of life by claiming that reincarnation was caused by desire, i.e., by the strength of the patterned purpose of human lives which is so strong that, itself non-physical, it outlasts the body and makes itself another body to continue its existence. This is not wishful thinking, because salvation to these Oriental religions is thought to consist of the killing of desire with the resultant end to existing individuality. Modern scientific evidence of the strength of the acting-pattern comes from the evidence that the matter composing any human organism is totally replaced several times in the course of the normal life-span. This carries at least a suggestion that the pattern of the organism is more stable than the group of atoms that compose it.

Now if we think of the non-physical pattern of a person's life as that in which the mysterious non-scientific thing we call consciousness appears in the course of evolution, then we can think of the pattern as being the person, i.e., the pattern or the patterned purpose which includes the consciousness and the desire and the will. It is the person in this sense that, according to the Old and New Testaments, is strengthened by God and Christ when the person is obedient. (II Corinthians 4:16. This strength or its reverse at the personal level may have repercussions at the protoplasmic level. I Corinthians 11:27-30.)

What possibility is there that the pattern could be transferred intact at death from the physical organism? We know no human person-patterns except those inherent in physical organisms which are aggregates of matter. (But what is matter? Apparently it turns out to be patterned energy!) Three imperfect analogies may help our imagination a little at this point.

Among the highly developed techniques for preserving great paintings is that of replacing the canvases of old masterpieces. The pattern of pigments is not the canvas, and yet if time destroys the canvas upon which the picture was painted, the pattern (compare

I Chronicles 29:15; Job 8:9; Psalm 144:4) of pigments which is the picture will be lost. What the experts do is to paste layers of paper and gauze over the paint. The picture is then laid face down on a table and slowly and carefully the original canvas and gesso are scraped away. Finally nothing is left but the pattern of pigments seen in reverse as it is upheld now, not by the old canvas, but by the temporary foundation. Then a new canvas is prepared and glued to the pigments. Afterward the picture is again turned over and the layers of paper and gauze are scraped from its face and the masterpiece reappears, securely upheld by a strong new canvas. At death could the living pattern which is the individual be removed intact by God onto his own power and then shifted to a new body that had been prepared for it? When St. Paul said, "It is no longer I who live, but Christ who lives in me," (Galatians 2:20) was he conscious that his human life, while still normally in this world, was being strengthened and undergirded by the Eternal Life, preparatory to transferring him eventually to a better situation than this world can offer? (I Corinthians 15:17-22). Some such idea is certainly characteristic of the Bread of Life passage in the Gospel According to John. (John 6:32-35, 48-51, 53-58).

Another, somewhat comparable analogy is that of preserving a fading photograph by rephotographing it using a better grade of paper and chemicals.

Still a third analogy, and one that seems natural to the modern mind, is that of a tape-recording. If the recording is played many times until the danger arises that the song may be lost through the deterioration of the tape, the tape may be played through once more and the song picked up by another recorder and retaped on fresh tape. The analogy is especially apt at the present time because scientists have used the tape-recorder analogy in regard to the brain's registering its sensation and thought, the idea being that all that we have ever known is "tape-recorded" on our brains, and that memory and thought involve a skillful selecting and recombining and replaying of parts of that record. If, for purposes of argument, we do think of the brain in tape-recorder terms, then there is no question but what much of the *content* of the record can be transferred even within our human life on earth from one "brain-tape-recorder" to another. This is regularly involved in the process of verbal communication: if I know a delightful joke it is "taped" on my brain. If I tell you the joke, then it becomes "taped" on your brain also.

This does not of itself prove that the living pattern which is the human self could survive the destruction of its own organism. We are at this point up against the subtlest form of the most basic and baffling of all problems, the relation of the subjective to the objective in the relation of the thinking-thinker to his thought. We have said that we can know the thinking-thinker directly only subjectively in knowing ourselves. We know ourselves directly as thinking-thinkers. But we cannot *know about* ourselves as thinking-thinkers objectively. Objectively we can only know what we have thought. What we *have thought* is of course transferable to the "tape" recording of another organism, as we saw in the example of telling a joke. But what is needed to satisfy the demands of the Christian picture of the life everlasting is that the Christian thinking-thinker, freighted with his continuity of memory, be transferable from his present organism to another "body" in some extra-cosmos environment in which he can experience intimate fellowship with Christ and the Father. (I Thessalonians 4:17; Philippians 1:23,24; Acts 7:59; John 14:3,16,17,23; Revelation 21:22,23; 22:3-5).

Of all New Testament writers, it is St. Paul who gives us most help in this regard:

> What is sown is perishable, what is raised is imperishable. . . .
> It is sown in weakness, it is raised in power. It is sown a physical body, it is raised a spiritual body. If there is a physical body, there is also a spiritual body. . . . Just as we have borne the image of the man of dust [Adam], we shall also bear the image of the man of heaven [Christ]. . . . Flesh and blood cannot inherit the kingdom of God, nor does the perishable inherit the imperishable. . . . For this perishable nature must put on the imperishable, and this mortal nature must put on immortality. (I Corinthians 15:42-44,49,50,53).

From this account it would seem clear that Paul is not thinking here of a reassembling of the physical components of our earthly bodies and of a transferring of them to the deathless state as the upholders of our conscious life. Instead he seems here to be thinking in terms of the abandonment of the disintegrating earthly body which has served its purpose, and the substituting for it a more powerful deathless body as the bearer and tool of that continuity of consciousness, thought, memory, will, desire, and sensation which is the person. This interpretation is borne out by his use of the grain of wheat that dies—the old husk disintegrates—in order that the life in it may grow in a new body. He says that "what you sow is not the body which is to be. . . . But God gives it a body as he has chosen." (I Corinthians 15:35-38). Jesus certainly did not think in terms of a protoplasmic existence, either "solid" or "rarified," in the resurrection life. (Mark 12:25).

The whole Pauline doctrine of the Christian being "in Christ" takes care for him of the method by which the Christian triumphs over death. "He who is united to the Lord becomes one Spirit with him." (I Corinthians 6:17). The Christian is to live in Christ, "rooted and built up in him." (Colossians 2:7) "In Christ Jesus you are all sons of God, through faith." (Galatians 3:26). "Therefore, if anyone is in Christ, he is a new creation; the old has passed away, behold the new has come." (II Corinthians 5:17).

CHAPTER 46

The Present Preparation in Heaven of Our Spiritual Bodies

There is one curious passage in II Corinthians which, using the figure of a tent for the body, (Compare II Peter 1:13, 14.) implies that while we live here on earth our spiritual bodies are already prepared and waiting for us in heaven; as if, while the painting is still on the old canvas, the new canvas is already prepared, ready to receive it.

> For we know that if the earthly tent we live in is destroyed, we have a building from God, a house not made with hands, eternal in the heavens. Here indeed we groan, and long to put on our heavenly dwelling, so that by putting it on we may not be found naked. For while we are still in this tent, we sigh with anxiety; not that we would be unclothed, but that we would be further clothed, so that what is mortal may be swallowed up by life. He who has prepared us for this very thing is God, who has given us the Spirit as a guarantee. (II Corinthians 5:1-5)

I believe that the theory this present book is developing can give an explanation of how this Pauline passage and several other relevant New Testament passages and some of the teachings of Jesus can be arranged into a coherent whole. When we ask ourselves how this heavenly body could be prepared and what constitutes it, if we base our explanation upon the character and nature of God, a doctrine of the life to come that appears wildly fantastic to the point of absurdity to the science-conditioned mood of the present day will seem theoretically possible. If we hold to the Christian doctrine of the all powerful, intelligent, supernatural Creator-God who created *ex nihilo*, then in the beginning there was nothing but God and he was powerful, intelligent, righteous-loving creative Mind. All that is which is not his mind is either a direct product of this Mind, or a derivative of the product of this Mind. The Divine Intelligence is rational-mind-plus. This "plus" includes the ability to think into independent four dimensional

406

space-time existence. This is what God did at the original Creation. *But a mind that can think our universe into existence in this way is not limited to merely rational mind's ability to remember. He would be able to remember multidimensionally, and remember if he wished into independent existence. After all, omnipotence is omnipotence.*

Jesus emphasized that God sees all that we do. He said that "On the day of judgment men will render account for every careless word they utter." (Matthew 12:36). Even the giving of a cup of cold water will not be unrewarded. (Matthew 10:42). We do not have to use many words in praying because God knows what we need before we ask him. (Matthew 6:7, 8). Not a sparrow falls to the ground without God's will. "Even the hairs of [our] head are all numbered." (Matthew 10:29-31). He mentioned this to reassure his disciples. "Fear not, therefore;" he said, "you are of more value than many sparrows." (Matthew 10:31)

I would like to suggest that just as the original cosmos was the product of God's creative thought, so the resurrection body involves the product of God's memory. It is only as one thinks through the implications of this idea that one realizes how exciting it is.

Let us take a human analogy. When a baby is one to four years old the events of his life have a double recording. They are recorded with increasing adequacy in his own developing youthful mind, and they are recorded also in the mind of his mother. When he is a grown man, his mother may reminisce to him about those early years, filling in the background situation of the family, refreshing his mind with added remarks about incidents he partially remembers, and telling him things about himself at an age when he was too young to remember. To some extent, then, his knowledge of his early self is genuinely filled in and reinforced by the assistance of his mother's memory.

Her memory of course is inadequate in many ways. She never knew her child's life completely and she has forgotten much that she once knew. Her recollection has grown dim, and her sense impressions in retrospect are less vivid than the original sensation. Even items she can remember she can only transmit to her son inadequately, neatly packaged in a temporal sequence code—our words and sentences—for him to reconvert as best he can to an approximation of the original incident.

But God's memory is subject to none of these limitations. A God who can remember all the designs of all the snowflakes can remember in complete detail all the circumstances of each situation in the life of each person. And time does not dim this memory. Furthermore, God is not limited like a human being to deducing the experience of others from their actions, words, gestures, facial expressions, and omissions. He knows completely the thoughts in each thinker's mind as the human being thinks them. In addition to this, our ability to register sense impressions is only a pale reflection of abilities that God has with far more robust strength and with greater perfection.

He who planted the ear, does he not hear?

He who formed the eye, does he not see? . . .

He who teaches men knowledge,

the Lord, knows the thoughts of man,

that they are but a breath.

(Psalm 94:9-11)

If it is the memory of God that constitutes for us the resurrection body, it is understandable why St. Paul in speaking of the resurrection body says of man's after-life:

It is raised in glory. It is sown in weakness, it is raised in power. It is sown a physical body, it is raised a spiritual body. . . . Just as we have borne the image of the man of dust, we shall also bear the image of the man of heaven. . . . For this perishable nature must put on the imperishable. (I Corinthians 15:43, 44, 49, 53)

If my interpretation of the resurrection body is correct, it explains the odd fact that through the centuries Christian teachers have claimed that a man's spiritual state at death determined whether he went to heaven or to hell, but his intellectual state hereafter was not thought of as a prolongation of his intellectual state at death. If he died genuinely submissive to God he belonged to God. If he died basically rebelling against God, as a rebel he was forever excluded from heaven. The choice was man's real choice and the responsibility for it man's. On the other hand, these teachers have not worried if Christian saints died with their minds so incapacitated by senility that they were only pathethic wrecks of their former selves. God has always been assumed to be entirely capable of refurnishing an individual hereafter with his earthly accumulation of thought and his full continuity of memory, (Revelation 6:9-11) when the broken physical instrument makes it impossible for a man to continue to be the guardian of his own intellect.

There is another infirmity characteristic of all people in addition to that of senility's damaging our instrument of thinking, and death shattering it. We are caught in the passing of time. Tomorrow is only more or less well calculated guesswork, and yesterday is but a memory that is already beginning to become dim. We have only today. Life separates groups of friends geographically even before death. Here in America beautiful buildings constructed by the devoted labor and fine craftsmanship of one generation are torn down by the next generation to make room for larger buildings in the name of progress. Augustine in his youth was haunted by the realization that all created things pass away. This frustration was one of the things that drove him finally to God. He says:

Whithersoever the soul of man turns itself, unless toward Thee [God], it is rivetted upon sorrows, yea though it is rivetted on things beautiful. . . . They rise, and set; and by rising, they begin as it were to be; they grow, that they may be perfected; and perfected, they wax old and wither; and all grow not old, but all wither. So then when they rise and tend to be, the more quickly they grow that they may be, so much the more they haste not to be. This is the law of them. . . . In these things is no place of repose; they abide not, they flee. (Augustine, *Confessions*. IV. x. 15.)

This haunting fear left him after his conversion, as it has left countless other Christians who could not express their joy and assurance as perfectly as Augustine when he said:

Blessed whoso loveth Thee [God], and his friend in Thee, and his enemy for Thee. For he alone loses none dear to him, to whom all are dear in Him Who cannot be lost.
(Augustine, *Confessions*. IV. ix. 14.)

The belief that things as they pass upon earth can be preserved by being gathered into God's memory is necessary from the Christian view of Christ, and hinted at in Christ's own teaching. It is essential to the Christian view of Christ because, if we think that God is the loving Father in heaven as Jesus claimed, we cannot think of God as wilfully discarding the memory of the earthly life of his Son. The raising of Jairus' daughter, the feeding of the five-

409

thousand, the Last Supper, Gethsemane, and Calvary were all incidents thoroughly enmeshed in the material manifoldness of our space-time world. To have preserved adequately the memory of Jesus' heroic gift of filial devotion the Father would have had to remember the scenes in which that devotion was enacted in a life and death of suffering service.

Christ's hints in his teaching that God remembers our lives in detail together with the scenes in which they are set are most definite in the Sermon of the Mount:

> Blessed are the meek, for they shall inherit the earth. . . . Rejoice and be glad, for your reward is great in heaven, for so men persecuted the prophets who were before you. . . . Do not lay up for yourselves treasures on earth, where moth and rust consume and where thieves break in and steal, but lay up for yourselves treasures in heaven, where neither moth nor rust consumes and where thieves do not break in and steal.
> (Matthew 5:5, 12; 6:19, 20.)

The treasure in heaven must refer to actions acceptable to God which can be turned over to his keeping as they slip into the past out of human control. The earth which the meek inherit must be the extramundane earth as eventually reconstituted by God. It is certainly not the present or future political set-up. Jesus had a view of unvarnished realism as to the situation of the meek in this present world. (Matthew 4:8-10; 10:16-22)

These hints reappear later in the New Testament. I Peter (1:4) speaks of "an inheritance which is imperishable, undefiled, and unfading, *kept in heaven for you.*" (Italics mine) II Peter (3:12, 13) speaks of "the coming of the day of God, because of which the heavens will be kindled and dissolved, and the elements will melt with fire," and adds, "But according to his promise we wait for new heavens and a new earth in which righteousness dwells." The book of Revelation says, (21:1, 2, 24) "Then I saw a new heaven and a new earth; for the first heaven and the first earth had passed away. . . . And I saw the holy city, new Jerusalem, coming down out of heaven from God. . . . The kings of the earth shall bring their glory into it." It must be remembered that to the writer of Revelation the old Jerusalem was a personally beloved city. So it is as if an American were saying, "the new New York" or "the new Denver." The New Jerusalem is probably thought of as having a recognizable

410

resemblance to the old Jerusalem. As the seer saw it in the vision "coming down out of heaven from God" the implication is that the heavenly Jerusalem already exists or is in the process of preparation. (And see Hebrews 11:13-16.) The remark about the kings bringing their glory into it is an indication of the vivid manifoldness of the hereafter as well as of the hereafter's having gathered into it what is good in this world. This is made even more explicit when the book of Revelation says (14:13) that the blessed dead "who die in the Lord. . . . may rest from their labors, for their deeds follow with them!" Paul's thought is in line with this when he declares:

Each man's work will become manifest; for the Day [of the Lord] will disclose it, because it will be revealed with fire, and the fire will test what sort of work each one has done. If the work which any man has built on the foundation [i.e., on Jesus Christ] survives, he will receive a reward. If any man's work is burned up, he will suffer loss, though he himself will be saved. (I Corinthians 3:13-15)

Although the emphasis in the New Testament is on God's great gift of Christ to the world and the joy of the everlasting companionship with Christ and the Father for the faithful "in Christ", there is in addition what seems the more prosaic suggestion that we have just been tracing that there is some sort of carry-over into the life everlasting of the deeds or attainments of men in this world. If God at the creation saw all that he had made and seriously considered it "very good", and if God was serious when he told man at the creation to "fill the earth and subdue it," (Genesis 1:31, 28) then the good earth, as conquered by man, must have some place in God's final successful accomplishment of his great experiment. To put it another way, the prayer ascribed to Moses in the ninetieth Psalm will some day be answered:

Let the favor of the Lord our God be upon us,
and establish thou the work of our hands upon us,
yea, the work of our hands establish thou it.
(Psalm 90:17)

For humanly speaking, man is like the grass that flourishes in the morning and fades and withers in the evening. (Psalm 90:5, 6) Only in God's strength is there permanence:

Lord, thou hast been our dwelling place in all generations.

411

Before the mountains were brought forth,
>or ever thou hadst formed the earth and the world,
>from everlasting to everlasting thou art God.

(Psalm 90:1-2)

If the prayer for the permanence of earthly accomplishment is answered and in some sense the work of men's hands is to be established, and if the deeds of the faithful are to follow them into the hereafter, then in some way the setting in which and through which the deeds were accomplished must also have a place in the everlasting fruition under the power of God. St. Paul faces this problem in just one passage and when he does he goes the whole way in claiming that nature will have a part in the glorious final outcome:

> For the creation waits with eager longing for the revealing of the sons of God; . . . because the creation will be set free from its bondage to decay and obtain the glorious liberty of the children of God. We know that the whole creation has been groaning in travail together until now. (Romans 8:19, 21, 22)

The Bible is characterized by reappearing themes, threads in its texture that at first seem inconspicuous but later appear in strength. This is the genuine foreshadowing of the New Testament in the Old, the Old Testament prophecy concerning Christ, although one must be careful not to take "proof texts" too mechanically.

The glorious grand finale with which the prophecy of II Isaiah closes relates to this final redemption of nature when all becomes well with the sons of God:

> For you shall go out in joy
>and be led forth in peace;
>the mountains and the hills before you
>shall break forth into singing,
>and all the trees of the field shall clap their hands.

(Isaiah 55:12)

Locally the quotation heralds the approaching occasion of Israel's return to Jerusalem after the Babylonian captivity. But even as the prophet penned the words he must have realized that they could not accurately be picturing the long dusty trek of a little band of returning displaced persons. He must have been dimly aware that overlaying his present picture he was getting a glimpse of the rejoicing of all nature at the final home-coming to the Ultimate Fatherland.

412

This passage in II Isaiah is the complete antithesis of the little book of Ecclesiastes. The importance of Ecclesiastes seems to me to be usually overlooked. It is admittedly not as great in its religious teaching as most of the books of the Old Testament; in fact it seems scandalously to deny some of their basic optimistic assumptions. But "the words of the Preacher" (Ecclesiastes 1:1) are negatively very important, for they serve, like the book of Job, as the closing of a door.

The Old Testament had gone on the assumption that this life is all that there is, that a man is part of his nation and clan, and that God is righteous. He chose Israel, and when the nation and men served him alone by living righteously God would protect and prosper them, and he would punish them if they turned from him and lived unrighteously. This was the ultimate framework within which Hebrew life was to be lived. Life was strenuous, robust, and desirable. Centuries of political vicissitudes and moral lapses and struggles tested this outlook on life. With the strong emphasis of Jeremiah on the individual the question became unavoidable of whether God does as a matter of fact reward the righteous and punish the unrighteous. The incidence of suffering in human life sometimes makes it difficult to fit this pattern of Divine action to actual human biographies.

The book of Job challenged the standard Hebrew frame of reference of the ways of God to man, pinpointing the argument to a lengthy description of the excessive misfortunes of a righteous man who suffered through no fault of his own. After the book of Job, the possibility had to be faced that the rewards and punishments of God might not be seen to be meted out with strict justice to the individual in this life. This was later to point in the direction of a life beyond this world in which God's justice could be perfectly allocated.

The book of Ecclesiastes not only challenges the idea that men receive their just dues in this life, (8:14) it also with greater skepticism challenges the old robust assumption that life is a desirable good and that it is worth living. The author substantiates his point by taking an example as extreme as Job. For King Solomon to whom he ascribes his musings upon life had in abundance everything that could make a human life fortunate and pleasant. The major emphasis of Ecclesiastes is not upon human suffering but upon the meaninglessness of life. According to the Preacher it is the thought of death that works backward and poisons all the happiness of life (3:19, 20). This is why "all is vanity and a striving after wind." (1:14) To what avail is the heaping up of possessions and pleasures (2:1-11) if God does not give a man power to enjoy them? (6:1-6) What value is there in striving to become wise if the same fate comes in the end to the wise man and the fool alike, (2:14-17) and if the same end comes equally to those who serve God faithfully and to those who do not? (9:2, 3) For

> Time and chance happen to them all. For man does not know his time. Like fish which are taken in an evil net . . . so the sons of men are snared at an evil time, when it suddenly falls upon them. (9:11, 12)

After Ecclesiastes the ultimate frustration of life if death is the final end is an idea that needed to be taken into account. And the belief in the life hereafter, when it finally came to Jewish thought, had to come in terms that would preserve the meaningfulness of this earthly life and the value of this earthly life, for biblical religion always affirms that this present world is basically precious, because it is the creation of the good God.

414

CHAPTER 47

The Heavenly "Books"

This long discussion of biblical hints of the final glorification of nature and the preservation of the good attainments of men by God for the life beyond has been necessary because it has been so largely ignored in this century. Most divines have come to the Bible so highly conditioned by modern books on religion that they are unaware of the extent to which these cautious hints as to the life to come are to be found in Scripture. The reason why this whole side of biblical teaching has been tacitly by-passed is that it obviously involves belief in the supernaturalness of God and a definitely miraculous element in his dealings with the world and men. And modern scholarly religious thought has been trying to forget the element of miracle in order to describe Christianity as compatible with science. The result has been that even the most cautious attempts to describe the hereafter are ruled out—ostensibly on the ground that in the hereafter it is God and not the stage-setting that is important. But modern thought will not admit that God ever acts directly in relation to an individual person. Instead God is described as "acting in history" and revealing himself by so doing. But since the deity of Jesus Christ is denied along with all miracle, the "acts in history" turn out to be simply a description of how men and nations and the lower nature have as a matter of fact acted. So the picture of God's character has lost its vividness in men's minds, and to most modern people God as well as the stage-setting of heaven is "a great white blur." I do not mean that we should dwell overmuch on the stage-setting of heaven. Any symbolism we use will be inadequate. But we think with the help of pictures, and any long-continued refusal to a do so results in the end in giving up thinking. The lack of thought about God and heaven has finally worked back to poison our present life, till our generation is saying with the author of Ecclesiastes, "Vanity of vanities! All is vanity." (1:2)

In attempting to fit a genuine picture of heaven into a consistent theological picture that has a place for science and at the same

time holds to basic biblical teaching, I have suggested that the resurrection body might be the refurnishing of the continuity of the subjective self with his own past as it had been held and edited in the memory of God. (Isaiah 43:25; Jeremiah 31:34) Since God sees all that we do or think, our lives can be thought of as "tape-recorded" by his Divine mind as well as by our own brain-instrument. As God, for purposes of creation, could change certain of his thoughts from the merely rational type to the full objectifiable "rational-plus" type, so he would be able at will to transmute certain of his merely rational memories to a "rational-plus" type. God could then refurnish us with his own "recording" together with some aspect of his Divine power, mediated through Christ's glorified body, that we could freely use in the heavenly setting. Since in heaven all obey and glorify him, having freely started the life of obedience upon earth, there are not the practical disadvantages that there would be on earth to having men in this world "use" the power of God, as they would be doing if nature only exists as he constantly upholds it. The "nature" of heaven *is* constantly upheld by God and so it is secure forever.

But the suggestion that the Divine mind "tape-records" men's lives is meant largely as symbolism pointing toward the reality. It is not of course biblical symbolism. The Bible knows nothing of tape-recorders! And yet it is closer to biblical symbolism than most people are aware. For the Bible has a great deal to say about books that are kept in heaven.

The idea of God keeping books has been much belittled, and even treated humorously as if it indicated a primitive picture of a limited God who had to have help at the Last Judgment to refresh his knowledge as to what men had done. Such belittling the idea of the heavenly books misses entirely the point of what the Bible is trying to say by means of them.

The Hebrews were always a history-minded and book-minded people. The two characteristics are naturally associated since books are a means by which men preserve what they can of the past. Since God was thought of as active and righteous, and since any righteous activity that we know involves consecutive choices in time, God is thought of in the Bible as being from everlasting to everlasting, not as inhabiting a static eternity which sees timelessly what we experience *seriatim*. Hence the problem arises of how God

keeps the past, and a suggested answer, on the basis of their human life, was that God writes it in a book. The thought of this will cease to seem crude to us if we think of it in terms of Dante's symbolism and say that in the Divine memory are "ingathered the scattered leaves of the universe, bound into one book by love." (*Paradiso* xxxiii. 85) There is no developed theme of the divine book or books in the Bible. The remarks about them are just thrown out from time to time. One gathers that God kept both the history of the past and his plans for the future in books. There are more references to the books in the Apocalypse than in any one section of the Bible, but Revelation was only making use of an idea that occurs from time to time throughout the Bible. (The references are Exodus 32:32, 33; Job 13:26; Psalms 40:6-8(?); 56:8; 69:27, 28 (?); 87:5, 6; 139:16; Isaiah 4:3 (?); Ezekiel 2:9-3:3; Daniel 7:9, 10; 12:1; Zechariah 5:1-4; Malachi 3:16-18; Luke 10:20; Philippians 4:3; Hebrews 12:23; Revelation 3:5; 5:1-9; 10:2, 8-10; 13:8; 17:8; 20:12, 15; 21:27.) The earliest reference to the book in which God writes history occurs in the golden calf incident in which Moses says to God that if he will not forgive the nation, "Blot me, I pray thee, out of thy book which thou hast written." (Exodus 32:32)

Before Hebrew thought took on the belief in a resurrection life after death it was realistically realized that "All flesh is grass," and that "The grass withers, the flower fades." (Isaiah 40:6, 7) But although men passed away, they took comfort in the fact that the word of God abides:

The grass withers, the flower fades;
but the word of our God will stand forever.
(Isaiah 40:8)

Men were comforted in the thought that God remembered them, that they were written in his book. (Psalms 56:8; 87:5, 6; Malachi 3:16-18) Thus the idea of the heavenly book or books gropes toward the faith that this life is not all there is for man: man may die and stay dead, but still the righteous are *permanently known about beyond this world*. So the tape-recorder symbolism I have used is simply a variation on a biblical theme.

The symbolism of the heavenly books has Christ's express sanction. After the seventy returned from their preaching mission, he told them to "rejoice that your names are written in heaven." (Luke 10:20, and compare Hebrews 12:23.) One does not have to stretch one's imagination very far to believe that his idea of the books was not a crudely mechanical one, but that he was using it figuratively to mean recorded in the mind of God. And this was probably often true of the thought of the biblical writers, inasmuch as references to books written in human hearts occur in both Testaments where the meaning is simply to remember actively and permanently. (Proverbs 3:1, 3; Jeremiah 31:33 quoted in Hebrews 8:10 and 10:16; Romans 2:15; II Corinthians 3:2, 3.)

If the meaning of the heavenly books has to do with remembering, there are also suggestions in the prophets of an intentional Divine forgetting. (Psalm 88:5, Isaiah 43:25; 64:9; 65:17, 18; Jeremiah 31:34; Ezekiel 21:31, 32 (?); Hosea 4:6.) This theme is taken up by Jesus in two passages in which he implies his role as judge on the Day of the Lord. In Matthew (7:23) he says that on that day he will declare to many "I never knew you; depart from me, you evildoers." And in the parable of the shut door he describes the "householder" as saying to many who knocked "I tell you, I do not know where you come from; depart from me, all you workers of iniquity!" (Luke 13:24-28)

If we follow along the theory that the situation for the life to come is created by the Divine mind which is rationality-plus and so can think into existence a new environment, making use for it of the perfected yeast of the old creation which Christ brought with him from the Resurrection, and of which, together with the Divine memory of the human project, use is made in constituting our "spiritual bodies", then we can think of God as excluding into the outer darkness what is evil, by willfully dropping from his memory what he does not wish to include in heaven. Using again the symbolism of the book, when an author is preparing a book for publication, as it is moving into its final form, he sends back the galley proof to the printer with certain passages marked with the symbol that means, "delete and close up." It is not that the author will forget the passages in the sense of being unable to recall if he wishes to that they were once incorporated. It is simply that the book can stand as a well knit artistic whole without them. As one looks at a landscape through powerful field glasses, one wonders where the distance has gone when the objects are brought into closer view. Nothing in the picture seems incomplete or falsified and yet a great deal of space seems to have dropped out. The human memory finds it easier to remember good than evil, and I think that this tendency of the human mind helped confirm the belief of the Old Testament writers, in the midst of social disasters, that the good, which is of God, is more permanent than the evil. When all the tremendous differences between the Divine and the human minds are allowed for, if man is made in the image of God, then the human experience of the human mind is useful in pointing the direction of the character of God. This selective character of the human mind in reconstructing the past into a unified whole, in which meanings that were unobserved in the tremendous clutter of details and sense impressions in the process of living stand out in proper perspective in retrospect, may well furnish a clue to the winnowing process by which the wheat of the earthly experiment is gathered up for permanent preservation and the chaff destroyed.

This thought of Christ's that there is a special kind of knowing that God does toward those who serve him is echoed by St. Paul when he says of the Christian state of wellbeing of the Galatians, "Now that you have come to know God, *or rather to be known by God*, how can you turn back again to the weak and beggarly elemental spirits?" (4:9 italics mine) This being known by God means something more than that God has complete information about a person as he has about everything and everyone in the creation. It means the intimate knowing of a friendship of established reciprocity.

Apparently this is related to what he wrote to the Corinthians when he explained to them that

No one comprehends the thoughts of God except the Spirit of God. Now we have received not the spirit of the world, but the Spirit which is from God, that we might understand the gifts bestowed on us by God. (I Corinthians 2:11, 12)

It has been said that "We love, because he first loved us." (I John 4:19) It would also be true that we know because he first knew us. According to the theory of this book, before nature was animate God understood, cared for, and appreciated it, and by this intelligent appreciation established with it a semi-interpersonal relationship akin to the semi-interpersonal relationship of the aesthetic experience. It was proximity of the Divine Knower knowing in this way that called gradually a reflection of his own life into existence

419

in independent matter, culminating in man. With man free choice is possible of whether he will obey God and so stay voluntarily in this position of being intimately known and appreciated, or turn from God. Where man turns to God through Christ this Divine knowing can be most intimate, can in fact be an indwelling of the Divine Spirit:

> Jesus answered him, "If a man loves me, he will keep my word, and my Father will love him, and we will come to him and make our home with him." (John 14:23)

It is the continuing relationship to the mind of God, in an ever intensified degree in the course of evolution, that constitutes the wellbeing of the creation, from the snowflake to the blessedness of the redeemed in heaven.

CHAPTER 48
Advantages of This Hypothesis

This book is not a full systematic theology, because not all of the relevant themes are treated, and most of those treated are dealt with incompletely. It is intended simply as a point of departure for further attempts to write an account of Christian doctrine from the biblical perspective that will take into consideration the findings of science. The book had to combat the confusing and disheartening influence that the discovery of the sheer size of the inanimate cosmos has had upon man; and at the level of the interpretation of life it had to combat the pervasive influence of the total impact of Darwinian, Marxist, and Freudian theories, which has been the anti-Christian implication that man is fully accounted for by forces lower than himself.

This means that the book had to present an over-all account of existence that is thoroughly teleological, keeping the account in line with the basic direction of biblical teaching, and at the same time weaving into the conservative Christian theological pattern a constructive use of such scientific beliefs as the "big bang" theory of the creation, the *second law of thermodynamics,* the expanding universe, the quantum theory, multidimensional mathematics, biological evolution, the anthropological and archaeological discovery of a "social evolution," the subconscious mind, and the psychophysical discovery of the intimate relationship of mind to brain.

It is to be hoped that other thinkers can carry on this task more adequately, but an attempt must be made to make a structural relationship between the theological and the scientific fields. Man must have a whole view of existence. At the present time this whole view is most easily attained by those who have such meager secular education that they are able to form their total picture of existence upon the Bible, without taking modern secular knowledge into consideration. Such people are in a sense religiously fortunate, for they can confine their thinking to the book that I as a Christian believe gives us a true account of Ultimate Reality, of man's ultimate frame of reference. But since God is to be served with all our minds and by using the world to his glory instead of withdrawing from it, it is necessary for those of us who have good minds and a college education to find some working relationship between the over-all picture of tested secular information with which modern times has been deluged and our basic Christian picture based upon biblical teaching. Man has to have a whole unified picture of existence at the back of his mind as a frame of reference for his thinking and action. The attempt to harmonize religion and science has too often either neglected to face squarely the scientific issue, or else has met science by keeping the Christian vocabulary but redefining it to such an extent that the basic biblical teaching and perspective are falsified. On the other hand, it is rather hard on religious writers to demand that they offer a definitive picture of the relation of science to religion when science is not sure that it has the ultimate scientific picture for the theologian to work with. But some broad scientific conclusions have seemed to be part of the working hypotheses of science, and these I have used.

When a strictly scientific hypothesis is tested, the optimum method is by experiment. If one has the hypothesis that such and such a chemical compound has lethal characteristics, one feeds it to guinea-pigs and observes the result. Obviously the creation of the universe and the long course of evolution are not repeatable experiments. There is, however, a non-laboratory, purely intellectual method of testing hypotheses that helps indicate whether or not a hypothesis is correct. This is to ask one's self the question, "If this hypothesis were true, how many questions and problems would it answer economically?"

From this point of view the advantages of this present theological construction seem noteworthy. It combats the fear that modern man has at the thought of the vastness of the cosmos, showing its tremendous extent as part of the supernatural God's plan to establish an adequate source of independent power for his creation to use over billions of years, in order to attain an other-than-himself that could reflect the Divine freedom. The "big bang", the expanding, and the dying of the universe have been compared with the biblical claim of Divine creation of the world and the prediction of its end. The phenomenon of entropy has been used to explain the origin of evil, in what seems to me a better solution of that theological problem than any I have ever read.

The book also takes the fact that the great themes seem to repeat themselves with variations in science and works the continuing repetition of themes through man's human history as a non-biological evolution. A theme that is traced through with especial fullness is that of God as teacher.

The book makes positive use of the theory of evolution, while describing evolution throughout as God-assisted and teleological. The theory covers the theoretical possibility of a positively demonstrable course of unbroken evolution from inanimate matter to man, and uses a discussion of the nature of aesthetic experience as half-way between an I-it and I-thou relationship, a kind of semi-interpersonal relationship to explain how God could come into active relationship with inanimate matter in evolution's earlier stages. This constitutes the best attempt that I know to explain *how* God can be thought of as guiding the course of evolution, so that one can hold both a consistent theory of evolution and the belief that man was created by God in God's image. And while the book keeps clearly in view the close correspondency between mental thought and brain action, the book has a carefully analyzed theory of revelation that allows for some genuine continuing intercourse between the supernatural God and men.

The full claim of Christianity to being the one exclusively true religion is upheld. This includes arguing for the full deity of Jesus Christ, and the genuine Incarnation and genuine Resurrection. There can follow from this belief a confidence in the resurrection body and in the life everlasting in the new heaven and the new earth for those who come to God through Christ.

Christ is building a kingdom, a new heaven and a new earth for which the life of the present world is the hot-house seed-plot, the place that was necessary for things to be born and voluntarily given to him, the people by voluntary self-surrender, the lower nature by becoming the well-used possession of the people who make the self-surrender. By our self-surrender to Christ we become part of his personal possessions, and so part of his total self-surrender forever to the Father. I suspect that from God's point of view this seed-plot function of earth and the voluntary surrender to him of what is born here is the great accomplishment and the great wonder, and that the problem of transplanting all that he can use from the earthly experiment into his new heaven and new earth is something that his unlimited power can accomplish with routine ease.

If this is the case, then our offering our own lives to him and helping others to do the same, and trying to live lives in line with righteous-love, and using the earth to his glory are our duty to him. All things belong to God and it is our duty and joy to try, with his help, to return to him his own with interest. Only what is given to him is safe forever. As "The Hound of Heaven" describes God as saying:

> All which thy child's mistake
> Fancies as lost, I have stored for thee at home:
> Rise, clasp My hand, and come!

Those who have loved and served God through Christ will inherit a kingdom which he inaugurates, controls, and preserves, built by him in part out of material that they have freely given him; and they will enjoy the privilege of being there with him forever and of having been allowed to have had a tiny part in working with him in the kingdom's formation. If others also enter heaven, they will to some extent have missed the joy of working as a comrade with God in the preparation for it. Since the treasure in heaven is so largely connected with fellowship with God, and since Christ told his followers to lay up treasure in heaven, and since Christ died in order to make this fellowship with God and heaven available to men, not to want it eagerly is the reverse of politeness to God.

For I think that those who belittle the desire for heaven and the thought of it because they advocate thinking exclusively about the welfare of their fellow men are making a short-sighted mistake. They are assuming that they can adequately bring about men's welfare, but a long view of life and history will show the inadequacy of what they can accomplish. The extent to which succeeding generations can pervert or misuse or abandon through ennui the gains for which a previous generation has struggled, and the extent to which the gains themselves are two-edged blessings carrying with them new dangers and liabilities, are often overlooked in the first flush of enthusiasm for a new cause. Thus the realization of the ideal of universal literacy has brought with it cheap and sensational journalism. The reduction of the working hours in the week to give men freedom to refresh themselves has brought with it the frustration of leisure they are unable to fill creatively, making them at least dimly aware of the emptiness of their lives. The development of better methods of agriculture to feed a starving world has resulted not so much in a well-fed population as it has in more starving mouths to feed. And behind all our present thinking and planning lurks the possibility that man will succeed in destroying all life on this planet by atomic power, thanks to skills developed by higher education.

The man who believes that goodness does not depend entirely upon our efforts for its preservation, but is confident that all items of good can have a double existence, the existence we give them in our structuring of society, and an existence as they are selected by God out of the welter of happenings to be part of the permanent furnishing of his kingdom, is a man who is better equipped to stand the long discouragements and frustrations of trying to establish justice and social well being than is the man who has no view beyond this present life. Even if we knew beyond a shadow of a doubt that the whole earth would be destroyed in three months by an atomic blast, it would still be our duty as Christians to go on serving God by living the kind of life within the world that would please him, to give him as much as we could, up to the last moment, that he could use in the life beyond.

CHAPTER 49

New Modern Fears This Hypothesis Can Meet

This book, which attempts to present the biblical understanding of man to a scientific age, is written in a way that should acclimatize to our religious thinking certain bewildering modern problems in addition to that of the atomic bomb. For example, seen in sufficient perspective, it is almost amusing that a century whose sophistication has "outgrown" the "primitive" belief in another race of extraterrestrial beings, namely the angels, is now speculating seriously on flying saucers and men from Mars. There is an almost medieval hobgoblin uneasiness in the modern thought, "If there is intelligent life elsewhere in the universe, is it completely different from our own?" But this terror is ruled out when we realize that evolution by its very nature is teleological, and so possible only if what is evolved reflects more and more characteristics of Deity. For this reason intelligent beings on other planets, while not necessarily photographic replicas of those on earth, would nevertheless have to have spiritual characteristics reflecting characteristics of God, and therefore the individuals of these unknown races would, like men, have to be related to God in either obedient or disobedient subordination, and so basically they would be like us.

But our fear of strange races is not confined to beings from outer space. We are now speculating on the question of whether our complicated electronic machines will ever become conscious, and whether, by-passing human reproduction altogether, men will succeed in creating protoplasm and human beings in test tubes, directly from inanimate matter. Both problems are basically one, namely the question of whether man, like God, will be able to assemble from the dust of the earth beings that have conscious intelligence. The only difference is that of whether the physical structure of these new consciously intelligent individuals is or is not protoplasmic. But the possibility of *"homo robot"* or *"homo testubus"* need not alarm us theologically. For the image of God in mankind depends upon the ability of the product of evolution to reflect the Divine characteristics of power, creativity, thought, the ability to

426

choose consciously, aesthetic appreciation, and above all righteous-love. If human beings, themselves a product of God-guided evolution, should short-cut the long process by directly assembling matter in such an adequately complicated form as to reflect these characteristics, these man-assembled beings would have human status and could freely try or not try to obey the requirement to do justly, to love mercy, and to walk humbly with God, and thus they too would be candidates for salvation. " 'God is able from these stones to raise up children to Abraham.' " (Matthew 3:9)

It should be pointed out that, if man succeeded in fabricating men in this way, we would not have solved the riddle of human life. For we would only have gained a complete account of the physical complication of matter that exists when intelligent consciousness takes place. But the relation of the subjective to the objective, the thinker-thinking to this physical aggregate, would still be an unsolved mystery.

Another pair of problems that troubles modern religious thinking has to do with the validity of religious experience. There are drug-induced LSD visions and luminous spiritual awareness induced by Hindu meditation. Why, men ask, are not these as religiously valid as the Christian's experienced relation to God? The answer relates to the Christian claim that the highest or guiding characteristic of the activity of the Godhead is righteous-love. In the case of drug-induced or yoga-induced visions, the visions tend toward a luminous coherent allness, and are static in the sense of something to be contemplated and not revelations of a righteous active will demanding obedience. Thus these static visions are not visions of the *living* God, because to live is to be active, and God's active nature is guided by his righteous-love. Love in the biblical sense is an active caring. It is not a diffuse feeling of static affection submerged in a contemplative vision. The goal God has planned for men is an active comradeship with himself forever. This involves personal adjustment of the individual life to the guiding aspect of God's nature, his righteous-love. Since righteous-love is active, the proper adjustment of man to God is not basically contemplation, but is, as the Bible makes clear, loving obedience. This is why most of the visions recorded in the Bible give God's followers directions for their activity. Thus it was normal for St. Paul to say to King Agrippa, "I was not disobedient to the heavenly vision." (Acts 26:19)

It should be noticed that contemplative visions are usually thought of as in some sense *achieved*, whether by drugs or discipline, as if man could take the initiative in the unveiling of the Divine. But the Bible suggests no technique for inducing visions,[1] and does not even outline a technique for prayer beyond insisting on an attitude of honesty, devotion, and obedience. For neither God-given visions nor the goal of prayer are humanly achieved.

If it were possible to humanly achieve them, human beings could to some extent manage God, which would be impossible. This raises the question of whether the static contemplative type of vision and the nature mysticism type of vision may not be largely luminous awareness of the accumulated result of the divine assistance God has already given to the world over a billion of years. That is, if our theory is correct, all gains made by the world to date have been made with the help of God, and the gains once made we have inherited from the earth as part of its accumulated "stock-pile" of gains. These tracks of God's activity are available to the discernment of all men simply as men, as part of their earthly heritage without special biblical revelation.

> Ever since the creation of the world his invisible nature, namely, his eternal power and deity, has been clearly perceived by the things that have been made. (Romans 1:20)

The range of human consciousness is normally narrow. If the range is widened by drugs or discipline, then sometimes the awareness of the tracks of God's activity upon nature can increase to a luminous degree. This would explain on the one hand why this type of vision has genuine spiritual validity of a sort and is sometimes made use of by God in his training of men, and it would explain on the other hand why these visions and the religious life based exclusively upon them are inadequate. This explanation is intended neither to encourage drug taking with its practical dangers, nor to belittle the devotees of Hinduism and its derivative branches. Surely, although Hindu contemplation does not reveal the Father of our Lord Jesus Christ, it does not follow that those individuals who have earnestly sought God by a Hindu regime of contemplation—not knowing the better way—will therefore be permanently

---

[1] I am omitting, as primitive only, consideration of the early bands of prophets mentioned in I Samuel as wandering about and using music and dance to stimulate religious frenzy. I Samuel 10:5, 6, 10-12; 19:18-24.

lost, for Jesus said, "To him who knocks it will be opened." (Matthew 7:8)

This book has also a theoretical answer to the modern question that is usually implied rather than bluntly stated. Bluntly stated it would run something like this: If we do the morally right thing and have high moral standards and work for the welfare of others why is not that enough? Why bring God into it? Apart from the obvious basic answer that we were created not for ourselves but for God, and that he wishes to honor Christ by having the whole earth obey him, this book offers a theoretical answer to this question at the man-centered level at which it is asked. The answer is that everything, even careful social arrangements for human welfare, that is not God-oriented and so subject to his sustaining control is trapped by entropy-death and will therefore perish. In this sense the harsh words of the Thirty-Nine Articles must be reaffirmed:

> Works done before the grace of Christ, and the Inspiration of his Spirit, are not pleasant to God, forasmuch as they spring not of faith in Jesus Christ, . . . yea rather, for that they are not done as God hath willed and commanded them to be done, we doubt not but that they have the nature of sin.

But in reaffirming this the proviso must be added that for those who are trying to lead the morally good life *as part of their search for God,* the morally good is an assistance toward this end, (Psalm 19:7) because *under these conditions Christ can accept the attempt as homage to himself.* But this qualification does not apply to those people who are not oriented to God in obedience, who are leading merely correct, genial, useful lives, the unsurrendered aspect of which is not apparent due to fortunate circumstances combined with a large inheritance of the social-spiritual gains of the past. For such good as these people possess is part of their earthly heritage and all things earthly are subject to over-all entropy, in this case spiritual entropy. That this merely worldly goodness is subject to disintegration is more than obvious at the present time. The slow process of "backsliding", unchecked by the power of Christ in lives surrendered to him, can be spiritually fatal.

Even with this present book's inadequate emphasis on man's need to be saved from positive sin by Jesus Christ, it must be obvious to all who seriously consider the matter that "the form of this world is passing away" (I Corinthians 7:31) and that "Here we have no lasting city." (Hebrews 13:14) Surely to a generation accustomed to think in terms of the "relativity" of all things to the individual it must be obvious that the extreme human emergency will inevitably occur whether it is heralded by the last trumpet, or whether the earth suddenly deserts us by a man-made atomic cataclysm or is melted by the intense heat of the collapsing sun (compare II Peter 3:10), or whether at a ripe old age we desert the world seriatim by natural death. In any case we are completely unable to assist ourselves in what lies beyond. Only Deity has everlasting life and power in his own right. The Son of God lived a human life and died and rose again from the dead in order to make possible the Divine undergirding and protection of men's lives forever, if they will surrender themselves to him to receive the aid that he died to bring them. If people who have been brought up in some awareness of Christianity are not leading lives consciously and confessedly surrendered to Christ, and if the reason is that they do not want to have to obey Christ—they would *prefer* to leave the Father and Jesus out of it—the New Testament certainly implies that they are on the road to the outer darkness.

For myself, I find the thought of death without Christ frankly frightening. In this area if in no other man's realization of his absolute need of dependence upon God for his well-being is unavoidable:

Now I lay me down to sleep.
I pray thee, Lord, my soul to keep.
If I should die before I wake,
I pray thee, Lord, my soul to take.
And this I ask for Jesus' sake. —
    For thine is the kingdom
    and the power
    and the glory — forever. Amen.

SELECTED BIBLIOGRAPHY

Augustine, Saint. *The Confessions of St. Augustine*, New York: E. P. Dutton & Co., Inc., 1939. (Everymans Library)

Baillie, John. *The Idea of Revelation in Recent Thought*, New York: Columbia University Press, 1956.

Barbour, Ian G. *Issues in Science and Religion*, Englewood Cliffs, N.J.: Prentice-Hall, Inc., 1966.

Barnett, Lincoln. *The Universe and Dr. Einstein*, New York: The New American Library of World Literature, Inc., 1957. (Mentor Book M71)

Blum, Harold F. *Time's Arrow and Evolution*, New York: Harper & Brothers, 1962. (Harper Torchbooks TB 555)

Buber, Martin. *I and Thou*, New York: Charles Scribner's Sons, 1958. (The Scribner Library SL 15)

Butler, J. A. V. *Inside the Living Cell*, New York: Basic Books, Inc., 1959.

de Chardin, Pierre Teilhard. *The Future of Man*, New York: Harper & Row, Publishers, 1964.

The Phenomenon of Man, New York: Harper & Row, Publishers, 1961. (Harper Torchbooks TB 83)

Dillenberger, John. *Protestant Thought and Natural Science*, Garden City, New York: Doubleday & Company, 1960.

Gamow, George. *Biography of the Earth*, New York: The Viking Press, 1959. (Compass Books C 53)

The Creation of the Universe, New York: The Viking Press, 1959. (Compass Books C7)

Heim, Karl. *Christian Faith and Natural Science*, New York: Harper and Brothers, 1957. (Harper Torchbooks TB 16)

The Transformation of the Scientific World View, New York: Harper & Brothers Publishers, 1953.

Jacob, Edmond. *Theology of the Old Testament*, New York: Harper & Brothers Publishers, 1958.

431

James, William. *The Varieties of Religious Experience*, New York: The Crowell-Collier Publishing Company, 1961. (Collier Books AS 39)

du Noüy, Lecomte. *Human Destiny*, New York: Longmans, Green and Co., 1947.

Otto, Rudolf. *The Idea of the Holy*, New York: Humphrey Milford Oxford University Press, 1925.

Plato. *Phaedo* and *Timaeus*, Jowett translation.

Pollard, Wiliam G. *Chance and Providence*, New York: Charles Scribner's Sons, 1958.

"The Cosmic Drama", New York: The Episcopal Church the National Council, 281 Fourth Avenue, no date.

Physicist and Christian, Greenwich, Connecticut: The Seabury Press, 1961.

Sartre, Jean-Paul. *Existentialism and Human Emotions*, New York: Philosophical Library, 1957.

Schrödinger, Erwin. *Mind and Matter*, Cambridge: at the University Press, 1958.

Sinnott, Edmund W. *The Biology of the Spirit*, New York: The Viking Press, 1959. (Compass Books C 17)

Temple, William. *Nature, Man and God*, London: Macmillan and Co., Ltd., 1951.

Underhill, Evelyn. *Mysticism*, New York: E. P. Dutton and Company Publishers, c1912-c1926.

Whitehead, Alfred North. *Process and Reality*, New York: Harper & Row, Publishers, 1960. (Harper Torchbooks TB 1033)

Science and the Modern World, New York: The New American Library of World Literature, Inc., 1949. (Mentor Books M28)

*   *   *   *   *   *

INDEX OF SCRIPTURAL REFERENCES

435

436

437

438

INDEX OF PROPER NAMES AND TITLES*

*Note that constantly recurring subjects: God, Christ, Bible, Hebrews, and Protestant are omitted entirely. Names of biblical books and persons are listed only where they supplement the index of scripture passages.